"Every Man Should Try"

"Every Man Should Try"
Adventures of a
Public Interest Activist

Jeremy J. Stone

PublicAffairs

NEW YORK

PHOTO CREDITS: *Photo on page 8 by permission of Jane Kahn. Photo on page 16 (left), by D.G. Brennan.
Photo on page 56 (top) by permission of the Library of Congress. Photo on page 56 (bottom) by permission
from the estate of I.F. Stone. Photo on page 86 by permission of Sally Shelton Colby. Photo on page 136 by permission of Ann Hoopes. Photo on page 194 by permission of Hattie Perry. Photos on pages 46 and 76 by
permission of FAS. Photos on pages 99, 136, 173, 181, 272 and 288 by the author. Photos on pages 8 (right), 16
(right), 77, 94, 126, 162, 196, 208, 223, 235, 249, 253, 261, 262 and 307 from the collection of the author.*

Book design by Jenny Dossin.

Icon art by Jackie Aher.

LIBRARY OF CONGRESS CATALOGING-IN-PUBLICATION DATA

Stone, Jeremy J.

Every man should try : adventures of a public-interest activist / Jeremy J. Stone.—1st ed.

p. cm.

ISBN 1–891620–14–2 (hc)

1. Stone, Jeremy J. 2. Science—Social aspects—United States. 3. Science—United States—Political aspects.
4. Scientists—United States—Political activity. 5. Scientists—United States—Biography. I. Title.

Q143.S745 A3   1999

327.1'7'092—dc21

99–12694

CIP

First Edition

10   9   8   7   6   5   4   3   2   1

One man can make a difference,

and every man should try.

JOHN F. KENNEDY

Contents

Introduction:

The Meaning of This Memoir

Six hundred years ago the famous Arab judge, general, politician, and minister Ibn-Khaldun wrote his great work of historiography, *The Muqaddimah: An Introduction to History* (1377), in order to explain to himself why all of his determined and creative efforts aimed at good government had always ended in disaster.

After thirty-seven years of public interest activities, I decided to reexamine a much less exalted effort. It seemed worth asking, in the spirit of Ibn-Khaldun, why some success was achieved on those occasions when it was, and why, in others, no significant, or lasting, impact seems to have been made. Was success no more than the result of collective effort? Was failure simply the result of numerous actors working at cross-purposes? Or could ingenuity, hard work, or the political judgment of an individual become a critical factor in success, and lack of it a reason for failure? Was President Kennedy right when he said, "One man can make a difference"? And was this why "every man should try"?

Certainly another part of the motivation for this memoir was personal, summed up in the aphorism that a life unexamined is a life not fully lived, combined with my becoming sixty years of age. I wondered if any of my work—my life, in a sense—had been provably worthwhile.

But another part of the motivation was civic—to determine whether my experiences had anything to teach others about the process of public interest activism in the modern Western world. Still deeper was a hope that something might turn up that would assist in the generic goal of encouraging my brand of public interest activism.

And what is that brand? There is, of course, a zoo of different nongovernmental groups; accordingly, public interest activism takes many different forms, and the degree and kind of ingenuity and creativity required of the participating individuals varies greatly. Public interest activists may be working with such a large group of activists with a similar goal or, for whatever reason, taking such a minor role in directing the campaign, that their activism is highly programmed and offers little strategic choice of topic or originality of tactics. By contrast, I had much autonomy.

Even for public interest activists who have much scope for creative maneuver, there are quite different modi operandi. For example, among my colleagues in public interest science, some are actually solving scientific problems as part of an effort to advance the solution of public policy dilemmas. Others are involved in giving science advice to government, such as organizing and drafting studies, administering or maintaining advice-giving organizations, or trying to ensure the functioning of the White House science advisory apparatus. Some are basically servicing the media with informed commentary on a range of high-tech and arms race issues. Others are working to put together the scientific basis for resolving issues where science impacts society while maneuvering to advance related solutions.

Whatever they are doing, to the extent that public interest activists like these are required to show ingenuity and enterprise in solving public policy dilemmas, they are called here, for want of a better phrase: entrepreneurial activists. Entrepreneurial activism has much in common, in the world of ideas, with capitalist entrepreneurship. Of course, the activist gets (only) psychic return rather than financial return. But he or she has to plan campaigns much as a capitalist organizes a business, and must develop a constituency for his or her idea, just as a businessperson develops a body of customers.

One fact of life of entrepreneurial activism is that, all too often, only the activists know exactly what it is they have tried to accomplish and how, because so much is carried out behind the scenes. In many cases, the actors they influence prefer to hide what influenced them or they just forget. And sometimes the activists themselves are quite ignorant of the extent to which success can be attributed to their valiant efforts.

With all this in mind, I decided simply to recount what had happened in about two dozen campaigns in which I had engaged. Thus the chapters of this volume are, in a way, case studies from the point of view of a single activist, but they are, I think, less dry than that sounds. The volume itself is, really, the documented life of an activist with more than five hundred notes. (To simplify consulting the notes, I have listed them in consecutive order at the end of the book, and to encourage the reader to consult them, the more interesting of the substantive notes have their superscripts in brackets, so that a [20] will come to be [20].)

Throughout more than a third of a century of activism—even during the last three decades, when I had the Federation of American Scientists (FAS) as a platform—I was still a very small actor on a large planet working on intractable problems held in place by strong forces. The reader will wonder how on earth I could have hoped, during this period, to have accomplished anything—much less hope, today, that the historical record might show some signs of it.

One explanation lies in chaos theory, in which a basic metaphor is the butterfly that flaps its wings in Paris and somehow causes a storm in New York. The sometime instability of a situation—not uncommon in political affairs, where ideas spread rapidly to powerful actors—can turn a small force into a big one. Activism is chaos theory applied in a political context that is, in the modern Western world, especially chaotic.

Accordingly, I decided to try to write a memoir that would remind the reader, as I sought to remind myself, by what narrow and often random margins of circumstance success or failure was determined, and by what quiet decisions important paths were taken or rejected. More generally, I wanted to know where the decision-points were in my activities and in my life.

For this reason the text is decorated with four symbols. A butterfly flapping its wings appears whenever I or someone else, through an act of will, enterprise, or decision, starts some kind of important breeze. It signals the reader that from this act something important happened, as will be seen later in the story. It looks like this:

Often, past and future events are linked by small connections that have more than the usual significance but are the results not of some deliberate act of will but just of random circumstance. Here the text shows a chain to symbolize a chain of circumstances. The symbol looks like this:

Sometimes, my life or my undertaking has been deeply affected by a decision that opened a door or closed a door in some fashion; here I show an open or closed door:

This memoir is not a book about the total achievements of FAS during the past twenty-nine years I have been its chief executive officer, and does not include achievements of other FAS staffers during that period—they will have to write their own books. I have dwelled only on those activities in which I played a leading role. On the other hand, it would have been quite impossible for me to accomplish anything during this period without the opportunity provided by FAS. The official support of its members and officials, the advice whenever needed, the autonomy of operation permitted, the balanced oversight provided, and the encouragement always available were all essential to my undertakings.

No less essential was the loving help of my wife of four decades, B.J., whose collaboration actually included learning Russian, some Chinese, and some Spanish, as well as editing my articles and memoir with unsurpassed skill.

Making a difference is, of course, the energizing motivation of public interest activists; having devoted a lifetime to trying to make a difference, they would hardly be human if they didn't wish to reflect on the extent to which they may have succeeded.

Accordingly, it is therapeutic for activists to write this kind of self-investigative memoir. It's a little bit like the movie *It's a Wonderful Life*, wherein an angel shows a depressed hero what his life may have meant. I commend it to my entrepreneurial colleagues.

Finally, only too conscious of the imperfections of this memoir, of the limitations of activist campaigns upon which it reports, and of how little anyone can know of what actually transpired, I wish to offer the concluding sentiments of Ibn-Khaldun's foreword to *The Muqaddimah*, where he writes, "The capital of knowledge that an individual scholar has to offer is small. Admission [of one's shortcomings] saves from censure. Kindness from colleagues is hoped for."

JEREMY J. STONE[*]

---

[*] Readers who wish to comment upon the book can reach the author at JStone@fas.org. Readers who wish to learn more about Federation of American Scientists (FAS) should write to 307 Massachusetts Avenue, N.E., Washington, D.C. 20002; telephone: (202) 546–3300, or e-mail to fas@fas.org.

PART I

Successful Odyssey with
the Anti-Ballistic Missile

First Thoughts on Anti-Ballistic Missile Systems

The most important arms control agreement of the Cold War was the Anti-Ballistic Missile (ABM) Treaty of 1972. The titanic battle to create this treaty, which banned anti-ballistic missile systems (except for a single site), took a full decade from conception to ratification and involved an army of arms controllers and government officials working in many stages.

Scouting activities for this army, over the same decade, are described in these first three chapters. The first chapter describes initial activity, in 1962–1964, in which an original approach to dealing with ABM systems ("no-first-procurement") is conceived. A related paper on ABM limitations of various kinds is presented in 1963 to the Russians through an international conference.

A follow-up paper is deemed sufficiently important that it is sent to the highest level of the Defense Department and presented, by special invitation, at the most important private meeting of U.S. and Soviet scientists being held at the time.

My decade-long odyssey in search of a U.S.-Soviet treaty on anti-ballistic missile systems began in 1963 with an electric thought whose arrival in the attic of my home in Elmsford, New York, I can still vividly recall.

If the Russians—who were then said to be experimenting with a missile defense system around Tallinn in Estonia, then part of the

USSR—could be persuaded, one way or another, not to build such a system, then America might be persuaded to desist from building its own system. Both sides would then avoid the waste of expensive, ineffective systems that would, still worse, accelerate each side's interest in buying offsetting offensive missile systems.

The idea appealed to me a great deal more than the work on which I had been engaged. In fact, my arrival at the Hudson Institute, in March 1962, had been traumatic. Its director and founder, the extraordinary Herman Kahn, had welcomed me as follows: "Jeremy, we have a problem with a twelve-month contract. Nine months have passed since we got the contract, and not a word has been set to paper. Now that you are here, we want you to be the one to fulfill it. It does not have to be great, just good." To my further horror, the subject of the contract, funded by the Defense Department's Office of Civil Defense (OCD), turned out to be a pet Kahn idea: the strategic evacuation of American cities.

It was a key belief of Herman's (called "not-incredible first-strike") that the Soviets should be persuaded that the United States just might launch a nuclear first strike against them if they invaded Western Europe. The strategic evacuation would, he reasoned, give such a threat credibility and commitment by emptying U.S. cities—thus arguably putting American citizens largely out of reach of the immediate effects of Soviet nuclear retaliation.

For a liberal like me, who then opposed even the prudential program of designating fallout shelters, this project was a creation of the devil. I seriously considered returning to the Stanford Research Institute (SRI) and asking for my job back as a research mathematician. I can still see myself with my head in my hands, sitting forlornly on my stoop in Elmsford, considering just that.

Persisting, however, I produced a study in which, on paper at least, the entire northeastern United States would be evacuated by car and rail in three days. Later when I briefed OCD in the Pentagon, its director asked whether I thought this plan would work.

"Thanks so much for asking," I said. "No, I don't think it would work at all!" I was intensely relieved to realize that OCD was far more pedestrian in its thinking than Herman, and that my study would go nowhere and do no harm.

How had a twenty-six-year-old, freshly minted Ph.D. found himself in this predicament? My college roommate—and the best man at my wedding—the distinguished economist Sidney G. Winter, had been working at RAND, an Air Force think tank set up after World War II. He recommended me to Herman, then planning to leave RAND and start his own institute. Sid then persuaded me to visit RAND and meet Herman, who, Sid said, was an influential person who could be influenced by me and for good purposes.

It was 1961, and storm clouds were forming in the Cold War with a Berlin blockade that led, in due course, to the Cuban missile crisis. Saving the world, even through Herman Kahn, seemed more important than whatever my meager mathematical talents would produce at SRI. I agreed to move as soon as my wife, B.J., finished her own Stanford University Ph.D. in mathematics. My decision was made more difficult by the fact that most of my friends and many relatives considered Herman Kahn an evil person.

Kahn had become famous for three-day lectures on the subject of his tome *On Thermonuclear War.*[1] He, almost alone, considered nuclear war something to which strategy should, and could, be applied. He alone considered it even winnable. Startled liberal commentators asked, "Is there really a Herman Kahn?"

But Herman was, at least, smart. Sid called him the smartest person "to his right" that he had ever met. Herman was said to have received the highest intelligence rating on the Alpha test given to World War II recruits up to the time he took it in 1942. He was very incisive but seemed, up close, much like a super used-car salesman. His friends spoke of the "wit and wisdom of Herman Kahn." Short and very fat, about 350 pounds, Kahn held people to him with a kind of intellectual sex appeal. He was always "on," spouting anecdotes and running through set-piece minilectures.

Believing that, as God had turned mud into men, he could turn ordinary mortals into strategists, he felt he did not need, or really want, to hire established experts. He therefore dominated the staff even more than would otherwise have been the case; although he welcomed debate, few could maintain opinions in opposition to him.

Soon after I joined the staff, the issue arose of my getting a security clearance, something that had been pending for four years. In 1958, after our first year of graduate work in mathematics, B.J. and I had been offered summer work at the prestigious RAND Corporation in Santa Monica, California, as consultants. The jobs offered the splendid salary of twenty-five dollars per day for each of us, and RAND had good working conditions. We obtained the necessary "interim" clearances for dealing with secret material that were required to work in the RAND building.

Our work was satisfactory. I had, indeed, published two RAND papers in the summer, one on a new method of doing linear programming and another on economic arbitrage.[2] We were invited to return for another summer, but on May 12, 1959, we learned that the interim clearances provided by RAND had been withdrawn by the Air Force.

The Air Force Office of Special Investigations (OSI) interviewed me under oath and asked questions about my relationship with my father, I. F. Stone, a well-known journalist. These interviews require vigilance. Sometimes, the all-important printed transcript turned out to be less than faithful to my obvious verbal intention. For example, by sticking a period into an oral statement that needed a comma instead, they changed the entire meaning:

Q. Does your father exert any influence over your thinking or over you?
A. As much as any man can say.[sic] My political views are my own.

The hearing, and later information provided me in 1977 under a Freedom of Information Act (FOIA) request, strongly suggested that OSI had no derogatory information whatsoever about me personally—I was young and apolitical. But the withdrawn security clearance prevented me from returning to RAND.[3]

Herman's hiring me and, perhaps, the Hudson Institute's influence reopened the security-clearance matter, and eventually I found myself sitting in the bowels of the Pentagon, armed with a pocket handkerchief, being interrogated by a lieutenant colonel, a captain, and a civilian employee of the Air Force.

My interrogators were polite, junior, and seemed politically naive. They wanted an explanation of why my father had opposed such things as the House Committee on Un-American Activities and new laws on wiretapping. I mentioned that the White House had recently used my father's credibility as an honest journalist in its White Paper on Cuba by quoting him as saying, after a visit to Cuba, that "Cuba has the smell of an Eastern European satellite state."

In any case, I was cleared two months later and, eventually, cleared for "top secret." (Two years later, after leaving the Hudson Institute, I decided to let these clearances lapse. This would make it easier to travel to the Soviet Union and write freely on arms control because no question would arise of my misusing classified information.)

The most dangerous episode of the Cold War, the Cuban missile crisis, occurred in October 1962, six months after my arrival at the Hudson Institute. To everyone who worked in these nuclear-war think tanks, this incident precisely mirrored in reality the "escalation ladders" and scenarios then in wide use. So when President Kennedy gave his October 22 speech saying: "It shall be the policy of this nation to regard any nuclear missile launched from Cuba against any nation in the Western Hemisphere as an attack by the Soviet Union on the United States, requiring a full retaliatory response upon the Soviet Union," I drove immediately to Princeton, where B.J. was at a conference, to be with her in case the world was in its final moments.[4]

At about the same time of the Cuban missile crisis, Donald G. Brennan, then an arms controller, became Hudson's president, with Herman remaining the director. Brennan was tall, with a stiff Pruss-

Herman Kahn, founder and
director of the Hudson Institute

Donald G. Brennan, president of
the Hudson Institute, and the author (rt.).

ian presence but with an ideology then much more congenial to my own. Herman and Don could not have been a more unlikely couple, not only politically but also physically. Hudson's symbol at that time could have been that of the 1935 New York World's Fair: obelisk (Don) and sphere (Herman). They instantly agreed on a Hudson Institute rule that any employees who were heavier than 300 pounds or taller than six feet four inches could travel first class.

Under Herman's leadership, the Hudson Institute produced voluminous studies that often said little but were saved by some "kicker" that could justify the contract. For example, the Army had asked for a study on the anti-ballistic missile, which it certainly favored. The Hudson study's main usable conclusion was to invent a "new" argument for the ABM that, indeed, might make the entire study worth the money to the Army.

What was this new argument? Following a nuclear attack, an anti-ballistic missile protecting a steel plant or other key resource could, it was argued in the study, make the difference between successful postwar recovery and disastrous collapse. This was a perfect example of the kind of mind-stretching argumentation, hypothetical and extreme, characteristic of Herman. I complained that I opposed the anti-ballistic missile and was not eager to work on studies like the one for the Army. Herman's response: "No problem, we can do a study for the Arms Control and Disarmament Agency" (ACDA, which was unsympathetic to the ABM). To someone running a policy institute and trying to raise money to keep it going, it was all clear. But, for me, the approach seemed too mercantile, although I was happy to do one ACDA study.[5]

After the electric moment in Elmsford, stopping an ABM race became my real preoccupation. I quickly prepared a paper for a conference in Michigan entitled "Should the Soviet Union Build an Anti-Ballistic Missile System?" It argued that the United States would desist from deploying an ABM system if, but only if, the Soviet Union did not move forward with its own ABM system. Donald Brennan's reaction was gratifying. Since he had edited a book then called the "bible" of arms control,[6] he was well placed to judge how important and original this was or was not.[7] To my thrilled satisfaction, Brennan tried to bring the idea before the secretary of defense. Now this was what I had come to Hudson for!

In a letter of December 3, 1963, to Adam Yarmolinsky, then "The Special Assistant" to Secretary of Defense McNamara, Brennan said the paper was "important and interesting enough to be brought to the Secretary's attention." The paper argued, he said, "with high persuasiveness" and "careful historical documentation" that the Soviets should not proceed. Did Yarmolinsky want to suggest any changes or to show it to Mr. McNamara before it was communicated to the Russians?

Herman Kahn's reaction was more skeptical. He supported ABM deployment and believed, as many did at that time, that all new technologies were bound to be implemented. Herman sent me to Princeton to talk to the astrophysicist Freeman Dyson, then on the Hudson board.

Hat in hand, I presented myself before the famous Professor Dyson, who proceeded to explain that the Russians liked defense, for historical reasons; why not let them waste their money if they wished? But the problem was, I responded, that the United States would feel obliged, politically, to respond with its own ABM. I was startled by the candor and simplicity of Professor Dyson's response: "I never thought of that."

Returning to Hudson, I prepared, by December 12, 1963, a sixty-page paper, "Anti-Ballistic Missiles and Arms Control."[8] 𝒥 I urged consideration of a "no-first-procurement policy for ABM systems" based on "more-or-less tacit understandings" and encouraged the secretary of defense to testify, in open session, on the likely costs of a Soviet ABM system. Furthermore, he should declassify information in the Department of Defense that bore on the waste and inefficiency of past Soviet efforts to build defenses.

The paper further argued that "certain decoys will easily saturate the Soviet system" and mentioned non-ballistic missiles as a possibility. It also suggested that we should threaten to build an ABM of our own that would "degrade the Soviet offensive missiles or require additional Soviet resources to keep up." (This is, of course, what some of President Reagan's staffers later considered his Star Wars program to be!)

The Pugwash Conference, begun by scientists in 1955 as part of an international peace movement and awarded the Nobel Peace Prize in 1997, had been deemed by Brennan, some years before, too multinational for really private discussions. Instead, he pressed for the establishment of a quiet U.S.-Soviet bilateral Pugwash. It came to be chaired by the Harvard biochemist Paul Doty. In early 1964 Brennan advised me that the Doty group would pay me a thousand dollars (about five thousand in today's dollars) for the use of my paper in a forthcoming meeting in Boston with the Soviets in late spring. Would I agree? Yes! But only if I could present the paper myself. Doty reluctantly agreed. 🄸

About this time, I decided to call the thirty-five-member Hudson staff together and give a lecture entitled "The Incredibility of Not-Incredible First Strike." ("Not-Incredible First Strike" was, as mentioned, Herman's favorite force posture—a credible threat to attack the Soviet Union with strategic weapons in response to some provocation in Europe. Recognizing how hard it would be to make this "credible," he advanced the notion that we should keep it, at least, "not incredible." I felt this was not possible.)

This talk was an unprecedented success. I had learned the Kahn technique of jokes, slides, and quotations and had prepared carefully. I had answers for all of Herman's interventions and it was the first time I ever felt I had defeated him in debate. But somehow this success just deepened my impatience with the Hudson Institute and with the entire profession. I resigned, 🔲 without a new position, and began writing a book on my experiences, after which I would return to mathematics.

Working at home, I quickly prepared a first chapter on "bomber disarmament," which I mailed widely to strategists, government officials, and the like.[9] How pleased I was to get a polite letter from the assistant secretary of defense for systems analysis, Alain Enthoven, even though he noted the enormous political obstacles that bomber disarmament would face. At least someone was listening.

More important, both the Princeton Center for International Studies, led by Klaus Knorr, and the Harvard Center for International Affairs, in the person of Thomas C. Schelling, said I could join for a year as a research associate. I chose Harvard. 🔲

Late in the spring of 1964, the Doty study group met with the Russians. On the American side, Doty was joined by Henry Kissinger, then a Harvard professor and strategist; Marshall Shulman, later the senior adviser on the Soviet Union to Secretary of State Cyrus Vance; and Jerome B. Wiesner, who had been a science adviser to Presidents Kennedy and Johnson.

On the Soviet side there was N. Talensky, a Soviet general (but really a specialist in Soviet military history); M. D. Millionshchikov, an academician and vice president of the Soviet Academy of Sciences; Vasilly Emelyanov, a metallurgist who had been a chief designer of tank armor during World War II and, later, the Soviet ambassador to the International Agency for Atomic Energy (IAEA); and I. Sedov, reputed to be a major figure in the Soviet military-industrial complex.

On hearing my view that the Soviet Union should not build an ABM, General Talensky said that it constituted an ultimatum and that, if this continued, he would walk out. I was stunned. Marshall Shulman, ever the diplomat, explained that my statement was just a warning (not a threat) that the United States would inevitably take action in the face of a Soviet ABM system.

Undaunted, I approached Millionshchikov after the session and said, "Well, at least one Soviet academician agrees with me; look at this quote from Artsimovich, who says that someday defensive systems might be worse than offensive ones."

Millionshchikov said, "Artsimovich always disagrees with everyone else."

Later Kissinger told the Russians a relevant joke, which they enjoyed hugely: As a Texas sheriff was beating a group of communists, one of them shouted, "Don't beat me, I am *anti*communist." The Texas sheriff continued to beat him, exclaiming, "I don't care what kind of communist you are."

The next morning, at breakfast, Emelyanov repeated this joke and said to me in friendly fashion, "That is the way you are, Stone, missiles or anti-missiles, you don't care, you beat them all." He had gotten the point. (And he turned out to be a great ally.)

Emelyanov also proved important in another way. He had advised me and my wife that he had learned English in his sixties in the back of a chauffeur-driven car in Moscow and that I could therefore surely learn Russian. I was not about to undertake such an onerous task, but I was not above asking my wife to do it. And this she did, beginning at once with summer school at Harvard in 1964 and at intensive summer school courses in 1965 and 1966 at Wyndam University in Putney, Vermont. In the ensuing five years, B.J.'s competence in Russian became a key element in my efforts to promote an ABM treaty.

CHAPTER **2**

Harvard Becomes a Base
for an Anti-ABM Campaign

At Harvard, from 1964 to 1966, while B.J. learns Russian, two books on arms

control are produced, as well as quite a few articles, all primarily devoted to

securing an ABM treaty; in 1964 a first trip to Moscow takes place to talk the

Soviets out of building an ABM.

I took up residence at the Harvard Center for International Affairs in June 1964 and began work on a book. I also prepared a string of memorandums for the Doty group, which I was eager to impress.[10] Meanwhile, I continued to write about the current status of ABMs.

By September 1964 Harold Brown, later secretary of defense, but then director of defense research and engineering in the department of defense, was concluding that for the "foreseeable future" the cost of an ABM system would be "substantially larger" than the extra cost needed to counter it by the USSR. Department of Defense (DOD) studies showed that missile offense had a two- to four-year lead over missile defense. In *The Bulletin of the Atomic Scientists*, I urged both sides to announce military budget reductions, which, it seemed, would "strengthen a tacit understanding not to provoke this new [and expensive] round in the arms race."[11]

Not everyone was persuaded by my views on the ABM. Henry Kissinger was one of the three leaders of the strategic wing of the center (along with Thomas Schelling and Robert Bowie). One day he introduced me to a touring member of the Board of Visitors by saying sardonically, "He is trying to show that the ABM is so ineffective that it won't work but so effective that it should be banned by treaty." Several years later, of course, it was the same Henry Kissinger who was successfully negotiating the very treaty in question and observing publicly that opponents of anti-ballistic missile systems were correct to observe that these ineffective systems were stimulating the arms race.[12]

From June 1964 to June 1965 at the Harvard Center for International Affairs, I completed my book *Containing the Arms Race: Some Specific Proposals,* which included as its first chapter much of my thinking about the ABM and moved on from there to bomber disarmament, missile disarmament, and, finally, a "negotiator's pause." The latter anticipated the "freeze" championed by Randy Forsberg almost two decades later. The chapter was stimulated by the American proposal in 1964 that the United States, the Soviet Union, and their respective allies "should agree to explore a verified freeze of the number and characteristics of strategic nuclear offensive and defensive vehicles." It was, really, Robert McNamara who invented the freeze.[13]

From June 1965 to June 1966, not finding any suitable position to move to, I stayed at the Center for International Affairs, courtesy of Thomas Schelling, and began work on a second book, *Strategic Persuasion: Arms Control Through Dialogue.*[14] At Harvard I had pretty well given up trying to attach myself to the Doty study group—which evidently viewed me as too young and lacking any special asset. My last effort was to see if the group could help me spend a year in Moscow, in residence, working on arms control. But Doty was characteristically aloof and noncommittal, and I could not figure out where I stood. 🔊

Accordingly, by the summer of 1966, I had decided to become my own individual Pugwash movement. 🔊 A Moscow Mathematical Congress provided an occasion. My first book was finally being published, and its good reviews would make an excellent calling card.[15] I was, obviously, not the world's greatest arms controller. But if I were *there*, in the center of the action, with all the relative advantage this implied, I might be able to make a difference. So I decided to give the Russians my advice personally. I wrote Glenn Schweitzer at the U.S. embassy in Moscow that I would be there from August 15 through September 5 and that I had already sent copies of my book to a "wide range of interested Soviet persons."

The main impression of a first-time visitor of Moscow was one of drab poverty. The airfield seemed almost grass-covered, with little traffic. The apartments were old and run-down. People seemed very poor. There were few cars, and they were old. One suddenly realized that the Soviet Union was just a developing country. Half of the Soviet population lacked indoor plumbing; per capita ownership of cars was fifty years behind the U.S. rate. When, subsequently, some Soviet friends smuggled my wife into a computer center—her Ph.D. was in numerical analysis, and she had computing experience—she was shocked to see paper tape. They were years behind. It occurred to me then—and I acted on it often later (as this memoir will show)—that if Western leaders could visit Moscow, much of their fear of Soviet power would seep away, and the arms race would slow.

Donald Brennan had traveled to Russia in September 1965, a year before me, and a Soviet citizen, Nina Shakova, became his guide. An English teacher for scientists in the Academy of Science, she was cheerful, attractive, intellectual, and divorced, with a daughter. During his travels with her, they became intimate—something that was promptly learned by U.S. security and caused Brennan, who had many clearances, some difficulty later.

Brennan returned from the visit persuaded that the Russians had irrevocably decided to build an ABM and that, in any case, their position had some merit. He was the rare case in which a Western scientist was infected with Soviet ideas—normally the flow went quite in the other direction.[16]

Brennan and I later drifted apart as his support for the ABM grew. By 1966, however, we were still in reasonably close touch, and he urged me to seek out Nina Shakova on my trip, which I did. She lived in a one-room apartment with her daughter, Natasha, and her mother, whom we called Mama. It was against an old Stalinist law

Nina Shakova in the Kremlin
in 1965

B.J. (center) with Nina's mother and Nina's
daughter, Natasha, who became a mathematician

to let foreigners see an apartment that did not have its own toilet and kitchen. But she let us visit at night, when the neighbors were out. We became very fond of the family. Their willingness to receive us and to tell us about Moscow life added a great deal to our visits.

With Nina, as with all other Russians we met, it seemed quite easy to determine who was working for the KGB, who was allied with them for privilege (such as travel abroad), and who was innocent of any desire to work with them. You could tell from their personalities and from what they said and how. Of course, anyone could be called in by the KGB, and all had to report to them—including high scientists. But some had been recruited, and others were just innocent bystanders. Shakova was innocent. For the most part, the KGB let her alone. The one time in our long association when our conversations indicated that they had called her in, she was badly frightened.[17]

Anti-ABM Lectures at Dom Druzhbi

As far as lobbying against the ABM was concerned, however, Shakova could not help. Instead, I lectured twice on the ABM.

Once was at the Institute for World Economy and International Relations (IMEMO), then on Yaraslavskaya Ulitsa, and headed by the academician N. N. Inozemtsov. It went well, but the audience was small in number and not very well informed. The second was at Dom Druzhbi (Friendship House), where the usual friendship organizations met. Well-dressed individuals who did not give their names—both characteristics made me feel they must be influential—convened, and I made my pitch. In particular, I gave them the following advice: "If you build an anti-ballistic missile system, we will build a much bigger one." When asked why, I replied, "We are rich and not afraid to spend money."

In fact, Emelyanov had returned from the Doty study-group meeting to write an article in the Soviet publication *New Times* that showed him expressing similar sentiments. He staunchly supported the Soviet line that defenses were good while quoting American strategists as saying, "If the whole thing is taken over by Big Business, arms spending will grow to monstrous proportions. . . . For it is a profitable business, and no capitalist is likely to forfeit his profits."[18]

In Moscow, Emelyanov encouraged me to write an article in the English-language *Moscow News*;[19] in retrospect, I think he felt it would make me more "kosher" inside the Soviet system and help lay a political basis for our dialogue. I wrote a largely platitudinous piece about the importance of scientists speaking the truth to one another and not abusing their common trust—I wrote, "They must put this trust to work in the service of disarmament and arms limitations."

A State Department political officer wrote to me on January 9, 1967, saying that my article was "something of an oddity for this journal," inasmuch as the *Moscow News* rarely printed anything that diverged from the party line; he wanted to know whether they had changed anything. They had not.

Toward the end of my visit, at a meeting at the Academy of Sciences, Emelyanov mentioned that General Talensky had died and that it was a great loss for the academy's arms-control group. Talensky, he said, had been their link to the Soviet Defense Ministry. B.J. and I decided to crash the funeral and took a taxi to the Red Army Club.

Attaching ourselves to the end of a long file of soldiers who were marching into the club to view the bier, we walked past a startled guard into the main room. Four friends of Talensky's, of whom one was Emelyanov, were standing guard around the coffin. Emelyanov looked startled but pleased as B.J. deposited the flowers on the coffin. In a quick look around, I saw at least two of the well-dressed men who had attended my Dom Druzhbi lecture.

Returning home in the privacy of the taxi, I burst, unaccountably, into tears. The poignancy of our representing Western arms controllers at the funeral of this well-intentioned general in the very heart of the enemy citadel overcame me.

Later, I received an unexpected appointment, requested earlier, with the famous arch-conservative *Pravda* editor, Yuri Zhukov. He turned out, in both physical and intellectual dimensions, to be a kind of Soviet Herman Kahn, a likeness that was confirmed when, in a cynical reference to my attendance at the funeral, he said, "You certainly have an ingenious way of getting appointments in Moscow."

Still, I was more and more convinced that my skills and personality were a key that could open some kind of Moscow lock. I was keenly aware, however, that the Soviet system, like a predatory male, enjoyed manipulating innocence.

I felt obliged, of course, to debrief someone about anything interesting that might happen during my trips. It had been reported, as a small part of a famous scandal of the day, that the CIA had threatened one of their sources with faked psychiatric documents, and I felt they played too rough for me.[20] I also considered it safer, all around, to be able to deny—on both sides of the Atlantic—that I had anything to do with *any* intelligence agencies in either country. Who knew when I or my wife might be picked up by the Soviet secret police and questioned or whatever. In the 1960s, travel in the Soviet Union was a rather unusual experience. So rather than get involved with the CIA, I chatted with officials of the Soviet desk of the State Department and some middle- to high-level friends in the Defense Department.

CHAPTER 3

Return to Mathematics, to Moscow, and to Washington

After "retiring" in 1966 to teach mathematics at Pomona—and despite continuing to write about the ABM and to lobby Moscow about it—a career as mathematics professor is found to be too dull. Efforts to retool as an economist also fail. A return to Washington permits participation in the climactic ABM debate of 1969.

In the fall, a new U.S. senator's visit to Moscow leads to the beginning of a surprisingly successful campaign to slow the arms race. In great secrecy, efforts are made to save the life of the daughter of the retired premier, Nikita Khruschev. Because of related circumstances, the KGB decides that the author works for the CIA—something he learns twenty years later.

I concluded, while in Cambridge, that I should return to teaching mathematics. I did not feel comfortable in political science per se, and I was unable to attach myself to the senior activists. I felt that the Pugwashites had not been preparing with sufficient care for their meetings. A misunderstanding about whether I was invited to a Polish Pugwash conference—which led to my arriving and being bounced—deepened a certain antagonism.[21]

Accordingly, after the trip to Russia and Poland, I moved to Claremont, California, where I took up a position teaching mathematics at Pomona College while my wife took a full year off to advance her Russian. The climate was ideal, and Pomona had very much the Swarthmore College ambiance I had known as an undergraduate. My associates in Cambridge believed that I had "retired" from political life. But my interest in the ABM debate continued, and B.J.'s Russian studies signaled our intention to run our own private Pugwash.

By the summer of 1967, B.J. and I had decided to return to Moscow, this time traveling from California to Japan, then by boat to Nakhodka (near Vladivostok), and from there by train to Moscow on the Trans-Siberian Railroad. In fact, the Russians required us to fly from Kharbarovsk on the east coast to Irkutsk. This seemed an effort to prevent us, both Jews, from jumping off the train when it passed through Birobidzhan, an autonomous region that had been set up as an ersatz Jewish homeland and that I had asked to visit.

In Irkutsk, on a boat on Lake Baikal, the KGB tried to set us up with a young girl who was carefully seated next to us. It just happened that she spoke English, was Jewish, had a father who was a journalist, and was the second best chess player in the Oblast. Central casting must have worked hard on this.

On the train for about a week with two female doctors traveling from Khabarovsk to Leningrad for a medical conference, B.J. got a great workout in speaking Russian. I explained Freud to the doctors, who knew nothing of it and found it "dirty."

In Moscow I gave a second lecture at Dom Druzhbi—to a group of people who said absolutely nothing; I concluded that they spoke no English, that the Soviet "system" was just recording what I said, and that the talk's organizer had been unable to drum up a real audience.

I also lectured both at Arbatov's new Institute for the USA and Canada and at IMEMO. By then, I had my second book to hawk: *Strategic Persuasion: Arms Control Through Dialogue.*[22] It was especially interesting to meet Arbatov, whom I was to encounter periodically for the next quarter century. He was an enormously interesting addition to the Soviet Pugwashites. He was far more aware of political realities and the political line than the scientists were. He was obviously well connected, as the head of an Institute, and he was smart.[23] You could be sure he understood what you were saying. For someone like me, who was trying to influence Soviet policy, he was a grand improvement as an interlocutor.

He found himself, of course, in a difficult political situation. Americanologists were as suspect to the Soviet authorities as Sovietologists were to McCarthyites. And the situation in the USSR was, of course, more tense than any of us could fully realize. When Arbatov, in the post–Soviet days, wrote his memoir, *The System*, he related a truly revealing anecdote. The KGB chief, Andropov, invited Arbatov to share a letter, written in a sincere tone, that the KGB censors had seized from a person with whom, in fact, Andropov and Arbatov had good relations. In the letter, the man complained that his (unnamed) superiors were "worthless" and "stupid" and were wasting his energy and time. Andropov was planning to turn the letter over to Brezhnev, who would have assumed that it was referring to Brezhnev himself, even though the general secretary was not mentioned. Arbatov tried to dissuade him. Andropov responded that this would be naive: "I'm not certain that a copy of this letter has not been handed over to Brezhnev already. After all, the KGB is a complex institution, and its chairman himself does not escape its attention. All the more so since there are people who would be delighted to compromise me in the eyes of Brezhnev for having concealed from him something touching upon him personally."[24] Even the KGB chief felt surrounded by the system.

Arbatov managed to stay afloat, however, with everyone watching everyone else. In later years he confided to me that it was he who had prevailed on Gorbachev to limit the president to two five-year terms in the new constitution. When I asked how long he had been running his institute, he said, "Twenty-seven years, but I still have work to do."

B.J. and I returned from Russia through Eastern Europe and got a clear picture of the enormous variety of living standards from Russia rising steadily to Bulgaria to Rumania to Hungary to Vienna to

London and finally to southern California, where even as an assistant professor I lived in a house with a heated outdoor swimming pool.

The Adelphi Paper and the Specter of Nuclear Weapons Use in Vietnam

At Pomona in 1967–1968, I was teaching a course in arms control besides courses in mathematics, and B.J. was teaching mathematics at Harvey Mudd College. Among the strategists opposed to anti-ballistic missile systems, I had sufficient standing to receive an assignment from the Institute for Strategic Studies (ISS) in London to write a monograph. And this monograph, *The Case Against Missile Defenses*,[25] was the most important paper I had prepared on the subject since my 1964 contribution to the Doty group. I eventually distributed about a thousand copies at my own expense to add to those distributed by ISS to its many members worldwide.

The paper attacked the idea that a proposed "thin defense against Chinese missiles should be used as a 'building block' for a larger defense designed to neutralize Soviet offensive weapons." As we shall see, it was, indeed, the Army's effort to use the "thin" (or "light") ABM as a building block for a "thick" defense that brought the ABM program to a screeching halt and made the ABM Treaty possible. ⧉

The Adelphi paper was scheduled to appear in the spring, and I decided to carry it personally to Moscow the next summer to make sure it was well read. But before the paper was printed, the specter of nuclear weapons use in Vietnam interrupted my teaching.

On February 15, 1968, in an article in *The New York Times*, the chairman of the Joint Chiefs of Staff, General Earle G. Wheeler, was quoted as saying, "I do not think that nuclear weapons will be required to defend Khesanh," a city then under siege in Vietnam, but he refused "to speculate any further."[26] Two days later, President Johnson went to the El Toro Marine Air Station in San Diego, purportedly to see some marines off to Vietnam, and, being in the neighborhood, on February 18 he stopped in to see ex-president Dwight D. Eisenhower, then vacationing in Palm Springs.

All my alarm bells went off. Eisenhower considered it a personal triumph that his threats to use nuclear weapons against China had brought about an armistice in the war in Korea. Johnson might think him both willing and able to give national "permission" to use or threaten to use nuclear weapons in Vietnam. This was the moment, I felt, when Johnson would have to fish or cut bait on any possibility of nuclear use, and that might be the reason he was visiting Eisenhower.

I summarized my fears in a memo on February 25, 1968; I mailed my analysis, entitled "A Crime Against Humanity," to every U.S. senator. Not content with that, I canceled classes for a week and flew to Washington to drive home my point. At the intermission of a play in Washington, I spoke to my friend from Harvard, Morton H. Halperin, then the deputy assistant secretary of defense for arms control and policy planning in the Pentagon (and now the director of policy planning at the State Department). He told me "not to worry."

Why was he so relaxed about this? Clark Clifford had just taken over as secretary of defense, and, as I learned years later, Mort already knew that Clifford wanted to withdraw from the war, not escalate it. But was Johnson contemplating such use? I am not sure that we can ever know, but I subsequently discovered that senior American scientists shared my concern.[27]

Third Trip to Moscow

B.J. and I decided, for that summer, to travel to Moscow via Constantinople and a boat through the Black Sea to Odessa and thence by train to Kiev and Moscow. Passing through New York, I attended a small meeting at the Carnegie Endowment that was attended also by the former secretary of defense Robert McNamara.

I had long sympathized with McNamara and his heroic efforts against the bomber lobby and the pro-ABM forces. He had also organized the Defense Department in a rational fashion for the first time in history. And he had been magnificent in handling the Cuban missile crisis. I felt I was in the presence of a giant among men.

Our journey took us to Odessa and Kiev, where we went to visit the dying and repressed synagogues. In the guest book in Odessa, a canny Jew had written a message: "The rabbi assures us, in private conversation, that there is no anti-Semitism in Russia."

In Moscow I offered an apparatchik a hundred dollars if he would have my Adelphi paper translated into Russian and give me a copy. This was done, and I gave a copy of the Russian translation to a startled U.S. embassy.

The whole thing gave me enormous satisfaction. Now, in Russian at least, what was I hoped the definitive work would be read. And the translator said it would be sent to the Ministry for Medium Machine Building, which was known to be the heart of the Soviet military-industrial complex.

The Soviet invasion of Czechoslovakia took place that August, while I was in Moscow. Over a lunch at Dom Druzhbi, a young Soviet apparatchik, Aleksandr Bessmertnykh—who rose, two decades later, to be the Soviet foreign minister—gave this astonishing explanation of why he believed this invasion was necessary: "Well, we did a poll, and it showed that 15 percent of the population still preferred capitalism, so we knew we needed more time before we could relinquish control."

After returning home, I got a last-minute invitation to attend a fall Pugwash meeting in Denmark that was specially devoted to the ABM problem. My degree of specialization in this problem had overcome the American delegation's preference for not inviting me. My wife and I returned to Europe for this meeting, but my visits to Moscow now seemed much more important than my individual participation in Pugwash.

Emelyanov was there, always friendly, but he asked a question that froze my blood. Why, he wanted to know, did the American Pugwash group not include me in more meetings? To me, this question meant, "If you are OK and sincere, that is, not CIA, why do not Bernard Feld, Paul Doty, and the rest invite you more often?"

I rose to the occasion. I recounted the true story of the animal experimenters who had a colony of chimpanzees in a cage with a complicated machine that would produce—if the right buttons were pressed—a banana. The experimenters learned, I told him, two things. If a senior monkey figured out, somehow, how to work the banana machine, all of the other monkeys would stand around, watch, and learn, and soon they, too, would be producing their own bananas. On the other hand, if a junior monkey somehow induced the machine to produce a banana, none of the others stood around to watch, nor did they learn; they just took his banana.[28]

Emelyanov laughed and said it was the same in the Soviet Union; they would say they wanted new blood, but in the end, they kept waiting to make sure the blood type was right.

"How ya' gonna keep them down on the farm after they've seen Paree" became a popular refrain about American soldiers returning from World War I. And so it was with my effort to return to mathematics. My teaching at Pomona suffered from my lack of interest in preparing adequately for the classes. I spent all my time reading books on China or something else—anything else. I resigned from my position. 🔲

While I was a junior at Swarthmore College, I had won a summer fellowship from the Social Science Research Council (SSRC) to design "An Experiment in Bargaining Games"; this was an effort to apply psychology to mathematical theories concerning the outcome of certain non-zero-sum two-person games. The results were published[29] in the scientific literature, and on the basis of that success, SSRC gave me a first-year fellowship to study mathematics at Stanford on the theory that I would apply mathematics to problems in the social sciences.

Remembering this happy experience, I applied for and secured a fellowship to return to Stanford to retool as an economist. But studying economics turned out to be, for me, every bit as boring as teaching mathematics.

During this year, in 1969, something totally unexpected occurred that, in retrospect, sealed the fate of the ABM systems and made possible the ABM Treaty banning such systems. It was the lucky break that ABM opponents needed. By complete coincidence, it involved the largely defunct chapters of the Federation of American Scientists (FAS), which, a year or so later, I took over as chief executive officer.

In sum, the Army had decided to base the dozen anti-missile sites necessary for a "thin" anti-Chinese defense near major cities, where the system could more easily be bolstered into a "thick" defense. This was a fatal error. FAS chapters began to complain about "bombs in the backyard," and people who would not otherwise have noticed the ABM system decided that it was dangerous.

I remember how embarrassed I was about this argument at the time. In fact, the ABM warheads were not, in my opinion, likely to go off by themselves, and they were not a danger to the cities. But the public reaction was extraordinarily favorable to the anti-ABM cause. I neither fanned this fire nor tried to douse it. In any case, nothing could have stopped it.[30] About this time, Senator Edward M. Kennedy joined the opposition, and under his leadership, Senate opponents of the ABM grew from a dozen to thirty-four, on their way to fifty—a development that turned out to be decisive in securing the ABM Treaty.

With the ABM debate in Washington heating up and my economics retooling foundering, I decided to leave Stanford University in February and relocate to Washington. In part, it was because Jerome Wiesner had decided to put together an anti-ABM book to be sponsored by Senator Kennedy. I had telegraphed Jerry an offer of help and been assigned a chapter on inspection techniques.[31] Sometime around February I tested the waters in Washington without B.J. and, later, asked her to quit her job and join me.

I felt comfortable in Washington. My family had moved there in 1940 when I was five years old. My earliest memory was of a Washington neighbor, a certain naval captain—Captain Willenbucher—coming to the door and shouting to my father, "It's war!" He had learned early of the attack on the Navy's ships at Pearl Harbor and had rushed four doors down Nebraska Avenue to tell the neighborhood newspaperman.

I had attended local public schools (Lafayette Elementary School and Alice Deal Junior High School) until age fifteen. In 1950, my father moved to Paris to serve as a foreign correspondent for the now-defunct *New York Daily Compass*. And although I later attended high school in New York and then went off to college and graduate school, I continued to visit Washington regularly, since my parents had moved back in 1952. So I knew the town.

I quickly made contact with the anti-ABM forces, which were then being led by Senator John Sherman Cooper (R, Kentucky), whose chief aide was William Miller, and Senator Philip Hart (D, Michigan), whose chief aide was Muriel Ferris. Together they were moving the anti-ABM Senate forces from some thirty supporters to the eventual fifty.

With the entire scientific community to draw upon, they had experts on the ABM with credentials that far surpassed my own. (The single most effective ABM opponent was Wolfgang K.H. Panofsky of the Stanford University linear accelerator.) But none was living on Capitol Hill. As McGeorge Bundy once wrote in a *Foreign Affairs* article, one of the most important aspects of influence is "being there." I came to learn, during the following months, how important it was to be on the scene soldering wires and making connections.

Watching William Miller, a real operator and later the U.S. ambassador to the Ukraine, was instructive. He would sit in a back office of Cooper's suite calling senior scientists, working the press, rounding up other aides of key senators, and, in general, developing a campaign. Three years my senior, he had prior experience as a foreign service officer and knew the ropes. I helped him whenever I could and walked the halls serving as an unpaid operative for the anti-ABM forces.

The Problem of MIRV

During my time at Hudson Institute (1962–1964), I learned in a classified document about the possibility that missiles might fire more than one warhead with multiple independently targetable reentry vehicles (MIRV), which raised the possibility of destroying enemy land-based missiles in a particularly cost-effective first strike. By 1969 MIRV had been well publicized and rightly criticized as a new escalation in the arms race.

In retrospect, MIRV was an enormous assist in persuading the Soviet Union to accept an ABM treaty, since it raised the specter of so many warheads being fired at an ABM system at once as to reduce its effectiveness to zero. This was certainly a major reason why McNamara had approved the development of MIRV. But at the time, we all looked upon MIRV as an unalloyed arms race disaster. As I wrote for the June-July issue of *War/Peace Report*, "In anticipation of the Soviet MIRV, the U.S. is about to buy ABM. In anticipation of the Soviet ABM, the U.S. is about to deploy MIRV. . . . It has been suggested that the political leadership of each major power is simply too weak to seize this opportunity and to respond to this urgency. . . . The question seems to be, will they try?"[32]

Not since 1949 had the Senate seen even a close vote on a major military issue. But when, on August 6, 1969, the ABM issue matured, the vote turned out to be perfectly balanced at fifty–fifty. The opposition had grown from twelve votes in 1967 to thirty-four in 1968 to fifty in 1969. Vice President Spiro Agnew broke the tie, allowing the ABM system to go forward. But the administration had been forced to shift its ABM rationale to "bargaining chip" in a negotiation aimed at a no-ABM Treaty. The vote was a perfect outcome for the ABM Treaty proponents. A win by ABM opponents might have doomed the U.S. ABM system, but at the loss of a bargaining chip in negotiations with the Russians. On the other hand, a big win by the ABM supporters would have left the United States with an ABM system but without a treaty. So this very close result was, in fact, optimal. It represented, after the Bombs in the Backyard debate, the second big break for the ABM Treaty. [33]

At the end of the summer, we made another trip to Moscow. There a mathematician friend invited me to a conference he was running in T'bilisi on "large systems." The paper I had written at RAND on a new way of doing linear programming was vaguely relevant. I used the conference as a pretext to fly to Russia to try, one more time, to lobby the Russians in Moscow into an agreement on banning anti-ballistic missile systems.

The conference turned out to be rather dull, except for a lunch with the famous mathematician Leon Pontrjagin. Blinded by an accident in his teens, he had nevertheless made major contributions to new fields of mathematics, including topological groups. He was considered, along with the American John von Neumann and the Soviet Andrei Nikolayevich Kolmogorov, to be among the three greatest mathematicians of their generation. He was also, regrettably, known as one of the foremost academic anti-Semites in Russia.

Senator Mike Gravel, Democrat of Alaska, and the Exchange Bill

Senator Mike Gravel of Alaska was elected in 1968, and soon after my arrival in Washington in February 1969, I drafted his maiden speech on the floor—an attack on the ABM system. We became friends, and later, on hearing that I would be in Moscow in the fall and that I could show him around, he decided to visit at the same time.

His reaction to the decrepit nature of Moscow confirmed my

view that having politicians visit the Soviet capital would be extremely valuable. On the spot he decided to introduce a bill that would subsidize visits to Moscow by congressmen, senators, governors, and some others. This bill was later introduced with the slogan "Saints and devils thrive on distance."

A subsequent review of two centuries of reports of Westerners visiting Russia confirmed my view that after taking the tour, the hawks would be tranquilized by the poverty and the doves made more vigilant by the lies. In testimony he presented, Gravel took my line that a closeup view of the Soviets would lead the politicians to "trust them less and fear them less."

After Gravel left Moscow, I was asked by an intermediary whether I would meet with Sergei Khrushchev, the son of the retired premier, Nikita Khrushchev; Sergei had a sick sister, Lena, and wanted someone to take a blood sample to America for diagnosis. The disease lupus erythematosis was suspected. We readily agreed, but the blood sample was not ready by the time we left. When it did arrive, we took it from the Soviet Embassy in Washington to Johns Hopkins, to be analyzed there by an expert on lupus, Dr. A. McGehee Harvey.

I had always felt a certain sympathy for Khrushchev, who seemed to me to be a pre-Gorbachev who wanted change. My wife and I decided to arrange a doctor's visit. We told Harvey that we could not fund a suitable medical fee. But if he and his wife wanted a week in Moscow, we could pay for their ticket and the Khrushchevs—who had rubles—could fund the return ticket with payment in their own currency. I asked him to observe medical ethics and not to disclose the family name of the patient. He readily agreed, and he kept his part of the bargain.

The daughter did have lupus and did eventually die. On our return to Moscow in 1970, I learned that Harvey and his wife had been strip-searched by the KGB. But why? The mystery persisted for twenty years, until Sergei Khrushchev wrote his memoir, *Khrushchev on Khrushchev*. In that book Sergei Khrushchev revealed that he had been stunned at our offer to send a doctor, but Lena's illness was so severe that he appealed to the foreign minister, Gromyko, who telegraphed the Soviet ambassador to the United States, Dobrynin, to provide help and visas. But the KGB evidently thought that my interest in helping the Khrushchevs was linked to an effort by the CIA to smuggle Nikita Khrushchev's memoirs out of the country. (In fact, of course, I knew nothing of the memoir.)

When Sergei took the Harveys to meet his father—without the Intourist guide—the KGB's suspicions were confirmed. Later, at the Harveys' hotel, the KGB pounced and searched everything, taking films and finding nothing. Still they told Sergei that Harvey was a CIA agent—and Sergei apparently partly believed it.

I was falsely accused also. In his memoir Sergei reports that he was told that "Stone and Harvey are veteran intelligence agents" and that he should report any contacts with them to the KGB.[34] (Harvey, when told of this twenty years later, advised me "not to worry; when I was in India, people regularly accused me of being a CIA agent." In fact, Harvey was just America's greatest expert on lupus!)

According to Sergei, many people suffered from this incident, even including "totally innocent people who filled out the Harveys' visa forms in our Washington embassy." His relations with Yuli Vorontsov—then the minister-counselor at the Soviet embassy (and now the ambassador)—who had turned over the blood sample to me, were broken. The mathematician Revaz Gamkrelidze, who had arranged my meeting with Khrushchev, was no longer allowed to go abroad. According to Sergei Khrushchev's memoir, "nor was Stone particularly welcome in the Soviet Union."

Premier Nikita Khrushchev with the Russian mathematician Revaz Gamkrelidze on July 3, 1971, in the last photo taken of Khrushchev before his death

(Khrushchev was later told that Stone was an "out-and-out spy" and an "active CIA agent").[35]

Twenty years later, Sergei Khruschev wrote to explain why he had released our joint secret in his book ("Now it seems to me, has come a time to reveal secrets") and to thank me ("I am extremely grateful to you for your humanitarian part in the fate of my sister and for your silence in those not very happy years.")[36]

In retrospect, it seems inevitable to me that persons reaching across the barricades would be accused of being spies—not just on one side but on both. Whole agencies were organized as watchdogs to bark at any unusual sign. In fact, I was admitted to the Soviet Union the next year, in 1970—and again when I applied in 1975. But there were always long waits at the internal border, which in retrospect I assign to the time required for the Soviet system to position someone to follow me around.[37] (In fact, the only thing I ever spirited out of the Soviet Union was a poem by Evgeny Yevtushenko concerning Robert Kennedy.)[38]

My fellowship with the Social Science Research Council having terminated in 1969, I had secured an International Affairs Fellowship from the Council on Foreign Relations for 1969–1970. And I had persuaded the council to let me live in Washington and visit New York only for monthly seminars that I would give. This permitted me to continue as arms controller-in-residence on Capitol Hill, which suited me fine. We rented a townhouse within walking distance of Congress, and I prepared to haunt the Hill.

Part II

Life in Washington: Unpredictable in Every Way

CHAPTER 4

Life with the
Foreign Policy Establishment

The Council on Foreign Relations inquires whether a council nonattribution rule has been violated when a U.S. Senate aide learns of a comment made by the Soviet ambassador in an off-the-record meeting. Two years later, confronted with proof that government officials are regularly violating this rule, the council is led to a constructive change in the rule.

But the council association proves its worth when a council clipping file reveals that a new magazine for which the author is being asked to become managing editor might have been the conduit for CIA funds.

The tension over MIRV almost cost me my fellowship at the Council on Foreign Relations (CFR), a prestigious nonprofit organization of about two thousand members devoted to discussions of foreign policy.

It began when the council invited the Soviet ambassador, Anatoly Dobrynin, to give one of its normal off-the-record speeches at a gala black-tie reception that I attended along with about seventy others on January 23, 1970. Dobrynin mentioned, in passing, to the entire audience that MIRV was dangerous and that something should be done about it. At that time, my good friend Alton Frye was the administrative assistant and legislative assistant to Senator Edward Brooke, a distinguished black senator from Massachusetts. With his magnificent legislative skills, Frye had rounded up no less than fifty senators who wanted to oppose the testing of MIRV—tests that, once done, would make subsequent arms control agreements on the introduction of MIRV unverifiable and thus impossible to achieve. Frye, learning about Dobrynin's remarks, called the Department of State to complain. Why, he wanted to know, was State constantly telling Brooke that the Soviet Union was uninterested in MIRV? Did not the Soviet ambassador's remark show the opposite?

John McCloy, chairman of the board of the Council on Foreign Relations—and, at that time, also the chairman of the General Advisory Committee of the Arms Control and Disarmament Agency—then asked the council's executive director to look into whether I had violated the nonattribution rule of the Council on Foreign Relations by telling Frye what the Soviet ambassador had said in an off-the-record session.[39]

I was therefore called on the carpet by the late George Franklin, the council's executive director and one of the world's sweetest men. I said I did not believe that it was I who had told Frye but pointed out—as so many in Washington tend to forget—that Congress is part of the government. Indeed, Senator Brooke and, by extension, Frye represented no less than half the legislature—fifty senators—on this issue. Why should Frye not be told? At least ten of the seventy guests worked for executive-branch agencies with intense interest in the subject of MIRV and arms control. Were not all of them writing memos for their superiors? What would happen to them if they told their superiors that they could not report the Soviet ambassador's comments because of the council's "nonattribution rule"? (They would, of course, have been sent to the loony bin.) Whom were we kidding about this? On hearing all this, Franklin told me not to worry. But I was sore.

At the termination of my fellowship, the council asked me to become a full (and lifetime) member. It seemed too "establishment" to me at the time, and I hesitated. I turned to an associate for advice—the Harvard biochemist Matthew Meselson—and he told me incisively that if I wanted to work in this field, membership was, really, a professional requirement. Recognizing the wisdom of this, I wrote a note to George Franklin saying—I am now embarrassed to report—that "on reflection, I have decided to join." George responded evenly that he was happy that "on reflection" I had agreed.

So I was a member when, a few years later, over lunch, Fred Ikle, then director of the Arms Control and Disarmament Agency (ACDA), congratulated me on something I had said at the council. Asked how he knew, he said that one of his staff had provided him with a relevant memo on it! This was my smoking gun.

I turned on the council staff, reminding them of my earlier tribulation, and insisted that the attribution rule be changed to legitimize the discussions that were, in any case, taking place between council members and between the council and government officials.[40] And, two years later, after intense study, it was. So far as I know, no problems have come up with the new rule.[41]

I came to love the council and the good fellowship of persons of quite different political views. It was indeed useful to be a member. For one thing, I recommended that Frye receive his own International Affairs Fellowship and, as a result, he later joined the council and rose to be its senior vice president. And the meetings were often quite interesting. But one thing was astonishing. In one election, there were nine candidates competing for eight positions—in effect, one's vote was reduced to *not* voting for just one person. And then it got worse; Winston Lord, the president of the council, proposed that the voting become eight for eight.

In a letter of February 11, 1985, Chairman of the Board David Rockefeller announced the abolition of all choice, which he described, in a nicely understated phrase, as "vesting somewhat greater authority in the Nominating Committee."[42] The reason lay on the front page of *The New York Times* some time before. Henry Kissinger—a lion of the foreign policy establishment and, indeed, the person who had proposed Lord for president—had been revealed in the *Times* as the odd man out in the last election. Only he had lost, of nine candidates. And because of the mathematics of a nine-for-eight election, he had done so with almost two-thirds of the voters voting for him.[43]

The ballots now provided absolutely no choice while solemnly requiring that each person vote for all eight candidates or the ballot would not be accepted.[44] After a few years of this, I could stand it no more.[45] I decided to rebel and reduced my proposal to a single sentence—always a good idea:

> In elections for the Board of the Council on Foreign Relations, the Nominations Committee should offer the Council membership substantial choice by putting forward a slate of candidates substantially exceeding the number of vacant positions on the Board.

Then, in a fashion that was unprecedented, I stood outside the doors of the Washington council office and collected signatures. As I got some, I mailed out new petitions with the affirming names attached. After a few such cycles, I had 109 famous names, including a very wide political range, from George McGovern to General Edward Rowny and many in between. Even President Carter pitched in with a private letter. As a consequence, the council set up a relevant committee, and the rules were changed.[46] This episode fixed in my mind the fact that most people will *not* rebel and many will go along—even with the ridiculous.

The ABM Debate Continues

During my fellowship year at the council, in 1969–1970, I was less of a scholar and more of an activist. The book that I had hoped would emerge from the fellowship did not materialize, but an article in the council journal, *Foreign Affairs*, did ("When and How to Use SALT"). The article emphasized the role of domestic politics and concluded that "an approach that puts domestic debate first may be not only an *alternative* to a formal treaty but a precondition."[47]

I was also busy publishing articles urging congressional involvement in strategic issues. The fifty-to-fifty vote on the ABM had been the only close Senate vote in the entire Cold War on a defense issue, and I hoped for more. On March 1, I was the first "guest" advocate on an installment of the then-famous television show *The*

Advocates. On that show the question was, "Should the Congress appropriate further funds to maintain, improve, or protect land-based missiles in the United States?" I opposed such efforts to use ABM systems for the purpose of defending intercontinental ballistic missiles (ICBMs). Five days later, on March 6, on *The Washington Post* op-ed page, I discussed two SALT approaches. The first approach would be a permanent agreement on total size that would permit, under the quota limits, ever-changing modernization (in the end, the United States took roughly this approach). The other was an "interim freeze," an "attempt to negotiate, in the course of a few months, a jury-rigged comprehensive freeze that would hold together for, let us say, two years." I urged the latter.

On December 28, 1969, the council of the Federation of American Scientists met in Boston in a fateful meeting. Founded in 1945 by Manhattan Project atomic scientists as the Federation of Atomic Scientists, it had welcomed other scientists in 1946 by changing the name so as to keep the initials the same.

FAS had played an important role from 1945 to 1948 in efforts to maintain civilian control of atomic energy. And it had continued to function through the darkest Cold War years in the 1950s and 1960s. But FAS had sunk to a rather low ebb by 1969, with an annual budget of about seven thousand dollars a year and, of course, a mostly volunteer staff.

A mainstay of the volunteer organization, the physicist and former Arms Control and Disarmament Agency staffer Leonard Rodberg, suggested that FAS double the dues and hire a full-time paid director. ♫ But the candidates he rounded up for this position seemed too young, too grass-roots oriented, and, indeed, too unkempt, in the eyes of FAS officials.

I was a member of the Executive Committee at that time and had prepared most of the arms control statements since joining in 1962. Recognizing that my career as a fellowship bum was coming to an end—two fellowships back-to-back was about as much as anyone could expect—I offered to step down from the Executive

Committee to serve as the executive director if, indeed, Leonard Rodberg himself did not wish to do so.

Leonard said nothing. So the council agreed eagerly with my proposal. I reflected that life as an activist in Washington would suit me much better than life as a scholar. But would there be enough money, even with Leonard's experiment of doubling the dues from $7.50 per person to $15.00? There were only about a thousand members at the time. In today's dollars, it meant, if everyone agreed to pay the higher dues, an annual budget of about sixty thousand dollars.

Enter *Foreign Policy* Magazine

I began considering treating FAS as a half-time job and considered, for the second half, becoming the first editor of a new magazine, *Foreign Policy.* Two distinguished persons were wooing me to do exactly this: the late Warren Manshel, an apparently wealthy stockbroker who later became the U.S. ambassador to the Netherlands (in 1978) and was now *Foreign Policy's* publisher-to-be and chief financial angel; and Irving Kristol, a leading conservative thinker who was then editor of *The Public Interest.*

After Mandel had wined and dined me at the Century Club and at the Hotel Pierre restaurant, at his home one night he said, "Midnight is striking—you have to make up your mind." He raised his offer from ten thousand to twelve thousand dollars a year; this was an offer of about fifty thousand dollars in current dollars for half-time work, and the work seemed attractive. But I was nervous. Sam Huntington, the renowned Harvard professor of political science, had recommended me to Manshel, and I remembered ⬥ Sam saying that Manshel had worked for the CIA and that "I am not sure he ever left it."

I repaired to the Council on Foreign Relations the next morning and consulted their clipping file. There I found a *New York Times Magazine* article on one of the CIA-front organizations much discussed in 1967: *Encounter* magazine.[48]

The article was written by none other than Irving Kristol, who had worked for *Encounter.* He denied being "witting" to its CIA involvement but said the magazine had been sponsored by the Congress for Cultural Freedom and acknowledged that "both the Congress and *Encounter* were subsidized by the C.I.A." And his article referred to "the executive secretary of the Congress for Cultural Freedom—who had a 'witting' connection with the C.I.A., as he has since candidly admitted."

I was able, that same day, to determine that Warren Manshel had worked for the CIA from 1952 to 1954; then, after this remarkably short formal involvement, he had become the—guess what— "Executive Director, Congress for Cultural Freedom" from 1954 to 1955. In 1955 he had returned to New York and joined a brokerage house (Coleman and Company). And in 1965, he became the publisher of Kristol's periodical, *The Public Interest.*[49]

I broke out in a cold sweat. How would it seem if it came out that I was editing a magazine published by the same people who had previously been backed by the CIA—one of whom had actually worked for the agency? In such a case, who would believe this was not another CIA publication like *Encounter?* Of course, the rules on CIA involvement in domestic organizations had changed, as noted earlier. But could not the CIA have found some way around them? (According to a document that had escaped from a Council on Foreign Relations study group, one year before my dilemma, some had urged the CIA, after the scandal concerning the National Student Association, to do just that—to go under deeper cover, i.e., not to support American organizations directly but, somehow, to do so indirectly.)[50]

I speculated that a stockbroker like Manshel who had a connection with the CIA could easily be provided with monies in the form of commissions for handling covert parts of the CIA's vast budget. Then, by prearrangement, some of those brokerage fees could be used to set up anything the CIA (and Warren Manshel) wanted.

I liked Manshel but decided to withdraw quietly and work for FAS full-time. On hearing that I was declining, which I had signaled to Sam Huntington but not yet to Manshel, Warren called on a sunny May Saturday afternoon. He was concerned, he said, that if it became known that I would not serve as managing editor for some reason that reflected badly on the new *Foreign Policy* magazine, he would not be able to get it started.

I told him that it was not my intention to defame his project. And though I didn't mention my suspicions, he obviously knew what they were. I was not then against what he might well be doing; I just did not want to be part of it. And when *Foreign Policy*'s next choice for managing editor, John Franklin Campbell, called me to voice the same apprehension, I did not share my fears with him.[51]

By this time, I was acquainted with three quite senior Soviet officials: Georgi Arbatov, director of his Center for the U.S.A. and Canada; N. N. Inozemtsov, director of IMEMO; and M. D. Millionshchikov, vice president of the Soviet Academy of Sciences. All were visiting Washington as part of a Soviet delegation to a Convocation for Peace. I had invited more than a hundred people to my cramped rented town house to receive them. The guests included Henry Kissinger, then the national security adviser, who arrived in a car accompanied by a guard with a pistol on his hip. It was May 2, 1970, the day the United States invaded Cambodia.

Later, in the town house next door, Millionshchikov became everlastingly grateful to me for the opportunity to describe to some American experts on "turbulence" how he had been able to derive a well-known constant for fluid flow through a pipe with the calculus of variations. It was, he confided to me, the first time in thirty years he had come up with something publishable, since his work at the academy was too demanding to allow him time for research.

In Moscow, the fall before, he had described to me the Kafka-esque scene at his dissertation oral in 1917. As was the custom at Ph.D. orals, three candidates presented themselves simultaneously to answer whatever they could. In this case, he had been brilliant, another student competent, and a third student had been able to answer no questions at all.

The chairman of the dissertation committee regretfully advised the third candidate that he had failed. The candidate rose up and said, "It is you who are wrong. This is the year of the great socialist revolution. Russia has become a socialist country. We three candidates have presented ourselves as a collective. The collective has answered all your questions and so it passes, and I, as a member of the collective, also pass."

Millionshchikov was astonished to see the frightened professors back down in a country that had, they well knew, not the slightest idea what socialism should mean. The student passed. Perhaps, from that moment, socialism in Russia was doomed.

CHAPTER 5

Stopping an Illegal
CIA Mail-Opening Campaign

A shot in the dark in preparing the FAS newsletter hits paydirt by frightening the Postal Service into halting its cooperation with the CIA in illegally opening mail not only from foreigners to Americans but also from Americans to foreigners. Meanwhile, the Soviet Union is eavesdropping on American society without much sign of Justice Department interest in stopping it. A topsy-turvy world.

Entrepreneurial activists are probably born, not made, and one of their distinguishing characteristics might be an inability to fit in with establishments—with respect to which they become dissidents—and an impatient restlessness with the requirements of traditional occupations such as teaching or research. For ten years after receiving my Ph.D., I anguished over my inability to fit in at such institutions as the Stanford Research Institute, the Hudson Institute, the Harvard Center for International Affairs, Pomona College, Stanford University (in economics), and the Council on Foreign Relations. How happy I am, however, in retrospect, that these deficiencies of ability or motivation were shunting me into an organization that was far more "me." Activists need a home.

After becoming director (later termed president) of FAS in June of 1970, I spent much time rejuvenating the nearly defunct organization. A significant part of the FAS's meager budget turned out to come from roughly seven thousand dollars in annual dividends from an Ohio insurance company—dividends that were realized from the FAS group life insurance program when our members defied the actuarial tables and lived longer than expected.

I was still so spooked by reading about *Encounter* that I flew to Ohio to make sure that these dividends were deserved and not some under-the-table contribution from the intelligence community.[52] (I was never against the CIA, especially not against the "white side" of the CIA that did estimates as opposed to covert operations. But I certainly wanted to make sure we were not embarrassed by an improper association with the agency.)

In 1968, as chairman of the FAS nominating committee, I had induced Herbert F. York, chancellor of the University of California at San Diego and once a high-ranking Pentagon official, to run for FAS vice chairman (and chairman-elect), so he became chairman in 1970 just when I needed distinguished and brilliant leadership. He reluctantly agreed to my paying myself at a full-time rate, even though FAS lacked the money to do so and he feared breaking the FAS bank. I managed to scrape through by paying myself back-pay later.

I began by redesigning the monthly newsletter with more original material in an attempt to make it more attractive to members than it had been before.[53] And I persuaded a distinguished former deputy director of the CIA (and assistant director of ACDA), Herbert Scoville Jr., to chair a Strategic Weapons Committee.[54] The committee promptly denounced a report of the conservative American Security Council that claimed that the United States was falling behind the Soviets; we responded that the United States was "ahead, not behind, the Soviet Union in any important measure of strategic force effectiveness."[55] Our report got national exposure, most notably in an article by William Beecher in *The New York Times*, for its allegation of "scare tactics." So at least something was happening.

Meanwhile, I was recruiting FAS sponsors to our masthead: John Kenneth Galbraith; Nobel Prize winners Hans Bethe, Owen Chamberlain, Donald A. Glaser, Harlow Shapley, and Harold C. Urey; and presidential science advisers Jerome B. Wiesner and

George B. Kistiakowsky. Organizationally, we were looking much better.

The February 1971 newsletter, the fourth one I prepared, was on "Privacy of Communications in American Life: Eavesdropping and Mail Covers." This newsletter was instrumental in persuading the CIA to stop a twenty-year-old—and illegal—practice of opening

---

THE VOICE OF SCIENCE ON CAPITOL HILL

F. A. S. *NEWSLETTER*

FEDERATION OF AMERICAN SCIENTISTS—Founded 1946—
A national organization of natural and social scientists and engineers concerned with problems of science and society.

Vol. 24, No. 2
February, 1971

Herbert F. York, Chairman
Marvin L. Goldberger, Vice Chairman
Jeremy J. Stone, Director

PRIVACY OF COMMUNICATIONS IN AMERICAN LIFE: EAVESDROPPING AND MAIL COVERS

The right of the people to be secure in their persons, houses, papers, and effects, against unreasonable searches and seizures, shall not be violated and no warrants shall issue but upon probable cause, supported by oath or affirmation, and particularly describing the place to be searched, and the persons or things to be seized.

—Fourth Amendment, U.S. Constitution

COURT-ORDER EAVESDROPPING

Reports of court-orders show that state and local law enforcement agents are usually using wiretaps, at great expense, in criminal cases they could normally solve in other ways. Thus in the most common cases, those of gambling and drugs, hundreds of incriminating conversations are overheard and much business is going on. These cases could be solved without bugging by undercover agents. In cases of extortion, the party being victimized can permit eavesdropping, or make recordings himself. Is wire-tapping often *really* necessary? Since a lot of police work can be done for the $1,000 the median tap costs, tapping may not even be cost-effective.

Presumably, there are cases which can be solved in no other way. But the advantages of permitting these solutions must be balanced against the political costs. Once we permit state and local agents to do *any* wiretapping legally, they must be permitted the right to buy the equipment. And once they have the equipment, it is evident that they cannot be trusted to monitor their own compliance with legal safeguards. They are cops, not attorneys, and catching criminals is their professional interest. From their point of view, unauthorized wiretapping is a "crime without victims." They engage in it in the higher interest of protecting society. No police bureaucracy is going to prosecute its officers for being overly zealous in tapping phones. Even if the public could catch these officers in the act systematically, the FBI is not going to pursue such cases, and the Justice Department attorneys are not going to prosecute.

In addition, permitting, as the law does, "any officer of a State or political subdivision thereof, who is empowered by law to conduct investigations..." to buy wiretapping equipment keeps Spy Shops in business. These shops sell bugging equipment under the counter, to private detectives and anyone else, in violation of law. We know that other crimes without victims, such as gambling and prostitution, are

Continued on page 2.

FAS NO-ABM RESOLUTION HITS SENSITIVE NERVE

On December 27, at its national council meeting, FAS called for an initial separate SALT agreement on ABM— one which would preclude missile defenses or limit them drastically. A related press release arguing for agreements of this kind was widely distributed. On January 9, the New York Times and Washington Post both carried stories revealing that the Soviet Union had earlier offered to discuss just such a separate ABM agreement in the secret SALT talks, if the United States would agree in principle to the idea.

The notion of a separate ABM agreement is a hard one for the Administration to avoid. An ABM limitation has been a presupposition of all other progress in the SALT talks and, unlike agreements on offensive weapons, could be resolved by itself. Many U.S. arms controllers have called for this kind of agreement for years. Indeed, it was the Soviet Union that earlier insisted on the principle that offensive weapons be discussed also.

Furthermore, the talks are now deadlocked on issues

involving offensive weapons, such as whether those European-based U.S. aircraft capable of striking the Soviet Union should be covered in any agreement on strategic weapons. Even if the contemplated agreement on numbers of offensive weapons could be reached, the agreement might be no more than a "sham" permitting all-important qualitative improvements – as FAS pointed out in an earlier statement.

An initial ABM agreement would undermine motivation for offensive weapons by precluding the defenses that neutralize them. It would save large resources and the Governmental debating time absorbed by the ABM each year. The agreement would be far more significant strategically than the Partial Test Ban Treaty. The information that the Soviet Union is prepared to discuss an ABM agreement is bound to influence the Senate debate this year. Copies of the Federation statement calling for an ABM agreement are available, in limited quantities, at the national office.

(See also page 5)

See page 4 for discussion of mail covers.

The front page of the FAS newsletter of February 1971, the preparation of which led to the termination of the CIA's secret mail-opening program, HTLINGUAL foreign mail. I knew nothing about my letter's impact at the time. But it typifies political chaos theory at work in Washington: An FAS butterfly flapped its wings, and a storm broke out inside the government.

It was not until four years later, in June of 1975, that the Rockefeller Commission released its report on the CIA's domestic activities and referred vaguely to an "association of scientists" that had started a chain of events. An alert *Science* magazine reporter called us and quickly ascertained that we were the association in question.

All of this began on January 13, 1971, when, as part of preparation of the newsletter, I wrote to the chief postal inspector, W. J. Cotter, asking, among other things, whether the Postal Service was permitting any other agency to open the mails improperly. It was essentially a shot in the dark, based on no more than vague suspicions.[56]

His February 10 response to me denied any wrongdoing:

> The U.S. Postal Service has traditionally considered the seal on first-class mail sacred. This Department has no knowledge of any efforts by State or Federal agencies to induce postal officials to violate mail cover regulations or to allow any class of mail to leave the custody of official postal channels for the purpose of permitting other agencies to obtain the information contained therein.

But guess what? Cotter knew all about it. In fact, he had been given his job as chief postal inspector expressly to ensure that the CIA would not be deterred from borrowing foreign mail from the Postal Service to look it over before delivery. Cotter was well qualified for the assignment—he had been working in the very CIA field office that ran the mail intercept. The program was called HTLINGUAL.

Nevertheless, my letter spurred an alarmed Cotter to call the CIA's director, Richard Helms, demanding that the program be stopped and observing that he now worked not for the CIA but for the Postal Service.[57] Helms asked for a month's respite, during which time he persuaded Attorney General John Mitchell to call the postmaster general, Winston Blount, and to instruct him to tell his chief postal inspector to lay off.

On May 19, 1971, in the deepest secrecy, the high command of the CIA met for forty-five minutes to discuss what to do about the threat I posed to their project. We now know exactly what they concluded: Let's continue unless we decide that Stone really knows something and we are about to get caught.

We know this thanks to another weird chain of circumstances, seven years later, worth recounting as an example of Washington at work.

It began in 1978 when I asked the CIA (and the FBI), under the Freedom of Information Act (FOIA), for information gathered about me. Later, I complained to the CIA that given my five trips to the Soviet Union, they must have more than I had received.

On October 22, 1975, out of the blue, a CIA FOIA liaison officer to whom I had complained called and said the CIA had, indeed, found something further mentioning me and was, in fact, sending it over by messenger! The agency's suddenly solicitous attitude and special delivery raised my eyebrows.

When I saw the memo, which recounts a decision by government officials to persist in activities they knew to be illegal, I immediately walked over to the Senate Select Committee to Study Governmental Operations to show it to the committee's director, my friend from the ABM campaign William G. Miller. He said, "Oh yes, we are having a hearing today for Cotter to explain his role in this. And we have this memo already." Indeed they were responsible for having it declassified.

The CIA had assumed that the chairman of the committee, Senator Frank Church of Idaho, would release the memo that very day at the hearings and decided that they had better preemptively fulfill my FOIA request. At the last minute, however, Church decided that it would violate the privacy of a person mentioned in the memo (Herbert Scoville), and he decided not to release it after all. By that time, however, the CIA messenger had already brought it to me.

The memo detailed the exchanges in a meeting of the highest

CIA officials. Besides Helms (described as the DCI or Director of Central Intelligence), there was the DDP (director of plans, or covert activities); the C/CI and the DC/CI (the chief and the deputy chief of counterintelligence); the D/S (the director of security), and the C/CI/Project (the head of the mail-opening project).

Written in urbane fashion, the memo said that the DCI opened the meeting with a "reference to an inquiry as to possible mail tampering by Government agencies, addressed to the Chief Postal Inspector, Mr. Cotter, by Dr. Jeremy J. Stone on behalf of the Federation of American Scientists." The officials noted that Scoville "had been briefed" on the project but "had not been a consumer of HTLINGUAL material for many years." The DCI was not, the memo said, "over-concerned about Scoville."

The operation, begun in 1953, had been revealed to the FBI in 1958. The DDP was "gravely concerned" about bad publicity and "opined that the operation should be done by the FBI because they could better withstand such publicity, inasmuch as it is a type of domestic surveillance." But the counterintelligence staff wanted to continue the practice and considered it "*foreign* surveillance."

(In fact, I know from personal experience that this policy included surveillance of Americans at home because a later FOIA request of mine, in 1978, produced several chatty letters that I had sent to people in Russia: Nina Shakova, the poet Evgeny Yevtushenko, the Cambodia expert Dmitry Muravyev, and the *Pravda* editor Yuri Zhukov [letters that, in fact, are now helping me date events for this book]. So CIA was opening *outgoing* mail of Americans and not just *incoming* mail of Russians.)

Helms grilled his staff about who had knowledge of the practice outside the CIA ("only the FBI") and at the Postal Service ("the little grey man" who got a "$50 monthly bonus for this duty"). The memo continued:

> The previous Chief Postal Inspector, Mr. Montague, had never wanted to know the extent of examination actually done, and was thus

able to deny on oath before a congressional committee that there was any tampering. Mr. Cotter would be unable to make such denial under oath.[58]

The memo concluded with Helms asking the chief of the project to "monitor the operation most discreetly, and bring any problem or difficulty to him."

So the project continued for two more years. But later, in 1973, Attorney General John Mitchell was in jail for his role in the Watergate scandal, and Postmaster General Blount had retired. Cotter seized the occasion to complain again. Helms had been fired by Nixon in December 1972, and the issue was turned over to the new CIA director, James Schlesinger, and his deputy director for operations (i.e., covert operations), William Colby. They finally stopped the program.

It later turned out that at least one CIA staffer, Dr. Melvin Crain, had tried to stop the project from inside but reported that "officials of the CIA told me they knew it was illegal and unconstitutional but it was needed to achieve our mission." Crain revealed that highly sophisticated equipment based in post offices in New Orleans and in New York had permitted the CIA to "open, copy, reseal letters and send them on their way without any telltale signs of tampering," and so quickly that "the normal flow of the mail was not disturbed."[59]

Soviet Eavesdropping

Not only was the government engaging in (unauthorized) espionage against its own citizens, but it was also failing to resist Soviet espionage. The Rockefeller Commission on CIA Activities Within the United States had revealed that the Communist countries were able to eavesdrop on private U.S. telephone conversations with an "extraordinary degree of technology and sophistication."[60]

I immediately wrote to the Justice Department, which contains the

FBI and is responsible for preventing espionage, asking why electronic countermeasures were not being used to prevent this spying on Americans. After two months of delay, the department responded that it could not make a "final determination as to any specific course of action" and that the government's "course of action must be determined on a national policy level." Put another way, the Justice Department would prosecute you or me for listening in on telephones—indeed, the government itself could not do so without judicial warrants—but it was not about to lift a finger to stop the Russians from doing so. Aghast, we charged that the National Security Agency (NSA), which had interests in listening in on the Soviet Union, was not eager to start a "jamming war" and preferred a tacit agreement not to do so. The government, of course, was protected by secretly scrambled phones. Only the American public was being left out to dry.[61]

Another anomaly arose in November 1975, when I finally spoke to Cotter and asked him whether the letter he had sent me was "deliberately misleading" or "knowingly false." He said, "Of course, it was knowingly false since I was witting." I well knew that a private citizen could go to jail for up to five years for lying to a federal official, even if not under oath.[62] Such a law had been used against someone who denied to a police officer that he was a Communist. The Cotter letter raised the reverse question: Could a federal official lie to a private citizen with impunity? According to the law, the answer was yes. We persuaded Senator Kennedy to offer a proposal that would make it a crime for federal officials to make knowingly false statements. But it was not passed.[63]

In sum, mail opening, wire tapping, and lying all offered clear evidence for the insight James Madison conveyed to Thomas Jefferson on May 13, 1798: "Perhaps it is a universal truth that the loss of liberty at home is to be charged to provisions against danger, real or pretended, from abroad."

Bureaucracies seem often to engage in a kind of preemptive surrender of difficult terrain, especially when pressed from the outside with the danger of exposure. Under circumstances of protective secrecy, however, few will ever know what motivated the shift. By its nature, therefore, public interest activists normally get little credit for their success when wrestling with modern bureaucratic systems. For example, we have no way of knowing whether our letters to the Justice Department, our press release, and our interviews to the press ever had any impact on Soviet eavesdropping. But after the mail-opening affair I never doubted that the effects on policy matters of my activities might be far in excess of any echoes of these effects I might receive.

CHAPTER **6**

R&D Gap Report Stimulates
Both Investigation and Smear

An analysis of the statements of a DOD official gives rise to an unprecedented investigation by the R&D subcommittee of the Senate Armed Services Committee and, in due course, produces for the author a particularly vicious smear in six hundred newspapers by the notorious columnist Joseph Alsop and a position on the Nixon administration's "enemies list."

The third highest official in the Defense Department, Dr. John S. Foster, the director of defense research and engineering (DDR&E), was repeatedly claiming that Soviet technological superiority was just a matter of time.

I was, by then, an expert at reading congressional testimony—this was, after all, how I had prepared my first book—and I burned the midnight oil and read everything he said. I focused on what *Science* magazine eventually called "contradictions and discrepancies in . . . public statements and on flaws in the methodology they [defense department analysts] used to analyze the supposed threat."[64] Dr. Foster seemed to be lacking discipline.

I collected his statements in a fifty-page, heavily documented staff study entitled "Is There an R&D Gap?"[65] One of the themes of this study was that the "R&D gap" was as much a mirage as earlier "bomber gaps" and "missile gaps" had been, the reflection of wholly unrealistic projections of what the Soviets could do.[66] The report concluded that "this entire episode has been a classical numbers game featuring selective disclosure, questionable assumptions, exaggeratedly precise estimates, misleading language, and alarmist non-sequitur conclusions."

Trying to work behind the scenes, like a good staff man, I first circulated the report to key FAS members and persuaded four of our officials to review the document, to comment on it, and to let me put their names on the report as an "Ad Hoc Committee on Military R&D."[67] Our May 6 press conference produced a good deal of publicity—even a Herblock cartoon carrying the ironic caption "More Money! The Russians May Be Outspending Us." *The Washington Post* gave it ten inches.[68] UPI put our statement on the wire to all its newspapers, and even Walter Cronkite quoted our main charge.[69] Packing all of our charges into a single quotable sentence had worked well. (The limited capacity of the media has to be kept in mind at all times.) This publicity was unusual.

Science magazine, in an especially kind three-page survey, told the whole story and lauded us from beginning to end. The article began as follows: "In a well-documented presentation before Congress, the Federation of American Scientists (FAS) has released a good deal of steam from the Defense Department's latest drive to inflate its budget on the basis of a threat from the Soviet Union." And it concluded by saying, "Whatever the final effect, in dollars and cents, of their actions, the FAS is offering Congress something they have lacked for many years: expert, independent testimony on the question of how much weaponry is really enough."[70] (This was not, in fact, the first time the FAS had testified before Congress. Indeed, in 1971, as a reward for my enterprise in persuading the chairman of the House Armed Services Committee to permit outside groups before his committee, I seem to have become the first witness representing such a group in American history.)[71]

All of this coverage induced the previously lethargic R&D subcommittee of the Senate Armed Services Committee to hold a public hearing on May 19.

I left my name off the paper, even though I had had little help in preparing it. But when the arrival of one of the witnesses was scuttled because of a canceled flight, I surfaced and filled in, with George Rathjens, in testifying. I also produced another five pages, overnight, pointing out that Chairman John C. Stennis and Senator Peter H. Dominick had long ago asked Foster for an unclassified report documenting his charges but had never received it. But I did not sign this either.[72]

The reader may find my staying in the background surprising. In fact, however, I saw myself as a mahout for senior FAS officials. The people I was organizing were somehow "larger"; they were former government officials with credentials. I served as staff, writing documents for their signatures, much as staff members do for senators.

I also feared professional jealousy from my colleagues, even though they were often good friends or longtime acquaintances. I needed their advice and experience, and their credentials were essential. If I got "above myself"—or got too much press—they might be less willing to pitch in. And if the organization became known, as some had suggested, as "Jeremy with a few phone calls," our effectiveness would decline.

From another point of view, also, I felt that I was more important to the effort than any one of them. I feared our opponents might come to think so, too. And if they managed to hit the central command post (me) with a well-aimed smear, it could be lethal to the organization.

As it turned out, however, this happened anyway, thanks to the great success of the hearing. As one observer put it, "some light has been let into a shuttered room in the Pentagon." It was widely covered,[73] and was referred to eventually in *Time* magazine.[74] But the result was, perhaps inevitably, an effort to destroy my effectiveness.

The late columnist Joseph Alsop, then an influential denizen of Washington politics, was known for his dark visions of secret enemy plots. On May 26, 1971, he published a syndicated column in six hundred newspapers charging that the FAS had prepared a "bitter personal attack" on Foster, that I was the federation's "chief mover and shaker," and that I was out to "get" John Foster. A lot of

Joseph Alsop in China

people, he said, wanted Foster "out of the way" because he was almost always right in his assessments of Soviet defense developments. He added, "There is every reason to believe that Dr. Stone completely shares the views of his father, I. F. Stone. And I. F. Stone has not departed a quarter of an inch from the Soviet line on any foreign or defense-policy question in the last two decades."

In sum, it was a charge of treason—trying to help the enemy get rid of an American obstacle. The charge was supported by guilt-by-family-association. And the charges against my father were a smear of his views. Even for Alsop, this was a remarkably low blow. True, I. F. Stone, a radical journalist, was far to the left of Joseph Alsop. But in 1956, after his visit to the Soviet Union, he had written the following passage—in italics—in his famous newsletter, *I. F. Stone's Weekly: "This is not a good society and it is not led by honest men."*[75]

And this was just the tip of an iceberg of other writings that did not follow the Soviet line at all—writings celebrated for their independence of mind. In fact, I. F. Stone was so celebrated for his work

I. F. Stone at work

that upon his death, he received a half dozen op-eds and editorials in *The Washington Post* praising his work—a hell of a lot more than did Alsop when he died. And they were much warmer, from colleagues who knew him for decades. Other papers reacted the same way.[76]

As for me, Alsop was suggesting, without any evidence, that I "completely" shared my father's views. He knew nothing about me whatsoever. His characterization was thrice in error. His column called me "exceedingly left-wing" when I was a mere liberal. It called me a "political scientist" when, in fact, I was trained as a mathematician. It called me a Princeton graduate even though I was a product of Swarthmore College and Stanford University.

It was an interesting experience, being smeared. I learned of the existence of the article in advance from an aunt, Judy Stone, who worked on *The San Francisco Chronicle*. Picking up an advance copy at *The Washington Post* at midday, I asked them not to run it. (It turned out that *The Los Angeles Times*, home of Alsop's L.A. Times Syndicate, had refrained from printing the column because the editors considered it "unverifiable.") The *Post* was unwilling to hold back but ran it on May 26. And it later refused, to my amazement, to let me include in my complaining letter to the *Post* the simple fact that the L.A. Times Syndicate had refused to run the piece.

I asked Scoville to defend me. That night, at his home, nervously looking over his shoulder, I saw that he planned to say, "Stone needs no defense," and to go on to discussing substance! I promptly took the assignment back and started to rally support myself. The next day, May 27, the *Post* printed my reply and a defense of my integrity signed by Bethe, Goldberger, Halperin, Meselson, Scoville, Victor Weisskopf, and Herbert F. York. Only George Kistiakowsky declined to rebuke Alsop, telling me, "One should never get into a pissing contest with a skunk."

The executive editor of the *Post*, Benjamin C. Bradlee, wrote a column that appeared the same day my letter was printed; Bradlee's piece was entitled "The Columnists' Inflated Rhetoric." He cited examples of rhetoric from the columns of Alsop and the team of Evans and Novak, including the smear—but he failed to mention me.

I was still sore and considered suing for libel. But *The New York Times* legal office provided me with some free advice: The courts now required, for "public figures" like me, "an almost prohibitive amount of hard evidence of gross recklessness."[77]

But two weeks later, Alsop was trying to smear me more effectively.[78] He persisted in the charge of treason: "Dr. Jeremy Stone and a good many other misguided American scientists have formed a powerful lobby [FAS was twenty-six years old at that time] primarily aimed, so far as one can see, to subordinating American strategic policy to Soviet strategic policy."[79]

In June 1973, it was revealed that President Nixon had an "enemies list" of approximately 150 people, 20 of whom were academics or scientists. I turned out to be on it—one of the most junior of a distinguished roster that included McGeorge Bundy; the president of Yale University, Kingman Brewster Jr.; the one-time presidential science adviser Jerome B. Wiesner; Arthur Schlesinger Jr., the historian and adviser to President Kennedy; the economist Walter Heller; the president of Harvard University, Derek Bok; and Polaroid's Edwin Land. I have always assumed that it was Alsop's attacks that persuaded the Nixon administration that I was such a bad person that I should be included on this list.

.   .   .

From all this I learned that columnists were, like federal judges, powers unto themselves. They could distort and smear, and most editors would somehow fail to notice.

I also learned that the smears sat around, for long periods, in dark corners of the minds of those who wanted to believe them. And they could cause you to lose a friend. But, in the end, it seems to have reduced my effectiveness only in parts of town where I had not, in any case, much effectiveness anyway. It confirmed my disinterest in working for the government. That, in the end, served me well. And it persuaded me that any real success would corroborate the aphorism that "no good deed goes unpunished."

CHAPTER 7

An Arrow Aimed at Kissinger
Hits the Watergate Bull's-Eye

Political chaos theory is illustrated well by an FAS editorial that caroms off Henry Kissinger one year only to produce a delayed explosion the next year at the feet of President Nixon on what is, perhaps, the most sensitive day of Watergate.

The March 1972 newsletter aimed at bolstering the information needs of Congress at a time when parliaments throughout the world were losing power to their executive counterparts.[80] Accordingly, our special report on the "Legislative Right to Know" focused on (a) the obligation of executive-branch officials to testify; (b) the use of executive privilege to deny information; (c) the executive branch's use of information to lobby the legislative branch; and (d) selective declassification.

The question of executive privilege, in particular, was much in the air. In early 1972 the Separation of Powers Subcommittee of the Senate Judiciary Committee released about six hundred pages of hearings on executive privilege—the executive branch's oft-invoked inherent right to withhold information from Congress. The Supreme Court had never ruled on it, even though about twenty presidents had used it. Congress was becoming restive.

The hearings were dominated by the careful and thorough research of Raoul Berger, who had published a timely book on the subject (*Executive Privilege: A Constitutional Myth*[81]). Berger wrote, "There is little if any historical warrant . . . for the notion that executive privilege was ever intended to be among the checks on the legislative power of inquiry."[82]

I became interested in the use of executive privilege by White House employees. On investigation I learned that as many as seven officials there functioned under one "hat" as confidential advisers to the president (e.g., science adviser to the president) while under another "hat" they functioned in the executive office of the president in a position set up by statute (e.g., director of the White House Office of Science and Technology). They often testified under the second hat though not the first.

The reasoning was that Congress could compel the testimony of any officials, in the White House or elsewhere, whose positions were created by statute. In theory Congress could, if offended, just repeal the laws creating those positions. Advisers were another matter; their salaries were paid by appropriated monies, but more indirectly.

I thought Henry Kissinger's situation from 1969 to 1973 was anomalous. He was an assistant to the president for national security affairs (the confidential adviser role), but unlike the science adviser he failed to hold any second statutory position.

Worse, he should have been holding such a position because he was functioning as if he did. He was fulfilling the duties of the executive secretary of the National Security Council, since all of the staff members of that body were, in fact, reporting to him.[83] Therefore, I drafted an editorial entitled "To Facilitate Congressional Testimony, FAS Proposes Second 'Hat' for Henry Kissinger." It urged him to accept this second title and to testify under it.

As usual, I secured help in polishing the draft, and I obtained the endorsement of distinguished experts. In this case they included Berger, Alton Frye (who had moved to the Council on Foreign Relations), Bernard Schwartz (a distinguished professor of law at New York University), and Lee C. White, who had been a legal adviser to both President Kennedy and President Johnson.[84] Our newsletter received editorial-page attention in *The Washington Post*, and I sent two copies to the White House.[85] Both may have had unusual effects.

The first copy went, on March 2, to Henry Kissinger. My cover letter thanked him effusively for his "historic work" on China and denied that we were motivated by dissatisfaction with his work. But it argued that his testimony—on matters that did not involve confidential communications with the president—would be useful not only to the Senate ("vent the pressures and frustration that leading Senators feel") but to the administration ("you would testify more effectively than anyone else").

Henry seems to have moved fast to cut off any campaign of this kind by enhancing a relatively new innovation, private meetings with congressmen. He had already met with the Foreign Relations Committees in social formats at the homes of key legislators. Now he held a meeting with them in Blair House and proposed to make such meetings "periodic."[86] Thus, within thirty days of my letter to him, by March 31, he was able to respond to me as follows:

> I have met with Senator Fulbright and Congressman Morgan [the chairmen of the two congressional committees covering foreign affairs], and we have agreed to arrange periodic meetings with their committees in which I shall discuss with them the full range of foreign policy issues and answer their questions. The first of these meetings has been held, and I believe you will find that all participants benefited from the very frank discussion which took place.
>
> Recognizing both the special circumstances of the present situation and the right of the Congress to be fully informed, I believe that this procedure meets these needs in a way which does not compromise the traditional right of future Presidents to safeguard the privileged nature of the relations between the President and his principal advisers.

So something *had* happened, and Henry felt obliged to write me about it presumably in the hope that FAS would not press the point.

I also sent an advance courtesy copy of the newsletter to the White House counsel, John Dean. ♫ Much like the shot-in-the-dark letter I sent to the inspector general of the Postal Service, which triggered an end to HTLINGUAL, this letter neither had John Dean in mind as a target nor seemed likely to have any immediate effect.

But a year later it did. The fuse of this time bomb was set on April 20, when John Dean wrote back saying he had found the newsletter "most interesting." In answer to my attached question, he said that neither President Nixon nor any other president had "ever asserted a claim that Presidential aides have blanket immunity from testifying before the Congress on any subject." He said this was shown by examples in my newsletter and "the testimony of [Presidential Assistant] Mr. [Peter] Flanigan before the Senate Judiciary Committee."[87]

I filed the letter away and forgot about it.

Eleven months later, however, the administration was stonewalling under the pressures of Watergate and trying to prevent the testimony of its highest officials on the grounds of executive privilege. On March 15, 1973, President Nixon said, "Members of the White House staff will not appear before a committee of Congress in any formal session."[88] Three days later Raoul wrote asking if he could quote the Dean letter, of which I had sent him a copy a year before for an article he was writing. Only then did I realize that this was big news. On March 21 I walked over to the Senate and handed the letter to a staffer working for Senator Sam Ervin—as I recall, it was Sam Dash.

That evening I saw Senator Ervin waving this letter around on the evening news. After all, it said President Nixon had never "asserted a claim that Presidential aides have blanket immunity from testifying." Now he was. Two days earlier, on March 19, Ervin had threatened the arrest of White House staff members who refused to testify.[89] Now Ervin had, in the FAS letter, a smoking gun. Subsequently, *The Washington Post* ran an editorial ("Executive Privilege, Precedent and Mr. Dean") saying that there was "no better evidence of the slippery, spurious nature of Mr. Nixon's current claim" than the letter of Dean to Stone.[90] The *Post* observed that Nixon's position was the exact opposite of the one he had urged, twenty-five years before, when, as a congressman, he had wanted the testimony of Edward U. Condon.[91]

The irony was that Dean's own letter, as White House Counsel, could be used to demand Dean's testimony and thereby scotch any White House hopes that Dean himself might be kept from center stage. In any case, the letter was, by sheer coincidence, released on the climactic day of Watergate. That morning Dean had told the president, "We have a cancer within—close to the Presidency—that's growing."[92]

On that same day, Nixon and his chief advisers, John D. Ehrlichman and H. R. Haldeman, were, with varying degrees of bluntness, advocating that Dean prepare a report that would "give the President a public alibi if the cover-up were to collapse"—but that would clearly help Nixon hang the problem on Dean.[93]

The next morning *The New York Times* ran an article on Watergate that contained four paragraphs about Dean's letter to me.[94] Later that morning, at 11:00 A.M., Attorney General John N. Mitchell advised Haldeman, in the words of Haldeman's notes, that "the only real problem the P has is invoking executive privilege." Incredibly, through sheer coincidence FAS had supplied the most succinct bit of evidence against the White House on the issue that the attorney general thought was "the only real problem."

. . .

Chemists speak of supersaturated solutions that will precipitate out crystals if even slightly disturbed. FAS's effectiveness in both these cases, if any, rested on the fact that we created a small disturbance in contexts that were politically supersaturated.

As Murrey Marder of *The Washington Post* noted, the Foreign Relations Committee had had about as much as it could take of—i.e., had been supersaturated with—Kissinger's running foreign policy without testifying. Any small public disturbance concerning this issue just might precipitate out a troublesome public outcry. Thus Henry had good reason to respond to our letter and newsletter by taking preemptive defensive action. And he was wise to report this preemptive action to us, because it effectively warned us that any campaign we might otherwise mount would not have the full support of the Foreign Relations Committees, now effectively bought off. Meanwhile, his civilized letter and careful argument maximized the chances that we would just drop the subject.

In contrast, our release of Dean's letter stirred what was surely the most supersaturated context in modern American political history. Senator Ervin was threatening to arrest White House officials, and an embattled president was grappling with an aide right on the verge of turning state's evidence that would destroy his presidency. Into this situation, our letter was dropped fortuitously at the most critical moment. It is revealing that even Raoul Berger did not realize what a hot item this letter was and wanted it only to use in some pedestrian publication. What makes news important is something that, all too often, only journalists can predict. And few can tell what effects these stories will have within the bureaucratic fortresses to which they apply.

CHAPTER 8

Jump-Starting FAS

Finding his niche as the chief architect of FAS's renewal, the author becomes, for his initial five-year period, its only real staff. Accordingly, its agenda is shaped, in good part, by his interests and limitations. Membership grows rapidly and then reaches a limit to growth. FAS buys a headquarters building and divests itself of its two remaining chapters. FAS remains an organization with a minuscule staff through the 1970s but in the 1980s begins to grow and by the 1990s has a stable staff of about a dozen.

Although founded on October 31, 1945, and hence twenty-five years old when I became its steward, the Federation of American Scientists had maintained a full-time office only for its first three years, after which it was run by part-time staff and volunteers, with the help of various chapters, through the fifties and sixties. In June 1970 I became the first full-time employee of the federation in twenty-two years. My first task was to replenish and reinvigorate its membership.

To accomplish this, I undertook to write and publish, single-handedly, an attractive newsletter that grew, throughout the seventies, into a monthly periodical of several thousand words.[95] Of course, I had experts to rely upon inside or, when necessary, outside the federation. Some of the ideas came from them. But the buck stopped with me, and I did 95 percent of all the drafting.

One totally inexplicable thing happened during this period, sometime in 1971, as my father's career as a journalist was coming to an end and before he became a Greek scholar. He telephoned and, without much in the way of introduction, asked if I had any interest in taking over *I. F. Stone's Weekly* on his retirement.

I was incredulous. As he well knew and had told his intimates, he was a radical, while his son Jeremy was a liberal. (Just as the children of tall parents regress toward the mean in height, so also, I suppose, are the political views of both radicals and reactionaries watered down in their progeny—if, indeed, they are not, as often happens, quite reversed.) How on earth could he expect me to satisfy the political preconceptions of his constituency or to function at his journalistic level?

Also, I did not consider myself a journalist or a political pundit; I was functioning as a scientist and my interest was in saving the world, not in commenting on the passing scene. It was always an embarrassment when people seemed to see some connection between my (FAS) newsletter and *I. F. Stone's Weekly*.

But most of all, he had never wanted to take over *his* father's business; why would he think that I would want to take over his? I did not feel that I was living in the shadow of a great man because I. F. Stone was not *that* famous, but I did feel in the penumbra of another person. And, really, I strongly preferred to create my own identity. Put another way, I did not really know what to say when Senator Thomas Eagleton once said, "You are a good man, but your father is a great one."

So I immediately said no and declined to discuss it—how to explain to someone that one did want to be known only as that man's son? He was hurt; the *Weekly* was his baby, and he considered it a great sign of his respect for me that he would be willing to put it in my hands. And, later, he indicated that he felt I was put off by the challenge of it all—which, indeed, I would have been had I even entertained the notion.

My grueling schedule at FAS was made more exacting by the fact that I wanted our newsletters to be substantive and accurate and because they covered such diverse issues. Of special importance in shaping them was the bottom-line fact that I was not an all-purpose scientist but only a mathematician. I was a graduate of the Bronx High School of Science in New York city. Indeed, I had finished its ninth through twelfth grades in only two years, on an accelerated schedule designed to make up for my having lived in France from 1950 to 1951. Despite the rigors of the accelerated schedule, I ranked in the top quarter of my class. So I was a reasonably good student. But this did not mean I loved physics or chemistry or had any aptitude for science.

As a freshman at MIT, I was so demoralized by the extensive memorizing required in freshman chemistry that I wrote a long poem, in the style of A. E. Housman, for the MIT *Voodoo* humor magazine. It began as follows:

Say, Lad, have you chem to learn?
Blot then for the Quiz to bluff
Blot, and if your memory burn
Write the answer on your cuff.
Blot it now and you shall pass;
Write it, it will help you blot.
Try you not to comprehend;
Better men than you could not.
Memory is as memory does;
'Tis now the mind grows cold
For man and boy will soon be mad
Before the night is old.
And what are we to do here
If blotting stays the thing,
And Robots have it easy
And Eniacs are king
Why, nothing to be very sure
Is left for us to do
But Housman-like to slip away
Our Throat and Wrists slit through.[96]

In general, the overly technical curriculum turned me off and exhausted me. MIT freshmen had an exam every Friday, alternately in mathematics, physics, or chemistry. This made my nervous system feel like a bridge whose structure was being shaken by the rhythmic marching feet of soldiers. I was close to becoming your average freshman suicide, as the poem indicates. I was, accordingly, extremely grateful when, in late summer of 1954, Swarthmore College permitted me to transfer there to major in mathematics with minors in philosophy and economics.

At the end of that summer, my father took me and my siblings to Albert Einstein's home. He looked much older on this occasion than he had when we had visited him four years earlier, on a similar visit; he died eight months later, on April 18, 1955. Of my decision to become a mathematician, he said that unlike physics, which was based on a community of shared knowledge, mathematics was a "tower of Babel" in which the finest mathematicians could not understand more than a fraction of the papers presented at international conferences.

Of my tribulations at MIT, Einstein remarked, "Well, you cannot stuff a full horse," and of Swarthmore, which he had visited to get an honorary degree, he said it was a "place where one can reflect."

My preference for the political and philosophical over pure science must certainly have shaped FAS's agenda and the subjects of the newsletter. In any case, it meant that I had to work especially hard when the newsletter touched on complicated scientific issues. I fell into a certain pattern. Each eight-page newsletter (about six thousand words) contained an editorial that had to be approved by the Council of the Federation or at least the Executive Committee. And to give the editorials more bite, there were often two to four experts who would affix their names under the boilerplate "reviewed and approved by X and Y, this editorial has been approved by the FAS Council."

I left my name off the editorials (except through the quiet reference to approval by the Executive Committee, on which I sat) to try to make FAS seem larger than it was and to avoid the dreaded charge, often whispered about, that FAS was a "one-person" organization. (For some reason, which I have never fully understood, this was a special obstacle to getting grants from foundations. Like a man who is told he would be hired if only he had experience—and wonders how on earth he is going to get experience without ever being hired—I wondered how one ceased being a one-person organization if this was a bar to getting funding to hire staff.)

In fact, on arms control issues, we did indeed have a core group of very well informed experts with high status off the staff. But otherwise we did not. I wanted FAS to be broader than just arms control and thought the members would be bored if we were no more than specialists on arms control. I had visions, which proved largely unworkable, of expanding our operation into other fields—like an all-purpose Academy of Public Interest Scientists. To prime the pump and show that we could do something in those fields, I would, quite often, adopt some other issue and get several feet of material to take home.

In evenings and on weekends—since the days were spent running the federation—I would digest this cellulose, boil it down into a (hopefully interesting) newsletter with some conclusion. The conclusion, which I would invent, draw from the literature, or have suggested to me in some phone call with an expert, would then be the subject of the editorial. This would take three weeks of each month. In the remaining week of the month, I would walk the newsletter around on Capitol Hill to what seemed the appropriate offices and committees. And I would then mail it to the press and try to get some resonance.

It was an exhausting routine, made more difficult by the absence, at that time, of computers and desktop publishing, and frankly speaking, I can no longer even remember how I was able to keep it up—although I did for about ten years.

Ralph Nader once advised me that the FAS's chief virtue was its ability to run issues up flagpoles. On issues outside arms control in which I had, personally, no great interest or expertise—and so long as I had few independent staff—that was about the limit of what I could do. I would draft a newsletter, try to draw attention to it, and then move on to something else. (Of course, on arms control issues, we pursued them over time.)

For example, the February 1973 issue, entitled "FAS Calls for Energy Reorganization," asserted that "energy seems to be the concern of every agency and the responsibility of none." In a separate statement, the FAS Council called for "cutbacks" in the operating levels of reactors along with a crash program of stepped-up reactor-safety research. (On these energy issues especially I got a good deal of help from FAS officials, since we had energy experts, and I knew nothing about the topic of each issue until I wrote the newsletter.)

We got some press. *The New York Times* covered our call for cutbacks,[97] and *The Washington Post* covered our call for a coordinated energy policy.[98] In July the Nixon administration proposed an "energy czar" in the White House. No doubt many others had greater responsibility for this shift, but surely we were in the mix of influence on this issue.

In May 1973 the issue was "FAS Proposes Further Legislation on Automobile Emissions"—a highly technical editorial on oxidation catalysts, carbureted stratified charge engines, and the Clean Air Act.[99] I think my knowledge of this topic was about a month old at the time. If anyone followed it up, it would have been the "consultants."

When the Arab oil boycott occurred, I began collecting books on oil and wrote a special January issue: "Arab Oil Boycott: A Blessing in Disguise?"[100] For the energy experts, it was—since it brought the higher prices they needed to force conservation and planning.

I was, as always, nervous about the newsletters concerning subjects I knew little about. I felt like a reporter without a beat working on different issues all the time. Worse, I was required to write at some length for a specialized and highly picky (scientific) audience who considered "error" to be a reason for intellectual hari-kari.[101]

But sometimes I did surprisingly well, as do many reporters. One day I received a letter that Harvey Brooks, the distinguished dean of Harvard's Department of Engineering and Applied Sciences, had sent to S. David Freeman, head of the Ford Foundation Energy Policy Project. Reviewing a draft interim report, he referred Freeman to our oil newsletter: "It covers almost the same ground as your section 1, but is much more sophisticated, contains many more facts, and seems to refer to many studies that your staff is apparently unaware of. It has a much more authoritative ring than your section 1."[102]

That this highest brahmin of the scientific community should consider my thirty-day wonder report on oil more authoritative than that of the world's biggest energy project struck me as a triumph of Parkinson's Law.[103] There is a moral here somewhere, and I think it is that a good reporter (which is really how I was functioning) with good sources (which I certainly had) can get to the bottom of things from a standing start. In later years I felt that FAS might do better hiring science reporters than scientists.

All these newsletters outside our areas of specialization were available to other groups who were championing and specializing in the specific issues involved. The other groups had the time and motivation to press them home. I was too busy. But by helping other groups I hoped that the special cachet of scientists and the endorsement of the FAS Council and the experts would pay some dividends.

During each summer from 1970 to 1978, during the two-month break from writing a monthly newsletter, I worked hard at preparing direct mail fliers, of great complexity, and filling them with such hard evidence as could be found to show FAS's effectiveness. Fractions of our budget as high as 20 percent would then be thrown into the mails in the hope of getting new members and getting the money back. Besides the fliers, the mailing would be hitched to some specific issue: Sign this petition and, if you like what we are doing, join up.

I did all this work with the help of only one secretary, and we had no other substantive staff. This worked for at least the first five years. FAS's membership grew 60 percent per year for a few years, rising from its low base of fifteen hundred until it reached about seven thousand.[104] But this process relied upon getting large mailing lists. The AAAS list of the hundred thousand subscribers to *Science* magazine was a staple. With a 1 percent return, it would provide a thousand new members. And if the costs of direct mail were only twenty-five cents and each new member provided twenty-five dollars, the money would eventually return and the members would be stockpiled to provide some profit in a second year.

There were, however, limits to growth. The AAAS list became overused, and the rate of return dropped off. The costs of direct mail rose. Other lists were not available (e.g., *Scientific American* refused to let us rent their list even though they permitted the *Bulletin of the Atomic Scientists* to do so as an exception to their rule.) And more and more members were required to offset the higher levels of falloff as the membership level grew.

As more groups entered the direct-mail market, the end for direct mail was near. I wrote an op-ed piece in *The New York Times* entitled "Bread from the Waters."[105] By then, in 1978, there were twenty-five hundred public interest groups with budgets ranging from $100,000 or less to $4 million (e.g., Common Cause). One of our members complained that he had received, from various organizations, 306 solicitation letters in eighteen months, including thirteen from the Union of Concerned Scientists, eleven from the American Civil Liberties Union, eleven from Amnesty International, and ten from Common Cause. People were not opening their mail anymore, and the overgrazing of their interest was hurting everyone.

In the 1950s there were as many as thirty FAS chapters and branches, as permitted by the FAS constitution, but the numbers declined through the 1960s. By 1970 there were only two left: the Boston chapter, which called itself the Union of Concerned Scientists (UCS), and the Los Angeles chapter. I decided there was no point in running a largely defunct system of chapters.

UCS was working on issues of nuclear reactors. According to the

FAS constitution, chapters could work on such national issues only when and if the national organization had already taken a position. But UCS knew more about the issue than the national office did and our officials were divided on the issue. I invited UCS to become a friendly independent group rather than a chapter. And this was done. The Los Angeles chapter became independent also, as the L.A. Federation of Scientists.

No one in Congress or in foundations ever seemed to care much about how many members we had. It was, really, just an issue of raising revenue. And for this, membership was not very cost-effective. (It would, of course, have been more effective if we had found and exploited an issue that permitted us to recruit members who were not scientists—perhaps as sponsors—so that we could solicit much larger numbers of supporters, but this we did not do.) What did seem to matter to the media and Congress was the quantity and quality of names on our letterhead. Accordingly, I worked hard at recruiting famous scientists, especially Nobel Prize winners. My main breakthrough occurred in the fall of 1972, when I persuaded a Nobel Prize winner, Edward L. Tatum of Rockefeller University, to write a letter commending FAS, which he agreed I could send to his Nobel Prize–winning colleagues.[106]

This letter helped boost our list of supporting Nobel Prize winners from about ten to over forty—then about 50 percent of all living U.S. Nobel Prize winners in science and peace. Since the prize winners are selected for their scientific achievements, not their political views, it meant that FAS could no longer be accused of being a "radical" organization. But some still considered it so. Once, in the anteroom of the Senate Armed Services Committee, I ran into Jude Wanniski of *The Wall Street Journal*. He had, he said, been sent to "do a job on FAS" but on looking at our material, he had decided that it was not "so bad." (He did, however, characterize us as a group "which lobbies against almost all Nixon science and defense policies.")[107]

From 1946 to 1969, the FAS office had bounced around various addresses in downtown Washington, D.C., mostly in the vicinity of

Sixteenth and K Streets.[108] In the spring of 1970, I realized the need to be very close to Capitol Hill and persuaded the Friends Committee on National Legislation (FCNL) to rent to FAS a large room, with a separate entrance, on its C-Street side (207 C Street, NE). This building, which was actually across the street from the complex of Senate office buildings, was as close as one could get to Congress. Our modest headquarters housed me, a half-time secretary who evolved into a full-time one, and an assistant on the occasions when we had one. Once, a highly conservative *Fortune* magazine writer investigating the nefarious opposition to the anti-ballistic missile interviewed me in this office. He mentioned an enormous figure being spent by opponents of the ABM ($3 million a year, I think). I laughed and advised him that this room was our entire headquarters and that we were, as he knew, a key element in the opposition.

By 1974 I decided to strive for the impossible dream of actually securing a building for our permanent headquarters. There are not many commercially zoned buildings on Capitol Hill, where a restoration society tries to keep the area as it was when these buildings were built in the late 1890s. But by writing to all owners of commercially owned buildings, we located one, on the distinguished Massachusetts Avenue. I solicited donations toward the $92,000 purchase price. To persuade donors that this was really important, I pledged $5,000 of my own capital and, in the end, found one $10,000 donation and two other $5,000 donations.[109] With this 25 percent down payment, we purchased and occupied the building.

Thus by November 1974 the mood at FAS was euphoric. Four of five components of FAS's rejuvenation were in place. The membership had grown by 450 percent, which made us a self-sustaining group with a full-time office. We had recruited a substantial segment of America's best-known scientists. We had constructed a tax-deductible arm, the FAS Fund, to secure donations. We lacked only resident experts, which, at that time, we wanted in medicine and public health; the environment and energy; and development, agriculture, and population.[110] A major failure occurred when we thought we had secured a challenge grant agreement from Max Palevsky to match one dollar for every dollar we raised toward endowed-staff chairs for each of these areas. But when, after three months of strenuous efforts, we did succeed in getting a pledge for half of what was necessary for the first chair, he reneged—saying that he thought his pledge was just a device to help us raise money!—and the whole project of securing chairs collapsed.

On the whole, after five strenuous years, the future looked bright. True, a competing zoo of groups was descending on the public and the foundations for support, we were small, membership had certainly peaked, and revenues were limited. But voices of conscience are invariably small voices. And our small voice was, indeed, being heard.

Jerome B. Wiesner renewed his affirmation that "there is no other group that so truly represents the conscience of the American scientists as the FAS." We wore this quotation like a talisman. Men whom we, and many others, respected, such as John Kenneth Galbraith, had been even more ebullient in their praise: "During the past two years my association with FAS has extended from Washington to Peking and from the SST to the war in Vietnam. I defend the view that it is the most useful single organization of which I have knowledge." And the British Nobel Prize winner Sir Peter B. Medavar had written, "Cynics have said that during the course of social evolution the human conscience has become a vestigial organ. That this is not the case is shown very clearly by the past and present activities of the FAS."

From a personal point of view, I felt uplifted and fortunate beyond belief. Here I was, a third-rate mathematician surrounded by Nobel Prize winners, world-famous economists, and scientists of all kinds. They were very hardworking, conscientious, and decent—easily as much so as I. In academic terms they were much smarter—the lords of their disciplines. And I was their steward, supervising an idealistic organization rooted in the conscience of the scientific community. Holy cow!

FAS group picture in 1987. Back row, left to right: *Jane Wright, Eleanor Jensen (comptroller), Bonnie Frederick, and Martha Fell.* Middle row: *Cely Arndt, Ned Hodgman, John Pike, Frank von Hippel, Thomas Longstreth, Christopher Paine, and Dan Charles.* Front row: *Mark O'Gorman, Thomas Stefanick, the author, David Albright, Bonnie Ram, and Brad Cohen*

Because I had served as a professor of mathematics at Pomona College for two years, I knew well, by this time, the disadvantages of a teaching profession about which, for many years, I had held romantic and unrealistic views. Not a week went by that I did not reflect on the psychological rewards of my current vocation compared with the intellectual isolation of teaching mathematics, even in the wonderful surroundings of Claremont, California. Outside the organization, in the hurly-burly of Washington political life, I saw around me all manner of persons with abilities greater than my own. It seemed that everyone in Washington who was not a Rhodes Scholar was a former clerk to a Supreme Court justice. As my mother would have put it, they were the "crème de la crème"; I felt myself, a magna cum laude from Swarthmore, to be just "la crème"—and it did not seem like much.

Harry S. Truman is said to have remarked, "On my first week in the Senate, I asked myself, 'Harry S. Truman, how on earth did you get here?' But in the second week, I asked myself, 'Harry S. Truman, how on earth did these other guys get here?'" For my part, I felt the first emotion without the second. Some of the senators seemed to have their limitations, but the very best of the reporters, staffers, and activists with whom I came in contact seemed highly skilled.

All in all, I considered myself a person who had escaped intellectual interment and who had entered into the promised land. Fueled by this sentiment, I labored like a person possessed, working weekends and taking no vacations for fifteen years.

In late 1976 an organization was formed to be a self-styled "foreign policy Common Cause"; it was named New Directions. President Carter's election took some of the promise out of it—after all, Carter's administration *was* a new direction. And mismanagement by its officials took some further steam out of it. In desperation the organization's key members were strongly urging me to run it—and FAS also—in a kind of citizen-scientist joint operation. I gave a lot of thought to it but decided there was not enough promise in New Directions and that it would become a millstone around my neck.

Instead, I offered to help New Directions with advice and, with that in mind, to find lodging for the organization near my own— lodging much less expensive than what they had and much nearer the Hill. In a transaction that a George Soros would appreciate, I bought the building next door to FAS headquarters without spending a penny. On my appeal, the bank renegotiated my mortgage on 307 Massachusetts Avenue into a mortgage on 305–307 Massacusetts Avenue together, using the appreciation in 305 to provide 25 percent of the value of the two adjacent buildings together. And with a five-year lease from New Directions, the bank was persuaded that the mortgage was secured.

Predictably, New Directions promptly went broke, but by that time I had rallied FAS members with a "mortgage-burning" fundraising campaign that gave us payment-free occupancy of both buildings. By the end of

The author receiving an honorary degree from Swarthmore College in 1986

1978, we had two buildings. My real estate successes notwithstanding, by 1980 I was ready to quit. Ten years seemed to be, for numerological reasons, the time to go. I was exhausted and drained. I had run out of ideas—a newsletter a month was a difficult nut to crack. Nothing seemed to be working. I felt I was on a treadmill from which I could not dismount.

I was forty-five years old, and I decided to go to law school; the law had always interested me, and I had illusions about its practice. But picking up some application documents at the Georgetown University Law Center somehow brought me to my senses. I realized, only a day before I was to announce my retirement at the FAS annual meeting, that this would be disastrous—as indeed it would have been. I slogged on. 🚪

In 1978 or thereabouts, I had received an anonymous, unsolicited offer of three thousand dollars from a member of the Rockefeller family. In what seems now to have been a ludicrous excess of vigilance, I considered whether to accept or not. After all, one Rockefeller, Nelson, was vice president of the United States, and we prized our independence. I later learned that a key official of the Rockefeller family office, Elizabeth McCormack, had asked my friend Alton Frye, then a vice president of the Council on Foreign Relations, if he knew any group that deserved funding, and he had suggested FAS. 📖 My eventual acceptance of this grant proved to be critical to our organizational life. 🚪 About a year later, this same source, recognizing that I needed to have at least one assistant, had offered us enough to fund one person for three years. I hired Deborah Bleviss to work on energy conservation in late 1979.

The anonymous donor, and a certain amount of entrepreneurship on my part, put down an FAS anchor. In eight years of the eighties, the members were advised that an anonymous donor was providing about $60,000 if FAS would match this sum. We were thus able to accumulate $120,000 in a capital account each of these years. And two years later, Proctor Houghton, owner of Houghton Chemical, provided challenge grants for a Space Policy Chair. The importance of this cannot be exaggerated, since on foundation grants alone one makes no "profit" and puts down no financial anchor. We put the money into town houses on Capitol Hill. In the end, FAS was working out of three such town houses and enjoying rent from three others.

By 1985, in an article about FAS—entitled "On Scientists as Lobbyists"—*The New York Times* observed that the original atomic scientists were dying off and "the 'grand old men' are being replaced."[111] We were still getting much valuable help from a few senior sponsors, but more and more of the work was being done by very well informed, increasingly professional, and highly political staff members who needed less and less help from famous academic scientists. FAS was stronger than it ever had been. The work was going smoothly. I was no longer writing every newsletter—I was turning out only about half of them—and the strain of operating the organization had much diminished.

In the last thirteen years, since 1985, the organization has been stable in size, with annual expenditures of under $1 million. The main organizational innovation has been the creation of separate personalized newsletters that FAS staffers put out themselves, free, to lists of interested experts and relevant policy makers: for example, Lora Lumpe's *Arms Sales Monitor* or Steven Aftergood's *Secrecy and Government Bulletin.* These journals made their authors famous in the relevant expert communities, led the media to acclaim the authors as experts, and persuaded the funders that something tangible was actually happening. Most important, self-publication of this kind unleashed creative energies and kept the staff members lashed to their word processors.

Over the past three decades of our work, the public interest sector has changed enormously, becoming larger, more professional, and more specialized so that new entrants have to compete with longtime activists with considerable experience. A kind of Darwinian evolution, arising from the necessity for groups to compete constantly for funding nourishment, has put some groups out of business and left the rest leaner and meaner and constantly looking for action. Increasingly, the various activist groups in a sector function through coalitions that are highly specialized.

Meanwhile, staider institutions, such as the Council on Foreign Relations, the Carnegie Endowment, the Brookings Institution, and many others have recently come to emphasize public policy activities at the expense of longer-term research, monographs, and op-ed essays instead of book-length pieces. The ever more professionalized public policy sector has to compete with these "new" entrants. In foreign countries also we see the multiplication of human rights groups, Open Society groups, security-oriented organizations, and so forth. In this crowded field, it takes ever more knowledge, creativity, and shrewdness for an activist to make a noticeable dent in events.

But the new organizational environment provides not only a thoroughly carved-up turf but also untapped opportunities. A staffer interested in progress in some field can spend his or her time rounding up other groups to forge a common campaign. This was unheard of in 1970 in the security field, when there were so few groups to be mobilized. And the new context, which puts a great stress on ever more detailed information, provides an opportunity for those, like our staffer John E. Pike, who disseminate information (e.g., providing the community with an enormously useful Web site).

In sum, as the millennium comes to a close, FAS, the oldest of the nuclear arms control groups, is still functioning in its original field and still finding new and related fields to conquer. Meanwhile, my almost three decades of work as FAS's CEO seems to have left me the dean (in point of service) of CEOs of the security-oriented public interest community.

CHAPTER 9

My Collaboration with Colby

Colby's "rebirth" in 1977 as an arms controller is explained. Colby and the author become a Washington odd couple.

I never met anyone with more of the "right stuff" than William Colby. The first time I ever laid eyes on him was when, as director of the CIA, he dared to confront a collection of vocal anti-CIA activists at a Capitol Hill conference. He was smooth and collected.

Later, shortly after he left the government, I found myself the only "dove" at a conference of the Young Americans for Freedom at which he was one of no less than twenty-five "hawks." I anticipated being completely isolated in my views. To my astonishment, I heard William Colby speaking eloquently about the arms race; when my turn came, I announced that I could not really do a better job of explaining what I felt. We chatted in the parking garage about the B-1 bomber, which Colby opposed.

The next day, at the Senate Foreign Relations Committee, I regaled a friendly staffer with the news, "Colby is a dove on arms control." 𝒟

"Well," he said, "let's have a hearing!" He sounded like Perle Mesta spotting an occasion to have a party. It was promptly agreed that General Daniel Graham, the arch-conservative director of the Defense Intelligence Agency (DIA), in the Pentagon, should be the right-wing foil. As a kind of finder's fee, I was offered a third seat on the panel.

When Colby and I met before the hearing to coordinate our statements, we did so at my house because, I had found, his residence was still shrouded in secrecy; "Bethesda, MD" was all it said in the phone book. He seemed decent and approachable. The hearings were successful, and Bill developed a theme that he much emphasized thereafter—that in his experience "satellite photography and electronic eavesdropping were now sufficient to verify arms limitations."[112] But the main result of the hearing was to announce to the arms control community what the CIA would have called a wondrous new "asset"—an arms control "dove" who was believed, by everyone, to be a political "hawk."

Soon Colby was seen everywhere on the arms control conference circuit. There was neither money nor fame in it for him. On one occasion, when we both traveled to Denver to appear on some kind of "advocates"-style show—he the witness and I the interrogator—we had a few hours together on the plane. I learned that his father had been a journalist, as mine was, and that our views in many areas were quite compatible. I also learned that our entrepreneurial paths had crossed, at a remove, in the case of the *Glomar Explorer*, an enormous vessel built by the CIA under the cover of the Hughes Corporation, purportedly as a method of scooping up mineral modules from the ocean bottom. In fact, it was designed to raise a Soviet submarine.

This vessel's cover story had been used by the American Mining Congress (AMC) as a tool to torpedo longstanding and statesman-like negotiations by the Nixon administration at the Law of the Sea Conference—on the grounds that the vessel showed that America was already harvesting minerals from the sea and that a Law of the Sea Treaty dividing up the ocean bottom would be a sellout. At the time, I was busy exposing an unholy partnership between the AMC and Senator Lee Metcalf (D, Montana), the chairman of a Senate subcommittee that was advancing a bill that sought to undermine the multilateral negotiations. I wished I had known at the time what was happening![113]

In March 1987 I invited Colby to join a conference at Airlie House that included some Soviet scientists who quivered at the prospect of meeting a former CIA director. I introduced him as one who had dropped behind enemy lines during the Normandy invasion to help advance the second front so important for Russia. (My introduction was careful to note for the record that Colby had never worked for me and that I had never worked for him.)

Still, Colby and I were just friendly acquaintances until I returned from my first trip to Cambodia. I had become consumed with the goal of preventing the return of the Khmer Rouge, which had, by some estimates, murdered a quarter of Cambodia's populace from 1975 to 1978. In 1989, U.S. policy was to support a coalition of three factions, all trying to unseat the then Communist regime of Hun Sen in Phnom Penh. This coalition's strongest partner was the Khmer Rouge. A victory for the coalition, I believed, would be victory for the Khmer Rouge. The policy had to be changed. (I later learned that the CIA analysts agreed and felt that the State Department's policy was wrong.)

I called Bill and asked if he would lunch with me. He invited me to the Cosmos Club, and when I saw that he shared my concerns, I asked if he would help me. 𝄡 He said the only problem was that he was a "hawk" on nearby Vietnam and was, indeed, completing a book showing how we might have won that war. He wondered how this would play out.

In the end, we agreed that these were not incompatible positions. 🎵 In fact, it made his Cambodia position (and his Vietnam position) all the more credible at home. And, as time went on, we became the "odd couple" on Cambodia. Before the dust had settled, we had written two op-ed pieces in *The Washington Post*[114] and had testified jointly before the Senate Foreign Relations Committee.[115]

Our unusual alliance was not limited to Cambodia. When, in 1992, the Serbs were laying siege to Sarajevo, I asked Paul C. Warnke and Robert Adams, the secretary of the Smithsonian Institution, to lunch with me to discuss what might be done. I suggested a U.S. effort to lift the siege, and when these two experienced observers showed sympathy for the idea, I went immediately to see Bill. He said he was an "old artilleryman" and started explaining how fire could be homed in on enemy mortars. He was all for the idea, and we soon published an article in *The Washington Post*, "Break the Siege of Sarajevo."[116]

Articles published in either *The Washington Post* or *The Los Angeles Times* are automatically sent to *The International Herald Tribune* for possible republication on its editorial page. Such republication is especially important in advancing ideas on European or Asian issues. In this case, as in the case of the Cambodian articles, *The International Herald Tribune* gave us a break. And the entire episode definitely seemed effective.

Bill was a reserved person, and his past as a CIA director added to this reserve. But by this time, we were friends. His wife, Sally Shelton (a former ambassador to Barbados and Grenada and now an assistant administrator of the Agency for International Development, or AID), and Bill had invited us to more than one Christmas or Thanksgiving dinner.

I was living on the outskirts of Washington political and intellectual life. I was not ostracized, as my father had been during the witch-hunts of the McCarthy era, but I certainly was not in great demand on the social circuit for one reason or another. In particular, there was no way I could help anyone climb the Washington social ladder. I lived quietly.

To my surprise, Bill seemed, in his seventies, to be somewhat outside Washington society also. Being a former CIA director, he was somewhat estranged from non-agency persons. And as one who had affronted so many CIA colleagues, through his cooperation with Congress and attention to legality, he seemed to have distanced himself from the agency. Of course, as his very well attended funeral in 1996 showed, Colby was deeply loved.

In the 1990s I confided to him, in private, many of my old war stories—most of them in this book. And when I would go off on some FAS mission, I would sometimes visit him in Georgetown, where he then lived. I would get that quietly respectful send-off that many others, embarking on more dangerous missions, must have also received and valued for its empathy.

Once when I had a serious moral problem uniquely relevant to his previous experience (and discussed later in this book), I saw that he was a real friend. And, in a search for secondhand books with which to write a related newsletter, I came across his book *Honorable Men: My Life in the CIA.*[117] In reading it, I realized how similar our attitudes were. He had tried to make the CIA an instrumentality of the law; without even knowing each other at the time, we had, in effect, collaborated in ending the mail-opening program. What happened is revealing.

Inside the government, he had been, at the time, secretary of the management committee for CIA director James Schlesinger, and was charged with preparing the matter for Schlesinger's decision. As he wrote:

> Two things bothered me about the project. First was the fact that opening first-class mail was a direct violation of a criminal statute; I looked it up in the law library to make sure. And secondly, I could get nothing beyond vague generalities from the Counterintelligence Staff when I asked what the operation had actually accomplished of any value over the years.[118]

That was Bill Colby, a rare CIA director who repaired, when unsure, to law libraries. Colby had also terminated Project Chaos, a program of spying on domestic dissidents, the program, I have little doubt, that placed a rather remarkable woman in my office in the 1970s whom I was forced to fire for obvious acts of organizational espionage.[119]

The more I read, the more I liked Colby. I saw, also, that in his treatment of his mentor, Richard Helms, he had put conscience and belief in law above friendship in forcing Helms to stand trial. I saw, also, that Bill believed in friendship.

In 1989 I purchased a splendid vacation home, a log cabin high on a cliff overlooking the Chesapeake Bay, in Calvert County, Maryland.[120] After hearing more than enough about this, and my theories about vacation homes, Bill and Sally decided to buy one, too. ⌬ Sally asked me for the name of the excellent realtor who had helped me, and I referred her to Denise Gardner of Solomon's Island. They told Denise they wanted someplace in the woods. But, on learning that Colby was a sailor and had a boat, she 𝄢 promptly insisted on taking them to an unusual site, almost completely surrounded by water, adjacent to Cobb Island, where a single house stood on a promontory.

William Colby and the author examining a chess-playing machine in Stone's cabin in Scientists' Cliffs, Port Republic, Calvert County, Maryland

Bill fell in love with it immediately, bought it, and, to my immense relief, actually used it and enjoyed it. (I was worried that I had nudged him into buying something that he and Sally would have no time to use.) But what could never have been anticipated, of course, is that he would have a heart attack or stroke while canoeing late at night and would topple out of the canoe and drown.[121]

During the week it took for his body to surface, the press had ample time to recount his exploits and to dwell on his admirably modest persistence. They talked, especially, of his difficult decision to tell Congress of past CIA misdeeds. What the journalists never mentioned, of course, is that Colby, in addition to all else, had had the independence of mind—in Washington, D.C., of all places—to befriend, and openly collaborate with, Jeremy J. Stone.

Washington rules go well beyond "gladiator, befriend not gladiator." They instruct political climbers not to be associated—not to "maintain relationships"—with those who might be judged, by others, to be of an inappropriate political coloration. Probably none are more conscious of the system than those who have been read out of it.

Washington, and Washington political outcomes, cannot be understood until there is a much better understanding of the magnetic lines of political force along which the iron filings of humanity are lining themselves up. Colby was completely different. He looked at each issue from a zero base of intellectual curiosity and brought to it a fount of common sense and wisdom. If we could bottle what he had and distribute it around, Washington politics would be an entirely different kind of place.

PART III

Creating Barriers to
the Use of Nuclear Weapons

CHAPTER **10**

The No-One-Decision-Maker
Approach to No First Use
of Nuclear Weapons

*A new approach to the control of the first use of nuclear weapons is conceived
in which a leadership committee of Congress would be required to agree before
a president could turn an undeclared conventional war abroad into a nuclear
war; in different periods this is run up a flagpole in three different ways. But
none works. In the end, a leadership committee without nuclear powers has
only minor success.*

In late 1971 a bill was being discussed in Congress that sought to
limit to thirty days the president's authority to employ armed forces
in combat without a declaration of war. While taking a shower, it suddenly occurred to me that the most important war power the president had was his ability to introduce nuclear weapons into a foreign
conventional conflict without a declaration of war. Why shouldn't Congress address this? Why shouldn't Congress be required, somehow, to
give its assent before the United States escalated a foreign conventional
war into a general nuclear war? The United States itself not being under
direct attack in the war abroad, and because no conventional war can
be lost in a day or two, there would be time for consultations. Thus
began one of the most frustrating and interesting campaigns,
including three quite different efforts made over two decades.

This was, in fact, a quite original approach to first use of nuclear
weapons, which appeared nowhere in the literature. It was not the

U.S.-Soviet ban on first use discussed as early as 1963 by Morton H. Halperin. Nor was it the unilateral forswearing of the first use of nuclear weapons advocated by many doves. It was, instead, a method of putting an additional "lock" on the revolver by involving Congress.[122]

The greatest strategic problem of the Cold War was the danger that Warsaw Pact conventional forces would overwhelm Western Europe. NATO's original approach had been based on building conventional forces to match those of the USSR and its allies. But this strategy proved beyond NATO's will and capability, and accordingly, during the period of unquestioned U.S. nuclear superiority, the NATO strategy evolved into the so-called trip-wire response, in which any Soviet aggression could induce a full-scale nuclear attack by the West.

By 1967, U.S. superiority had waned, however, so NATO turned to a strategy of "flexible response," which claimed to have the advantage of facing an enemy with "great uncertainty" about what NATO would do if attacked.[123] But if a president authorized the first use of nuclear weapons in such a conflict, he would be, I reflected, escalating a foreign conventional conflict that posed no immediate threat to U.S. survival, into a nuclear war that threatened to destroy the United States immediately. And since the Russians could not overwhelm Europe within hours or a few days, should not the president secure, somehow, the authorization of Congress before making war to this extent? This was the original idea, that escalation to nuclear war was tantamount to launching a new war.

I got the comments and suggestions and, above all, the endorsements for a statement of a very distinguished group of experts; we released our statement at a December 9, 1971, press conference.[124] We emphasized that this new policy would not undermine the U.S. threat to engage in nuclear retaliation for nuclear attack. We even agreed to support firing nuclear weapons on presidential authorization if faced with an "irrevocable launch" from the other side; our entire concern was with nuclear responses to foreign *conventional* hostilities.[125]

In due course, the Senate Foreign Relations Committee reported out the War Powers Bill. In the committee report, Chairman Fulbright wrote, "I concur wholly with the Federation of American Scientists that Congress must retain control over the conventional or nuclear character of a war," and he proposed amending a section of the bill.[126]

Fulbright subsequently offered a floor amendment providing that except in a declared war or "in response to a nuclear attack or to an irrevocable launch of nuclear weapons, the President may not use nuclear weapons without the prior, explicit authorization of the Congress." The amendment was defeated 68–10. Accordingly, the first effort to adjoin this idea to a War Powers Bill failed. But we felt that the Senate had not been prepared for this vote, and indeed, no hearings had been held. We waited for this defeat to cool down.

Four years later, in the spring of 1975, the issue of first use of nuclear weapons arose through threats made by Secretary of Defense James Schlesinger against the North Koreans. Aroused by this, Congressman Richard L. Ottinger (D, New York) introduced in the House of Representatives a resolution, H.J.Res. 533, simply stating that "Congress declares it to be the policy of the United States to renounce the first use of nuclear weapons." More than one hundred congressional cosigners put their name on it until they were advised that it had long been U.S. policy to threaten first use of nuclear weapons in Europe to discourage an invasion. They promptly withdrew their support.[127] *The Washington Post* had an editorial calling this "The First-Use Hubbub."[128]

On August 6, 1975, the thirtieth anniversary of the bombing of Hiroshima, I decided to travel to Japan to issue a press release explaining to the Japanese what the original atomic scientists had been doing since the bombing to prevent a recurrence. The press conference, called by the mayor of Hiroshima, was well received, with some Japanese newsmen bowing low and backing out—a show of respect never seen in the National Press Club in Washington! More relevant to my planning, I learned that the famous Huntley Brinkley

Hosting, at FAS headquarters, the mayors of Hiroshima (Takeshi Araki) and Nagasaki (Yoshitaki Morotani) in 1976 following the author's press conference in Hiroshima in 1975 opposing "one decision-maker" for first use of nuclear weapons

NBC news show had picked up my complaint, from Hiroshima, that "no one decision maker should be permitted to set in motion a process that might kill more than one billion people." Getting heard at home sometimes requires speaking abroad.

I now began to think of embodying our idea in a congressional resolution.[129] On returning from Hiroshima, I tried to generate support from like-minded groups. The Arms Control Association (ACA) pitched in by declaring that "persons other than the President should be directly involved, and not merely 'consulted,' in the decision to be the first adversary to use nuclear weapons in a given situation. As a practical matter these other people should be members of Congress."[130] But the Council for a Livable World (CFLW) was not helpful, even after being approached by Senator Alan Cranston (D., California), whom its board members loved. All CFLW would endorse was that "a resolution along the lines under consideration by Senator Cranston and the FAS" should be aired at hearings discussing a variety of ways to "strengthen the line between nuclear weapons use and nonuse"; they added that they would like to participate in the hearings.[131]

In effect, this "no-one-decision-maker" proposal was caught between the millstones of the hawks (who saw it as undermining the deterrence of conventional attack) and the doves (who saw it as somehow constructing a mechanism that *could* authorize first use, which they opposed completely). It was, accordingly, a proposal without a political base. ACA was an exception that proved the rule since its members represented, really, an alumni association of the Arms Control and Disarmament Agency—doves but disabused through government experience.

Senator Cranston was interested in introducing something along our lines, but the staff members with whom I was put in touch were dragging their heels—they thought it would undermine his campaign to become the Senate democratic whip. Meanwhile, Congressman Les Aspin, who later became chairman of the Armed Services Committee and then secretary of defense, was working on a resolution that would preclude first use without a declaration of war.

Nothing happened. I discouraged Les's effort in favor of Alan's. And then Senator Cranston decided to modify the issue in a way that I could not support, and the whole thing collapsed.

Eight years passed. I cannot now recall the genesis of the idea to throw the matter into the courts—I think it was a letter from an activist in Pennsylvania. But the point was to abandon efforts to have Congress pass an affirmative resolution and, instead, to assert that the president did not have the authority, in the first place, to act other than as we wished, in consultation with Congress.

I began preparing an article that, in the end, was entitled "Presidential First Use Is Unlawful."[132] The gist of the article was to follow a line of President Jefferson's: "Considering that Congress alone is constitutionally invested with the power of changing our condition from peace to war, I have thought it my duty to await their authority for using force in any degree which could be avoided." Or, as the late Supreme Court justice Arthur Goldberg testified, "The President . . . constitutionally has no war-making powers except perhaps to repel, as I have said earlier, a surprise attack, an emergency, following which he must immediately go to Congress."

During the 1975 effort, the Defense Department had written to FAS supporters, saying that the basic authority to order the use of nuclear weapons "is vested in the President, the authority being inherent in his role as Commander-in-Chief." Sometimes, they also invoked a perverse implication of a section of the Atomic Energy Act of 1946 aimed at civilian control that gave the president the authority to move nuclear weapons from civilian hands to the military when needed.[133] It was interpreted as legislative authority to "use" nuclear weapons.[134] The Defense Department pointed to the vote we earlier lost 68–10 as giving added authority.

But we argued that first use "in effect moves the nation into the line of fire—into the war zone" and was an "entirely new war in common-sense terms." In legal terms it was moving from trying to "repel" an attack on U.S. forces abroad to "initiating just that kind of much wider commitment that the Founding Fathers wanted to be made by Congress."[135]

The NATO Treaty itself was not at all an "automatic" declaration of war. As Dean Acheson testified in ratification hearings on April 27, 1949:

> This naturally does not mean that the United States would automatically be at war if one of the other signatory nations were the victim of an armed attack. Under our Constitution, the Congress alone has the power to declare war. The obligation of this Government under article V would be to take promptly the action it deemed necessary to restore and maintain the security of the North Atlantic area. That decision would, of course, be taken in accordance with our Constitutional procedures.

Foreign Affairs magazine, to whom my article was first entrusted, could not decide whether it agreed or not. William P. Bundy, the editor, wrote that my manuscript had thrown him a "knuckle ball" and that "an idea this big must not come off half-cocked. For that very reason I am keeping our exchanges for the moment to myself." After long delays, I turned to *Foreign Policy*. (When advised that *Foreign Policy* had decided to publish it, a staff member of the older, more prestigious *Foreign Affairs* commented, "Well, they have less to lose.")

Foreign Policy, by contrast, held a news conference upon publishing the article in the fall of 1984 and submitted it for a prize. I persuaded the noted constitutional lawyer Raoul Berger to join me at the press conference, at which he said, "The president can only repel attacks, not engage in wider wars, without authority from

Congress, and a nuclear war would obviously be a qualitatively wider war than any conventional one."[136]

How were we to get the public to take this legal issue seriously? One way, mentioned in a footnote in my article, was to have someone "indicted for sedition for an overly pointed enunciation of the views expressed here." Under this method, a radical activist would appeal to military officers not to obey orders to fire nuclear weapons in conventional hostilities unless Congress had declared war or some equivalent. This had been done in Great Britain in May 1985, when twenty-two persons sent a message, "To Members of the Armed Forces," saying "first use" of nuclear weapons was illegal under international law.[137] They quoted from the *British Manual of Military Law*, which states that members of the armed forces were "bound to obey lawful orders only."[138]

Such advice to disobey, in America, if proffered with criminal intent, is prohibited by a statute, 18 U.S.C. Section 2387, which states the following:

(a) Whoever, with intent to interfere with, impair, or influence the loyalty, morale, or discipline of the military or naval forces of the United States:

   (1) advises, counsels, urges, or in any manner causes or attempts to cause insubordination, disloyalty, mutiny, or refusal of duty by any member of the military or naval forces of the United States is subject to a fine of not more than $10,000 or ten years imprisonment.

But for the same reason such a person, if convicted, might have some standing to contest the presidential power.[139]

The sedition approach would certainly have gotten publicity, especially since the military services were intensely nervous about the propagation of the disease of "authorization uncertainty." In September 1975, a decade earlier, in a class for Air Force officers who would later work in underground Minuteman missile silos, a major

97

named Harold L. Hering had asked a simple, honest, straightforward, and highly moral question: "How can we be sure that the order entering the command post is a properly authorized one?" The Air Force immediately began moving him out of the service.

In hearings on his case, Hering said he was concerned about the need for checks and balances that would take into consideration the nature of nuclear warfare, "when time limitations would leave a missile combat crew without visible evidence, such as a formal declaration of war by Congress, that a launch order was in keeping with constitutional guidelines."[140] Hering had not refused to launch a nuclear weapon and was not a conscientious objector, but he had made a formal request to know what safeguards existed to protect against an unlawful launching "by a President gone berserk or by some foreign penetration of the command system."

We spoke up in Hering's defense.[141] He was retired despite internal appeal; a board of inquiry ruled against him on the two counts that he had failed to "discharge his assignments properly" and that he had a "defective attitude toward his duties." He decided not to seek the legal funds necessary to file an appeal.

Hering's experience showed that the sedition tack touched a very sensitive nerve. But in the mideighties, as before, I did not have the stomach for such an approach. I was not radical enough. During the Vietnam War, I had even opposed civil disobedience in a debate in *Commonweal* magazine over what actions were appropriate in opposing the war. While others urged "disobedience now," I argued, "Probably there are no short cuts."[142] So, from my point of view, the immediate task was to try to round up some support by real lawyers.

Constitutional Lawyers Debate
Presidential First Use

So joining with the Lawyers Alliance for Nuclear Arms Control, FAS ran a November, 1985, weekend symposium at the Airlie House

Conference Center for constitutional lawyers, pro and con. Edited by Peter Raven-Hansen, a collection of the papers was later published under the title *First Use of Nuclear Weapons: Under the Constitution, Who Decides?*[143]

Since the last time I had raised this issue, the Supreme Court had reached, in 1983, a far reaching decision invalidating about two hundred statutes that, some thought, put a stake through the heart of my proposal as well. The

Some of the constitutional lawyers convened at Airlie House, Airlie, Virginia, to discuss the constitutionality of presidential first use of nuclear weapons. From left: *Stanley Brand, Chairman Peter Raven-Hansen, Robert Turner, Allan Ides, and Stephen Carter*

case in question, known as the Chadha case, entered the courts in 1974—around the same time Senator Cranston was trying to work up a bill on first use—and it was finally decided in 1983, the year before my *Foreign Policy* article appeared. In essence, the Supreme Court ruled that Congress could not pass laws that included a provision that delegated to a house of Congress, or a committee of Congress, the right to veto regulations subsequently adopted by the executive branch to implement the law in question. In other words, the Supreme Court ruled that, if Congress did not like the way the executive branch was implementing a particular law, it would have to pass an entirely new law to stop it and could not control the law's implementation through oversight by a subset of Congress. This seemed to suggest that Congress could not ever delegate to a subset of itself—which was, of course, essential to a leadership committee's functioning in this nuclear realm. The court's decision deplored such a "convenient shortcut" in legislative processes and pointed out that, in the fullness of time, Congress could pass a new law changing any unwanted regulations. But what we were proposing was not a convenient shortcut but an essential streamlining. The answer seemed simple enough to me:

The first-use of nuclear weapons may not be so immediate an issue that one decision-maker need be given the authority to decide it, but it is a time-urgent matter and does not permit the usual congressional procedures. Nor does this question involve a veto over regulations; instead, it is a committee method of effecting a constitutionally granted congressional authority over war.[144]

Professor Allan Ides of the Loyola Law School in Los Angeles agreed and said the statute was, from a legal point of view, a combination of two acceptable elements. The first was a congressional ban on first use of nuclear weapons. He argued that such a total ban did not interfere with any implementing regulations of the executive branch and so was not at odds with the Chadha decision. The second element was a grant of specific authority to a committee (in this case the leadership committee) to *revoke* that ban. (He argued that Chadha did not prevent revoking because revoking the ban gave the executive branch *more* authority.) They pronounced it constitutional. Charles Tiefer, the deputy general counsel to the clerk of the House of Representatives, also held that the committee-delegation aspect of the statute was constitutional. He took an even more fundamental point of view. He said that the famed Chadha decision did not—and was not meant to—apply to statutes in a wide range of foreign policy areas where the congressional and the executive branch share constitutional authority.

Not surprisingly, conservative legal scholars did not agree. Professor John Norton Moore of the University of Virginia had genuine doubts whether even the congressional ban on first use was constitutional in the absence of some relevant piece of international law enhancing Congress's authority. He also viewed the committee delegation as unconstitutional and the proposal as one that interfered with the commander in chief's operational authority to use weapons consigned to him.

It was a split decision—but one that advanced these notions from a private campaign initiated by a nonlawyer and a group of scientists to something that deserved legal attention. Unfortunately, we did not secure the critical mass of senior constitutional experts that would have permitted a march on Congress. And we did not find a clear way to force the case into the courts.

Fourth Approach:
Leadership Committee of Congress

It was clear by now that there was no political will in Congress to control the first use of nuclear weapons. But what if we sought to create a leadership committee of Congress *without regard to nuclear weapons?* Perhaps, once created, it could be later used for the purpose we desired. We began thinking of a congressional leadership committee for consultation with the president in national emergencies. We began emphasizing that there was a class of time-urgent issues on which Congress, as a whole, might be unable to consult effectively and on which a leadership committee might be useful. These included not only war-powers issues but also national emergencies of other kinds in which the Congress could not be assembled to function in a timely fashion. In 1985, with the help of a consultant, Scott Cohen, the former chief of staff of the Senate Foreign Relations Committee (under Senator Charles Percy—R, Illinois), we began a campaign to set up such a committee.

A series of presidential actions ensued (Grenada, October 26, 1983; Libya, April 14, 1986; Panama, December 19, 1989; Iraq, August 8, 1990). After each of these episodes, Scott and I asked leading members of Congress whether they thought there should be some delimited body within Congress with which the president should consult before undertaking such actions. People's eyes would open with interest for a few days after such emergencies but then glaze over again.

In fact, in each such emergency, the president would normally "consult" in some pro forma way, usually by informing a selected but unspecified collection of congresspeople of his own choosing. And they would have no opportunity to talk among themselves, as a committee, about what to do. President Reagan, for example, invited fifteen congressional leaders to the White House before bombing Libya. They were informed that FB-111's based in England had been dispatched on a bombing mission two hours earlier.

In response to his questions to the administration, Robert Byrd, the majority leader, was told that no one in Congress had been consulted in this case despite the fact that the third section of the War Powers Act states, "The President in every possible instance shall consult with Congress before introducing U.S. Armed Forces into hostilities."[145] Byrd promptly wrote the president a letter, cosigned by the chairmen of the Foreign Relations, Armed Services, and Appropriations Committees, suggesting that the War Powers Act be "refined" to define a specific consultative body; he suggested members of Congress occupying eighteen specific positions—the same ones we had urged earlier.[146]

Finally, on August 19, 1990, Scott and I wrote a relevant op-ed piece for *The New York Times*[147] entitled "If Congress Is Afraid to Declare War." ♫ We said that the congressional designation of the relevant consultative group was just a matter of "good housekeeping" for Congress and that it required no new law and no fight with the executive branch. Our piece ended by observing that Congress could do more in the war-powers area; but, we wondered, "Can it in good conscience do less?"

This seemed to get action. Six weeks later, on October 2, Congress took the initiative. A leadership announcement designated eighteen members who had been asked by the leadership "to make themselves available as a group for regular consultation with the President," and the Senate majority leader encouraged the president "to consult on a regular basis" with the group.[148] So a precedent was set, at least for that session.

. . .

In retrospect, if I had been more determined and more radical, I think I would have found someone to engage in sedition—I might even have engaged in it myself. But the risks and costs would have been large. Raoul Berger had counseled accurately: "The notion of having army officers act contrary to presidential orders would alienate many of your well-wishers."[149] There were also many ways in which the courts could have addressed the sedition issue without resolving the fundamental political issues of first use. The sedition strategy seemed, in the end, a prescription for fruitless martyrdom.

In any case, the subject of the first use of nuclear weapons was an important one. I do not regret the time spent on it. And, as the reader will see in the next chapter, I made one last effort, in quite a different way, to put the world on the road to no first use.

CHAPTER II

Urging No First Use of Nuclear Weapons on the World Court

A legal theory is devised whereby the International Court of Justice (known as the World Court) could, if it wished, ban the first use of nuclear weapons. The court is lobbied in unusual ways. Its unexpected and Delphic decision tells us quite a bit about the calculus of its decision making and the interplay between law and politics in which the tautological can become politically potent.

In the summer of 1995, while working on related newsletters, I pondered the fact that the United Nations General Assembly was given to passing resolutions, almost every year, condemning the use of nuclear weapons. But the votes were always about a hundred in favor and twenty against, with the nuclear powers opposing; because they were not sufficiently unanimous, these declarations had little effect on international law. Recalling that the other weapons of mass destruction, chemical and biological, were already deemed illegal by various conventions, I wondered whether a resolution would pass if it took the following form: "Resolved: The use of any weapons of mass destruction such as biological, chemical, and nuclear weapons is hereby prohibited."

My thought was that the nuclear states might vote for this with the reservation that they understood it as a contract—something they would obey only so long as others did not violate it. This had been the approach to the ban on poison-gas warfare. The Geneva Protocol precluded chemical warfare under any circumstances. The

United States and others endorsed it. But they continued to build such weapons in case the other side violated it.

Under these circumstances, my draft resolution would have, in effect, banned only "first use" of nuclear weapons and, indeed, literally, only first use of a weapon of mass destruction, since it would have permitted use of nuclear weapons following chemical or biological weapons use. But this seemed to me worth doing. And as part of the plan, a high-sounding resolution that seemed to do more, much more, would be adopted and this would help the antinuclear campaign.[150]

As I pondered this idea, I learned something that I should have known before. A group of antinuclear activists, grouped together since 1992 under the aegis of a World Court Project, had persuaded the United Nations General Assembly to ask the International Court of Justice this question: "Is the threat or use of nuclear weapons in any circumstance permitted under international law?"[151] In effect, the World Court Project had decided to try to circumvent the General Assembly's failure to ban nuclear weapons by asking the court a yes-no question. The case was to be heard in November 1995. I decided to try to reshape the resolution idea into something the court, rather than the General Assembly, could say. The reformulated declaratory proposition was simple: "The use of any weapons of mass destruction such as chemical, biological, or nuclear weapons is, and ought to be declared, illegal under international law."[152]

I decided to try an amicus brief. A splendid international lawyer, Burns Weston, polished my draft (twice) and helped put it into a proper form. The brief explained that the Federation of American Scientists was not a group of lawyers but nevertheless had a strong interest in the subject, knew what the political traffic would bear, and wanted to be helpful. I mailed it off to the court.

At the last minute, I also decided to try to place an article summarizing the amicus brief in *The International Herald Tribune*, where the judges would be likely to read it. And after sending it off and mailing separate copies to the fourteen sitting judges, I decided to go to The Hague (nothing ventured, nothing gained) and see the opening of the proceedings.

It seemed impossible to me that the World Court Project could be successful. Judges on the World Court vote as their nations want 80 percent to 90 percent of the time, either in the hope of having their nine-year terms renewed or because they are chosen to have views compatible with their nation-state's perspective. How could such a court—which included seven judges from countries that either were nuclear states or were allied with them—do other than split if it were given no other option than to abandon even nuclear deterrence (i.e., nuclear retaliation for nuclear attack)? Our no-first-use proposal, dressed up as an absolute ban, seemed the only politically feasible alternative.

It was very exciting watching the hearings open and seeing, for the first time, the World Court. But the judges rarely ask questions of the petitioners, and when they do, the answers are provided for the record. So life is easy for the lawyers. A day of this was enough for me.

On Tuesday morning, at the Amsterdam airport, I saw that *The International Herald Tribune* (God bless it) had printed my op-ed piece summarizing the amicus brief. Thus the judges would all see it! I later learned, quite indirectly, that the court had debated, that morning, whether to accept the amicus brief as part of its records; the court had declined to do so. In its fifty-year history the court had only once solicited an amicus brief (which it never received) and had *never* accepted one. It was a tribute to our brief, and the fact that it had been published, that the court considered accepting it. Normally, whoever had the temerity to send such an unsolicited communication received a polite note of rebuff stating that the document had been put in a special reading room where the judges could read it if they wished. Such briefs were not, however, made part of the record.[153]

But I knew nothing of this as I entered the aircraft. Instead, I was walking on air. It was, in fact, to become a red-letter day. In the first place, I was sexually harassed by an attractive stewardess. And in the second place, I had another idea.

This idea was rooted in an unusual experience involving the Gulf War. In August 1990, I had dimly recalled that back in 1978 President Carter had instructed Secretary of State Cyrus Vance to say something related to no first use of nuclear weapons at the UN. Carter had wanted, no doubt, to adopt a doctrine that was as close as possible to a flat out "no-first-use" doctrine on nuclear weapons. But "no first use" unqualified was clearly impossible in the face of fears of the overwhelming Soviet conventional attacks on Western Europe. First use of nuclear weapons, as a response, had been the touchstone of Western strategic policy since the early fifties.

No doubt Carter had asked whether he could say, at least, that the United States would not use nuclear weapons against non-nuclear states. The sticking point here was North Korea, which might lurch forward and seize South Korea's capital of Seoul unless deterred by some overwhelming threat. Accordingly, the Carter administration drafted a policy statement designed to "grandfather" the Korean conflict. It said, in effect, that the United States would not attack nonnuclear states, even if they were carrying out an aggression, so long as they were not "allied to a nuclear-weapons state or associated with a nuclear-weapons state" in carrying out their attack.

This would take care of North Korea, which, based on memories of the Korean War, would never attack, it was felt, without support from Russia or China. In a wholly pointless addition, the administration further decided not to offer this assurance to states that were not cooperating with the Nuclear Non-Proliferation Treaty, thus leaving out India, Pakistan, and Israel (none of which needed this assurance). As a result, the "negative security assurance" got fairly complicated and arcane, and, as a further result, it was little discussed and few people ever heard anything about it.[154]

When Iraq invaded Kuwait on August 2, 1990, fears began to circulate that the United States might use nuclear weapons in the war. I then dug this negative security assurance doctrine out of a reference book. But, unsure whether the Bush administration supported this Carter administration doctrine of a dozen years before, I wrote to the director of the Arms Control and Disarmament Agency (ACDA), Ronald F. Lehman II, on August 15 and asked him. His response of August 28 said that, indeed, the Carter assurance had been "reaffirmed by successive Administrations" as recently as August 21, three weeks after the war with Iraq broke out. And it had been called, on March 13, 1990, a "firm and reliable statement of U.S. policy" by the U.S. ambassador to the Geneva Conference on Disarmament.

Six months after the war began, on February 5, a front-page article in *The Los Angeles Times*—"American Support Grows for Use of Nuclear Arms"—quoted an unnamed official who said, "We have never forsworn nuclear use in the past, and if we did so now, we'd lock ourselves into making the same statement in every future crisis." Accordingly, on February 7 FAS released the exchange of letters between Lehman and me in a statement entitled "Nuclear Weapon Use Already Precluded by U.S. Policy." This exchange of letters has become a kind of footnote in history. It confirmed that the U.S. policy opposing the use of nuclear weapons in wars with nonnuclear states was deemed by at least some government officials to apply to the worst possible case: Iraq was a false adherent to the Nuclear Non-Proliferation Treaty, was engaged in a war with the United States, and was threatening to use prohibited weapons of mass destruction, such as biological and chemical weapons.

By the summer of 1994, the world had reached the point where it had become inconceivable that any of the aggressor states would be "allied to a nuclear state or associated with a nuclear weapon state" in carrying out an attack on U.S. forces or our allies. Put another way, Iran, Iraq, Libya, and North Korea were not going to get any help from nuclear powers in attacking our interests, nor were they allied with Britain, France, China, or Russia. And these potential aggressors were all, of course, nominally part of the Nuclear Non-Proliferation Treaty.

As a result, the qualifying phrases of the negative security assurance had become quite irrelevant. I drafted an editorial for the September–October 1994 FAS *Public Interest Report* (*PIR*) entitled "Nuclear Weapons: A No-First-Use Doctrine Exists for All Non-Nuclear States." (Of course, some states were not signatories to the treaty—India, Pakistan, and Israel are the only ones of significance—but these, though not covered, were not countries the United States would ever threaten with nuclear weapons.)

All this was in my mind when I boarded the plane to return home. Furthermore, I knew that by this time the other nuclear powers (e.g., Britain, France, and Russia) had adopted parallel versions of this negative security assurance as part of the effort to win support in 1995 for extension of the Nuclear Non-Proliferation Treaty. And China had adopted a no-first-use policy in 1963.

With a blinding flash, it occurred to me that one could, with mathematical precision, prove that *nobody*, for all practical purposes, was threatening first use against *anybody*. The nuclear powers were not threatening the nonnuclear states. And the nuclear states were not threatening one another. First use against a powerful Soviet Union became moot after the collapse of the Soviet regime rendered Russia too weak to present a conventional threat to NATO. Russia had offered China a no-first-use pledge. Was Britain threatening France, etc.? I knew vaguely that there was something called customary international law in which a policy followed by *nearly* all states could become binding on *all* states. Suddenly, this seemed a perfect solution to the problem faced by the court. Obviously, the court would not denounce the policy of nuclear deterrence—the threat of nuclear retaliation for nuclear attacks. Nor should it opt out of the case on some procedural grounds. Instead, it could pronounce nuclear first use as a policy that had been abandoned by the community of states.

On returning to Washington from The Hague, I wrote up my

ideas as an op-ed piece and sent it to *The International Herald Tribune* on the very slight chance that lightning might strike twice.

One of the judges had acknowledged my amicus brief by letter and perhaps recognized that FAS had a right to be heard as the conscience of the original atomic scientists. Accordingly, I sent the judge an advance copy of my latest article, as well as my exchange of letters with Lehman. I received a brief acknowledgment stating that the material had been of "intense interest."

It was obvious that the judges knew little about strategic analysis, doctrine, or facts. Emboldened by the acknowledgment, I wrote a third op-ed-length piece observing that the pleadings they were receiving from interested parties were no substitute for testimony or evidence from disinterested parties. I had earlier lunched with a real expert on the World Court, Keith Highet, and learned there was an untried way to get such evidence. As a result, my article observed, I hoped learnedly, that the court ought to try, under its unused Article 50 of its statute, to seek expert opinions. I sent this off, and it was politely acknowledged. But I doubted very much it would have any effect.

I then learned, through a call to Paris, the stunning news that the *Tribune* was actually thinking of running my second piece. My old friend Dick Falk, a legal expert for the World Court Project, had commended the amicus brief and liked this idea also; he said that he would, if I wanted, work with me to develop the legal basis for the concept of using customary law. Burns Weston also offered his help. Thus encouraged, I decided to return for the last three days of hearings, which included the day at which the alphabetically rearguard United States and United Kingdom would testify.

On the first of these days, November 13, the *Tribune* printed my article; given the sparse coverage of this World Court proceeding, my ideas on this subject were getting more attention than all the other commentary put together.

The British pleaders were magnificent in style and made our own officials, who pleaded immediately thereafter, seem like provincials. Officials from both countries told the court that the "specific cir-

cumstances" and "sizes" of nuclear weapons made any court determination about first use a technical issue beyond its competence. But
the British, in what a psychiatrist would call "leakage" from a reticent
patient, said that the international community had "sensibly elected
to draw a veil of constructive silence" over the issue of legality of
nuclear weapons.

On returning, I prepared a rebuttal to the U.S. and U.K. testimony—the title was "No Such Thing as a Limited Nuclear War: U.K.
and U.S. Try to Mislead the Court"—and sent it to the same judge.
After all, I wrote, since the 1950s all strategists had agreed that there
was no reliable "fire-break" between nonuse of nuclear weapons and,
on the other hand, bilateral spasms in which virtually all deployed
nuclear weapons are fired. No matter how small the bomb first used
or how limited the circumstances, the head of state—not techni-
cians—would make the decision. And in the minds of those chief
executives would be the inevitability of escalation to full-scale
nuclear war. It was, in fact, embarrassing to watch the U.S. representative from the Defense Department tell the court that limited
nuclear war was possible—something no serious book on strategy had
countenanced for decades.

When this rebuttal was acknowledged by one judge, I was
already hard at work on another: "Divide the Question Rather
Than the Court: Truths No State Dared to Plead."[155]

When that was acknowledged, I prepared and sent to the court a
final tutorial entitled "What Is Extended Deterrence?" In this piece
I tried to educate the court about the way in which the NATO doctrine had developed, and I gave reasons why the abandonment of first
use could be accepted.

In the end, I had published two op-ed pieces for a newspaper the
judges would likely read, and I had sent the court four more brief
analyses.[156] I rested because I had nothing more to say. I had tried to
provide the court with the accumulated wisdom not of the legal
profession but of the arms controllers. Although the court had
refused to acknowledge my amicus brief—and had led me to wear a

button on later trips bearing the words "failed amicus"—I felt that I had been a true "friend of the court." I later confirmed that the op-ed pieces had been distributed internally through the court. There was nothing more I could have done.

Seven months later, on July 8, 1996, when the court announced its advisory opinion, I was there. The long background opinion of the president of the court, as read, and the first four agreed court conclusions that he recited seemed unremarkable.

But after the fifth conclusion was read—a two-sentence observation that had been passed only by a seven–seven tie and a tie-breaking vote of the chief justice—there was a crush in the press room so great that when I tried to get a copy of the opinion, my glasses were almost broken and a bag I was carrying was ripped from my shoulder.

On these two sentences, instead of a seven–seven polarization between third-world doves and NATO or nuclear-state hawks, the court evinced a center of seven judges who left, in dissent, two hawks, two doves, two cop-outs, and a Frenchman. Since the center half included the president, who has a deciding vote in ties, the center was a majority. This two-sentence decision, designated as point E, read, in its entirety:

> It follows from the above-mentioned requirements that the threat or use of nuclear weapons would generally be contrary to the rules of international law applicable in armed conflict, and in particular the principles and rules of humanitarian law.
>
> However, in view of the current state of international law, and of the elements of fact at its disposal, the Court cannot conclude definitively whether the threat or use of nuclear weapons would be lawful or unlawful in an extreme circumstance of self-defense, in which the very survival of *a* State would be at stake. (emphasis added)

This decision called the use of nuclear weapons "generally" unlawful but it said it did not know whether the "threat or use" was "lawful or unlawful" in the extreme cases in which the "very survival" of a state would be at stake.

The president of the court, in his summary conclusion, stated that with the requirements that the court had demanded, "the use of such weapons in fact seems scarcely reconcilable."[157] On the other hand, with regard to just about any "imaginable circumstance" of nuclear use considered by the nuclear powers in the post–Cold War era, the court said it was uncertain. And under international law, the court's uncertainty permits states to do as they wish. Thus basic nuclear deterrence itself was certainly not ruled unlawful. Under this "extreme-circumstance" doctrine, the United States could threaten the wide-scale use of nuclear weapons against Russia in an effort to deter the Russians from destroying the United States.

More surprisingly, the United States could also continue to threaten first use of nuclear weapons to prevent conventional attacks designed to overthrow foreign governments. For example, the United States could threaten Russia with the use of nuclear weapons to deter the overthrow of the Federal Republic of Germany by Russian conventional forces, or it could threaten North Korea with nuclear weapons if that Communist regime threatened to overthrow the government of South Korea. And "a" state (in our example Germany or South Korea) has the right to protect itself—qua government—even if its population were not threatened by nuclear death and would, perhaps, in the face of a conventional attack, rather be red than dead.

In sum, the court did not dare to deny NATO its residual first-use threats. From a legal point of view, the court felt obliged to do so because, in its eyes, collective self-defense by states is fully protected under the UN charter (so the Federal Republic of Germany can ask the United States for a protective umbrella). And, from a practical political point of view, Court President Bedjaoui, an Algerian, could not have gotten the seven votes he needed to make up his majority had he not done so. In particular, the German judge, Carl-August Fleischhauer, wrote that the "inherent right of self-defense ... would be severely curtailed" if nuclear weapons were ruled out in "collective" self-defense. It is significant that in President Bedjaoui's summary for the court, he uses, instead of "a", the word "the." Had the word "the" been approved by the six other judges, the court would have ruled against the first use of nuclear weapons unless they were themselves threatened with overthrow from a conventional attack. It was that close.[158]

So both second use and NATO first use, and indeed, also first use against invading nonnuclear states, are permitted if they threaten the survival of some government. What about circumstances that are "not extreme"? The ruling says that nuclear weapons are "generally" prohibited, and that any use or threat of use must conform to the principles of "necessity and proportionality."[159] But there are circumstances that fit between "generally" and "extreme" circumstances in which the "very survival of a State" would be at stake.

So perhaps, under this opinion, the United States could threaten the use of nuclear arms against Iraq if Saddam Hussein were threatening to use chemical or biological weapons in war.[160]

It may seem strange that the court's advisory opinion consistently treated "use or threat of use" of nuclear weapons as a single indivisible phrase. (In short, the court ignored my op-ed piece entitled "Divide the Question Rather Than the Court.") Why did it? The court failed to make the commonsense distinctions between use and threat because international law considers it illegal to *threaten to do* what is illegal to *do*.[161] And the court failed to distinguish between first use and retaliatory use because it saw the real issue as the gravity of the threat confronting the state being attacked.

Above all, the court was unwilling to highlight the nearly universal significance of the negative security assurances on which I had put such store. Perhaps this is where the court felt it was hampered by a lack of "elements of fact at its disposal"—none of these facts had been put in evidence, and they did have to be applied. But it did incorporate them, with vague references to undertakings of states.

Experts Confused

Eight days later, in Washington, a panel of six experts convened to discuss the decision before an audience of about one hundred listeners; the group was sponsored by the Arms Control Association, the American Society of International Law, and the Lawyers Alliance for World Security. The panelists included the representatives of the departments of state and defense who had appeared before the court.

None pointed out that the decisions permitted first use in NATO (and would have done so in general except for a quiet court incorporation of the negative security assurances—which the U.S. government may be quietly abandoning). Three of the panelists actually misstated what the court had concluded. For example, one panelist said we should now take our nuclear weapons off our ships since first use was now prohibited in the defense of other states like South Korea.

The incredible fact was this: The World Court had devised an opinion so Delphic and subtly drafted that even a week later, the world's experts failed to notice that the ruling had, really, built its case around the existing policies of the nuclear powers. When I pointed this out from the floor there was general incredulity until the representative of the World Court Project, in what lawyer's would call advice against interest, said: "Jeremy is right." (Our two public interest groups had a greater insight into what the World Court had done than the government bureaucracies—something that is increasingly common in a world full of highly motivated activists.)

In a certain political logic, by providing much useful rhetoric, the court made an advance that would help rally antinuclear activists everywhere against nuclear weapons use. But the legal calculus used by the court departed from common sense (threat might be an appropriate deterrent when use is not), from strategic analysis (first use versus second use), and from real-life problems (such as use of other prohibited weapons of mass destruction).

In any case, fifty years after our atomic-scientists movement had been created to prevent the further use of nuclear weapons, we had managed to get our two bits in before the World Court—despite the absence of a state sponsor and despite the fact that we argued something that no state pleading had had the sense to try. We had shown that, at least in our case, one could lobby the World Court.

In the end, as one shrewd and experienced observer advised me, the court had done something that courts do in difficult cases: It had given the decision to one side (the nuclear powers) and the language to the other (the antinuclear forces).

PART **IV**

Improving Relations

with Superpowers

CHAPTER 12

Catalyzing Exchanges
with an Ill Premier Zhou Enlai

An early (June 1972) entrance to China is achieved through luck and the seizure of an opportunity. A first scientific exchange is stimulated. After a dinner with Premier Zhou Enlai suggests something is amiss, an effort is made to gain entry for a delegation of cancer specialists — badly needed as it turns out — for Premier Zhou himself.

It was not only with regard to executive privilege that Henry Kissinger and a mere mortal like myself were connected, but also with regard to China. I was working on it while he was, and I got there only three months after President Nixon. But China brought along with a sense of high success, a number of heartaches that are only now fading.

B.J. and I had been preparing to go to China before it seemed at all possible. We had decided, after our fifth trip to Moscow in the fall of 1970, that there was little more we could do on the ABM issue in Moscow, official U.S.-Soviet talks having begun. I therefore asked my linguistically agile wife to drop the study of Russian and to try to learn Chinese with a view to the seemingly impossible dream of allowing us to work on issues pertaining to the People's Republic of China (PRC). She began by taking an intensive course in Chinese for an academic year. In the summer of 1971, she was in Middlebury, Vermont, so deeply immersed in a summer Chinese-language program that I could be with her only one day per week. But this turned out to be the right summer to be trying.

While on a trip to Hanoi in April and early May of 1971, two antiwar activists, Ethan Signer of MIT and the biologist Arthur Galston of Yale, discovered, to their delight, that visas applied for in Ottawa for a visit to Beijing were supplied to them in Hanoi. In May 1971 they were the first American scientists allowed into Beijing in two decades—and they got there two months before the secret visit of Henry Kissinger. When they returned, I realized they were both FAS members!

I called Arthur, congratulated him on his success, and said the job of linking China to America was too big for any one person. Would he chair an FAS committee on U.S.-China relations to try to open the door wider? He would. At the end of May 1971 I sent a letter bearing Arthur's signature to the president of the Chinese Academy of Sciences, Dr. Guo Mo-Ruo, explaining that FAS was not connected to the U.S. government but rather represented two thousand "progressive, socially concerned scientists" working for world peace.

After B.J.'s summer program was over in Vermont, we went directly north to visit the People's Republic of China embassy in Ottawa, Canada, in hopes of impressing the staff there with our sincerity and B.J.'s Chinese. We urged scientific exchange, the dispatching of a delegation from FAS, and the sending of books from America on science.

This was the same July in which Henry Kissinger made his secret, historic mission to Beijing—a visit that made our dream possible. And, to the amazement of the State Department and many of my colleagues, we received a friendly, encouraging answer from Guo Mo-Ruo on August 3.

At the suggestion of a startled State Department staffer who regarded all this as big news, I wrote to Henry Kissinger.[162] He encouraged our "efforts to improve exchanges," said he would "keep in mind" some of my suggestions on making arms control relevant to China, and said he was "impressed with B.J.'s rapid progress in Chinese language study."[163]

In late 1971 we wrote again to Guo Mo-Ruo to propose a visit and, in mid-December, received a letter stating that our request was being considered "positively." Two months later President Nixon embarked on his "week that changed the world": a visit to Beijing, from February 21 to February 28. After another two months, in mid-April, we wrote a letter making it clear that we were waiting expectantly and were puzzled by the delay.

Within eight days we received a reply saying that we were indeed invited, but that the invitations to us had crossed with our letter. We did not believe this, but considered it a form of exquisite politeness to make us feel welcome. Later, in Beijing, when I met my letter-drafting counterpart, my worst suspicions were confirmed. He asked what the word *positively* really meant. I explained. It became evident that the Chinese had understood it rather more as meaning "sympathetically."

But on realizing that they had inadvertently raised our hopes, they had felt obliged to follow through. Or perhaps our April letter of impatience gave them an excuse to raise the question with Zhou Enlai, who, it was said, was making all decisions about Americans traveling to China at that time. In any case, this incident shows that nothing succeeds in this complicated, politicized, and bureaucratized world without a large element of luck.

I had formed a delegation composed of our chairman, Marvin L. Goldberger, and his wife, Mildred; the Chinese legal scholar Jerome A. Cohen and his wife, Joan; and my wife and me. We were met in Canton on May 21 by Lee Mingde of the Chinese Scientific and Technical Association of China; after arriving, we saw a woman give birth by acupuncture anesthesia and then proceeded to Beijing on the same day.

I found it weird to be inside this ancient civilization, whose members were visibly distinguishable from oneself; I felt like an intruder in a sea of blue ants. And the Chinese reserve and politeness, which made overt dealings so pleasant and comfortable, could produce a sense of uneasiness. One felt culturally inferior, wondering what the Chinese really thought of us barbarians. As one of my friends remarked, one hour after leaving China, (a) you feel hungry, and (b) your head falls off.

From my point of view, the overriding purpose of our visit was to catalyze the initiative of scientific exchange with China. My intense obsession with this was later to cause some interpersonal problems.

I was asked by a Chinese official, quite early, a question that I knew was central to our mission: Was the National Academy of Sciences (NAS) an official organization of the U.S. government or nonofficial? China was preoccupied at that time, and still is today, with keeping Taiwan part of China. It would violate China's "one-China" policy if it were to have exchanges with a governmental organization that had links with Taiwan—as NAS did.

In retrospect, I rate my answer as A-plus, but my acceptance of their eventual response merits only a C. I answered, "I am an expert on this question since I have recently had occasion to check the official government organization manual. It says that the NAS is 'quasi-official.' That means that you can consider the Academy to be 'official' or 'nonofficial'—whichever you prefer. And in either case, I will give you arguments for it."[164] I indicated that FAS was much smaller than NAS and would be suitable only for anchoring exchanges for a suitable transitional period. A week later, this official returned and said, "Thank you for assuring us that the NAS is 'nonofficial.'"

In retrospect, it is perfectly obvious, from that statement, that the Chinese had decided what answer they wanted and were signaling what line we ourselves should take. Harder to accept was the corollary that we should abandon any effort to invite a delegation to America. To do this on the basis of an indirect statement about the nature of NAS was more than could be expected from our (Western) mentalities. Accordingly, we continued to press for scientific exchange in general, and for our receiving a delegation in return. I was maniacally insistent on this. I felt the weight of the entire Chinese scientific community on my back—all of whom, I felt sure, would want this exchange to begin.

In Beijing, we met with our host, the seventy-two-year-old Zhou Peiyuan, a nuclear scientist trained at Cal Tech who had been forced to flee to Canada to get back to China in 1949. (At that time, the United States was trying to prevent nuclear-trained scientists from getting to China.) He was now functioning as the chairman of a revolutionary committee in charge of Beijing University. The Cultural Revolution, which would not end until four years later, was raging. Many organizations had "toppled" their leaders and were run by revolutionary committees.

In between meetings and trips to explore the city, Goldberger gave a lecture on physics, Cohen gave one on law, and I gave one on arms control—no doubt the first discussion of arms control from a Westerner in twenty-five years in China. That the United States was considering a space-based ABM system seemed to them science fiction—although our Bambi project had envisaged just that. Another proposal, which I had picked up from Morton Halperin before leaving, was a nuclear-free zone involving Korea, Japan, and Manchuria—still an idea worth working for.

If left to me, we would have spent all our time in Beijing struggling, at every opportunity, to discuss scientific exchange. But the "delegation" had many other interests. My efforts to control things by distinguishing between delegation "members" and "spouses" only antagonized Mildred Goldberger and Joan Cohen, who wanted a say in group activities. And this friction made life difficult for my chairman, Marvin Goldberger.

Our Chinese hosts advised me, "We want everyone to be happy," and they suggested a trip to Shanghai, Xian, and Luoyang—ancient seats of the Chinese capital. I could not refuse, and Joan was ecstatic.

Although we did not know it at the time, Shanghai was the site of the left-wing extremists of the Cultural Revolution, the Gang of Four, and we were treated there with a touch more suspicion than in Beijing. I probably did not help things by asking a guide, "Has Chairman Mao ever made a mistake?"

"That," the guide responded, "is an abusive question." Indeed, it was.

I never ceased to be amazed at the brilliance of the Chinese repartee.

I felt that the Chinese would, someday, be very strong and would, in addition, be providing mankind with most of its great scientists and diplomats. Their future would be bright. They are an enormously talented people. In a toast I said so—I think some of them considered this a "racist" approach—and expressed the hope that America would be their friend.

During these travels we saw factories, universities, hospitals, communes, a May 7 (reeducation) camp, museums, plant nurseries, acrobatics, the Ming Tombs, the Great Wall, the Imperial Palace, and the Summer Palace. After splendid visits to Xian and Luoyang, we traveled to Canton, from which we were to depart the following day. Over lunch, to the amazement of all of us, our guide asked, without any warning or explanation, "Would you like to return to Beijing?"

Mildred announced, "Of course not, we are leaving tomorrow," or something to that effect.

I blurted out, "Cool it, Mildred" and began asking our guides what they meant. I, at least, knew it meant *something*. (I had been called, by others on the delegation, the chief tea-leaf reader; I did feel then, and do now, that I was more attuned than any of the others except Jerome Cohen to the subtleties of Chinese discourse.)

The Chinese guide said little more, though we discussed the issue for an hour. All he permitted himself was to admit, "I have put to you a hard problem"—a remark that confirmed the purposeful nature of the invitation.

Mildred Goldberger—and hence Marvin, too—was not about to return to Beijing on such a vague offer and felt, with plausibility, that it would involve further and more detailed talks in Beijing on the problems of cultural exchange. Joan had commitments that required her to leave. But Jerome Cohen was eager for any additional days in China. Sensing that something was up, I announced that B.J. and I would return for three days. And so, to my horror, the delegation was split—something I had feared would happen. So only three of us returned to Beijing.

On our arrival, we were told we would dine with the head of the American desk in the Foreign Ministry, Cai Zemin, a high official who eventually became the ambassador to the United States. (I remember our discussing at length why it would be so difficult for China to announce that it would resolve the Taiwan issue only through peaceful means—an issue still very much with us today, a quarter century later.) We were told that the next day we would meet with Vice Foreign Minister Qiao Guanhua, which was incredible! In the nearest he ever came to an apology, our guide said, immediately upon our arrival in Beijing, when we learned the news of these two appointments, "I had to follow my instructions to the letter." Needless to say, had we known, the Goldbergers would have returned with us. In Asia one cannot be too alert, and one needs to have one's radar turned on full at all times.

Still more was to come. At the end of the meeting with the vice foreign minister, which lasted four hours, we were told that that very evening, on June 16, we would dine with Prime Minister Zhou Enlai.

Our Dinner with Zhou

For the dinner the Foreign Ministry had called back from distant parts of China three other people: Richard Dudman of the *St. Louis Post-Dispatch* (an old friend of my family's); Harrison Salisbury of *The New York Times;* and John K. Fairbanks, America's greatest China scholar. Premier Zhou gave a toast to cultural exchange, and there followed a discussion of the diplomatic problems that could slow this process, especially the absence of diplomatic relations and the influence of Chiang Kai-shek's government in Washington.[165] In particular, long-term visits of Chinese students could be complicated by the presence of Taiwan students at American universities. I proposed some ways of circumventing this problem and said, "There are many ways to skin a cat"—a remark that provoked some problems in translation.[166]

First row, left to right: *Premier Zhou, Tang Wen-sheng (Nancy Tang, the interpreter), the author, and B.J.;* second row: *Foreign Minister Qiao Guanhua; John Fairbanks (America's most distinguished China scholar) and his wife, Wilma; Jerome Alan Cohen; Vice Rector Zhou Peiyuan of Beijing University; and Madame Zhou Peiyuan*

More important, Zhou noted that such problems did not arise for visiting delegations of Chinese scientists who could pass through universities with a connection of one kind or another to Taiwan. According to Harrison Salisbury, this was the first time that policy on exchanges "had been put so specifically at the top" of the Chinese agenda.[167]

I had been warned by the Chinese cadres, who by then knew me only too well, that I was not to raise "business" questions at the dinner (i.e., the issue of scientific exchange). Indeed, they had earlier told me to "relax." (My response, which visibly unnerved them, was that "Chairman Mao would not have given me that advice.") In any case, I was not to be put off. As Premier Zhou escorted me to the exit, I said, "Premier Zhou, our scientists want to come to China. But we demand reciprocity. We want your scientists to come to America."

Asked at what university I worked, I said I worked in Washington but represented scientists at many universities. He responded, "Then you will introduce us to many scientists."

Zhou was, as all reports show, deft and diplomatic to the *n*th degree. He bestowed upon me a treasured gift: a photograph, taken as this exchange took place, memorializing our visit as he looks respectfully at this thirty-six-year-old minor functionary from far-off Washington.

During the discussion before dinner, I had raised the question of exchanges on strategic issues, arms control, and so on. Premier Zhou said that they would be much more interested in exchanges on non-military issues such as medicine. He began gesturing as if with a cigarette and said that his doctor had told him he should stop smoking.

Something about the way he did this triggered my radar. In fact, Zhou was known for calibrating every gesture. I thought that he, or someone important, was ill and that this was an important signal.

During a subsequent trip to China, in 1986, I read, in a biography of Premier Zhou, that he had, indeed, learned that he had cancer in 1972.[168] The full story came out only in 1994, when Chairman Mao's doctor, Li Zhisui, wrote about Mao and his attitudes toward medicine.

The month before we met, in mid-May, Premier Zhou informed Dr. Li that a Politburo member, Kang Sheng, seemed to have cancer and that Zhou wanted to tell Mao. Dr. Li confirmed the diagnosis of bladder cancer. Dr. Li knew that it was an "unwritten rule that no politburo standing committee member or any member of Mao's staff could undergo major surgery without permission from the Chairman."[169] Mao refused, saying cancer could not be cured and the treatment would only hasten death. "Don't tell the patient, and don't perform surgery. Then the person can live longer and still do some work," he ordered.

Kang's plight induced Zhou to have a physical exam, and his urine revealed cancerous cells. Chairman Mao was at first reluctant to believe the doctors and, when he did, refused to allow the treatment. He ordered the tests on Zhou stopped and said, "Leave the patient alone and let him live out his life happily. If I have cancer, I definitely will not have it treated." He refused tests on himself.[170]

Zhou wanted the operation but was not willing to go ahead without Mao's consent. He was still "waiting for Mao approval" for surgery in July 1974, when Mao was diagnosed with the fatal and progressively debilitating Lou Gehrig's disease (amyotrophic lateral sclerosis).[171] Zhou suggested asking the Chinese delegation to the UN in New York to gather information about Western treatment for this disease—but was told the United States had no effective treatment either.[172]

Of course, I knew nothing about this when I asked Zhou Peiyuan, after the dinner, whether FAS could send a delegation concerned with issues of cancer; I asked him to specify what kind of cancer would be of greatest interest, and he said he would investigate and respond.

He said later that they would be interested in "all kinds of specialists combining theory and practice." Back in the United States, I worked up a delegation of senior specialists—the best in America. Everyone was eager to visit China. I promptly wrote a letter proposing the delegation and sent it off in the mail.

There was no answer. I attributed it to a thoughtless article Jerome Cohen had written on his exit from China, discussing the meeting with Zhou and speculating that Mao had throat cancer. The publicity surrounding this could have turned off Chinese interest. After all, self-reliance and Chinese traditional medicine were two key Maoist themes.

For a long time and still to some extent today I writhed over not having handled this better. In about 1980, when our original guide, Li Mingde, arrived in Washington as a science attaché, he responded to my expressions of regret by saying that the letter had "never arrived." This redoubled my feeling that I ought to have tried harder—sent another letter or dealt through the Chinese mission in New York. (I had visited the mission and talked to Ambassador Huang Hua about it but had not given him another letter.) In any case, I felt less than effective.

But after having read of Mao's aversion to operations for cancer, I am not sure anything would have come of it. Dr. Li says that Zhou had cancer of the bladder, colon, and lung; he added, "Strangely, the cancers were independent of each other, not the result of metastasis."[173] So perhaps little could have been done for Zhou in any case. He died on January 8, 1976, and Mao followed him, eight months later, on September 9. Mao had never even visited Zhou in the hospital.

Five months after our May-June visit in 1972, the Chinese reciprocating delegation arrived. It had been sent to Sweden, Great Britain, Canada, and the United States and was on the road for three months. On its arrival at Dulles airport, I was overcome with emotion at the thought of what this meant to millions of Chinese scientists in particular and, in due course, to the Chinese population itself.

The Chinese had decided to have their host be the Committee on Scholarly Communications with the People's Republic of China (CSCPRC), which was a consortium of the National Academy of Sciences, the Social Science Research Council, and the American Council of Learned Societies. The final decisions on this had come, we later heard, in negotiations in Paris between the United States and China. The formula worked out was that CSCPRC would host the delegation "in cooperation with the Federation of American Scientists."[174]

It was painful not to be able to be the host of this first delegation, which, until the fall, we thought we were.[175] But CSCPRC were a group that could follow through with subsequent exchanges, as we could not. Officially I was "happy with the way it has worked out."[176]

Still the Chinese were very sensitive to our feelings. They thanked both FAS and CSCPRC for inviting them, and they told everyone that they were here at the "joint" invitation of FAS and CSCPRC.[177] And FAS gave the farewell banquet for them in San Francisco on December 18—at the suggestion, I think, of CSCPRC.[178]

Our activities in promoting scientific exchange with China dwindled thereafter. Perhaps because he had been cheated of seeing Zhou, or because of his high scientific rank and excellent diplomatic behavior in China, Marvin Goldberger was promptly invited back. But he distanced himself from FAS by not advising headquarters (me) that he was going, and by not reporting to us when he returned.[179]

I felt that the small foothold that I had fashioned was eroding. And since the scientific exchange had now begun, there seemed nothing immediate we could do in any case. I quietly dropped out and began work on other things.[180]

But remembering Zhou's hope that I would introduce their representatives to many scientists, and having the warmest feelings for him, I bestirred myself to try to introduce Chinese Liaison Office staffers to various Americans in Washington. But I did not return to China for fourteen years.

CHAPTER **13**

Congressional Travel to the USSR: Cold-War Antidote

The author is persuaded by his own visits to Moscow in the 1960s, and by history, that congressional travel to the Soviet Union would slow the arms race and produce much sounder U.S. policy by tranquilizing hawks and sobering up doves. He makes a half dozen abortive efforts to stir such travel, over fifteen years, truly succeeding only when he secures the help of a handful of elite women prepared to wage a door-to-door campaign on Capitol Hill.

Visiting the Soviet Union tranquilized the hawks. They saw, immediately, a totally unexpected third-world poverty and longstanding, deeply felt, Russian fear of war. At the same time, visiting the Soviet Union disabused the doves. Nothing about the undemocratic and totalitarian way in which Russia operated could do anything but stir the apprehensions of dovish visitors.

In 1937 André Gide, the French sympathizer with the Soviet revolution, wrote a disabused report that was a sensation, asserting, "In the USSR, everybody knows beforehand, once and for all, that on any and every subject there can be only one opinion."[181] In 1948, a Soviet bureaucrat told John Steinbeck, "We are very tired of people who come here and are violently pro-Russian and who go back to the United States and become violently anti-Russian. We have had considerable experience with that kind."[182]

In 1956, as noted earlier, my father had come back and written something about Russia, in italics, that he knew would startle many of his left-wing readers and, perhaps, jeopardize his publication: *"This is not a healthy society, and it is not run by honest men."*

In 1970, a liberal journalist couple, Delia and Ferdinand Kuhn, wrote, "Looking back on our journey, we were more troubled by the closed nature of Soviet society than anything else we saw or heard."[183] And in 1976, Robert Kaiser of *The Washington Post*, reviewing his three years in Moscow, reported that the Russians were "less formidable than we have imagined, more vulnerable and more nervous." And he went on to say that our exaggerated fear of Russia and its expenditures was, in part, "a tribute to our own foolishness."[184]

These sorts of reactions were evident to me from my trips to the Soviet Union in the sixties. And later research revealed similar sentiments in the statements of the few American senators who visited the USSR. The conservative John Stennis (D, Mississippi) had gone to Russia in 1958 and reported, "Frankly, I was not prepared for what I saw." He doubted that "Russia now plans a direct military attack upon us" and talked of its inefficiency.[185] Senator William Roth (R, Delaware) concluded, in 1974, that Communism is a "highly inefficient economic system."[186] When Senator Sam Nunn (D, Georgia) came back in 1978, he announced, "It is difficult for Americans to grasp the terrifying slaughter and suffering that befell the Soviets during World War II, which left a permanent and indelible scar on the Russian psyche."[187]

From my point of view, the situation was perfect: Congressional travel to the Soviet Union would slow the arms race. "Trust them less and fear them less" became the slogan of the campaign to get congressmen to visit the Soviet Union. It was also pretty obvious that the reverse was true: When Soviet leaders visited the United States, they saw a democratic society that was *not* poised to attack them (leading them to trust us more) while observing wealth beyond anything that they had imagined (leading them to respect and even fear us more).

My campaign began in Moscow when I introduced Senator Mike Gravel (D, Alaska) to some friends in September 1969. At a dinner at the home of Revaz Gamkrelidze, an associate ("corresponding") member of the Soviet Academy of Sciences, Gravel made a toast to the idea, which he intended to champion, of sponsoring leadership visits. Back in Washington he talked to Soviet ambassador Dobrynin about it and proceeded to introduce a bill on November 7, 1969.[188]

Our main point was that visits by nonpolitical citizens could go on forever without making much difference: The percentage of people seeing the other's society would remain minuscule[189] and the political effect negligible. The problem was that the *leadership* of the two sides had little idea of what the other side's society was like. We needed to stop sending only athletes, doctors, educators, and scientists and begin sending political leaders.

But Gravel's enthusiasm for this idea, which could not be contained, embraced more than just the two houses of the national government: He wanted to subsidize trips for local and state officials as well. He proposed dispatching a thousand political leaders and their spouses for up to two weeks (half would be from Congress, and the other half would be made up of fifty governors, the mayors of the hundred largest U.S. cities, and the majority and minority leaders of the fifty state legislatures). This program, we estimated, would cost only $5 million—one-half of an intercontinental missile's cost. Gravel also wanted to facilitate trips to the United States for more than a thousand members of the Soviet leadership, with their spouses, under procedures for financing that were to be negotiated.[190]

On its introduction, Senator Robert Byrd (D, West Virginia) found the idea "intriguing" and Senator Mike Mansfield (D, Montana), the democratic majority leader, used the same word. At a public hearing on February 6, 1970, Averil Harriman and George Kennan, our two most distinguished former ambassadors to the Soviet Union, gave favorable testimony. Of the American public officials polled, 75 percent responded favorably, and only 5 percent were opposed. The Soviet state newspaper *Izvestia* carried an article reporting favorably on the bill.

On April 10, 1970, the Senate Foreign Relations Committee approved the bill with only one dissenting vote—the $5 million was to be spent for the thousand visits over five years. But predictably, the right wing began to attack the bill as "junketing"—although why anyone would want to go to Moscow for its nonexistent nightclubs, sun, and beaches was unclear. In fact, our tabulations showed that six times as many congresspeople were going to Western Europe and five times as many to the Far East. Nobody wanted to go to Moscow.[191]

Congressional Quarterly was keeping close track of all foreign visits of all members of Congress and wrote a detailed article about them annually. This was, they told me, the issue that invariably attracted the most media attention. Pandering to local cynicism about their representative's desire to travel, these reports could turn off enough voters to influence elections.

The Gravel bill was brought to the floor on April 20, and Senator Robert Dole (R, Kansas), who was then serving as a kind of informal watchdog for the Nixon administration, championed the opposition, saying, "I do not believe that going to any country as large as Russia or as small as Israel would engage one to learn enough to give us more guidance in voting in Congress."[192] (Fifteen years later, in a change of heart, Senate Majority Leader Dole was writing President Reagan urging the president to arrange with Gorbachev ways "to institute [parliamentary exchanges] on a more regular basis.")[193]

It looked like this rallying of conservatives by Dole would defeat the bill, but the majority leader, Mike Mansfield, was found and brought to the floor. He rounded up the supporters, and we won 38 to 23.

The bill was, however, bottled up in the House Committee of International Relations because, we gathered, the White House did not want it. It feared that the legislators might get out in front of the president in the organization of détente and might complicate its efforts. So the State Department announced that if members of

Congress really wanted to go, State would be happy to oblige them if only the bill were killed.[194]

In November I wrote Henry Kissinger observing that President Nixon's effort to "turn confrontation into negotiation" had now proceeded apace. Could Nixon now let down the floodgates on such exchanges—perhaps proposing them himself during his upcoming visits to Beijing and Moscow?[195] But in December 1971, with regard to China, Kissinger was still talking of the importance of getting exchange "in other than political fields." And Kissinger's Soviet policy was even more determined to avoid political travel.[196]

By 1974 President Nixon had himself been not only to Moscow but also to Beijing. I wrote Kissinger again, asking him to "let my people go." A week later I got my answer on a car radio: Henry Kissinger was saying, "We are all in favor of having scientists, sportsmen, tourists, artists, and other *nonpolitical* persons travel to the Soviet Union." (emphasis added)

In 1977 we decided to analyze the voting records of the senators who had been to the Soviet Union.[197] We concluded that 55 percent of the thirty-three senators who had voted dovishly had visited the Soviet Union. But only 40 percent of the forty-four senators with intermediate voting records had visited there. And of the twenty-three senators who voted hawkishly all of the time, only 22 percent had made the trip. Senator Strom Thurmond (R, South Carolina) told a colleague that of course he could not go there because he was so anticommunist that they would throw him in jail. In an article publicized in *The Washington Post* conveying these statistics, we even played the China card, observing that "at the present rate of travel, it seems likely that within a very few years more senators will have been to [Beijing] than Moscow."[198]

In 1982 we geared up the campaign again. To provide the necessary materials, we got the backing of President Ford[199] and twenty former senators, along with some former secretaries of state and defense.[200] Our research showed that since Russia opened itself up to travel, there had been visits by 284 different senators but only ninety-five senatorial visits. Typically they were going to interparliamentary conferences in Moscow or somewhere in that direction (e.g., New Delhi). If one subtracted presidential aspirants, SALT II treaty investigations, and interparliamentary union visits, there were only about twenty-five senators in the last twenty-five years who had taken the trouble just to go and look around.

On March 27, 1982, we sent a news release on our survey to the AP and UPI wire services. It showed that over 75 percent of the House of Representatives and 60 percent of the Senate had never obtained "first-hand impressions and information" about Russia. The names showed that twenty-two of the thirty-six members of the House Foreign Affairs Committee had not been to the Soviet Union.[201] And we listed all of the names to draw attention to the situation. We also announced that 70 percent of the Soviet Politburo had never been to the United States.[202]

The publication of our release resulted in some forty newspaper editorials in support of congressional travel to the USSR.[203] I also published an article in *The Washington Post* entitled "Let Our Senators Go! (to Russia)."[204] Then-congressman Paul Simon (D, Illinois) promptly issued a press release lauding this article and saying he had never before seen a "newspaper or magazine, radio or television station criticize senators or representatives for *not* traveling."[205]

In July 1983, a few months later, Senator Dole became a supporter of sorts. He introduced a Senate Resolution (182) stating that it was the sense of the Senate that travel by senators to the Soviet Union "serves the interests of the United States and should be, and is hereby, encouraged."[206] But this was to give senators "protection" from junketing charges; it did not help them finance the trips.

The Women Volunteers Put It Over the Top

In 1984 my wife and I were dining with our friends Townsend Hoopes and his wife, Ann. Ann was the longstanding cochairperson

Ann Hoopes lobbying

of the McLean Foreign Policy Group, an organization of women who met monthly to discuss
foreign affairs and to hear distinguished speakers. Motivated, she later told me, by concern
about Reagan's "Star Wars" proposal, she asked
me whether there was anything these women
could do. 🔔 I asked her if she could organize a
team of women to visit offices of members of
Congress who had not been to the Soviet
Union to prod them into doing so. She agreed,
and we met on July 17 to get it started.

From this chance conversation came the
final and by far most successful effort to promote congressional
travel to the USSR. We formed the Project for Congressional Travel
to the Soviet Union. Beginning in November 1984, a team of about
a half dozen female D.C. residents, led by Ann, systematically visited
the offices of all 420 congresspeople who had not yet traveled to the
Soviet Union.[207] At that time, 15 percent of the House members and
50 percent of the senators had made such visits. The women were nervous at first, but their social skills served them well as they learned
Lobbying 101: how to go door-to-door in Congress.

On February 28, 1985, the team organized an FAS lunch for

Hoope's team in action: From left: *Ann Shirk,* con-
gressional *staffer, Martha Newell,* two *staffers,*
Kathy Kenety, Betsy Marshall; other side: *Ann*
Hoopes, Cely Arndt (obscured), staffer

twenty senators. The event's
theme was underscored by Russian dolls and bowls, homemade
cookies, and Russian bread and
flower arrangements. Marvin Kalb
of the State Department was the
featured speaker. Majority Leader
Dole attended. When senators began telling their favorite trip anecdotes, Senator John Warner (R,
Virginia) explained, with some
pride, that his toast in Moscow

had so angered the admirals who were receiving him that they threw their drinking glasses into the fireplace. (Warner had no idea that this showed enthusiasm, not anger.)

On March 6, the project hosted forty-five members of Congress for the same purpose. William Colby was the featured speaker—as a former director of the CIA, he was perfect for a "know-your-enemy" campaign. No one said even one unkind word about this project, and as an outgrowth of this lunch, Representatives Claudine Schneider (D, Rhode Island) and Morris K. Udall (D, Arizona) introduced a resolution that paralleled the one introduced by Dole in the Senate.[208]

At about this time, the project decided to write a brochure and to organize a grass-roots campaign; Ann wrote a letter to "The Women of America" with this conclusion: "We are going for the nerve here. A few hundred such visits can change the political and psychological map of the personalities that have the power. Help us nudge the existing system into sanity."

Our campaign began to show signs of progress. In 1985 there was an upsurge in congressional travel to the Soviet Union, with fifty-five representatives and thirteen senators traveling individually or with committees, as opposed to 1984, when only three senators and three representatives had done so. Both the U.S. embassy in Moscow and the Soviet embassy here reported large increases in applications by members of Congress for travel to the Soviet Union.[209] The Soviet embassy told Ann that twenty-six delegations had applied for trips and that enough was enough, "call off your dogs."[210]

We also now had something that individual citizens could do. A handsome brochure for citizen action—prepared at FAS by our staff associate Ned Hodgeman—was entitled "Raising the Rate of Exchange." On its cover was our key injunction to citizens: "All you have to do is ask: 'Congressman, in light of your pronouncements on appropriate U.S. policy toward the Soviet Union, may I ask . . . have you ever been there?'"[211]

The Russians had long wanted, along with many other countries, bilateral parliamentary exchanges with the United States, no doubt to enhance the international image of their parliament, which, obviously, the United States viewed as a fraudulent rubber-stamp operation. And they no doubt thought, also, that this would be a way of approaching the U.S. government through that "soft under-belly" of our legislature. I was still for such exchanges—any method of fostering Soviet and U.S. leadership visits was okay with me.

Although parliamentary exchanges with any country could take place, U.S. law requires them only with our immediate neighbors, Mexico and Canada. I observed and pressed the idea that the Soviet Union was, also, an immediate neighbor across the Bering Straits. And it seems to me that this notion found its way into a speech by President Reagan.

In April 1985, when I was visiting Moscow as part of the FAS–Soviet Academy traveling "school" on arms control, Evgeny Velikhov arranged for me to meet with Lev R. Tolkunov, the chair-man of the Soviet Union's Council of the Union (its House of Rep-resentatives). There I pressed for parliamentary travel. (Tolkunov told me that in 1974, Majority Leader Mike Mansfield had ex-plained to Tolkunov that he could not organize a parliamentary exchange group with the Soviets—as we had with the Mexicans and the Canadians—because the United States would then be obliged to organize them with all other countries.)

Tolkunov may have briefed Gorbachev, because when the Soviet leader received Speaker of the House Tip O'Neill the very next week, the issue finally got the spin and prominence we wanted. Gorbachev stated, "We know the role played by Congress in Amer-ica's political life, and we attach great importance to developing contacts along the parliamentary line as one of the elements of invigorating Soviet-American relations. The time is such now that people, *shaping the policy of the two countries*, should by all means converse with one another."[212] (emphasis added)

When Gorbachev said he considered parliamentary exchange to be a central method of invigorating U.S.-Soviet relations, I decided to try to create a Soviet analogue of the National Committee for U.S.-China Relations, which had done so much to handle the logistics of Chinese travel. In the summer of 1985, I retained a former undersecretary of state, Benjamin H. Read, who knew, and was respected by, everyone in town. In fifty interviews of relevant Washington policy movers and shakers, Ben found little or no opposition and much enthusiasm. He concluded that moneys secured through legislation and from foundations could set up such a thing.

But at this point we ran into delays and obstacles that obliged us to abandon the project. Soviet fears of incidents, perhaps, or the desire of some Russians, perhaps of Arbatov's Institute, to monopolize the exchanges, may have done us in. Where we wanted an exchange that was as open and frequent as possible, the Soviet side might have wanted it to be controlled and limited. The last straw was an interview I had in the Soviet Foreign Ministry in July 1986 with an official who made it clear that nothing would happen on what we considered to be a worthwhile scale.

In April 1985, en route with Velikhov to a Carter-Ford arms-control meeting, I organized a lunch for Velikhov and Congressman John D. Dingell, the chairman of the House Committee on Energy and Commerce. Velikhov, who was the chairman of the Energy Commission of the Soviet Union, promptly invited Dingell's whole committee to come visit the USSR. This was, we thought, our first success in our efforts to link the standing commissions of the Soviet parliament to the committees of the U.S. Congress. However, at the last minute, Secretary of Defense Caspar Weinberger withdrew permission for use of the plane the committee had planned to use.

In February 1987, I was again in Moscow and had the opportunity to talk to Valentin Fallin, the former Soviet ambassador to East Germany. He was then the influential director of the Novosti press agency and a candidate member of the Central Committee. He remembered my interviewing him when he was at *Izvestia*. Prolix and sometimes vague, he nevertheless seemed well meaning. I asked him to tell Gorbachev that the Soviet leadership would not understand the necessity for his reforms (perestroika) without a trip to the West themselves. Could he, Fallin, poll the Central Committee concerning their visits to the West, or lack of them, and present Gorbachev with the results showing how few officials had had this experience? We gave Fallin our statistics on such Soviet visits by high U.S. officials.

He was cautious, saying, "If people speak on these visits, they will be critical. Your side will forget about internal disagreements if our people come." He added, "According to Gorbachev, our aim is not to quarrel." But on hearing that the leaders could come as "tourists" and not just to discuss policy, if they wanted, he was encouraged. He said he would do the poll and would discuss the matter with a Politburo member.[213]

In any case, we did not give up on our basic campaign. In June 1987 we were advertising for fifty interested and committed individuals who would lead, on a state level, a national campaign to get senators and congresspeople to travel to the Soviet Union.[214] By July we had them mailing our booklet (*Raising the Rate of Exchange*) to their members of Congress. In November I could be found testifying on our efforts to the Helsinki Commission, and I tried to get their support at least for an "exchange of parliamentarians" if not for "parliamentary exchange." In other words, we were quite prepared to have reciprocal visits of parliamentarians without formal exchange. The commission had a very good record for having traveled to the Soviet Union, and it knew that such travel would help with human rights.[215]

.   .   .

In the end, of course, although we catalyzed the travel of quite a few delegations, we never got the sort of exchange program we had hoped for. A formalized program of regular Soviet visits here was more than the Soviet Union was ready for. Their parliament was so phony that many of its members—milkmaids and Stakhanovites— were, in the eyes of their government, completely inappropriate for a visit to the United States. So I do not feel that my failures with *that* side were due to ineptitude.

With regard to the American senators and representatives who did travel, it is difficult to gauge how much overall effect these visits had, but it could have been very real in some cases. One dramatic and relevant example of the effect on Americans of exposure to the Soviet Union was revealed in 1997 in the case of General George Lee Butler, who had been in charge of the Strategic Air Command that targeted Russia. Asked to explain his psychological evolution from nuclear warrior to disarmament champion, he mentioned his first visit to the USSR, where he saw "severe economic deprivation. . . . More than that, it was the sense of defeat in the eyes of the people. . . . It all came crashing home to me that I really had been dealing with a caricature all those years."[216]

Even one senator, speaking privately about a visit, can exercise a powerful influence on the group mind that is the Senate. At one point, through Velikhov, I was able to arrange a visit to the Soviet Union for then-senator William Cohen (R, Maine; now the secretary of defense), who had never been there, and Senator Joseph Biden (D, Delaware), who had.[217] On his return, Cohen took me aside at a meeting and pulled out a poem that he had written. A quick examination showed that for him one trip was quite enough: His poem reflected the essence of Russia, and I told him so.[218]

PART V

Human Rights and the Defense
of Sakharov: 1973–1987

CHAPTER 14

1973–1979: Defending Sakharov Through NAS and Moscow

After an initial defense of Sakharov in Finland, in 1973, has real resonance, FAS policy toward the Soviet Union is reshaped. A subsequent boycott of a Moscow conference seems to have assisted Elena Bonner in getting a visa to Italy. In 1975 an electric visit to Sakharov and the refusenik scientists in Moscow is written up in the FAS newsletter. Through chains of circumstance involving a public dispute with the imperious president of the National Academy of Sciences, the newsletter catalyzes a change in the attitude of the American scientific community toward the defense of oppressed colleagues abroad by institutionalizing human rights committees inside the scientific societies.

My defense of Andrei Sakharov, which lasted for fourteen years, began in far-off Finland at the end of August 1973. The Aulenko, Finland, Pugwash Conference started rather inauspiciously when efforts were made to persuade me to withdraw a submission to the conference entitled "Superpower Détente Could Threaten Soviet-American Scientific Cooperation." The paper, only a few hundred words long, was, a Pugwash official told me, "too terse and logical" to be ignored and was upsetting the Russians. Shaped by my training in mathematics, it was hard to ignore because it was formulated as a "proof" with two lemmas (each proved) and a conclusion.[219] I reproduce the summary proof below:

Lemma I. Superpower détente may lead to fewer American restrictions on free circulation of scientists but greater Soviet restrictions.

[e.g., Soviets might become more concerned about ideological penetration and brain drain.]

Lemma II. Détente may lead American scientists to feel freer to criticize Soviet treatment of Soviet scientists. [e.g., U.S. scientists might become less concerned about war and less concerned about being associated with anticommunists in their criticism of the Soviet Union.]

Conclusion: Détente may lead to rising American scientific protests about the treatment of Soviet scientists and may imperil Soviet-American scientific cooperation.

I declined to withdraw the paper, ⟨⟩ and the Russians began distancing themselves from me; it seemed they would not speak to me. This included Georgi Arbatov and others I knew. But this paper may well have been my most precise prediction. As I show in this and the next two chapters, it was also a self-fulfilling prophecy in which my own activism, triggered especially by a subsequent visit to Moscow, played a significant role.

The conference was important for another reason. On August 29, forty Soviet academicians denounced Andrei Sakharov in *Pravda*, the official organ of the Soviet Communist Party, and it appeared that a campaign was being developed against him. The academicians said that Sakharov had spoken out "against the détente policy of the Soviet Union," that he had become the "instrument for hostile propaganda" against their country, that his activity was "fundamentally alien to Soviet scientists," and that they wanted to "emphatically condemn his activity, which discredits the honor and dignity of Soviet scientists."

Both Artsimovich and M. D. Millionshchikov had recently died, and I seized the opportunity of a memorial session to make some pointed comments to all 120 attendees of the Pugwash conference—comments that drew Western applause, with the Soviets sitting on their hands. Readers will recall the scene to which I refer:

In 1964, when I first met Millionshchikov, I was presenting a paper against the ABM, and everyone on the Soviet side was denouncing me.

146

I went up to Millionshchikov, whom I came very much to love, and said, "At least one Soviet academician agrees with me; look at what academician Artsimovich has said." Millionshchikov responded, without hesitation, "Artsimovich always disagrees with everyone else."

But now it is 1973, and the treaty banning ABMs was ratified by the Soviet Union just last year. So we see that one academician can be right even when all others disagree! Accordingly, it is possible that academician Andrei Sakharov could be right even while forty academicians say that he is not. So he should be with us at these conferences, and we should defend him.

This anecdote was so apt that Arbatov suggested to others that it showed that I was a "professional" propagandist.

The famous Peter Kapitza was at the meeting, a physicist so great that Stalin had refused to let him leave the country to return to England. He was the only Soviet scientist friendly to me, and the reason was revealing. Kapitza had lived under a kind of self-imposed house arrest for a half dozen years because of his criticism of Beria. Of all the people at the meeting, only he had the prestige to resist the demands in Moscow that all delegation members must sign the *Pravda* statement denouncing Sakharov. So we were dissidents together in a common cause, he and I. And I feel now the honor this historic figure did me by defecting from the Soviet chill with which I was surrounded by showing me personal warmth.

I would not have expected all this to have any effect whatsoever—except to impair my relations with the Soviets. Certainly I did not expect my actions to inspire anyone. But I realized later that, under the longstanding conditions of U.S.-USSR confrontation, Western scientists in dialogue with the Soviets had learned to expect that their counterparts, if affronted, would bang an enormous pair of cymbals, pick up their papers, and leave. Under the emerging conditions of détente, however, walkouts were not a part of Soviet instructions.

Awareness of these new circumstances began to dawn in Washington. On September 8 the National Academy of Sciences sent a cable defending its "associate member Andrei Sakharov" and saying that "harassment or detention of Sakharov will have severe effects upon the relationships between the scientific communities of the U.S. and the USSR and could vitiate our recent efforts toward scientific interchange and cooperation."[220] This was a key act in the effort to protect Sakharov. An article in *Science* magazine detailed its origin at some length because, although the sentiments were obvious, NAS did not take this step easily.[221] *Science* said the letter's authors were encouraged by reports from the "scientific grapevine from Pugwash" noting, "In two instances, the crisis concerning Sakharov was mentioned or alluded to." A reporter observed, "In years past the Russians would have gotten up and walked out of the room. Instead, they 'just sat there' while other delegates warmly applauded."[222]

In the October 1973 FAS newsletter, prepared on my return, I began developing the theme that became the basis for FAS's policy toward the Soviet Union—and for the later defense of Sakharov. Entitled "The Responsibility of Scientists Under Conditions of Détente," the lead editorial argued that FAS had been correct in putting peace first on the agenda under the conditions of the Cold War. But now, under conditions of détente, I argued that FAS should give more emphasis to freedom for our foreign colleagues. The council approved these views, unanimously I think, although some of the older members who had courageously devoted many years to resisting the crude forces of American anticommunism were loath to join in what seemed at first to be a reversal of that position.

The newsletter stated that American scientists should no longer provide the Soviet Union with the "special dispensation" we did not provide to other countries: refraining from comments on Soviet intellectual freedom. "So long as nuclear armed states exist, it is entirely appropriate—as a security matter—for citizens everywhere to advocate the intellectual freedom required to ensure that détente is not lightly discarded."[223] We also warned that détente could lead to more repression in the Soviet Union. Scientific cooperation was essential to scientific advances and, for this, Soviet scientists needed free speech and travel. "Acts of intellectual courage," I wrote, "must be protected and encouraged."

In a speech I was invited to give to State Department employees at their Open Forum, I explained our position and indicated that we had decided to become, in a sense, a "balance wheel to U.S. government policy." It meant that we would pursue détente when the State Department pursued Cold War, but in the context of détente, we would feel free to pursue our own hostility toward Soviet repression of our Soviet colleagues.

The State Department was especially interested because at that time Senator Henry Jackson of Washington was attacking the Nixon-Kissinger policy of détente with amendments that would deny most-favored-nation trading status to the Soviet Union until it eased its policy on Jewish emigration. Our position became a minor straw in the wind of that giant struggle, but it was noticed. A *Washington Post* story about the Jackson and Mondale amendments devoted an unusual five paragraphs to our position, which had been released in a press conference the day before.[224]

Up to this time, U.S. scientific concern for Soviet colleagues had been shown by 150 scientists at the National Institute of Health (NIH), whose petition threatened noncooperation unless the emigration of Jewish scientists was permitted. But there was not a lot more going on.

To help change the atmosphere, we sent our October 1973 newsletter to the hundred thousand members of the American Association for the Advancement of Science (AAAS) and others in a direct-mail solicitation. We said we would send a delegation to Moscow if enough joined us. We generated two thousand signatures and sent them to the Soviet ambassador, Anatoly Dobrynin, on August 12, 1974.[225] We also testified about our policy to the House Foreign Affairs Committee.[226]

By 1975 the Helsinki Accord had been signed. It seemed natural to visit Moscow, to see if the accord would make any difference and to have our long-promised on-the-site visit. The FAS chairman was strongly opposed to this, and tried, without success, for ninety minutes on the phone, to dissuade me, even though he had been a core signer of mass appeals for help for Soviet scientists. He failed. [227]

The Second Sakharov Hunger Strike

On May 9, 1975, we saw a brief mention of a three-day hunger strike by Sakharov designed to persuade the authorities to give a visa to his wife, Elena Bonner, for an eye operation in Italy. (This was actually Sakharov's second hunger strike; the first hunger strike in 1974 was the only one on which we did not help.)[228]

In order to amplify this, we put out a release on the same day saying we would boycott an upcoming meeting on "Scientists in World Disarmament" of the World Federation of Scientific Workers (WFSW) and called on scientists to join us. The British news service Reuters put out a three-paragraph report, carried in *The Washington Post*, in which we called the Soviet refusal "barbaric" and said that Mrs. Sakharov might go blind if not given the treatment in Italy.[229]

To our amazement, the Soviet embassy actually called, and we affirmed that we would attend if the visa for Bonner was granted. It was, but only on the last day of the conference, July 18. A few FAS members who attended in a personal capacity felt that the visa had been granted in a response to our boycott.[230] (At this time, as will be shown below, WFSW wanted FAS to join their federation; they needed an American affiliate that was more than a paper organization. This gave us a certain influence.)

The momentum building, in November I returned to Moscow. B.J. and I met all the leading Jewish refusenik scientists—scientists who had applied for exit visas and been refused. For applying, they were blacklisted and could not obtain work. These included a corresponding member of the Soviet Academy of Sciences, the chemist Benjamin Levich; the mathematician Ilya Iossifovich Piatietsky-Shapiro; the cybernetic specialist Alexander Levich (dean of the refuseniks); and others.[231] We also met non-Jewish dissidents: Valentin Turchin, a doctor of physics (courageous enough to have started a Moscow office of Amnesty International); Yuri Fyodorovich Orlov, who had been blacklisted for writing a letter to Brezhnev in defense of Sakharov (and who later became a cause célèbre while imprisoned for several years); and corresponding member Igor Shafarevich (a mathematician who had joined with Sakharov in a groundbreaking organization, the Soviet Committee on Human Rights).[232]

In Val Turchin I saw the face of our own FAS members: independent-minded, honest to a fault, and good-natured. And in Sakharov I saw the mirror image of the movement that had created FAS: atomic scientists burdened with the guilt of discovery and impelled toward greater political awareness and activity.

Turchin took B.J. and me to Sakharov's dacha, where we arrived at about 11:00 A.M. on November 8, 1975, in the area where other high government officials had their dachas. (Sakharov possessed *three* Hero of the Soviet Union Awards, as many as Brezhnev, and so had the right to have his dacha in this protected area, near Defense Minister Grechko and surrounded by many police checkpoints.)

I began by explaining how we had tried to help get his wife, then in Italy, her visa. He seemed to think this boastful and, in a characteristically gentle way, told me a pointed, humorous story. He said that both Willy Brandt and the king of Belgium had taken his wife's case directly to Leonid Brezhnev, and in both cases, Brezhnev had said the same thing: "First I have heard of this."

I said, "Do you know the significance of July 18, the day she received her visa?"

He said, "No, this is interesting because she was told on one day that the visa was denied and she said, 'So I will go blind and it will be on your head.' The next day she was called back, and the visa was granted."

I explained that July 18 was the last day of the WFSW meeting, that WFSW had been told they were responsible for the visa, and that we had boycotted WFSW to put pressure on them to do something. He paused and then accepted me—not, of course, as having settled the entire issue but as one who had "played a role" and who proved it by knowing aspects of the problem he had not. (This was confirmed in a letter from Andrei of December 20, 1978, in which he asked for support for a second visa for Elena to go to Italy and referred to the "great support which the FAS and you personally demonstrated in this matter in 1975." And it was further confirmed when a Quaker activist, Terry Provence, visited Sakharov and was told by Andrei that he considered Stone to be "articulate, creative, and brave.")

Andrei was lonely for his wife, he said, with whom he was deeply in love. But he had, at least, his stepdaughter Tanya Yankelevich; her husband, Yefrem; and their new, still-swaddled grandchild, Matvey. They were all crowded together in the dacha kitchen with his mother-in-law; it was a scene out of *Doctor Zhivago*.[233]

I offered to write a letter urging Pugwash to include him in their talks, but he considered this a "false" issue since he would not be allowed to leave the country. When I amended the idea to meetings in Russia, he agreed. We wrote to the Pugwash Continuing Committee urging this.[234]

Asked to provide a statement to FAS members, Sakharov lucidly dictated a statement that revealed much about his attitudes.[235] He warned that Soviet authorities try to "shape the relationship" between American and Soviet scientists along "very strict lines of ideological control" and that a good example "involves the Soviet participants in the Pugwash movement." He thought that U.S. government decisions were "over-flexible and too agreeable." He wanted us to work to permit scientists to go to conferences if invited

to them and not "just the scientists whose political qualifications are deemed correct." He urged the "personal defense of concrete persons." And he urged concern for "disarmament, environment, and all the rest." Above all, he urged unity among scientists, a unity that he thought would be most easily achieved by scientists because they were the "least egotistic part of society."

Except for the criticism of our government as overly agreeable— not our point of view—the rest could have been taken from our own editorials. He was a true counterpart of FAS.

We left Sakharov's dacha in the late afternoon and took the 5:00 P.M. train back. Plainclothesmen were in evidence at the train station and lurked on the return train. As we left our taxi a few blocks early to hide our destination, we saw them sitting in a car. We approached them, and B.J., on my instruction, said in Russian, "Why are you following us? We have done nothing wrong." They said, "You are guests." But whether it meant we needed extra protection or extra surveillance was unclear.

In the darkening gloom, we walked on a few blocks to dine with another refusenik. The reader can imagine how much these contacts with refuseniks galvanized my concern. Especially moving was the visit to the "refusenik seminar" of Mark Ya. Azbel in which Jews refused exit visas tried to keep up their science by lecturing to one another. An important incidental purpose of the seminar was to provide a place where visiting foreign scientists could meet with Jewish refuseniks in a scientific context.[236]

But the most important meeting in shaping FAS policy was the meeting with the highest-ranking refusenik, corresponding member Benjamin Levich. He made two complaints about the National Academy of Science's lack of commitment to the refuseniks, which, in the end, became bombshells in changing NAS policy. ♫

Levich told me that the NAS foreign secretary, George Hammond, had broached his own case and those of other refuseniks but had not pressed the issue when the acting chief scientific secretary of the Soviet Academy, G. K. Skryabin, had said, "It is not up to us." (And, according to the story, Skryabin had later told the refuseniks, maliciously, "You see, they complained and bounced right off us; do not expect any help from them, they are calmed down.")

Levich's second anecdote was that on an earlier visit, Levich, expecting a meeting with the NAS's president, Philip Handler, then in Moscow, had called him, but that Handler had refused to meet with him.

Levich also gave me a powerful quote from Einstein:

> A prime responsibility of every academy is to encourage and defend the scientific life of the country. Despite this fact, scientists of German society, as far as I know, have become silent witnesses to the fact that a considerable part of German scientists, students, and teachers have been stripped of the possibility to work and obtain for themselves the means for subsistence. I haven't the slightest desire to belong to any scientific society capable, even under outside pressure, of conducting itself in such a fashion.[237]

Our visit to Moscow ended with a bang. While leaving off letters asking if we could send an observer to the trial of the human rights activist Sergei Kovalev, we found ourselves at the apartment of a very nervous V. F. Turchin, who had reason to believe that Sakharov was undergoing a police search—or was about to be searched—and they were quite worried until they were able to reach him. It gave us the flavor of life in the dissident community.[238]

I paced up and down on the plane on the long flight home, thinking about how to handle these issues. But I did not anticipate the full explosion that resulted.

I wrote the December 1975 newsletter as a trip report.[239] I put the Levich complaints in a small "box" in the corner of page 9, where they could not be missed, under the headline "Complaints About the National Academy of Sciences," and I added the Einstein quote.[240] I then secured the names and addresses of all one thousand members of NAS and mailed them the newsletter with a letter drawing their attention to the complaints and to Sakharov's and Einstein's injunctions; I asked them whether they could be relied upon to "sympathetically consider" relevant petitions. 🕮 We asked them to affirm the following: "I will do what I can to encourage the National Academy to defend scientists in difficulties for the above indicated actions."[241]

One hundred fifty of the thousand members of NAS responded affirmatively, but the president, Philip Handler, responded explosively. This explosion, which I did not anticipate, made the campaign to raise the consciousness of the scientific community a success. Accordingly, some background may be appropriate.

My Relations with Philip Handler

I had never met Philip Handler and, really, had never wanted to. He once confided to an intimate, "If the Federation [FAS] continues as it is, there will be *two* voices of science in Washington." To him, this was heresy; for me, it would have been a great success.[242]

But there was more to it than institutional rivalry. It was clear that Handler harbored a certain antipathy, common in the scientific community, toward activism. In one of his speeches, he said:

> We have learned that the scientist-advocate, on both sides of such a debate, is likely to be more advocate than scientist and this has unfavorably altered the public view of both the nature of the scientific endeavor and the personal attributes of scientists.[243]

According to Handler, "Once the scientific community has presented the facts, however, it must leave final decisions to the policymakers and the public."[244]

Handler was known to be an imperious and skillful infighter. I kept my distance. I knew, from time to time, we would be criticizing NAS, or might want to. I remembered what Spartacus had said in Howard Fast's novel: "Gladiator, befriend not gladiator."

The month before I left for Moscow, I received just such an invitation to get into the ring with NAS—an urgent phone call from the director of the Arms Control and Disarmament Agency, Fred Ikle. Fred said that ACDA had contracted with NAS to do a study entitled "Long-Term Worldwide Effects of Multiple-Nuclear Weapons Detonations." NAS, he said, was about to release the study, and he feared it would give the wrong impression. Could I help? He sent me a copy of the study and the cover letter from Handler.

Parkinson would have loved this incident. ACDA had expected, of course, that NAS would write a report detailing the terrible effects of nuclear war.[245] According to Handler's cover letter, however, the chief question posed by NAS was, "Would the biosphere and the species Homo sapiens, survive a nuclear war?" Failing to find a single mechanism that could provably destroy the planet, it had concluded, "Yes."[246] This affirmation had been watered down in the press release to "probably yes."

Most bizarre of all, the report had focused on the Strangelovian scenario that some nation might consider it advantageous to trigger World War III. Since the NAS study would have persuaded such a nation that worldwide effects were minimal, Handler's cover letter felt obliged to backtrack and say that the results of a nuclear holocaust were "entirely unpredictable."

I threw together a statement and got the approval of the FAS's executive committee for its release to the press on October 4. It said the academy had "studied the wrong form of the right question" and added, "Evidently, with its customary alacrity, the National Academy of Sciences has gone about answering, after eighteen years, Nevil Shute's 'On The Beach.'"[247] (One executive committee member, a member of NAS as well, felt that the title of the press release went too far and was in poor taste: "The National Academy of Sciences Seems to Lack Public Policy Sense." In retrospect, I can only agree with him.)[248]

Standing outside NAS, I hawked the press release. The worst part for Handler was that *The New York Times* report showed that Dr.

Ikle and I were on the same wavelength; both of us were quoted as saying that the report's conclusion was "irrelevant" to public policy.[249] *Science* magazine said that ACDA was "dismayed at the tone of the report." It even reported that Handler had contacted *Science* to express "anguish and concern" that "his letter, and the report itself" had given an impression opposite to the one he wanted—that there would be "no hiding place" for anyone.[250]

This October flap occurred in the month before I met Sakharov and two months before I was mailing letters to Handler's members asking them to note his acts of omission in Moscow. So he was still smarting from a perceived defeat.

Handler fired off an eight-page, single-spaced, letter to the FAS's chairman at that time, Philip Morrison, demanding "an appropriate public apology to the Academy, to Dr. Hammond and to me." He said that otherwise these "calumnies" would "damage my ability and that of our Foreign Secretary to serve the Academy and the ability of the Academy to serve our country."

He said my two campaigns had been "an effort to derogate the National Academy of Sciences" and that my letter to NAS members with the December newsletter was using against NAS "the very tactics which the PIR [FAS *Public Interest Report*] advocates be used against the Soviet Government." For Mr. Stone "deliberately to seek to turn our friends and members against the Academy is an ugly act." It was all "*cheap, yellow journalism*" (emphasis in original). He explained all that he would have told me had I only asked—and this question of my not phoning him for his comment (I *had* phoned his foreign secretary) became the major charge against me. (He being a fellow president of a scientific society, I had felt I should not badger him; I invited his press secretary to have Handler call me and left it at that.)[251] In retrospect, I should have pursued him more directly. But the FAS executive committee backed me up and declined to apologize.[252] And the former NAS foreign secretary Harrison Brown supported me also, telling *Nature* magazine, "If anything, the Academy has erred on the side of not doing enough publicly."[253]

Handler's colorful letter was, in fact, the instrument of our eventual success. It was so quotable as to be irresistible to the press. ⟨⟩ *Science* magazine ran a long article entitled "Academy vs. Federation of Scientists: Handler Accuses Stone of 'Ugly Act.'"[254] This article dealt, unfortunately, more with the dispute about journalistic procedure than with the substance.[255] But this, too, we turned to our advantage. We took the newsletter in question and mailed it to some 125,000 scientists ♪—most of them received *Science* magazine—and told them they might want to know more about the debate. We sent the whole FAS newsletter in question and a request for support and membership.[256] We also circulated a four-page analysis of NAS's position.[257] The entire debate was going out on Voice of America, which must have made me seem quite anti-Soviet in the Soviet Union.[258]

During my 1975 trip, I had promised to try to get support for three scientists in different disciplines: the biologist Sergei Kovalev (who later, after the breakup of the Soviet Union, became Russia's most celebrated defender of human rights); the physicist Andrei Tverdoklebov; and the mathematician Leonid Pluysch, whose internment on psychiatric grounds was the most celebrated such case of that period and upon whose behalf even the French Communist Party had protested in vain.

We held a press conference for Kovalev and then wrote to thirty thousand American biologists in his defense. ♪[259] With regard to the physicist Tverdoklebov, we held a press conference of March 2, 1976, and when we could not get the American Physics Society list promptly, we rounded up 62 of 120 NAS physicists and sent a press release about it to the Voice of America. ♪ A subsequent letter from Turchin was kind enough to say that this Voice of America statement had saved Tverdoklebov from prison and had resulted in the milder punishment of internal exile.

In the case of the mathematician Pluysch, we decided to try to manipulate the Soviet system, and we may have succeeded. On November 28, 1975, we sent a letter to Mrs. Pluysch expressing our intention to send a report on his case to seven thousand scientists and to send "subsequently, a copy of our conclusions to every American mathematician by mail." 𝒮[260]

By mid-December we read, in a column by Vera Rich in *Nature*, I think, that rumors in Moscow suggested Pluysch might be released. So on December 18, we wrote to Ambassador Dobrynin indicating our plans to send a relevant letter defending Pluysch to every American mathematician (and even enclosing a copy of the proposed letter). We said we would not send it if the rumors could be verified. A week later Reuters reported that Mrs. Pluysch had been asked to submit an application for an exit visa. On January 4, AP reported that Soviet authorities were saying they would release Pluysch. And on January 8 they did. One observer thought that it was conceivable that the last straw in Pluysch's case was the possibility—which our involvement suggested—that his case would jump the Atlantic and become a major issue in American scientific circles, an eventuality that Ambassador Dobrynin may have moved to prevent. But of course, our actions may have had nothing at all to do with it.

Appalled by the lack of support from our fellow professional societies, we prepared a second newsletter entitled "On the Obligations of Scientific Societies to Defend Scientists Abroad and Encourage Public Involvement at Home." 𝒮[261] It called the strictly professional disciplinary societies the "real problem children." We said they were "staffed by directors of long tenure, their placidity unruffled by the annual rites of passage of one (more-or-less-honorary) Chairman to another." They understood responsibility to mean "obligations of restraint" rather than "demands of conscience." Their officials were often "ill-informed, philosophically vague and unempathetic."

By now FAS members were complaining that I should write about something else, anything else; they felt that FAS was not a human rights organization only. But I had one more problem to resolve. What could individual scientists do? And how could we agitate without breaking the links of scientific cooperation with the Soviets—which none of our scientists wanted to do?

I solved this problem in the next issue, March 1976, which was headlined "On a Method of Helping Colleagues Abroad: 'The American Refusenik.'" ♫ The idea was that American scientists would "refuse" to cooperate with Soviet scientists until a specific "adopted" Soviet scientist was given his rights. Thus *individual* scientists would break off relations, but only conditionally and, it was hoped, temporarily. And since most scientists were not activists, enough of them would remain to carry on scientific exchange. We would, in effect, harass the exchange system but not break it off. The idea was spread around.

This solution was particularly important because, as I soon realized, NAS had no idea how to handle this problem. When it issued a release, it suggested it would refuse to participate in joint scientific ventures unless the harassment stopped.[262] But the Soviets were not about to stop being the Soviets, and the harassment would never stop completely. So this policy would only lead to disaster for scientific exchange.

Best of all, with the refusenik policy, the scientific community could tell the government that we, the scientific community, had a punishment suited to the crime. It could be told to butt out and stop threatening to break off all scientific exchange—something not easily restarted and something that would mean permanent isolation of Soviet scientists and permanent denial of U.S. access to the results of Soviet science.[263]

In testimony before the House Foreign Affairs Committee on the Helsinki Accord, we noted that the agreement's call for cooperation in science left it to the institutions and scientists themselves "to determine the opportunities for mutually beneficial cooperation and to develop its details." We said we were "not advocating, and will not advocate, wholesale breaks in scientific exchange" between any two nations. And we explained the American refusenik method.[264]

As a direct result of this confrontation, the National Academy of Sciences was forced to create a Committee on Human Rights, whereas until then, all such matters had been dealt with by the president (Handler) and the foreign secretary in conjunction with certain advisers. Now the issue of human rights had been institutionalized.[265] And where before it had been assumed that aside from rare cases the issue of human rights was not the business of NAS, defending foreign colleagues now became an integral function of the academy.[266] And as it went with NAS, so it went with the other scientific societies. With the prominent exception of the American Physics Society, most did not then have a committee on human rights. But most did thenceforth, after some urging from us.[267]

By 1977, we had been successful enough in institutionalizing concern for human rights of scientists inside the scientific community that we stopped hiring staff within FAS to work on this issue. But I continued, of course, to monitor it.

Elena Bonner Sends a Strange Secret Appeal

In September, Elena Bonner flew to Italy for a second time, for treatment for the same eye condition that had provoked Andrei's first hunger strike. During her visit, on October 9, she and the rest of the world heard the news of Sakharov's Nobel Prize, and she eventually traveled to Oslo to receive it.

After the award was announced but before it was granted, we received a letter, dated October 26, from a British psychiatrist, G. A. Low-Beer, with a request that was hard to understand. He said that he had had a conversation with Elena Bonner, that she had asked him to write to me, and that she sounded "very despondent." He wrote:

> You may have read in the papers today that the Sakharov flat was ransacked by hooligans of the official type. She fears that they might have left some incriminating material hidden in the flat which could then be used against them. . . . She feels that life has become intolerable for her, her husband and the family. She thinks it would be futile for her husband to ask for an exit visa.

Andrei Sakharov, Elena Bonner, B.J., and the author

In view of this, she would like you to issue a statement saying that in view of the continual harassment and official attempts to make life intolerable for the Sakharov family, the Soviet Government should supply them all with exit visas and allow them to leave. For reasons which I have already stated, she does not at the moment wish to be associated with such a statement, but the ransacking of her flat, which was reported in the British papers today, together with other "reliable" information which I am giving you now, should form the basis of such a statement.

My own personal impression is that Mrs. Sakharov is very anxious to leave the Soviet Union and that her husband is of two minds. I think that a statement on the lines suggested by Mrs. Sakharov would somehow give her husband a choice in deciding what to do next. Should you wish to talk to her yourself, her telephone number is . . . .[268]

According to Sakharov's *Memoirs*, Elena Bonner's visa for her trip to Italy arrived in August "just as Tanya and Efrem received their visas to emigrate,"[269] and all five of them, including the grandchildren, Matvei and Anya, left for Rome on the same flight on September 5, 1977.[270]

So Elena Bonner was free to defect to the West from Italy, and Tanya and Efrem were already out. The psychiatrist believed, evidently, that we were being urged to make a statement to manipulate Sakharov's decision about whether he could live without her.

This is one of only two occasions when I felt it would be wrong to respond to a Sakharov family request; the second, in 1987, is discussed later. In any event, Andrei and Elena were, of course, never permanently separated.

CHAPTER 15

1980–1982: Defense of Sakharov via Dobrynin and the Media

In 1980, after Sakharov is exiled to Gorky, FAS "adopts" Sakharov and boycotts the Soviet Union itself. When Sakharov announces a major hunger strike, in 1981, a desperate telegram is sent to him in Gorky warning that help may not arrive in time; Sakharov's response arrives in time to help galvanize major public and private support.

Through the 1970s Sakharov had become the central figure to whom the dissidents and the Jewish refuseniks turned for help, which he would often provide by calling in Western reporters in search of a story. The authorities were, for the time being, tolerating his agitation. The numbers of dissidents and refuseniks had diminished through imprisonment and emigration, but his appeals continued.

Sometimes these appeals would be broadcast widely, such as through an op-ed piece in *The New York Times* explaining how the Soviet Union had reacted to President Carter's letter to Sakharov.[271] Sometimes they would be sent personally to individuals, such as the letter he addressed to "Drs. Morrison and Stone" appealing to FAS to defend Naum Meiman and Yuri Gol'fand and to inform our members of their plight.[272] Sometimes they would come in a long letter in Russian, signed by Sakharov and his son-in-law Efrem Yankelevich, which B.J. would translate.[273] We even received a personalized tape about one refusenik he wanted to help that included Sakharov's voice offering "greetings to Stone and to his wife, whom

I remember very well because I met them last year."[274] He was spending all his time appealing.

But then Sakharov went too far. During Christmas week in 1979, after the Soviet invasion of Afghanistan, he released a statement of protest. In the political rubble of détente, there was no longer any reason for the Politburo to tolerate him.

On January 22, 1980, they stripped him of all state and government awards and said he had been "conducting subversive activities against the Soviet state for a number of years" and had "lately embarked on the road of open calls to reactionary circles of imperialist states to interfere in the U.S.S.R.'s internal affairs."[275] Exiled to Gorky, a city off-limits to foreigners because of the military aviation plant located there, he was put under a regimen just short of house arrest.

He and Elena were very closely watched. During the first month they received their mail. But after the Sakharovs tabulated how many were pro and how many con, and mentioned this in a wiretapped room, all the pro letters ceased to arrive. They were so closely watched that one day, when they conspired to disappear in some bushes during a walk, a helicopter promptly appeared overhead. On another occasion, a purposeful remark by Elena about the terrible trash across the street, and her intention to send a picture of it to the West, induced three Army trucks to clean up the yard the next day.

I invited Bernard Feld, then the editor of the *Bulletin of the Atomic Scientists* in Chicago—our slightly younger cousin organization—to join me in a request for a visa to travel to Gorky to discuss Sakharov's situation.[276] Only one week after the exile, we wrote to the Soviet ambassador to the United States, Anatoly Dobrynin, that we represented the American counterparts of the atomic scientist Sakharov. If the Soviet government "does intend to permit academician Sakharov to meet with any foreign colleagues in future," we would like to do so promptly.[277] This was the time to find out if they would permit visitors.

Meanwhile, FAS and NAS were working hard to prevent Sakharov's expulsion from the Soviet Academy of Sciences.[278] In the end, after a worldwide protest, the Soviet Academy did not expel Sakharov but only censured him for actions "directed against the interests of our country and the Soviet people, actions helping the heightening of international tensions and denigrating the lofty title of Soviet scientist."[279]

This was an important first victory for world science in the defense of Andrei Sakharov. On matters relating to Sakharov's expulsion from his academy—as opposed to issues involving his exile or his hunger strikes—it seemed plausible that threats involving scientific exchange could be especially effective.

In June 1980 I tried to visit Moscow to express our concerns, but in midsummer, after we pressed our case with the Soviet embassy, the president of the Soviet Academy of Sciences, Alexandrov, wrote that he could say "nothing new" about the Sakharov affair and wondered if Stone did not want to "consider again the value" of a visit to Moscow at this time.[280] When I persisted, the embassy simply declined to provide a visa.

We thereupon wrote to Dobrynin that we were breaking off relations with the Soviet Union and the embassy staff, leaving open only the possibility of communications from him personally—and thus preserving our standing to send complaints to him. This was a major step for us, since U.S.-Soviet disarmament was an absolutely fundamental FAS goal. 🔲

Sakharov could not leave Gorky, but his wife could. Elena Bonner would travel to Moscow from Gorky and smuggle out letters, probably through the U.S. embassy. From time to time, we would get a message. For example, a letter of December 9, 1980, read as follows:

Dear Dr. Stone:

Five years have past since you came to visit us in our dacha in Zhukovka. At that time, our children, Tanya and Efrem, and our grandchildren were still with us and took an active part in our meeting. Elena was then in Italy, but she knows you from having heard about you. Now our life has greatly changed. Our children are in the U.S., and we are very lonely without them, and we worry about them. I am in Gorky; my wife, with great difficulty, commutes between Moscow and Gorky. . . .

I know much, though of course not all, about the important work which FAS is conducting in my defense. I heard your speeches on the radio, in spite of the jamming. They pleased me very much.[281] Thanks for "adopting me." Undoubtedly your speeches were well suited to the more detailed and broader development of a campaign. It seems to me quite proper that FAS and SOS [Scientists for Orlov and Sharansky] look upon my defense as a part of the campaign in relation to all the repressed scientists in Russia—Orlov, Kovalev, Sharansky, and all the others. . . .

It is also important that you emphasize the similarity of my position on questions of disarmament with the position of FAS.

I have already more than once announced publicly and written in letters, and I am using this letter to write you personally, that I consider it important to include in the campaign for my defense the exit problems of our son's fiancee, Lisa Aleksayeva. For almost three years, she has failed to receive permission to emigrate, and her request has not been answered in more than a year.

There is no other reason for holding on to her except the unlawful one of using the situation to put pressure on me. But indeed this gives me a basis for asking those participating in my defense also to speak up for her right to leave to get married. . . . I suspect that it would be not unhelpful to know that I turned for help on this question to the Soviet Academy of Sciences, in a letter to E. Velikhov and later in a letter to A. Aleksandrov, but without any result. Efrem has the text of these letters.

With gratitude and respect,
Andrei Sakharov

On the first anniversary of Sakharov's exile, we wrote to Ambassador Dobrynin (with Frank von Hippel, then the FAS chairman, cosigning the letter) saying that "the silencing of Andrei Sakharov continues to be a permanent impediment to exchanges between our office and your embassy staff."[282] A month later, I wrote asking for an "off-the-record" discussion of related problems—but never got one.[283]

In June I wrote asking for a change in the "conditions of confinement" of Sakharov, including "visits and communications" with colleagues. And we complained at length about the pressures being applied to Lisa Aleksayeva.[284] In October in response to rumors in the newspapers, we wrote supporting an exchange of Sakharov, Orlov, and Sharansky for an East German, General Zorn.[285]

Third Sakharov Hunger Strike

That fall, FAS and a few other individuals and organizations received personal announcements of Sakharov's intention to hold a well-prepared and extensively publicized hunger strike, his third. In a letter dated October 9, 1981—but delivered to everyone much later, after the hunger strike had begun—he wrote, "Having despaired to break through the KGB-built wall by any other means, (we) are forced to begin hunger strike demanding that our daughter-in-law, Lisa Aleksayeva, be allowed to leave the U.S.S.R. to join our son."[286]

Announced by Elena Bonner on November 16 in Moscow, the hunger strike was begun on November 22 and lasted seventeen days. On the thirteenth day, the point at which Soviet regulations call for intervention with labor-camp hunger strikers, Andrei and his wife were hospitalized.

Despite Elena's press conference in Moscow a week before, the references in the press were a total of about two inches of coverage in *The Washington Post*, plus a *New York Times* article on a letter signed by a few dozen Nobel Prize winners (many of whom had been rounded up by the FAS office).[287]

We—and not only we—were in despair about whether the hunger strike would work. In an editorial, *Nature* magazine wrote,

"It is possible that on this occasion their isolation has led them to misjudge the future."[288] Three days after the strike began, we cabled Sakharov in Gorky: 🎵 "Attention has now been drawn to this problem. It may not be possible to secure results immediately. The Federation of American Scientists asks you to discontinue the hunger strike while your supporters work to help you achieve your goal. The world needs you. Do you have the right to risk yourself in this way?"

The KGB evidently let the telegram through, no doubt because it seemed to serve the KGB purpose, as they did a similar telegram from Joel Leibowitz, a former chairman of the New York Academy of Sciences.

On November 30 we received Sakharov's answer, which concluded, "I can no longer believe in the kind of promises of the authorities not backed up by action! I ask you to understand and take this into account. With esteem and thanks."[289]

During the interval between the telegrams, in a random offhand discussion with a *Washington Post* reporter, I complained that the newspapers were in danger of going from one-inch stories to full-page "obits"—with nothing in between to alert their publics that a major story was brewing. Might they not be held guilty of poor editorial judgment? 🎵 He told me what to do.

On his advice, I appealed to the *Washington Post* and *New York Times* foreign desks and asked each to "query" its Moscow correspondents for stories. Two days later both papers displayed lengthy stories on the Sakharov hunger strike. From then on, a reporter advised FAS, the "story was assured."[290]

These stories appeared on December 2 along with a splendid *Post* editorial, "Tragedy in the Making." This was the perfect backdrop for our release of our December 1 telegram from Sakharov. 🎵 The release said that FAS had "no doubt of Sakharov's determination and had put aside all other duties and is working full-time to avert the disaster which his death would represent."[291] For the KGB's benefit, we sent the same sentiments to Sakharov by cable.

The telegram and the long-awaited news stories from various Moscow correspondents gave us something with which to work. Armed both with the telegram and the Moscow press reports—and especially with the underlying fact of Sakharov being without food for *ten days*—we got what we felt were important results.

Placing quiet telephone calls, we were able to induce, among others, two former secretaries of state (Cyrus Vance and Henry Kissinger), at least one former president of the United States, one American winner of the Lenin Prize (Linus Pauling), and a former ambassador to the Soviet Union (Averell Harriman) to call the Soviet ambassador in Washington and express their concern.[292]

On December 5 the press reported that President Reagan had made a "brief and deliberately low-key statement" urging Lisa Aleksayeva's release out of growing concern that the situation could become a "source of major new tensions."[293]

Two or three days later, the Soviet government gave up.

In the end, the Sakharovs were not force-fed. Each was told that the other was dying and was urged to eat. But they held to their fast. On the seventeenth day of the strike, on December 8, a high KGB official came to Gorky and assured Sakharov that if he discontinued the hunger strike, his daughter-in-law would be permitted to go to the West.

In his memoirs, Sakharov reviews the affair and says, "No one can say which was the drop that caused the glass to overflow, which act of support was decisive."[294] Little did we know that still another hunger strike was coming and that we would be involved in that one also.

For now, however, the Soviet leader, Leonid I. Brezhnev, had thrown in the towel, and eventually he permitted Bonner two foreign visits; in one of them she even visited her children in Boston without attracting attention.

. . .

In retrospect, the KGB made a mistake in letting our telegram through because it prompted Sakharov's response, which in turn galvanized our effort and our ability to mobilize others. Activists should heed the lesson of this episode: Even powerful opponents normally, in the heat of battle, make mistakes.

Our second contribution, the rounding up of phone calls to Dobrynin from so many famous and influential nonscientists, shows that when the conditions are right, one can mobilize the greatest support with ease—whereas when the conditions are not, it is possible that nothing at all will work. Here again we see the role of supersaturation in politics, which is to say that public interest change can be most easily precipitated when conditions are ripe to respond to small perturbations.

All things considered, I think that FAS played as significant a role in defending Sakharov through this third hunger strike as it had in the second, in 1975. But basically, Sakharov saved himself through his determination and unwillingness to take no for an answer, even from his most faithful (and nervous) supporters.

His success, in turn, depended upon certain characteristics of the hunger strike tactic. Prolonged hunger is deeply feared by all primates, and the humans of the industrialized world are normally quite unfamiliar with it. Accordingly, the notion that Sakharov had been *ten days* without food not only struck a deep empathetic chord in all who heard of it, but also galvanized observers into action as if every day might be his last. Fortunately, humans are capable of surviving hunger strikes considerably longer than people think. This fact provided the necessary time to generate the institutional, bureaucratic, and political concern needed to turn the Poltiburo around.

In sum, tactics often determine results in subtle ways. Political activists, no less than generals, must give a lot of thought to how their efforts are likely to play out.

CHAPTER 16

1983–1987: Would Moscow Give Sakharov to Kennedy?

Reagan's "Star Wars" speech impels a return to Moscow and a halt to the FAS boycott. A secretly arranged meeting takes place with Elena Bonner, who hints at new hunger strikes. Later Sakharov writes the author in an effort to warn the world of such an act, but the Sakharov family deliberately holds up the letter. An idea is generated to have Sakharov given to Senator Kennedy, as other dissidents had been, and a two-year effort goes forward to work out a deal. Finally, in late 1986, Sakharov is released from Gorky. In 1987 three evenings are spent with Sakharov, mainly reexamining the past.

On March 23, 1983, President Ronald Reagan gave his famous "Star Wars" speech, which we viewed as an arms race emergency threatening the ABM Treaty in which we had put such store and on which we had worked from 1963 to 1972. Our response to it, and its impact on work on SALT and START, are described later. But the speech also had important repercussions on our work with Andrei Sakharov. In particular, it forced our return to Moscow.

Shortly after the speech a Soviet journalist dropped in to get our reaction to a long list of Soviet scientists having signed an "Appeal to All Scientists of the World from Soviet Scientists" denouncing the Reagan speech. Rather than provide an offhand reaction, I proposed to Frank von Hippel, then the chairman of FAS, that we send a joint formal letter to Soviet Academy of Sciences president A. D. Alexandrov saying we shared his concern that ABM systems were a danger to world peace and that they could stir up the arms race. We did so.

Drawing on my early experience in the debate of the 1960s, and in an effort to help Sakharov, we said, "As participants in those early debates, we well remember the early support in this struggle of such members of your Academy as the late Academician Artsimovich, of Academician Andrei Sakharov, and later of the late Academician M. D. Millionschikov."[295] We invited Alexandrov to distribute our letter to all academy members.

We received a call from the Soviet embassy; could two officials call on us? On their arrival, they produced, with a great flourish, a return letter from President Alexandrov. It was, however, little more than a friendly acknowledgment and did not propose any joint action against the ABM.

I told the visitors that we had boycotted the Soviet Union for the last three years on the specific ground that we had been denied a visa to go to Moscow to complain about Sakharov. What if, in the face of this emergency, we made a trip to Moscow to discuss the arms race with the full understanding that we would, while there, make known our views about Sakharov? Honor having been served, I said, we could return to civilized discussions of arms control—which was, after all, the goal of our organization.

And so that is what we did.

The visit to Moscow took place in November 1983. I arranged with the American embassy to meet Elena Bonner, then visiting Moscow. She was brought to the embassy by a staffer at 11:00 A.M. on Saturday, November 26, while I, with a camera—as if at Checkpoint Charlie—waited for any interference from the Soviet guards as she "crossed the lines."

The embassy was jittery—and rightly so—about Soviet eavesdropping, and the arrangements for this visit had been discussed with me under a freezing "cone of silence" right out of a *Get Smart* episode.

We had not met before, since she had been in Europe when I visited Andrei at their dacha. But we had, of course, been in correspondence. B.J. and I had received a small gift from the Sakharovs—a wooden doll with their names discreetly written on the bottom—and she knew, of course, something about our work. Her eighty-year-old mother had stayed at our house in Washington; and we were quite friendly with Tanya and Efrem and had brought pictures of the family with us for her.

We gave her a camera and, more important, the most powerful handheld computer then on the market, a Texas Instruments device that could be programmed with up to six hundred instructions. It was for Sakharov, to give him something to occupy his mind.

Elena Bonner in a secretly arranged meeting with the author at the U.S. embassy in Moscow while Andrei Sakharov was exiled in Gorky

While we spoke, Elena discussed the campaigns being waged against them. An anti-Semitic article entitled "E. Bonner and Children Incorporated" had begun as follows: "In its effort to undermine Soviet structures from within, the CIA has gone to Imperial Zionism and created a special section for 5,000 agents.... A. D. Sakharov has become the victim of one of the Zionist agents of the CIA [i.e., of wife Elena Bonner]." As a result of this campaign, the Sakharovs had received 2,500 abusive letters saying, for example, "Divorce this Jewish woman."

The Sakharovs feared using the official doctors (lest they harm Elena deliberately), some of whom had lied to them or about them in judicial proceedings. And Bonner complained about lies that were being told about Sakharov's affairs to U.S. delegations by various people—especially Soviet Nobel Prize winner N. Basov and President Alexandrov. She said that Western scientists should insist that Sakharov participate in any disarmament talks held in Moscow.[296] She complained that an NAS group had failed to meet with her in October 1982 after applying, in advance, for such a lunch. She claimed that an embassy official had appeared, shamefaced, and reported that the Soviet authorities had threatened the U.S. National Academy of Sciences that the semiannual disarmament talks with them would be broken off if they met with her. (The academy saw it quite differently.)[297]

I explained the FAS's recent three-year rupture of relations with the Soviet embassy over its refusal to give us visas to complain about Sakharov. And I said that we had come only on the stated understanding that we could complain about the case while here this time. Still, our own talks on disarmament with Soviet scientists might be broken off. She did not thank us for this or any other of our efforts. An Amnesty International official had told me years earlier that the dissidents in Russia never do. She just looked down, smiled, and said she understood. One got the clear impression that what were strains for us were, really, victories for her. And she may well have put no store in talks about arms control and considered us, really, foolish for thinking that a dialogue on arms control with the Soviets was of any value.

In fact, Bonner thought all the visitors were out of their depth. "Foreigners," she said, "could not appreciate the force of propaganda here and, in general, the quality of totalitarian life. Every Soviet dissident was a miracle, like a bit of sand in the gears that turned out to be a diamond. The government is composed of deeply cynical people who think only of their personal position and nothing more."

The dissidents were, indeed, remarkably durable, and of course, their personalities varied all over the map. But I have never forgotten my first meeting, in New York, with the just-exiled Valery Chalidze, who had served with Sakharov in forming a Soviet-based committee on human rights. Asked politely, on his first day in America, whether he thought he would become an American citizen, he said, "I do not think so. I have read the oath of citizenship, and they would have to make certain changes."

Sakharov himself was unfazed by the strains of opposing the system. As will be seen, he was thoughtful, logical, and quite detached in dealing with problems. But he certainly did not believe in trading "chits," as politicians do.

So one could move heaven and earth, as Jerome Wiesner did, to get Sakharov his first trip out of Russia. But that did not mean Sakharov would agree to speak to potential donors on behalf of the Sakharov Foundation that Jerry was trying to create. To say other than exactly what he thought—just because someone was helping him—would have been for Sakharov, I suppose, some kind of lapse in integrity. I wonder if he believed even in social white lies.

The main thing I learned in Moscow, which I did *not* report in the newsletter, was that the Sakharovs were thinking of announcing yet another hunger strike—only twenty-four months after the last one, which had lasted seventeen days![298]

Bonner gave me a letter that she wanted delivered to the Soviet Academy. Since I was at the airport, about to leave the country, I offered it to one of my hosts, Andrei Kokoshin (then the head of the military-political division of Arbatov's Institute for the USA and Canada, later the deputy defense minister, and still later the secretary of the national security council). He turned white at the very idea of accepting this letter for transmission to the academy.

A few weeks later, when Velikhov was in the United States, I showed it to him. In Elena Bonner's book *Alone Together,* she makes much of this issue of letter-delivery, saying: "We think Dr. Stone kept his promise, and that the Academy administration therefore knew about Sakharov's coming hunger strike and what had prompted it. Just like the previous time, they did nothing to avert it."[299]

In fact, this is incorrect on a number of grounds:

A. The letter did *not* threaten a hunger strike. It did indicate that the issue had become "for us a question of life or death" but it suggested that *Elena Bonner's* life was at risk.

B. I was not asked to pass along the hints of a hunger strike to Velikhov.

C. On January 13 Sakharov released this letter to Andropov to the press, so the academy certainly had it by then.

D. In general, Elena Bonner had no way of knowing that the Soviet Academy "did nothing to avert" the hunger strike. Whether the academy did, or did not, do anything to try to fulfill her desire to help Sakharov, she could only have known that it did not succeed.

Ironically, the historical record shows that it was Elena Bonner's daughter Tanya Yankelevich and her son-in-law Efrem who prevented the world in general (and the Academy of Sciences in particular) from learning that Andrei Sakharov was, indeed, definitely thinking of another hunger strike.

On January 13, 1984, when Sakharov released the letter to Andropov publicly, he sent the Yankeleviches in Boston a letter addressed to me personally that did specifically warn, "I've begun thinking of a hunger strike again, however horrible or monstrous it may sound. But is there any other way out?"[300]

Efrem and Tanya deliberately kept this letter from me for three months, until late April. Even while visiting my Washington home for an overnight stay that spring, they advised me that they were "still translating" a letter for me from Sakharov!

When they finally sent it to me, I immediately tried to get *The Washington Post* and the Associated Press, among others, to cover this. But a three-month-old warning of a hunger strike that clearly had not occurred was not considered newsworthy. When, finally, a reporter for *Science* magazine agreed to write about it, he called Efrem for comments and was promptly persuaded by Efrem *not* to publish. So the Yankeleviches seemed still to be hoping that the hunger strike—designed to secure an exit visa for their mother—might not occur. Or they were afraid that Elena's contingency planning in Moscow by Elena might be upset if this possibility became known.

Withal, the hunger strike began on May 2. The first newspaper reports were on May 9, with *The New York Times* reporting that Sakharov had said he would "fast to the very end if they do not let her go abroad for medical treatment."

By coincidence, Velikhov was in America from about May 4 through May 12, and so he was present when the storm broke. I escorted him in Washington, where Ivan Selin, the chairman of the board of American Management Systems (AMS) gave a party for him on May 6 and where he met with NAS and Les Aspin on May 8. I also took him to Boston, where he attended a gala birthday party for the physicist Victor Weisskopf and then left for Russia on May 14.

By May 20 we were cabling Velikhov, then the vice president of the Academy of Sciences, warning of the effects Sakharov's death would have—we stated that "the entire [presidential] election will be influenced by this tragedy, and in an undesirable direction."

An enormous worldwide campaign was under way. On May 24 Tanya Yankelevich met with Pope John Paul II and reported, "He promised us his full support."[301] The science academies of four major countries (the United States, Great Britain, France, and Sweden) urged the Soviet Academy to "help Academician Sakharov and his wife in getting the health care they require and request."[302] The Norwegian Nobel Committee wrote on May 25, expressing "concern and dismay." Editorials were everywhere.

On May 26 we cabled Sakharov to remind him of all the dire consequences that would attend his death and added, "Please keep this in mind when you consider, for example, whether Western medical attention and visits with Western relatives must take place now and in the future outside the Soviet Union, or could take place inside."[303]

On May 28 we cabled Velikhov that "the quiet presence of an FAS official in Moscow might be useful perhaps in providing assurances" and that "Larry [Larry Horowitz in Senator Kennedy's office] and his office agree" and that, if the academy agrees, would invite us and provide visa support.[304]

That got nowhere, and at the end of March, I went to a Pugwash conference in Geneva. At the conference I tried something else. I wrote a telegram addressed to President Chernenko but sent it to Velikhov, asking him "if possible and useful" to transmit this not only to Chernenko but also, with copies, to the foreign minister and to Ponomariev, the Communist Party secretary of ideology. It said, "If the Soviet government is unable to persuade Sakharov to end the hunger strike, we respectfully request the opportunity to try to do so using our established close relationship with him to accomplish this goal."

I also asked for visa support to get into Moscow. This apparently hit a real nerve—certainly because of the highly ranked persons we listed as desired recipients of the letter. Our request elicited an angry letter from the Soviet Academy's chief learned secretary, A. S. Khohlov, to FAS's chairman, Frank von Hippel:

> J. Stone's addressing to the Academy of Sciences of the USSR by telex of May 31, we regard as interference in our internal affairs. Such actions of J. Stone can complicate to a great extent relations between us and undermine bases of mutual understanding established between Academy of Sciences, USSR and FAS. Due to this reason we are unable to arrange acceptance of J. Stone's visit to Moscow and in future we shall refrain from meeting with him on such matters.

By June 5 the Russians were denying that Sakharov had died, and the Soviet press agency Tass was saying that he "feels well, takes regular meals and leads an active way of life."[305] No one knew anything and, in particular, no one could confirm whether or not Elena had joined in the fast.

By June 7 Efrem and Tanya were at the economic summit in London, trying to meet with aides to the seven leaders, and the U.S. State Department spokesman said that the United States had been in "quiet diplomacy" with Moscow on this issue for "several months."[306]

The Russians were angry, and an irritated Foreign Minister Gromyko was saying that Moscow "will not be told how to deal with the Sakharovs by other countries. The conversation on this subject ends here."[307]

In November 1983 after Elena Bonner hinted at a new hunger strike, I began working on a way in which Sakharov and Bonner might be expelled from the Soviet Union and sent to the West. It seemed feasible in principle. Officials in Moscow were split on a course of action. We knew that some Soviet officials thought that he knew too many secrets ever to be allowed to leave the country. Some were even saying that he was so brilliant that "he still might invent something against us."[308] But others thought that fifteen years without a security clearance and thirty years away from real weapons work were quite enough to permit his exit.

Thanks to a chance meeting with a Kennedy staffer, Jan Kalicki, at a Midwest arms control meeting right before my 1983 trip to Moscow, I had been authorized to invite Velikhov to a December 7 forum on nuclear winter that Kennedy was organizing. [🖱] Neither of us thought he would come on such short notice, but he did.

Kennedy threw a wonderful party for Velikhov and his delegation and gave him a number of presents, including a bust of Einstein.[309] I was Velikhov's host during the visit and took the delegation to Princeton and Boston from December 6 to December 12.

In Princeton, while discussing gifts, I had a brainstorm. Maybe the Politburo would "give Sakharov away" as a gift. And to whom better than Senator Kennedy! They were eager for him to visit Moscow. Kennedy had been instrumental in springing other dissidents in just this way by negotiating terms for a Kennedy visit to Moscow.[310] And Moscow could, perhaps, elect Senator Kennedy president with such a gift—or think they could.

I pursued this idea for the next three years as it moved up and down and up and down. In the process, I learned that Senator Kennedy had a potentially useful back channel of his own. Eventually I became a link between Mrs. Bonner, during her visit to the United States, and Senator Kennedy. But even the Bonner family had to be kept in the dark about some sensitive matters at that juncture.

FAS had arranged to have a traveling school on arms control in which Velikhov and we would host each other's delegations and hear lectures on arms control. We were scheduled to go to the USSR in late March, two weeks after the death of President Chernenko (March 10, 1985). I asked Senator Kennedy's office to send Larry Horowitz or a letter with me. Kennedy wrote this note, which I delivered:

Dear Mr. Vice President:

I regret that important U.S. Senate meetings prevented me from sending Larry Horowitz to Moscow with the Jeremy Stone delegation. I asked Jeremy to deliver this letter to you in order to convey my warmest greetings and to convey my concerns on a matter of mutual interest.

As you know, the issue of Andrei Sakharov has complicated U.S.-Soviet relations. Now, according to press reports this week, he has threatened to resign from your Academy—an action which would provide a new obstacle to the improvement of these relations. Recognizing that this is viewed as an internal issue by your government, I did nonetheless want to express my readiness to participate, if asked to do so, in any solution to the problem.

As you know, I have been thinking about a visit to the Soviet Union. If it were helpful to the constructive solution of the problem I would alter my schedule to make myself available at any time.

I look forward to seeing you again soon, either here or in Moscow.

My very best personal regards,

Sincerely,

Edward M. Kennedy

I had also had a brainstorm about how to urge Sakharov's release from Gorky. While sitting next to Velikhov at a lunch on April 1, I quietly advised him that the greatest enemy of Star Wars was, in fact, in the Soviet Union. He asked, "Who?" I pulled out Sakharov's comments on the ABM from his 1968 book *Progress, Coexistence, and Intellectual Freedom.* "If you permit him to speak," I advised, "he would be a terrific asset to the anti-ABM campaign." I gave him and Arbatov copies of the remarks, and I advised both of them that these statements would be printed in our *Public Interest Report*.[311] (In retrospect, however, it is obvious that the pre-Gorbachev Politburo was too hidebound ideologically to consider such a tradeoff.)

On April 4 in Moscow, Sergei Kapitza took me to lunch with his mother, the widow of the famous atomic scientist Peter Kapitza, whom I had met in Finland. A very brave man, Kapitza had offended Beria by declining to work on atomic weapons (not for political or moral reasons, however). As a consequence, she and he had lived under conditions approaching house arrest for a dozen years, until Beria died. During this time they left the house only together, lest one of them be killed by the KGB.

She also gave me some insight into Mrs. Bonner's power over Andrei—which is, of course, confirmed in almost every chapter of Sakharov's *Memoirs*.[312] She said that once, Peter Kapitza—who was senior to Sakharov and respected by him—asked, in the presence of Elena, if he could speak to Andrei alone. Elena did not offer to step out of the room, and so Andrei refused. Mrs. Kapitza said that all of the wives in her circle hated Elena Bonner.

After this visit to Moscow, which was my main chance to influence the START talks (to be discussed later), I returned to Washington at the same time as Velikhov. On April 8, after a lunch we and a few others had with Senator Kennedy in my home, I observed to Velikhov that no one was "using" the fact that Sakharov had "integrity"— he would do whatever he said with regard to staying in the West or telling secrets. Why not ask him what he would do? The problem, Velikhov said, was his wife. I replied that in Gorky the wife was "very powerful because he had no other influences, but in

Academician Evgeny Velikhov and Senator Ted Kennedy at lunch

America there would be other people to talk to." He thought this was "very interesting," and I mentioned the Star Wars angle again.[313]

On the same day, Sakharov began his hunger strike again, to demand that Elena "be allowed to go abroad to visit her mother, children, and grandchildren and to receive medical treatment." He was removed to the hospital and force-fed and ended his strike on July 11—only to begin it again on July 25 so as to be back in the hospital by August 1, the tenth anniversary of the Helsinki Final Act embodying the human rights for which he was fighting.[314]

Sakharov was so intent on getting Elena permission for this trip that he offered to both President Gorbachev (who had become president on July 2) and Gromyko to "discontinue my public activities apart from exceptional circumstances."[315] By August 13 he had dropped from 175 pounds to 138. He discontinued the strike only on October 23, when Elena was assured she would get a visa the next day.

The hunger strike had lasted, with one two-week break, for six months!

On April 17 Larry reported that Velikhov said he was interested in the Kennedy idea but would need certain assurances and would meet with the secretary general, in person and in private, at the end of April, to try to deal with the problem in May. Larry said he might be making an "advance trip" to Gorky.

On April 18, I sent Velikhov a telegram with a prearranged signal that Kennedy's office was moving forward with the gift approach of releasing Sakharov as a goodwill gesture.

I now gave Larry a letter for Sakharov dated May 7; in it I explained what we were up to and what we felt Sakharov would have to do—in case Larry made enough progress so that Sakharov himself became the obstacle. I appealed to Sakharov to agree not to campaign against the Soviets if they would release him to the West. I wrote:

[I]t was my view that the solution to your confinement required some kind of concession as well as the intercession of the Senator. Accordingly, I urged Soviet authorities to use the principled character of your mind as a solution to the very problems it created for them. We all understood that you could be depended upon to hold to any agreements reached. Thus your character is, again, determining your fate.

Needless to say, it was already understood on both sides that you were, despite all, patriotic, had never revealed Soviet secrets before, and would not do so in future. But there were fears of a rapid intense round of denunciation—fears exaggerated by the exaggerations of Soviet propaganda about you which many Soviet officials had come to believe.

I went on to describe the costs to arms control of his hunger strikes and the urgency of resolving them; I also explained the impossibility of consulting Efrem and Tanya, but I expressed my feeling that they would agree. I further opined that if this did not work out, Mrs. Bonner would want to return to the Soviet Union— which would be foolish.

Finally, I pointed out that this proposal had "taken one year and a half to mature and the election of a new secretary-general. We will not have a chance like this soon again."

Larry's trip to Moscow was unfortunately postponed, as shown by the fact that my files show the same letter, retyped with the date July 11 as I redated it to give it to him again. For the five months, from June to October 1985, Larry kept up a lively back-channel communication with his interlocutors in Moscow, frequently giving me cryptic indications about Sakharov's well-being.[316]

On July 23 I was given to understand that the Russians had made a major offer to Senator Kennedy to visit Moscow, upon which all this scheming had depended—but that it did not include anything for Sakharov. It did include, I was told, five hours with Gorbachev, being on television twice, addressing the Supreme Soviet, and something about parliamentary exchange.

Kennedy turned it down. We were still in business!

On September 9 Sakharov's stepson, Alexsei Semyonov, called on the White House and on September 12 began a hunger strike in front of the Soviet embassy (or as close as they permit). The very same day Larry told me that "Soviets cable urgent meeting Vienna."

I considered this the direct result of Soviet nervousness about Alexsei's hunger strike. When I visited him on the street corner—with Tanya saying, "Jeremy, don't discourage him"—I felt very strange. Alexsei's hunger strike was stimulating alarm in Moscow and I could feel the pulse of that alarm directly through Larry's cables. I couldn't encourage him without revealing what was up. And, in any case, I was not at all sure what was the right thing to encourage.

Then Moscow said a week later would be all right. On September 16 they proposed stepping back the urgent meeting to September 27 in Helsinki, and Larry cabled back something on the order of "cut the baloney." More time passed, and on October 16 Larry told me that Gorbachev had said "no for the foreseeable future"; the foreign minister was annoyed at Shultz over something that had happened in Helsinki!

Given all this, it was a surprise when, on October 23, Elena Bonner got her visa and thereafter was permitted to go abroad. What had happened?

Dobrynin's memoirs show that the Politburo had discussed Bonner's request on August 29, 1985. The chairman of the KGB, Viktor Chebrikov, spoke in favor of granting the application but "categorically opposed permitting Sakharov to accompany her because of his knowledge of the development of Soviet nuclear weapons in minute detail. If Sakharov got a laboratory abroad, he would be able to go on with military research."[317] But the issue of Sakharov's release from Gorky persisted.

At the invitation of the Supreme Soviet, Kennedy decided to go to Moscow to meet Gorbachev and to see what he could do. A few days before he left, I passed through Boston on my return trip from China, and on January 29, 1986, I called on Mrs. Bonner at 54 Maplewood Avenue, where Tanya and Efrem lived.

She was quite willing to have the campaign directed toward

Sakharov returning to Moscow, as opposed to leaving the USSR, and she was willing to make a deal in which both would cease commenting on issues that enraged the Politburo. She thought the Soviet official who would be most likely to be able to negotiate this with Andrei was Velikhov.

I told Kennedy that Bonner was not aware of the "enormous and unique influence" the senator had in the Soviet Union but that after I explained it, "the family began to realize it and warmed up to your involvement and, in particular, made it clear that they would not attack you." (At this Kennedy looked astonished at the temerity of Mrs. Sakharov.)

The Bonner family also mentioned that they had a document whose release would embarrass the president of the Soviet Academy; they suggested that Gorbachev be advised to make concessions to "distance himself from the past brutalities" that they were prepared to disclose. (This document was Andrei's letter to the president of the academy describing his hunger strike of 1984.)

Elena Bonner had returned to Gorky in June, after meeting with Prime Minister Margaret Thatcher, President François Mitterrand, and Premier Jacques Chirac—all of whom were urged to work for Sakharov's return to Moscow and not for emigration.[318] Four months later, on October 23, 1986, Sakharov wrote Gorbachev a letter in which he stated his position and promised that he would "make no more public statements, apart from exceptional cases when, in the words of Tolstoy, 'I cannot remain silent.'"[319] Gorbachev called him in response on December 16, saying, "I received your letter. We've reviewed it and discussed it. You can return to Moscow. The Decree of the Presidium of the Supreme Soviet will be rescinded. A decision has also been made about Elena Bonnaire [*sic*]."[320]

Sakharov himself was never sure that his letter did the trick. In his *Memoirs*, he said, "I have no way of knowing whether it was this letter that prompted our release, although I suspect it was not. I've heard rumors that our case was under discussion during the summer of 1986 or even earlier; it's just possible, however, that the letter was the imperceptible tremor that touched off the avalanche." Just like us butterflies, for causation, Sakharov's theory had, in the end, to fall back upon chaos theory.

In February 1987, on the occasion of a Moscow Forum, B.J. and I passed three long evenings at the Sakharovs' home. Elena was angry. I had refused the Sakharov family's request to falsely assert that Efrem was needed by me for translation purposes so that he could "break the ice" and get a visa for a return visit to Russia.[321] "We will never forgive you," she said. Even the mild-mannered Andrei wanted an explanation.

But I was ready for this with the only kind of explanation that Andrei Sakharov could accept—a *principled* answer. We said we had always responded when his health and safety were at risk, even when that was the result of actions he had taken for his family. But otherwise, we could not be involved in family affairs and would put our arms control work first. (The FAS chairman, Matthew Meselson, had suggested I tell Andrei that he would resign if I did not take this position.) Andrei pondered this calmly, as I knew he would, and then turned to other matters.

We discussed all of the human rights issues that had swirled around him over the preceding twenty years, including how his warning of his hunger strike came to be published in *The New York Times* two weeks after it had begun, through no fault of mine but because of his family's actions. He smiled and quoted Antoine Bolulay De La Meurthe: "It was worse than a crime, it was a blunder." But he noted that Efrem made fewer mistakes than did Talleyrand.[322]

Sakharov seemed quite well, although I could not help feeling that the hunger strikes had taken a terrible toll. He had recently been quoted in *Pravda*—an important sign of his evolving acceptance—and he seemed destined to continue to play many important roles: loyal opposition leader inside the Soviet Union, creative and constructive critic in arms control negotiations, and human rights watchdog for all those in trouble.

He died two years later, on December 14, 1989, at the age of sixty-eight. It was the same month in which he had completed work on his *Memoirs*. It is ironic that it was not his complaints about the human rights of named or unnamed political prisoners or refuseniks that aroused the public, but rather his more personal and pedestrian demands for more foreign medical care and the right of his wife to travel to visit family. It was not so much the selfless quality of Sakharov's personality that caught the world's imagination as it was his determination to support his family, the ones he loved.

Had Sakharov gone on hunger strikes for other political prisoners and not for his family, his campaigns would have been neither sustainable nor sufficiently dramatic. There were too many political prisoners. There was only one wife and one family. The Soviet machine could be defeated only on the narrowest possible front.

Bonner and Sakharov, in their own way, were butterflies flapping their wings in far-off Gorky. The gigantic human rights storm they generated reduced the temperature of détente throughout the Northern Hemisphere for a decade. As an arms control advocate, I favored détente, but I was captured by the personal and moral drama of Sakharov's life, and I was honored to follow his courageous lead and to be involved in the maneuvers related above.

I am not sure how I could have done more for Sakharov—considering my base of action and political capital. After all, even Dobrynin was helpless. He wrote:

> Our embassy nevertheless regularly warned Moscow about the extremely negative effect the trials of Soviet dissidents were having on American public opinion and on Soviet-American relations, but Moscow ignored it all. Brezhnev's regime remained convinced that the Western campaign for the dissidents was a matter of ideological warfare aimed at undermining Soviet society. Personal anger against Reagan was an additional factor in their stubbornness.[323]

But whatever ingenuity I, and others, applied to help Sakharov was evoked by his determination. And when we faltered, as I did more than once, worrying that his strategy might fail, he refused to be discouraged and forced us to continue. He was a general fighting well in front of his troops and rallying them by example.

His intellectual motivation was rooted in the international rights of mankind. That his visceral motivation in all but one hunger strike stemmed from a highly personal love of wife and family is, perhaps, as irrelevant as sincerity is irrelevant to political acts. No one in my lifetime so deserved the Nobel Peace Prize.

PART VI

Earthquakes, Freedom of the Press,
and Astrology

CHAPTER 17

Booms and Earthquakes:
Saving the East Coast a Scare

Carl Sagan asks the author to decide whether and when to hold a press confer-
ence announcing an impending East Coast earthquake allegedly heralded by
mysterious East Coast booms both in Nova Scotia and off the U.S. Coast.
Rather than alarm the entire East Coast, an urgent investigation is under-
taken, which unearths the fact that the Nova Scotia booms, which have
alarmed Canada, are in fact due to Concorde shortcuts.

Efforts ensue to track down the source of the U.S. Coast booms, leading to a
wild-goose chase looking for a new method by which sound might propagate.

In a congressional office at 5:00 P.M. on February 27,
1978, word was passed to me that an FAS sponsor, Carl Sagan, had
left a message to call; it was labeled "most urgent." ♫ He advised me
that Thomas Gold, an astronomer, and Dr. Gordon J. F. MacDonald, a former charter member of the president's three-man Council
on Environmental Quality, thought the mysterious East Coast
booms then being headlined in the newspapers were precursors of an
earthquake. Would I "handle" it?

Dr. Gold had a theory that methane might belch out of the earth
during earth movements and then spontaneously ignite. Dr. Mac-
Donald had heard of peculiar animal activities: bottom-dwelling
fish being caught in large numbers in Canada, the Canadian lobster
crop disappearing, and red snappers appearing on the surface. He
began studying past earthquakes and felt that he had examples in
which booms had been precursors to earthquakes. He also believed

that the Chinese had reliably used booms as warning signals of earthquakes. Gold and MacDonald had prepared a press release and asked if FAS would convene the press.

The government, they said, was preparing a report that military aircraft were responsible, but it did not identify the aircraft, and it was emphasizing either unusual winds or unusual temperatures (neither of which, MacDonald felt, existed). The Naval Research Laboratory (NRL), he felt, would paper over its uncertainty about many events by saying that "supersonic-capable aircraft" were at issue—but since they were there during working hours generally, and had been for years, this was considered less than persuasive. There were rumors that the Naval Research Laboratory had its conclusions rewritten at the last minute to emphasize "ducting" of sounds due to weather, but what this meant was unclear. Otherwise, it was said, the report would have just left many events unexplained.

I decided to defer a press conference until I had looked into this further rather than upset 100 million people here and in Canada with hard-to-predict economic and social consequences.

Remembering that the Chinese were especially expert on earthquakes and had maintained an "earthquake register" for almost three thousand years, I stopped at the Liaison Office of the People's Republic of China and asked that the register be searched for earthquakes with booms as precursors. In due course, in a first in Chinese-American emergency cooperation, the Chinese sent a cable from Beijing with two examples of similar situations, involving bottom-dwelling fish and gas and lightning strikes—one of which seemed to anticipate an earthquake and one of which did not. Lynn Sykes of Columbia's Lamont-Doherty Laboratory explained that the traditional seismologists and the Chinese did not consider booms as precursors, but as the sound of unfelt foreshocks.

Gordon MacDonald had found a 1906 letter suggesting booms were associated with the San Francisco earthquake and he also had examples from Turkey and Charleston in 1883. But he did not have an historical case in which there were: (a) months of booms, (b) no seismic activity, and (c) a subsequent earthquake. This disturbed me, but earthquakes are, after all, rare events.

More serious to the MacDonald/Gold theory, the mysterious events seemed to be occurring mostly during daylight hours. Dr. William Donn, also at Lamont-Doherty, advised me that these patterns were unprecedented in his fifteen years of observing with very sensitive microphones; he speculated about Russian secret weapons and said weather could not be the cause.

The zoos I called for animal reactions to possible underground movements had no unusual information to report, nor did FAS members at Woods Hole.

Complicating the situation was the alleged existence, according to MacDonald, of mysterious lights over the East Coast. Gold felt they might be methane detonating. MacDonald felt the probability of a major earthquake was on the order of 1 percent a year ordinarily (four in the last four hundred years) but that, in the next few months alone, it might be 5 percent. I urged further delay, to which he and Gold agreed, with MacDonald's provision that the press conference definitely be held on March 14—ten days off.

Because of an unusual snowstorm on March 6, MacDonald failed to join me at a meeting at his office in the Virginia countryside, but I was able to question his assistant, and she informed me that much of Dr. MacDonald's information on sonic-boom data and animals had come from a Ms. Hattie Perry of Nova Scotia. 𝒥 The assistant handed over these hitherto undisclosed Perry reports.

Ms. Perry had logged instances of both mysterious booms and mysterious rumbles in forty detailed pages. Recognizing that this was the Rosetta Stone, I abandoned meeting with Gordon and raced home to study it. Remembering that Concorde had begun flying about three weeks before and recalling from my experience opposing the supersonic airplanes in 1971 that they caused booms, I stopped calling the directors of East Coast zoos and began calling Concorde pilots.

It turned out that Hattie Perry was indeed getting boomed by

Hattie Perry of Barrington, Nova Scotia, who provided the Rosetta Stone that permitted the diagnosis that Concorde was producing the booms in Canada

Concorde—not every day, but sometimes, probably on days that were hot in London and Paris. The Concorde was forbidden to fly over land at supersonic speeds, but a shortcut over Nova Scotia could save it a few minutes. And these few minutes could be important to the Concorde on days that were hot. This was because, on such days, with the fuel expanded due to the temperature, the fuel tanks could barely contain enough fuel to get the Concorde to its destination with the required fuel reserve.

And what of the mysterious rumbles in which her house would vibrate but nothing loud would be heard? These, I realized, were "secondary booms" that were reflected off two main refracting layers in the stratosphere, at approximately thirty and sixty miles. Calculations showed that the Concorde flights originating from JFK or Dulles airport and flying 125 miles south of Nova Scotia were creating secondary booms that impacted her house with very-low-frequency sounds that caused her wall or door to rattle.[324]

This completely explained Hattie Perry's data except for that data concerning animal behavior of which Gordon had spoken. But on calling her on March 5, I discovered that she had other explanations for the animal data. It was, she said, "not all that unusual," and she "didn't put much stock in it." They were worried, she said, because they had heard that Mitre Corporation (where MacDonald worked) believed that an earthquake might be in the wind. Gordon had been on Canadian radio!

I thereupon advised the Canadian embassy (remembering that concerned high-level Canadian officials had been calling MacDonald while I was in his office) that in Nova Scotia it was Concorde, not to worry. And I made an appointment with the president's science adviser, Frank Press, to advise him of it.

I called J. D. Brown, a deputy superintendent at the Naval Research Laboratory, and explained what I had done. He made a generous comment: "You have my heartfelt thanks. This clearly falls in with what we wish we had done."

But What of the American Booms?

So we had solved completely both the main booms and the secondary booms being felt in Nova Scotia. The entire earthquake scare there had been resolved. But this still left American booms. We could correlate some vague rumbles on Long Island with Concorde; they were secondary booms from the period in the flight path before the plane went subsonic.

But there were still unexplained American booms. I thought I saw correlations between these unaccounted-for booms and the takeoffs from London of the Concorde. But the correlations would have required the booms to travel faster than the ground speed of sound. Could this happen?

As a nonphysicist, who had just learned about the "super" (secondary) booms reflecting off upper stratospheric levels, I thought, perhaps, anything could happen. Perhaps there were "hyper" booms as well. Nobody had any clear idea about this speculation until I called Richard Garwin. Without even putting down the phone, he thought for a minute and said, "Yes, there is a way."

He later released a paper explaining how shock waves, fired a hundred miles up into the thermosphere by the Concorde, could— because of their strength and the supertemperatures of that altitude—maintain their coherence and bend downward again while keeping roughly to the speed at which they were propagated upward.

I briefed Frank Press on Friday, March 10, and then, at his request, briefed the secretary of transportation on Monday, March

Richard Garwin — who provided a theory (here providing the author with an FAS Public Service Award in 1995 in the U.S. Capitol)

12. I had little paper triangles and maps of the entire system of worldwide Concorde flights (e.g., including flights to Dakar). With these I showed Frank why various strange phenomena might be related to certain Concorde flights.

He, an experienced scientist, correctly separated out the firm conclusions (Nova Scotia, secondary booms, and so on) from the more speculative and told *Science* magazine that the latter were "an interesting speculation that deserves further study."[325] But since the Naval Research scientists there for the briefing did not really understand the still-mysterious booms on the East Coast—which had started the flap—they could only agree to reopen the investigation, which they did.

Over the weekend, between the briefings of Science Adviser Frank Press and the secretary of transportation, I began worrying about the Concorde more generally. It had just been put into service, and I now realized, from Dick's reasoning, that it was throwing large amounts of energy upward into a very thin atmosphere. Was it doing any harm? After all, there had recently been some weird weather.

I began calling experts. I reached Hans Arnold Panofsky, the elder brother of Wolfgang K. H. (Pefe) Panofsky, who was an expert on atmospheric sciences. He cautioned me that the weather was formed at much lower altitudes and not normally influenced by the altitudes we were discussing.

In any case, I spent a weekend as "defender of planet earth," trying to see if anybody knew anything relevant. The Naval Research Laboratory reconvened its experts, and Dick went out to explain his theory with me in tow. He began deriving formulas on the blackboard while saying, over his shoulder, "Do you fellows know this one?" Evidently, he was deriving relevant formulas without knowing whether the experts in the field knew them or not! I was flabbergasted.

At one point, it seemed that the jig was up. One scientist said, "You have an exponent '2' on 'e' where there should be no exponent." Dick said, "Well, wait a minute," and went on deriving formulas while he thought about this in the back of his mind. And then he said, "Well, both formulas are right." How on earth both formulas could be right was then, and is now, beyond me. But Dick survived the scrutiny of the experts. They *knew* he was wrong but could not prove it.

Dick was, of course, infinitely experienced in all this. And he warned me, early on, that physicists could "always come up with a theory if there were data." But if there were not enough data, the theory would not be accepted. And really, in the end, I did not have enough data to support even a minor theory.[326]

Some months later, FAS received a call from a meteorologist, Richard Wood, from the U.S. Weather Service's Tucson office. He said he thought he knew what had happened off the East Coast—could I get him the weather maps for the days in question?

Wood had learned, in 1975, that mysterious booms in Tucson had been caused by supersonic flights, far beyond the normal range, because of the presence of an unusually swift jet stream blowing in the direction of the supersonic flights. The jet stream, with 250-kilometer winds, could push the supersonic booms along.

Wood confirmed that, on the days in question on the East Coast, the meandering west-east jet stream had been in such an unusual snakelike configuration that it was blowing due north around Charleston. It had blown the supersonic booms of offshore aircraft right onto the shore. Thus supersonic aircraft that had caused no audible booms for years were causing them on those unusual days.

In the end, the NRL computers proved right about the mysterious booms, but because the computers did not explain the phenomenon in a way that humans could understand, the unusual weather conditions involved had not been persuasive to critics.

Gordon MacDonald was still not entirely convinced. In a report he concluded that only 413 of the 594 boom events could be associated with known supersonic aircraft and that many of the remaining 181 events had a natural origin.[327] But I felt I had saved him and Gold from great embarrassment by discovering, in a few days of looking around, that it was Concorde in Nova Scotia and not the possiblity of a Canadian earthquake, as Gordon was suggesting.

In the end, I did more than Carl Sagan had asked; I made the right decision on the press conference, and not just as an educated guess but by resolving much of the uncertainty that was breeding a crisis atmosphere. My main emotion, on remembering all this, is a feeling of having narrowly escaped complicity in sounding an unnecessary and provocative alarm for which FAS would have taken the fall, plus my satisfaction in the simple calculations that confirmed it was Concorde that was harassing Hattie Perry.[328]

CHAPTER 18

Trying to Protect Freedom
of the Press from the H-Bomb

In 1979 The Progressive *magazine seeks to print "The H-Bomb Secret: How
We Got It—Why We're Telling It," and the government seeks to suppress its
publication. No such prior restraint order had yet been upheld in the history
of the United States—the Supreme Court having vacated temporary restraining orders in the Pentagon Papers case, the only other such federal case. Fearing that either the secret of the H-bomb might be revealed and/or the freedom
of the press inhibited, the author sends an amicus brief to a federal judge
describing a supralegal process of resolving the dispute. In a dramatic
moment the judge accepts the idea and warns the parties that he will issue an
historic preliminary injunction if the parties do not accept it over the lunch
hour.* The Progressive *refuses to accept the judge's warning and, for the first
time in American history, a federal court issues a preliminary injunction providing for prior restraint of the press.*[329]

Not long after a Princeton student named Phillips had gar-
nered considerable publicity by showing that he could design an
atomic bomb, a researcher, Howard Morland, came to FAS asking
for quiet assistance on an article on the hydrogen bomb. I asked
him whether he was seeking to become the "Phillips" of the hydrogen bomb. And when he said yes, I said we would not cooperate
because we saw no useful purpose in this project. The Federation of
American Scientists had been built around the effort to prevent the
proliferation of weapons of mass destruction—not to encourage it.

An MIT student, Ronald Siegel, received a draft of Morland's article, "The H-Bomb Secret," slated for publication in *The Progressive* magazine. Nervous about what was happening, Siegel gave it to his professor, George Rathjens, to examine. Rathjens, who had resigned as FAS chairman a few months earlier to function as an adviser to the ACDA director, Gerard Smith, promptly called *The Progressive*'s editor, Erwin Knoll, to try to talk him out of publication. Failing at that, he called the Department of Energy and suggested the article needed a classification review.

At this stage, of course, I had not read the Morland article, nor did I have then, or now, any expertise in H-bomb construction. Indeed, when offered the chance by the defendants to have myself cleared to read the article, I declined on the grounds that it would make it impossible for me to comment on the case. But had I read the article, I would have been alarmed by the belief of its author that it might well help other countries build their hydrogen bombs. Morland wrote:

> The physical pressure and heat generated by x- and gamma radiation, moving outward from the trigger at the speed of light, bounces against the weapon's inner wall and is reflected with enormous force into the sides of a carrot-shaped "pencil" which contains the fusion fuel.
>
> That, within the limits of a single sentence, is the essence of a concept that initially eluded the physicists of the United States, the Soviet Union, Britain, France, and China; that they discovered independently and kept tenaciously to themselves, *and that may not yet have occurred to the weapon makers of a dozen other nations bent on building the hydrogen bomb.* (emphasis added)
>
> Why am I telling you? . . . [Not] because I want India, or Israel, or Pakistan, or South Africa to get the H-bomb sooner than they otherwise would, *even though it is conceivable that the information will be helpful to them.* (emphasis added)

Morland's rationale was overdrawn and insufficient:

I am telling the secret to make a basic point as forcefully as I can: Secrecy itself, especially the power of a few designated "experts" to declare some topics off limits, contributes to a political climate in which the nuclear establishment can conduct business as usual, protecting and perpetuating the production of these horror weapons.

After reading a Walter Pincus article in *The Washington Post* on this subject and consulting with FAS officials, I sent a cable to *The Progressive* urging consideration of the damage that the article could cause both to nonproliferation and to the first amendment.

The first amendment guarantees, of course, a free press. Federal prior restraint on publication—as opposed to government complaints after publication—would have been a first in America. Even the publication of the Pentagon Papers by *The New York Times* had not, in the end, been permanently restrained by the U.S. Supreme Court. Thus a permanent "prior restraint" order would have been a very serious new precedent against the freedom of the press. Subsequently, the AAAS Committee on Scientific Freedom and Responsibility sent a comparable telegram urging, in cases of this kind, "voluntary editorial changes by the publisher after discussion with the Government if necessary."[330]

I had a brainstorm. 🕮 Securing the assent of the FAS Council to my idea, I mailed an amicus brief to the court giving gratuitous advice as amicus briefs do. The brief stated the following:

> We would suggest that one or two senior weapons scientists be joined by one or two senior representatives of the U.S. media, and the two- to four-person mediating committee be chaired by some respected lawyer or retired judge or justice. The resulting committee of three to five would then work together with the two parties and report to the judge on their progress, or lack of it, in dealing with the specific deletions at issue. At least this could facilitate subsequent litigation by narrowing the issues. The members could be chosen to be acceptable to the two sides.

After the government moved to suppress the article, a scientific consultant, Dr. Theodore M. Postol, gave *The Progressive* an affidavit saying that the Morland article could be easily derived from the *Encyclopedia Americana* article by Dr. Edward Teller. The government disagreed. And the FAS's (and America's) senior scientific consultant on this subject, the Nobel laureate Hans Bethe, had provided an affidavit stating, "Based upon my experience on the Bethe panel, whose task it was to analyze the nuclear capabilities of foreign nations, it is my judgment that public dissemination of the Morland manuscript would substantially hasten the development of thermonuclear weapons capabilities by nations not now having such capabilities." Affidavits went back and forth.

I flew to Milwaukee to be on hand for the March 26, 1979, decision. As I entered the court, I asked the judge's secretary if he had, indeed, received the amicus brief. To my surprise, she said, "Oh, the judge would like to speak to you," and ushered me into his chambers. He then asked whether the brief was endorsed by FAS or was a personal idea. I assured them that it had been endorsed by the FAS Executive Committee (a fact recorded in the amicus brief itself) and could be taken, under our rules, as the opinion of the organization. He said, "Fine." The secretary led me to an excellent seat to watch the morning proceedings.

It was very interesting. The judge summarized the case at some length and took note of an article that explained how the French had missed elementary ideas in the 1930s and had inexplicably lost a year's time. He thought the article could "provide a ticket to bypass blind alleys." Morland, in his deposition, had stated that "if the information in my article were not in the public domain, it should be put there so that ordinary citizens may have informed opinions about nuclear weapons." But the court said it could "find no plausible reason why the public needs to know the technical details about hydrogen bomb construction to carry on an informed debate on this issue." The court concluded that the information was "analogous to publication of troop movements or locations in time of war and falls within the extremely narrow exception to the rule against prior restraint."

The article was not just an embarrassment to the government as were the Pentagon Papers. Those documents, the court argued, simply contained "historical data relating to events that occurred some three to twenty years previously" with no "cogent reasons" advanced by the government as to why the article affected national security. In this case there was a specific statute, Section 2274 of the Atomic Energy Act, that prohibited communicating restricted data to any person "with reason to believe such data will be utilized to injure the United States or to secure an advantage to any foreign nation."

Accordingly, Judge Warren said, if necessary, he would issue a preliminary injunction against *The Progressive*. But he said "bad cases make bad law." At this point my jaw dropped as the judge began to talk about the amicus brief "submitted by the Federation of American Scientists through its director, Dr. Jeremy J. Stone"; the judge pronounced himself "greatly impressed with it" and agreed with us that a "non-legal resolution" would be in everyone's interest and would set a desirable precedent.

He said, "Now, therefore, acting on this suggestion, the court herewith poses to the parties a final choice." He declared a two-hour recess to see if the parties would agree to mediation, in which case each would be asked to submit to the court two senior weapons scientists and two representatives of the media. The court would choose two people from each category and would then itself approach a respected lawyer or retired jurist to chair the group. The panel would meet with the participants and would report back in ten days on its progress in dealing with the specific deletions at issue. At that time the court would either dismiss the case by stipulation of the parties or, in the absence of an agreement, would issue a preliminary injunction. If the parties did not accept this plan by the end of the recess, the court would "regretfully issue the preliminary injunction."

I walked around the town on air, wondering if it could be possible that this cosmic matter could be resolved by our suggestion. It wasn't. But it was close. The government agreed. I was advised that *The Progressive*'s board had also agreed. But its editor, Erwin Knoll, said he would resign as editor if the FAS proposal were accepted. And the board backed down. The judge issued his restraining order.[331]

The case continued. Some people may have tried to force the secret out, and it was reported that the relevant diagrams were being printed on T-shirts and worn on Australian beaches—where an antinuclear activist was said to have taken them. (Why antinuclear activists thought it so important to "get out" the H-bomb secret was always unclear to me.) On September 17, 1979, the Justice Department asked the court for permission to withdraw its civil suit. The authors of *Born Secret*, a book about the case, think there were "other suspected reasons" for the withdrawal: "A court decision that the untested Atomic Energy Act was unconstitutional could wreak havoc with the system for protecting nuclear data. And continuation of the litigation might have led to more disclosures of information that either should be protected or would embarrass the government."[332]

By November 1979 the article was published. In his editorial explaining his decision to publish, *The Progressive*'s editor dealt with the FAS proposal, stating that he had "patiently explained to our friends that the Founders, in their wisdom, had not written a 'mediation' process into the Bill of Rights." His editorial made no reference whatsoever to the problem of the proliferation of H-bombs—before or after he had learned the secret was adjudged to be in the public domain—but simply viewed the matter as a case of attempted censorship.

There are two ways to look at the *Progressive* case. In the first, which the insurgents have adopted, one can look at the case in retrospect. Here there *was no secret* at all. The government was foolish to try to restrain the magazine because, in fact, the article was oversold, revealing a secret that was no secret.

In the second way of looking at this, in prospect, *The Progressive*, and Howard Morland, were actively trying to discover and print something that they did not know was public knowledge. Morland's article concedes he might be revealing something that would help other countries build H-bombs, while editor Knoll never used as justification for his publication that the secret was already out. Meanwhile, the most senior atomic scientist in the country, Hans Bethe, who had chaired a panel on just this question, was giving depositions urging restraint.

Although national-security justifications for secrecy were abused over and over again during the Cold War (and still are today), and although the H-bomb secret may have been much nearer the unclassified surface than many had believed, I do think there are legitimate reasons for the government's keeping some matters concealed from public view. If, for example, the same problem turns up in the realm of biological warfare, I do hope that everyone will not be quite so eager to prove that the deadly secret can easily be derived from the public literature and that some future Howard Morland does not insist that it be placed on the Internet to prevent the government from "suppressing" his article.

CHAPTER 19

Confronting Reagan on Astrology Eight Years Too Early

Governor Reagan's interest in astrology and fortune-telling is spotted in 1980 during his run for the presidency. After an investigation, a letter is secured from Presidential Candidate Reagan denying that he lets astrology influence his life—a denial ultimately proven quite wrong but one that, ironically, might have served the Republic well.

In the spring of 1988, when advance P.R. stories about former chief of staff Donald Regan's memoirs began to circulate, I received a call from the McNeill-Lehrer News Hour. In the news business today, with modern technology, nothing is ever lost. Accordingly, the staffers knew that I had inspired small news stories, eight years before that candidate for president Ronald Reagan believed in astrology. Would I appear on the show to discuss the new disclosures about the president and his wife? On this bizarre issue, after years of waiting patiently beside my phone, I finally made it onto the most important news show in America.

It all began with a syndicated article in *The Washington Post* on July 13, 1980, by Angela Fox Dunn suggesting that Ronald Reagan was superstitious, consulted horoscopes, and believed in clairvoyance and fortune-telling. For example, Reagan thought that 80 percent of the people in New York's Hall of Fame were Aquarians like him. He also talked of Jeane Dixon as having a "foretelling" part of her mind and quoted a prediction she made about him that had come true.

I then called America's most famous clairvoyant, Jeane Dixon, who

gave me a twenty-five-minute interview. She had told Reagan that his "ultimate destination on this earth" was to be president and that he was the reincarnation of someone who had been a great American and a great leader.

Thus apprised, I wrote to Reagan, conveying a letter endorsed by five Nobel Prize winners, saying that, as scientists we were "gravely disturbed" that he might believe in astrology and fortune-telling. We asked that he clarify his position since we did not believe a person whose decisions were based even in part on such "evident fantasies" could be trusted with the grave responsibilities of the American presidency.[333]

Our subsequent investigation revealed that the leading astrologer in Las Vegas had been getting phone calls from the Sacramento White House asking for advice until the astrologer had asked for the exact moment of birth of the (unknown) person involved. Then the calls stopped. (Apparently, no one knows the exact time of day Reagan was born.)[334]

We also found a newspaper story in *The Los Angeles Herald-Examiner* asserting that the syndicated astrologer Joyce Jillson, a featured columnist in *The Chicago Sun Times*, had been paid several thousand dollars by the Republican National Committee for an astrological rundown on the prospects of a half dozen of the prospective vice-presidential candidates. (According to a later story, these were done in a rush so that Reagan could take them with him on a vacation to Mexico, where he went to rest before the Republican National Convention.)[335]

We called Jillson in 1980, and her husband, a lawyer, returned the call. He said his wife was a very *professional* astrologer and would never normally breach a confidence. In this case, she had thought that the Reagans wanted this known because so many people read the astrology columns that it would help him get votes by showing he had the "common touch."

On August 27, 1980, with the presidential election only two months away, Reagan sent me the following letter:

Let me assure you that while Nancy and I enjoy glancing at the daily astrology charts in our morning paper (when we are home, which isn't too often these days), we do not plan our daily activities or our lives around them.

I can honestly tell you they have never played a part in decisions I have to make nor will they.

I'm afraid there will be many things written about me in the next four months which will be more fiction than fact.

Thanks again and warm personal regards,

Sincerely,

Ronald Reagan[336]

Apparently, this was completely untrue, even when it was written in late August. Nancy Reagan tried to advise the press that her interest in astrology had arisen only after the attempt on President Reagan's life in 1981. But the astrologer Joan Quigley, in her memoir, refers to the Reagans' use of her astrological expertise "during the crucial last three months of the campaign" in 1980—which would include August.[337]

Quigley claimed influence on the Reagans in two significant ways: first, in influencing Ronald Reagan's schedule, and second, in influencing their attitudes toward Gorbachev.

For the first claim, she has the firm support of Donald Regan,

Presidents Reagan and Gorbachev working together, as the astrologer Joan Quigley predicted they would

President Reagan's chief of staff, who wrote, "The President's schedule and therefore his life and the most important business of the American nation was largely under the control of the First Lady's astrologer."[338] This must have been very annoying to Regan, and to Mike Deaver and Howard Baker before him.[339] But the traditional interest of astrologers—and their credulous clients—in auspicious moments and days may not have much effect in shaping reality. The president, after all, is an eight-hundred-pound gorilla who can sleep wherever he wants and whenever he wants. If he wants a particular date, he can have it. The astrologer does not, by insisting on some auspicious moment, prevent the occasion itself from occurring.

But it was on the question of Gorbachev that Quigley—if she is to be believed—may have been quite influential. Some excerpts from her book give the flavor:

> "Mercury in Aquarius likes ideas. Gorbachev's openness to new ideas is phenomenal!" I repeated this many times in different ways in an effort to convince her [Nancy Reagan]. . . . I finally convinced her that despite the way Russian leaders used to be, Gorbachev was different. I warned her repeatedly that it would be disastrous for Ronnie to go to Geneva with mistaken preconceptions and his old outmoded bias.
>
> "I know you are right," Nancy said. "But it won't be easy to change Ronnie. First, I'll have to persuade him. You know as well as I do how he feels about Russian leaders. I'll have to make him realize what you say about Gorbachev is true."[340]

How much of this is true or even, for that matter, important? As far as the truth is concerned, Quigley appears to be a typical California flake. And what she claims was her assessment of Gorbachev—an appraisal with which I totally agree—is quite consistent with her general philosophy. Indeed, when the Gorbachev foundation brought Gorbachev to the Fairmont Hotel in the fall of 1995, I saw the whole spectrum of Californian new age philosophers holding him in enormous esteem. Quigley's own attitude toward Russia had been shaped by an invaluable trip to Moscow. In her case, all it took was a veteran of the Bolshevik revolution approaching her in Red Square and asserting, in the standard terms, "The Russian people don't want war, we want to be friends with the Americans."[341] But that she persuaded Nancy Reagan of all this, I do find believable.

Whether Nancy Reagan had some effect on her husband, backed by the full weight of a trusted astrologer's predictions, is harder to say, but it is certainly possible. Now imagine a world in which the Reagans' reliance on astrology was "busted wide open" in 1980 by the press, perhaps based on some report from an organization like ours. Since many people are vaguely interested in astrology and few consider it evil, this might not have cost him the election. But it might have suppressed the Reagans' readiness to consult an astrologer. And this might have been for the worse, if Quigley did, indeed, have any influence on his attitude toward Gorbachev.

In sum, the Reagan affair with Quigley illustrates the unpredictability of political reality. Actions that seem to cut one way can cut another, even without taking into consideration the opposing forces that every political action evokes.

PART VII

Two Successes in the SALT and START Disarmament Talks

CHAPTER **20**

Should SALT II Be Ratified, and
What Form Should SALT III Take?

*Defenders of SALT II become alarmed that the author's published criticisms of
it might actually lead to its defeat. Meanwhile, behind the scenes, in a great
success, the president is persuaded to propose "Shrink SALT II" at the Vienna
summit as a proposal for SALT III. A few months later, in another success,
the entire Senate Foreign Relations Committee supports the idea. But the
Soviet invasion of Afghanistan makes SALT debates irrelevant.*

The struggle over ratification of the SALT II Treaty
occupied the arms control community from October 1978 to
November 1979. During this period, my penchant for committing
truth—in this case about SALT II's inadequacies—alarmed the
administration. To my amazement at the time—though I understand it better now—they actually thought that this butterfly's
views might imperil the ratification of the SALT Treaty.

Over this same period, I was trying to persuade both the administration and the Senate Foreign Relations Committee to adopt a
proposal for the later disarmament talks, optimistically entitled
SALT III, which would take the form of "shrinking SALT II"—
that is, simply reducing the levels and sublevels of SALT II by a
fixed percentage, say, 5 percent per year. Both struggles came
together in the fall of 1979 when the chairman of the Senate Foreign Relations Committee had to decide, perhaps under administration pressure, whether or not to hold a hearing to air my
(dangerous) views on SALT II.

Meanwhile, the administration had already proposed my views on SALT III to the Russians at the June 1979 Vienna summit. But this was a state secret that few knew. In the end, the Senate Foreign Relations Committee also approved these views on SALT III. Much of what happened here is not yet known, and perhaps this memoir will contribute to an understanding of it. Whatever our state of knowledge, there are clearly some morals to these intertwined campaigns to influence two branches of government.

The General Advisory Committee (GAC) was an advisory board of the Arms Control and Disarmament Agency (ACDA), with distinguished citizens at large serving as an advisory group. The friendly and dignified Thomas Watson Jr., the head of IBM, was the chairman of the group. Its executive director, William Jackson, had worked for me at an earlier stage, and he decided to invite me to address the group on the subject "After SALT, What?" ▓ On receiving this invitation, I began to think of what might be right to propose for such a group. It often seems true that hearings can elicit from experts ideas that they would not otherwise advance. And this was such a case.

On November 9, 1978, at 9:00 A.M. I repaired to the meeting room the group was using—the State Department Crisis Center—with eight pages of testimony and some large cardboard charts. I proposed that the United States and the Soviet Union agree to dismantle annually a small agreed-upon percentage (e.g., 2, 5, or 10 percent) of their strategic delivery vehicles (such as long-range bombers and missiles), with each side having the "freedom to choose" what to destroy in any given year.[342] I called this plan "Percentage Annual Reductions," or PAR. A chart showed that weapons would approach zero only asymptotically—like compound interest in reverse, they would never hit zero but only approach it, which is what one wanted. Long-run, dramatic, and flexible, the plan would seemingly preclude the kind of tedious negotiation that had characterized SALT II. The leaders would simply have to agree on the single (percentage) number that would define the subsequent reductions—or so I maintained.

My paper argued that this approach "seems the only alternative" after SALT, and, indeed, derived this conclusion from a series of points of view: International Political Requirements; Military Realities; Negotiating; History and Consideration of the Ultimate Goal. I speculated about side issues: modernization, third powers, grey area systems, and Minuteman vulnerability.[343] I called it running the arms race in reverse.[344]

The reactions seemed good. In fact, Paul Doty, a member of GAC, pulled out a copy of *Daedalus* and stuck an article under my nose, his eyes examining my face closely. It turned out that he had proposed the same idea in an article, "Strategic Arms Limitation After SALT I," and he seemed to be trying to figure out, from my reaction, if I had swiped the idea without attribution.

In fact, I rarely had time to read the academic literature and had missed it. And Doty's article was, on examination, very pessimistic about reductions of any kind because it related to SALT I rather than SALT II.[345] But I staked no claim to originality anyway. Indeed, I had included a prominent front-page footnote saying I had been encouraged by learning that FAS's chairman, George W. Rathjens, "had once proposed something like this to a committee of the House of Representatives."

A strange aspect of the morning was the fact that the air-conditioning was so loud in the Crisis Center that one had to use microphones to talk around a conference table. *The Washington Post* published my letter complaining that the "ultimate absurdity" was a State Department crisis center in which one could not hear another person talk.

Tom Watson enjoyed both the talk and the letter and he wrote me:

> Your presentation to the GAC was great, and the best that we've had in our ten-month history. It was forceful, but you delivered it so modestly that you didn't scare off the questions. Thanks very much for the new ideas you gave us.

I noted the column about your comments on the State Department's Crisis Room where we meet. You are dead right, but it seems to be an insuperable technical problem. Maybe now someone will find a cure.[346]

This seemed a terrific opening and I wrote Watson that his letter had "emboldened me" to ask if he were "both willing and able to ensure that Mr. Carter" had a chance to review the idea before I offered it to some senator. He called and left word that he would be delighted.

GAC later talked him out of it and he wrote that he had concluded it would be "inappropriate for the GAC to carry other organizations' letters to the White House." He urged me to use my own methods.[347]

I sent the president a letter on December 13, 1978, spelling out how the proposal might reconcile the views of "hawks," "doves," "strategists," "Russians," and Senator Jackson and his supporters, and how it would relate to SALT II ratification.[348] To make sure it was read, I was able to have it published in *The Washington Post* on Sunday, December 31.[349] (How could he fail to read it?) It concluded with these words: "If the two sides are not willing to accept PAR as their underlying approach, one wonders if anything will ever work to achieve the disarmament that all participants declare is their goal."

I then began to sharpen the idea by observing that the freedom to choose might be limited somewhat. Specifically, one would apply the percentage reduction not only to the overall limit (e.g., 2,250 strategic delivery vehicles) but also to the limit on numbers of MIRVed launchers (1,250), thus ensuring that neither side simply dismantled only the unMIRVed weapons first.[350] As the shape of the SALT II Treaty became more apparent—it turned out to have five limits and sublimits—I became more expert on what this shrinkage would, in fact, produce.

The two sides, obviously, had different numbers of weapons, both overall and of the different kinds that SALT was limiting. For reasons of national pride—and because a 1972 provision authored by

Senator Jackson required it—the limits being negotiated were, however, equal. As a result, any reduction in those limits was not, ipso facto, a reduction in numbers of weapons deployed. The limit might decline for some time before it "bit" a specific party and forced a weapons reduction. It all depended upon how close the party was to that limit in the first place. And because the Soviets were closer to the most important limits, the PAR approach, applied to the SALT II limits, had quite desirable features for U.S. planners, posing no threat to their plans for quite some time. (The United States was, in any case, concerned with modernization rather than increases in numbers at this point.)

On May 1, I briefed General Jasper Welch in the Pentagon. He understood immediately that this would sell in the Pentagon, and he promised to undertake a classified study on the subject.[351] I asked if I could have a "sanitized," unclassified version when he was done. He agreed and I was delighted. Later, I briefed Colonel Frank Jenkins, who was working for the Joint Chiefs of Staff, and got ready understanding and sympathy. In both cases, using blackboard and chalk, I felt like a real scientist explaining how a calculation could change the world. (In fact, of course, the calculations could have been done by a high school sophomore.) I spent the next few months lobbying the Senate Foreign Relations Committee.

President Carter Reveals His Summit Proposal

On May 6, 1982, a Swedish TV program interviewed ex-president Jimmy Carter and reported that at the June 1979 Vienna summit he had tried to give SALT more punch with some reductions of precisely my type. On the plane going to Vienna, according to Carter's memoirs, the president got General Jones to agree to 5 percent annual reductions.[352] He summed up his proposal this way: "I wanted immediate implementation of SALT II with its strict limits, an additional 5 percent annual reduction in these limits for the five years of its duration, a commitment to lower SALT III limits by at least 50 percent below those of SALT II, and the application of similar restraints on limited-range nuclear weapons in Europe."[353]

Had this been accepted by Brezhnev, SALT could certainly have been ratified because the charge that it had "no disarmament" would have been avoided and, indeed, because the reductions, in this form, would have had real strategic advantages for the United States. According to Dobrynin's memoirs, Carter handed his proposals to Brezhnev in an elevator in the American embassy at lunchtime on a yellow pad on which he had jotted them down.

That night Brezhnev convened a meeting to discuss "Carter's paper." Defense Minister Ustinov "was dead against the proposals as too far-reaching" and was seconded, at once, by Chernenko. Gromyko said there was time to consult the comrades at the Politburo and no need to respond immediately. Thus, Dobrynin recalled that "the semiofficial proposals made by Carter were mothballed."[354]

The FAS Flap over SALT II Ratification

While this was going on, Washington was consumed with debate over SALT II itself: Should it be ratified or not? On the whole, the hawks were saying that the treaty did not do much to limit the arms race while the doves were emphasizing what it did do. The normal polarity of debate had been reversed. It seems fair to say that the doves would have been more ready to denounce the SALT II Treaty as ineffective and flawed, had it been negotiated by a Republican administration, and the hawks less ready to denounce it.

For example, in November 1970 I was widely quoted as saying that the Nixon administration's approach to SALT I "is a sham because it's not stopping anything that either side really cares about doing."[355] The arms control community took the same approach to the inadequacies of the Nixon administration negotiation of a threshold test-ban treaty that included too high a threshold: 150,000 tons of

TNT. FAS officials applauded both of these stances. But critical comments about SALT II generated real unease among some of them.

A Russian observer once commented to me that the Pentagon gets what the Pentagon wants. He was right. And in the SALT negotiations, it was child's play for the Defense Department to insist that the negotiations not limit any of its existing forces or desired programs. As a consequence, the SALT II limits were arranged like scaffolding around a building—delimiting a structure without impeding it. No doubt the Russians had the same approach. My view was: "Like two alcoholics who find it easy to agree that another drink will not hurt, the superpowers have designed an agreement that will keep them 'bellying up to the bar' through its 1985 termination date."[356]

The February *PIR* was entitled "SALT: Pros and Cons for Doves." Besides three statements for SALT II, I included an analysis of the dovish case *against* the treaty, entitled "Thinking the Unthinkable: Need SALT Be at Issue in the SALT Debate?" Later I wrote a piece for *The New York Times* that set off the greatest flap within FAS in decades. I stopped short of opposing the treaty but ended the piece with a trial balloon:

> Could a coalition of those Senate hawks interested in protecting Minuteman ICBM's and those Senate doves interested in avoiding the replacement ICBM—the MX missile—and starting disarmament force the superpowers to work out suitable additional provisions? Maybe not. But one thing is certain. Overstrain is not the only danger confronting the SALT process. When, by 1985, it becomes painfully evident how modest this treaty was, SALT—as a comprehensive agreement on offensive weapons—could die of ridicule.[357]

In fact, when the Soviets invaded Afghanistan in December of 1979, thereby rendering SALT II ratification impossible, the terms of the treaty were tacitly agreed to and maintained much as I had predicted they would be in this article if it were blocked with a view to improvement.[358]

Herbert (Pete) Scoville, a mainstay of the arms control community, honestly felt that my activities were imperiling the ratification of SALT II, and I see this possibility more clearly now. A person's newsworthiness in Washington is enormously increased if he is deemed to be changing sides in some sense—this being, for journalists, on a par with "man bites dog." Hence, a dove critical of SALT II (like a hawk supporting it) was of interest. And the vote totals on SALT, almost from the beginning, seemed to require almost all of the undecided to vote yes to get the two-thirds vote in the Senate required for treaty ratification. If, then, Jeremy Stone did not like SALT II, others could, perhaps, be excused for voting against it. Or, what is more likely, an expert's reservation might embolden a few normally supportive senators to adopt an equivocal postion—as some of them did. And the seductive idea of sending it back for improvements was, for SALT II supporters, "dangerous."

I had not expected such a response since I did not consider my views so different from everyone else's. In particular, at about that time, *The Bulletin of the Atomic Scientists*, from our cousin organization, had editorialized that SALT II was "being metamorphosed into a monster." And President Carter had already told *The Atlantic Monthly* that he would try for interim compliance if the votes were not available. (Of course, this lack of votes was not yet entirely clear.)

Anyway, Pete, determined to redress my views publicly, drafted a letter for *The New York Times* and began to find supporters. He rounded up many of my most important senior advisers: Ruth Adams, Hans Bethe, Marvin Goldberger, George Kistiakowsky, Richard Garwin, and Jerome B. Wiesner. Also listed were sponsors or members such as Abram Chayes, Paul Doty, Sidney Drell, Gerard Piel, and Charles Townes. The letter had an unfortunate ad hominem tone and implied some uncertainty about whether I was really for arms control—it featured phrases such as "Stone apparently believes . . . "; "If Stone is really interested in arms control and in the SALT process ... "; "By poor-mouthing its accomplishments and naively implying . . . he is probably increasing the likelihood that it will not be ratified."[359]

This was no minor event. After the letter's publication, State Department officials bruited it about that "Stone had been repudiated by his organization." The high level of concern, and the conscious political maneuver, were brought home to me when a reporter told me that the president's science adviser, Frank Press, had advised a concerned FAS sponsor and a major newspaper that "Stone is being isolated inside his organization."[360]

I inspired a second letter to *The New York Times*—this one supporting me—which was prepared by one of the world's greatest drafters of statements, John P. Holdren (then of Berkeley and now at Harvard University), and endorsed by Frank von Hippel. It read, "We do not agree that the SALT II agreement deserves the unqualified support provided in the letter, and doubt that its signers do either!"[361]

I prepared a three-thousand-word defense of my position, which I printed in our newsletter.[362] As the March newsletter was coming out, and ten days before my above-quoted *New York Times* op-ed essay appeared, three senators wrote to President Carter saying the proposed SALT II treaty was "very difficult, if not impossible" for them to support. On March 5 Senator McGovern gave another warning speech, saying his "ultimate decision" on the treaty depended on President Carter's approach to pressures that were sacrificing long-term hopes for comprehensive arms control just to "win a few hardliners' votes for a very modest interim step which has significant merit only if a comprehensive agreement comes next."[363] Meanwhile, hawks were having a field day linking, or trying to link, preferred items to SALT ratification: MX missile procurement, major increases in NATO spending on theater weapons, linkage of SALT continuation to the world political situation, and so on.

From my point of view, if the hawks and doves were calling for the same thing—real cuts—it might occur. And Senator McGovern championed the approach.[364] On June 15 McGovern wrote the chairman of the Foreign Relations Committee asking for a specific hearing on "realistic hopes for SALT III." And he told the committee staff that he wanted to know what Jeremy Stone thought and that Stone should testify.

Though invited orally by the committee staff, I got the impression that somehow the invitation was not firm and that the committee (staff or chairman), perhaps under the influence of White House lobbyists, was waiting to see whether my testimony would just be critical of SALT II or entirely opposed to it. Although "critical" would have been what the chairman (and the administration) preferred—and that was indeed my position—I felt it would be wrong to be required, no matter how politely and tacitly, to show my hand before the invitation was formally extended. It was silly, but I rebelled. With the fifty copies of my testimony visible in my hot little hands, I told the chief of staff, William Bader, that I would turn over the documents when I got a written invitation to do so—which he said was just delayed for clerical reasons.

At this stage a journalist to whom I had confided this problem called the Foreign Relations Committee staff. ♫ The committee's prestige was at a low ebb, and the staff got the impression that if the hearings were canceled, there might be an inquiry into the reason. My invitation promptly appeared; I handed over the testimony.[365] The testimony revealed that I was *not* opposing the treaty but trying to tack onto it a condition related to SALT III—namely that SALT II should be shrunk.

The chairman, Senator Church, opened the hearings by saying something that he should by then have known was not true—that the witnesses were opposing SALT II. The two witnesses, I and Richard Barnet of the Institute for Policy Studies, were both supporting the treaty with dismay, not opposing it. And the committee staff, who usually prepare and at least review the chairman's opening remarks, had received the testimony and knew this critical fact.

I brought charts and a pointer, and I commended Senator

McGovern's notion "mentioned this morning" in earlier hearings of shrinking the overall limits as a "very good idea." But I put forward the sophisticated version of PAR, which was "Shrink SALT II" in all its levels.

During these SALT II hearings it was not uncommon for others to urge reductions in the limits and sublimits of SALT II or even to use my phrase "shrink SALT II." But they were less supportive than I would have liked of my exact notion—and President Carter's secret proposal—of using the very *same* percentage on each limit and sublimit.

The author testifying to the Senate Foreign Relations Committee on how to shrink SALT II as a proposal for SALT III. From left to right: *Senators Charles Percy, Jacob Javits, Chairman Frank Church, George McGovern, Joseph R. Biden. Hidden are Senators S. I. Hayakawa and Paul S. Sarbanes*

Paul Warnke, when pressed by Senator McGovern, said shrinking all SALT II limits in proportion "could be a useful approach." But Wolfgang K. H. (Pefe) Panofsky said he was still uncomfortable with "too specific a prescription to have exact proportionality in the various subcategories" because one might want a larger reduction for MIRVed ICBMs for reasons of stability.[366]

In the end, Senator McGovern lined up an overwhelming majority of the Senate Foreign Relations Committee for my general approach. The remaining problem was how to deal with this question of whether one percentage would apply to all categories or whether there might be different percentages applied to different SALT II limits. I was working closely with his office, and a memo sent to McGovern on September 24 about working out a deal with Senator Moynihan shows that the language we were considering then was as follows: "The Senate understands by the statement of principles that the two sides do intend, as a priority item in SALT III negotiations, to seek to reduce the ceilings and subceilings of

SALT II on an *equitable and proportionate* basis and, on this understanding, consent to the Treaty's ratification [emphasis added]." On November 1 Senator McGovern secured the unanimous consent of the Foreign Relations Committee to a "McGovern-Chafee" SALT III declaration that incorporated this approach.

But guess what? At the last minute, the White House sent word that it would support the paragraph on shrinking SALT II only if the "equitable and proportionate" basis was weakened further. I was told this in a hallway by McGovern's aide, Alex A. Knopp, and can still remember the scene. Horrified, I said, "Are you going to accept this?" and he said, "Yes."[367]

At this point Senator John Chafee walked down the hall, and I broke off to raise this with him. But he was not the main author of this resolution—just the Republican anchor of it—and he said something like "What's the difference?" More sober heads than mine said, "Jeremy, everybody knows what it means!"[368] But I was somewhere between disappointed and devastated. Of course, gaining the support of a committee meant accepting a very watered-down approach. But I still cannot understand why the White House insisted on diluting a formula for dealing with the Russians that it had already proposed to the Soviets in secret. Apparently, the staff did not know what had been proposed at the Vienna summit three months earlier.[369]

One thing sticks in my mind. At an early stage of my campaign, I had called on the State Department's director for political-military affairs, Leslie Gelb, now the president of the Council on Foreign Relations. He had taken one look at my idea—a single percentage that the two leaders of the United States and the USSR could agree upon—and said, "Jeremy, this is the kind of idea which will appeal to you and to President Carter and to no one in between in the bureaucracy."

He was almost right. It had appealed enough to the Defense Department—once they saw how much it favored our side—but, for the expert observers and the bureaucrats, the political advantages of the "single" number were downplayed. They wanted to go back to haggling. They implicitly assumed that our side could adjust these categories and subcategories as it wanted. Or they saw subtle adjustments in the category totals as more important than a simple and lasting agreement. The ultimate irony, in any case, was my inability to get through the U.S. Congress a precise formulation that—although I did not know it at the time—the administration had already proposed to the Soviets.

The Death of SALT: Afghanistan

Senator McGovern said his vote for SALT II's ratification depended upon the adoption of his resolution. And at that time, according to a friendly Senate pro-SALT office, ratification needed all of the eighteen undecided, including McGovern.[370] However, Frank Church had been told in confidence by the administration that American intelligence reported the existence of a brigade of Soviet troops in Cuba. (It seems to have been there since the Cuban missile crisis.) As Carter remembered it, Church "saw an opportunity to meet some of the conservative political attacks on his liberal voting record," which included visits to Cuba and complimentary statements about Castro. He called a press conference, tried to "escalate the report into an earthshaking event," and said that SALT II would not pass unless the troops were removed. Carter considered this "absolutely irresponsible."[371]

Church delayed SALT hearings and on November 2 appended a Foreign Relations Committee understanding to the SALT II Treaty requiring the president to assure the country that the Soviet brigade in Cuba was not a threat. According to the experienced observer Raymond L. Garthoff, the "margin of support" for SALT II was so thin by the fall of 1979 that even the "modest negative effects" of the brigade report were "possibly enough to kill it."

The shaky situation of SALT II was much in the minds of Soviet embassy officials, who more than once called FAS and others to try to figure out whether SALT II was likely to pass. Some observers felt that SALT's precarious situation in September and October could have figured in the Soviet decision to abandon détente in favor of the Christmas 1979 invasion of Afghanistan.[372] But by October the Politburo had already dispatched military specialists to see how Afghanistan would react if forces were sent in. Their report, filed in December, that such actions would mean war was ignored by Andropov.[373] There is little doubt, then, that the Soviet Union would have intervened in Afghanistan even if SALT II had not been in trouble—indeed, even if it had been ratified. (Garthoff supported this contention in a 1996 telephone interview with the author.)

In the end, SALT ratification turned out to be a secondary issue on the global scale. All of this churning around in America, of which my struggle to "Shrink SALT II" was itself a minor piece, was no more than a minor fluctuation sitting on top of much larger forces and pressures unleashed by instability in Afghanistan.

To the extent that SALT II needed to become a preliminary to real disarmament, McGovern and I may have been correct to encourage criticism of it as lacking disarmament. When the Republicans took office, the Strategic Arms *Limitation* Talks (SALT) were promptly recast as the Strategic Arms *Reduction* Talks (START) and the new president proposed reductions, no matter how ill-considered, that eventually did turn into disarmament.

CHAPTER **21**

START Talks: The Sakharov Finesse, Stone Variety

The main obstacle in the START talks is the Soviet demand, in response to
Reagan's announced interest in the ABM, that the United States pledge not to
abrogate the ABM Treaty at least for a term of years. A bear-hug strategy is
devised in which the Soviets would agree to ongoing continuing disarmament
subject to the condition that the ABM Treaty be maintained. Washington and
Moscow are lobbied to this end with good effect. The deadlock begins to crack in
Moscow when Sakharov takes a similar line that comes to be known as the
"Sakharov finesse." But the bear-hug version is the one eventually adopted.

I had a strong interest in the ABM, which, readers will
remember, I had worked on from 1963 to 1972, when the ABM
Treaty prohibiting these weapons was signed. Over a decade later, in
March 1983, I began receiving phone calls from distinguished FAS scientists who had been invited to the White House for a dinner with
the president with no reason having been given. They wanted to know
what was happening. Rumors swirled about satellites having been
shot down, problems in Central America—you name it.

It turned out to be the evening that President Reagan gave his
"Star Wars" speech calling for a Strategic Defense Initiative (SDI).
After it was given, I remember calling the White House press room
and telling Sam Donaldson that the best people he could ask for an
opinion on the speech were, even then, having dinner with the
president! The next day, however, I was one of the very few around
who seemed to want to be on TV on the subject; some of our lead-

ing experts did not want to denounce the president so soon after sitting at his table! Nine different domestic and foreign TV stations interviewed me in the next forty-eight hours. I knew all the most incisive anti-ABM lines, several drawn from my intellectual betters.

About that time, a philanthropist named Jay Harris decided to set up some kind of Space Policy Group; at the suggestion of a specialist in the starting of nonprofit peace organizations, Lindsey Mattison, he offered us two years' upkeep for one staffer to get such a thing started. We hired John Pike, who, in the end, became the most visible opponent of ABM for the next ten years, from 1983 to 1993. The issue had gotten far more complex than the one I had dealt with in the sixties, and many technical details were beyond me and required full-time work.

In fact, the U.S.-Soviet ABM debate had now a reversed polarity from the one I knew in the sixties, when we were trying to persuade the Soviets not to build an ABM and to give up on "defenses." Now Reagan was urging defenses, and the Russians were trying to persuade *us* to give them up. Disarmament was at stake. McNamara had summed it up well in the sixties when he said that either side could just build more missiles to overcome any ABM the other side might have. Under this logic, the Soviets were certainly not going to engage in missile disarmament in the face of the specter of a U.S. ABM system that could shoot down missiles.

My idea was a simple one combining my two main themes: no ABM and continuing reductions year by year. What if the Russians held the ABM Treaty hostage with such ongoing disarmament? What if they reversed themselves and said they *would* engage in continuing disarmament but only so long as the United States did not violate the ABM Treaty? It would take self-control and nerve on their part. But it would work. They would always have time to rebuild the stock of their missiles if we abandoned our commitments and started to build an ABM. And their threat to rebuild the stock of their missiles would lock us into the ABM Treaty. This was my "bear-hug" strategy. In due course, it appeared in my March 17

Washington Post article under the title "A Bear Hug to Avoid Star Wars? Moscow Could Offer Steady Reductions of Offensive Nuclear Arms."[374]

Velikhov, Frank von Hippel, and I had agreed that Velikhov's Committee of Soviet Scientists (CSS) and FAS would have a traveling "school" to give lectures on arms control, with biannual meetings, alternately in Washington and Moscow. By chance, the first meeting was in April 1985 in Moscow, where I was able to present my lecture on the bear-hug strategy to the largest and most distinguished audience I have ever had in Russia: about forty distinguished guests from research institutes, along with defense, foreign ministry, and press observers. The lecture was videotaped by the Russians.

The current undersecretary of state, Strobe Talbott, is certainly the finest chronicler of U.S.-Soviet arms control negotiations, with no less than three relevant books. In his splendid work *The Master of the Game: Paul Nitze and the Nuclear Peace*, he quoted my speech:

> You people are saying that if we go ahead with Star Wars, there can be no disarmament. I agree, but you should turn it around. You should see that if both sides go ahead with disarmament, there can be no Star Wars. Disarmament in and of itself might be the answer to Star Wars. With offensive reductions underway, there would be no political support for Star Wars [in the United States]. On the other hand, if there are no offensive reductions in prospect, there will be all the more support for Star Wars. You need political restraints, not further legal assurances concerning the ABM treaty.[375]

This was the bear-hug strategy in its delinked form: Just do it! Start disarmament and let things take their course.

After the April 1 talk, I had an appointment with Arbatov and was joined by a few of his aides who had attended my lecture. I explained the argument. Arbatov immediately objected and denounced the idea. Only one of his assistants dared to defend my approach—Alexei Vasiliev. Arbatov immediately cut him off and said, "There would be blood all over the floor." He meant that feelings ran high in Moscow against SDI and few would have the nerve to face it down with my disarmament approach, unaided by assurances on SDI from Washington.[376]

I called on the famous strategist and negotiator Paul Nitze on my return home. Among other things, Nitze had been secretary of the Navy, deputy secretary of defense, and was now special adviser to the president and secretary of state for arms control. Strobe Talbott, a veteran of many discussions with Nitze, recorded the situation in his book:

> On May 3, after his return to Washington, Stone called on Nitze and urged percentage reductions in offense, linked to "perpetuation" of the ABM treaty. Nitze was at first resistant, then listened attentively and receptively, although with a touch of discouragement and apprehension. "Jeremy," he said, "people in this Administration already treat me like a radical dove without any interest in national security."

I remember this meeting well because, by that time, I knew how Paul Nitze operated. He was the complete negotiator, always taking careful notes and scrupulously observant of the smallest details of Soviet behavior. Meeting him, I felt like a spy coming in from the cold and giving a negotiator a view of what his counterparts looked like from the rump side.

I had attacked Paul Nitze in 1977 for his strident attacks on Paul C. Warnke at the time of the latter's confirmation hearings for director of the Arms Control and Disarmament Agency (ACDA). And I had resolutely opposed his attacks, launched from his Committee on the Present Danger, on SALT II. Furthermore, Nitze had once blackmailed the Foreign Relations Committee by telling them that he would not appear on a panel if I were on it because I was not an "opponent" of the SALT II Treaty but only a "critic." We were far from close.

But I respected his intellectual skills and restless intelligence. I knew that he was the only avenue to arms control in the Reagan administration, and not only because he was the main adviser to Secretary of State Shultz on this subject. There just was no one else at all who was as sympathetic and influential on these issues.

Paul Warnke had once confided to me that in his opinion, Nitze might attack any treaty he did not himself negotiate but that he would, if given the chance, try his utmost to secure his own arms control treaty. (I had also played a few games of tennis with Nitze on his estate once and had seen, firsthand, how competitive he was; he definitely was the complete negotiator.) Nitze had himself endured confirmation-hearing attacks when he was nominated as Secretary of the Navy in November 1963. (It was alleged that in 1958 he had flirted with such notions as turning U.S. strategic forces over to NATO, or even to the General Assembly, under certain utopian presuppositions.)[377] Such a person could not be all bad.

I had brought to my appointment with Nitze complete documentation on percentage reductions: the beginning at GAC; the write-up in *The Washington Post*; the vetting by the Defense Department; the secret proposal by an earlier president, Jimmy Carter; and the unanimous approval of the Senate Foreign Relations Committee. In short, this proposal had a damned good pedigree.

My approach to Nitze was, "Have I got something for you! This is exactly what you need. You can tell the Senate you got reductions through the threat of ABM breakout and that you gave away nothing—in the Nitze style! And you can say you secured an outcome that had already been thoroughly examined and approved: percentage reductions."

In my vision, Gorbachev would also be able to make a similar boast that he was holding back the ongoing threat of Star Wars by threatening to break off the continuing reductions to which he had agreed. Meanwhile, Nitze would be telling Congress that he had forced the Soviets into continuing reductions through the ongoing threat of Star Wars. The bear-hug strategy was a *mutual* bear hug

with *mutual* hostage-taking. It was, in short, symmetric and beautiful and they both would get what they wanted without giving up
anything they wanted. Talk about win-win strategies and win-win
outcomes![378]

In Talbott's retelling, Nitze, Shultz, and McFarlane then managed
to get Reagan's approval for such an approach preparing a supersecret
document embodying the idea and briefing an inattentive president
in a "most low-key, cursory fashion" so as to elicit a "presidential shrug
and a nod."[379] The supersecret document, dubbed the "Sunday
Paper," was later summarized in a "Monday Paper" of talking points;
it was the bear-hug strategy with two details filled in: inclusion of intermediate-range nuclear forces (INF) along with strategic ones and spec-
ification of which interpretation of the ABM Treaty would prevail.
It even had an agreement of "indefinite duration."

Needless to say, I was privy to none of this glorious news at that
time, and I learned about it only when Talbott's book was published
in 1988. But Nitze encouraged me to return to see him and sent an
aide, Colonel Norman Clyne, outside after one meeting to say,
"Nitze thinks you are one of the few honest critics around."
Accordingly, I had my hopes up, and he *had* seemed interested.

At the November 1985 summit in Geneva, President Reagan
handed Gorbachev a "massaged" version of the Monday Paper with
its "nub" still there. It said that "in addition to accepting a 50-per-
cent cut in strategic offensive forces, 'the sides should provide assurances that their strategic defense programs shall be conducted as
permitted by, and in full compliance with, the ABM Treaty.'"[380]
[From my point of view, two presidents had now handed over proposals I had originated to two premiers; not bad for a butterfly.] But
according to Talbott, Reagan did not explain that the ABM program would continue only as R&D. Gorbachev said, "But this
allows SDI to continue," and they could not reach an agreement.[381]

At Reykjavík on October 11, 1986, Gorbachev offered a 50 percent
cut in offensive weapons so long as both sides remained in compliance with the ABM Treaty for at least ten years.[382] In a confused atmos-

phere of hectic talk of other utopian proposals, and many efforts to sabotage agreement by arms control opponents, the talks failed.

Sakharov Finesse: An Unadopted Variant of the Bear-Hug Strategy

Strobe Talbott puts considerable weight on the so-called Sakharov finesse in the Soviet acceptance of START. Sakharov presented it at a forum in Moscow in February 1987, his first major appearance after his release from Gorky.

During that forum I spent three evenings with Andrei Sakharov at his apartment. As a consequence, I can describe his thinking and mood both before and after his historic presentation drawing on my contemporaneous account in the FAS *Public Interest Report.*[383] Andrei was obviously nervous about his forum presentation. He was pleased to see that my two-page paper was similar to his own in arguing "disarmament now." As he read my six points, he looked slightly surprised and pronounced it "very reasonable."

We began discussing suitable terminology. "Negotiating" linkage was the Soviet position—no agreement on reductions without agreement on SDI. "Action" linkage was our position [i.e., mine and Sakharov's]—start the disarmament now and stop it only if SDI is "deployed" (his position) or if a narrow interpretation of the ABM Treaty is violated (my position). Both of us, we agreed, were for "conditional" disarmament, which, we decided, was a better adjective than "contingent."[384]

The next morning at the forum, Sakharov was tense, surrounded by cameras. I saw him tell the forum that the Reykjavík talks had failed because the United States wanted a free hand. He explained, however, that SDI would not be effective because of space mines and other countermeasures, and because large numbers of satellite battle stations would be needed. SDI supporters, Sakharov argued, wanted to ruin the USSR, and this could be very dangerous. He did not think the United States would dare deploy SDI, but if it did, the USSR would know how to defeat it. In any case, the breaking of the linkage between disarmament and a halt to Star Wars research would resolve the deadlock and make agreement possible.

On Monday night, and again on the next Thursday night, he thanked me for the support on the issue of linkage; even his wife, Elena Bonner, was warm in her thanks for this.

It was at times like this that I felt so fortunate to be an entrepreneurial activist instead of a think-tank operative or government bureaucrat. I was actually able to brief Sakharov and encourage his views before he spoke. But in his enthusiasm for disarmament and his scorn for ABM systems, he proceeded to a logical rather than a political conclusion. For Gorbachev to take Sakharov's formulation conditioning reductions on actual ABM deployment would have been to throw away the ABM Treaty unnecessarily since the Russian threat would not have been keyed to its violation. My formulation, which threatened to break off disarmament if the ABM Treaty were violated in any way, was the obvious and natural position that eventually prevailed.

But whether his exact formulation was politically feasible or not, Sakharov gave the Russians the necessary shot of confidence that SDI would not work. As a scientist of great stature, he helped stop a kind of panic about an unreal danger. Sakharov gave the Moscow community the courage to give Gorbachev full support. Two years after Arbatov had told me my bear-hug strategy would not work because there would be "blood all over the floor," the Russian side had calmed down, and Sakharov had helped to get them calmed down. Now the delinked bear-hug strategy was feasible.

It was just as I had thought when, in 1985, I handed Velikhov a copy of Sakharov's 1968 position on ABM systems from *Progress, Coexistence, and Intellectual Freedom* and whispered that the world's strongest opponent of Star Wars was locked up in Gorky. Why not let him out? By releasing Sakharov, Gorbachev had, indeed, gotten some help on Star Wars.

On September 21, 1987, NBC news reported the following:

A high-ranking Soviet official has outlined . . . the Moscow strategy in arms control over the remaining months of the Reagan Administration. This Soviet official said that once the agreement on short- and intermediate-range missiles is complete, they want to move toward a 50 percent reduction on long-range missiles. Star Wars would be treated as a separate issue, he said, but Moscow would nullify the agreement on long-range missiles if work on Star Wars went too far.[385]

How far was too far? This report did not say. A few months later, on January 15, 1988, I had an opportunity to take this matter up with Gorbachev himself in a roundtable discussion at the Kremlin in which he met with the advisers and Board of the International Foundation for Survival and Humanity. This was the first meeting of Sakharov and Gorbachev, and I was standing there, taking a picture of them both, when they had their first conversation. Sakharov said, modestly, "It's good to have freedom and responsibility again." Gorbachev, without missing a beat, said, "It's good that you believe that with freedom goes responsibility."

When, at the meeting, my turn came to ask a question, I mentioned the idea that Professor Samuel Huntington of Harvard had propounded that elaborate Maginot lines, like Star Wars, normally come at the end of arms races as desperate efforts that don't work.[386] Such efforts seemed, in his terms, the "frantic belated efforts of the challenged state" to assert an absolute superiority over its arms race challenger. And when they do get to this stage, it seems a sign that the energy in the arms race is exhausted.[387] I suggested to Gorbachev that perhaps, in this context, SDI should not be taken

At the Kremlin reception for the International Foundation for Survival and Humanity. **From left to right: Anatoly Dobrynin, Gorbachev, E. P. Velikhov, Federico Mayor (director-general of UNESCO), and the author. Others around the table, not shown, included Andrei Sakharov, Jerome P. Wiesner, Frank von Hippel, Wade Greene, Roald Sagdeev, Armand Hammer, and about eight others**

too seriously. (I had lectured about this in Berkeley about a year earlier and concluded that in historical perspective, Star Wars might mean the arms race was really over.) Gorbachev answered, "But you don't want me to permit an arms race in space, do you?" Still, I had made the point.

In the end, two years later, as was inevitable really, what was agreed was the elder brother to the Sakharov finesse, the bear-hug strategy—involving ABM Treaty violations of any kind rather than ABM deployment in particular. For example, on October 1, 1989, *The Washington Post* reported that a letter from Gorbachev to President George Bush had: a) withdrawn the Soviet demand that both sides agree to adhere to the ABM Treaty for at least ten years; b) asked that the two sides reach an "understanding" that violation of the ABM accord by one is grounds for the other to withdraw from the arms accord; c) suggested that the two sides clarify what research and testing on space weapons constitutes an ABM violation; and d) said that the two sides need not agree on this issue before signing and implementing the strategic arms accord.

In sum, the Soviets had agreed to go ahead without linkage but had made clear that they considered that violations of the ABM Treaty (and not just the "deployment" of which Sakharov spoke) would be grounds for their withdrawal.[388] It had been four and a half years since I had proposed that reductions could keep the ABM Treaty hostage and two and a half years since Sakharov (and I) had proposed that the hostage-taking could be done tacitly. The mills ground very slowly.

Indeed, it was on July 31, 1991, nine years after negotiations began, that the START Treaty was signed as a bilateral agreement between the United States and the Soviet Union. The Cold War was already over. Five months later, on December 25, 1991, the Soviet Union collapsed.

.   .   .

Nongovernmental experts have considerable advantages. In discussing how the outsiders on the two sides sought to shape the Reagan-Gorbachev arms control proposals, Talbott wrote:

The approximate American equivalent of Velikhov and the Soviet *institutchiki* were the RAND specialists who had been helping McFarland refine the terms of the great sting and Jeremy Stone of the Federation of American Scientists, who had been consulting with Nitze.[389]

But, in this process I had several advantages. In the first place, I was lobbying the Soviet side as well as the U.S. side, which, effectively, they could not. And in the second place, I could move more quickly, as small organizations invariably can.[390] Third, the people I was in touch with—Velikhov, Sagdeev, and Arbatov—were exactly the Soviet "outsiders" whom Talbott described as "the best known and most effective spokesmen" on whom Gorbachev was relying.[391] And they were often ahead of the negotiators.[392]

What can we conclude from all this? When governments face painful decisions, their internal procedures for securing consensus are under strain, and their normal processes do not work. In these cases one must do more than work on a government-to-government basis to influence the outcome. The goal should be to find a person (or persons) inside the government who shares one's views. After infecting them with the virus of one's ideas, it can then be left to them to manipulate the levers and controls of a government they know better than we and in which they are not hostile intruders.

This was, really, the main conclusion of my book *Strategic Persuasion: Arms Control Through Dialogue*. And now, reviewing this history, I feel that in working with Arbatov, Velikhov, and Sagdeev, I was faithfully implementing its central idea.[393] (And I was successfully applying this approach to the U.S. side through Paul Nitze.)

Arms control was, really, a coalition of doves in both camps against hawks. But only when they were in touch with one another could their full effectiveness be felt. Our contacts with the "flying squad" of experts that Gorbachev relied upon was critical to whatever success we had.

More generally, Gorbachev was the "dove in place" for which we all devoutly wished—and the key to change in Russia. He was ready to be inoculated with every conceptual virus we had. But when he arrived, the establishment of experts was profoundly reluctant to accept his sincerity. On December 8, 1988, for example, Gorbachev made a magic UN speech calling for reductions in military force. The next day, every single commentator on *The Washington Post* op-ed page had something bad to say about it.[394]

It seemed crazy to me not to help Gorbachev. In late February 1989, hearing rumors coming out of Russia that Gorbachev was in trouble, I wrote a *New York Times* op-ed essay entitled "Let's Do All We Can for Gorbachev." I wrote, "He represents an asset and an opportunity. If we fail to seize this opportunity in time, who among us will not later regret it profoundly?"[395] The public turned out to be much at odds with the pundits. The piece sparked such an unusually large and positive response that I received an unprecedented thank-you letter from the deputy editorial-page editor.[396]

The *Times* editors knew what Gorbachev meant and what he was doing. Two months later, on April 2, 1989, the *Times* editorial board announced, in a two-foot-long editorial, "The Cold War Is Over." And I was the first of about a dozen experts quoted in this editorial. It meant a lot to me to be mentioned in such an historic editorial.

Still, it was another six months before a *New York Times* headline could announce, "U.S. Offers to Aid Gorbachev's Plan to Revamp System; in a Change in Tone, Baker Says Washington Could Provide Advice and Technical Help." In general, the caution of experts, and the inertia of governments, was so great that the arms negotiations had not begun to be successful until the Soviet Union had begun to collapse. To that extent, all of the above efforts on arms control itself became moot. But the disarmament debate and dialogue helped the superpowers stay well back from the brink during the most dangerous period of the Cold War. And it also helped set an indispensable example for movements for world disarmament and nuclear nonproliferation in the post–Cold War period.

PART VIII

Strengthening Defenses Against Proliferation, Crime, and Terrorism

CHAPTER 22

Forging a CIA-KGB Connection While Working for Neither

The author finds himself moving beyond a congressional "travel campaign" into an effort to get a deputy CIA director to visit Russia and, from there, to a quiet effort, which moves quickly at first and then slowly, to persuade the CIA to work with the KGB on matters of common interest such as proliferation, crime, and terrorism. To overcome reluctance, the author targets North Korea as an example and exhibits KGB willingness to participate. In the end, the talks start exactly there.

It all started, quite innocently, on October 14, 1988, at an open meeting of the American Association for the Advancement of Science (AAAS). The speaker was the deputy director of the CIA, Robert M. Gates, and he was speaking on Mikhail Gorbachev and the Soviet Union. In closing, he invited questions, "no matter how irreverent," and I could not resist the bait. "Dr. Gates," I said, "I think we can all agree that none of us would take sex education classes from a virgin, no matter how well-informed that person might be on sex. In this connection, may I ask if you have ever visited the Soviet Union, that is, had personal intercourse with it?"

The attentive reader will immediately realize that this was no more than a provocative restatement of the already embarrassing question we had developed for our congressional travel campaign (Chapter 13). But it got a big laugh. Gates finally admitted that he had not been to the Soviet Union and said the "welcome mat" was not out in the USSR for intelligence officers.

Not willing to quit while I was ahead, I persisted. "How many other CIA officials who helped you with that speech were also virgins?" At this point, the old boy network kicked in. The moderator of the AAAS-hosted speech was Sidney Greybeal, who had worked for the CIA for fourteen years (rising to become division chief of foreign missile and space activities).[397] He announced, "We are not going to permit questions that denigrate Government agencies or speakers." Greybeal later advised me, in private, that he thought no intelligence officials were *allowed by the United States* to travel to the Soviet Union and that, in his opinion, the question should not have been asked!

After the talk, I approached Gates and, in friendly conversation, explained my point of view on visits. "Would you," I asked, "visit the Soviet Union if I could get you an invitation?" He had, after all, said it was a question of a "welcome mat." His answer was professionally gray. But I was determined to pursue it.

When I saw that his admission of not having been to the Soviet Union was reported in *The New York Times*, I felt he would have more than the normal motivation to go.[398] I wrote to Ambassador Yuri V. Dubinin, who had, he once indicated to me, somehow determined that I was an American "Velikhov." (Of course, Velikhov was a real scientist, a senior member of his scientific academy, and a *real* operator; but I did not try to dissuade Dubinin.)

My letter explained the humorous situation and recalled the "truly useful effects" of the meeting between the Chiefs of Staff of our two countries, Marshall Akhromeyev and Admiral William J. Crowe. Would the Soviet government have any interest in inviting Gates as a "tourist" or as a guest of the KGB, "where, we read, new departures are taking place"?

I mentioned the possibility that a "certain communication between intelligence officers" might be relevant to "prevent terrorist activity by third parties or whatever." But my main goal was, as the ambassador well knew, to prevent high officials of both governments from "flying blind" in their assessments of each other.

I sent a copy of this letter to Gates, saying that "I would not normally presume to bypass your undoubtedly marvelous collection techniques but thought you might welcome receiving a blind copy of this letter to Dubinin directly."[399] (I was enjoying this.)

Absolutely nothing happened; no response. But a month later, Andrei Sakharov was permitted to come to America as a guest of the International Foundation for the Survival and Development of Humanity. At a dinner for him at the National Academy of Sciences, I approached Ambassador Dubinin and told him the story; he asked me to send the letter again, marked "personal."[400]

On December 13, 1988, I wrote to Gates: "While I have had no word yet from Ambassador Dubinin on the initiative we discussed, I assume that the agency is, by now, studying one relevant question: 'Is there a role in bilaterals for the intelligence community?' May I contribute some ideas to this study?"

I *know* that someone must have tipped me to this, because frankly, I would otherwise never, never, have used the jargon (to me) "bilateral." Thus, on the mere hint that I might have stirred up interest in contacts between the intelligence communities, I sent a two-page letter to the director of the CIA, William Webster, mentioning six possible areas of common interest: proliferation of weapons of mass destruction, terrorist activities, drug trafficking, threat perception, third-world developments, and mutual misconceptions. But my emphasis was still on just getting some exchanges of visits started "while General-Secretary Gorbachev is there to insist that such exchanges are consistent with his world view."

On December 18, with no word from Moscow, I had lunch in Washington with Georgi Arbatov, still the director of the Soviet Institute for the Study of the USA and Canada. By this time, I had known him for more than twenty years. I asked Arbatov to take the matter up with the KGB chief, Vladimir Alexandrovich Kryuchkov, whom he said he had known for a long time. Arbatov considered Kryuchkov (who turned out to be one of the anti-Gorbachev coup plotters) a "decent individual" who had been among other decent individuals selected by Andropov—including, of course, Gorbachev himself. He agreed to report back on any reaction to my proposal when we saw each other again at the upcoming January 16 meeting in Moscow, which both of us, and Gorbachev, were planning to attend.[401]

I had written Senator William Cohen, a member of the Senate Intelligence Committee, to alert him to what I was trying to do and had enclosed my letter to Dubinin. I got a characteristically thoughtful and serious two-page letter from Cohen on December 28. One paragraph, in particular, seemed very promising:

> The efforts you have undertaken to encourage reciprocal official visits on the parts of Soviets and Americans have played an important role in improving communications and mutual understanding between our two countries. *They provide an excellent base on which to build further cooperative steps.* (emphasis added)

Cohen indicated that the Senate Intelligence Committee had the same restrictions on its members and staff that the intelligence community did in terms of unofficial visits, but that it did encourage "official travel" to embassies or consulates.[402]

Right after the New Year's holiday, I received a call at 9 A.M. from a person unknown to me, Vyacheslav Zakharovich Borovikov, the first secretary of the Soviet embassy in charge of security. He wanted to provide an answer to my letter to Dubinin. Obviously, he represented the KGB—for a while I assumed that he was head of the KGB station, but he later said that he was not.

Remembering a hint I had once received from William Colby not to do anything seemingly furtive, I invited him to meet with me at my office, and I immediately sent Judge William Webster, CIA director, a letter reporting on my conversation. (At this stage of my life, I had never visited CIA headquarters and simply put my letter in the mail.)[403] In my office, Borovikov said my letter had been reviewed at the "highest level"—which always meant Gorbachev—

and had been considered with "understanding and support." He continued, "If any of the highest-level officials of the CIA wanted to meet their counterparts in Moscow, it could be done in entire security and confidentiality. If there were any practical considerations in this respect, they would be happy to deal with them."

When I drew him out, Borovikov indicated the visitors could apply as guests of the ambassador. He indicated that the visits need not involve meeting counterparts—but could just be visits. "Highest-level" CIA officials, he said, meant director and deputies. Asked if the KGB chief would be permitted to meet with Americans, he said he "thought so" but it would be decided, again, at the "highest level"—meaning Gorbachev, not Kryuchkov.

He asked me, in effect, to be an intermediary on this and to inform him and the CIA of any developments. I ventured the gratuitous advice that if the Russians wanted exchanges, they should offer some helpful information that could hardly be refused and that could provide a basis for further exchanges. I promptly transmitted information about all of this to Gates, who was moving on to the White House as deputy national security adviser, and Webster.

On January 5 *The Washington Post* reported that our ambassador in Moscow, Jack Matlock, had two days earlier had an unprecedented ninety-minute meeting with the KGB chief, Kryuchkov, on January 3. The article said that Matlock had asked for the appointment, and that Kryuchkov "appears to have made a favorable impression" (this is the very same Kryuchkov who later conspired to overthrow Gorbachev). When a Foreign Ministry spokesman was asked if the Soviet ambassador would be calling on the director of the CIA, he said "such a step could not be excluded."[404]

I invited Borovikov to visit the day before I left for Moscow. When Borovikov and I got together on that January 9, I offered to meet with Kryuchkov or one of his deputies—but nobody lower— to try to help bring this intelligence dialogue about. (I felt that the lower-level people ran spies, turned agents, and so on, but that contacts with high officials were more consistent with what I was try-ing to arrange.) I again emphasized that I did not work for the U.S. government, that the ideas were my own, but that I would inform the U.S. government of anything I was told.

Borovikov was not sure whether Matlock's visit to the KGB chief was coincidental or related to my initiative. He said the invitation was not really to Gates personally but that if authorized to speak for the intelligence community, Gates could come in his new White House capacity as deputy national security adviser. He seemed a bit upset when I said, "Because you represent an intelligence service and because all such services are trained to manipulate people, I want to note, for the record, that I would immediately break off any contact and abandon this project if there were the slightest effort to pressure me or any of my friends or associates here or there [I had a few friends in Moscow] in connection with this dialogue. But I am sure that you are all too sophisticated and too well aware of my record of independence for that."

He said he wished I had not said that, but he added that there would be "no tricks." It must have sounded naive and virginal to him; I sensed that he felt that it marred my record for sophistica-tion and would make his colleagues less willing to deal with me. But when dining with the devil, I was determined to sup with a long spoon.

It was evident, however, that the KGB wanted the diplomatic entities out of it. Borovikov had advised Ambassador Dubinin only tangentially of his meeting with me. (This was a longstanding pat-tern in Russian affairs; even Czarist ambassadors had no authority over the Czarist secret police.)

While I was in Moscow, no contact with the KGB was proposed by anyone, but I did participate in a roundtable meeting with Gor-bachev. Upon returning on January 17, I received a letter from Gates. He said "events had moved too rapidly" for him or Judge Webster to respond immediately but that he found my "suggestions and initiatives quite interesting." On the other hand, "The U.S.

Government must be careful that it does not send the wrong signal to those who would be watching such developments that we might be sharing information beyond that normally exchanged in diplomatic channels." Gates repeated that "the situation seems to be changing rather quickly," and he expressed interest in hearing any "new insights about your original ideas." He said he was moving to his new position as deputy assistant to the president for national-security affairs; on the bottom, he wrote in longhand, "Maybe now I'll finally get to the USSR."

On February 1 William Cohen suggested to me that Ambassador Dubinin just apply for a "private, one-on-one, appointment" with William Webster—paralleling the appointment in Moscow but with "no public announcement anticipated" (as there had been in Moscow). Later, Cohen authorized me to advise Dubinin that the suggestion had come from him.[405]

In a letter of February 6, I urged Dubinin to accept. I said that "it seems evident that the [Soviet government] would prefer that such contacts finesse the foreign ministries of both sides" but that this is "not possible on the U.S. side to the same degree" as it would be for the Soviet government. It seemed to me that the dialogue on common interests "would likely be under the general oversight of a U.S. ambassador somewhere (e.g., Vienna)," albeit with the participation of members of the intelligence community. And discussions held in Washington to get it started "would probably have to involve yourself."[406]

In a footnote added at the last minute, I indicated that Cohen planned to be in Moscow in March and that I hoped he would be able to discuss his ideas for dialogue with Kryuchkov. In a February 6 meeting with Borovikov, I handed him the letter to Dubinin.

I heard nothing further. On March 23, six weeks later, I wrote Dubinin with another copy of the letter. ("Not having had any reaction from you to me or to Senator Cohen, I am sending you a second copy in case this letter was lost.") Still nothing. (Much later, I learned that Dubinin did, indeed, get his meeting at the CIA and that Senator Cohen's call had encouraged CIA director Webster to agree to the meeting.)

Gates got his first trip to Moscow in May 1989, and only because Secretary of State James Baker believed in taking a large inter-agency contingent with him for Soviet talks. Whether the visit had an effect on his thinking, I did not then learn. But in a later inter-view he said the impact on him of the visit was "more cultural than political," that Moscow was a lot dirtier than he expected, and that he saw "some guy with tomatoes for sale, all spoiled." The visit also "validated what I had read and heard about" and he knew that it was "better in Moscow than in other places." As laughable as it might seem, this is the stuff for which we wanted congressional and executive-branch travel.

The Effort to Get Information on North Korea

By December 18, 1991, two years later, I had returned from a week's visit to North Korea, where I was hosted by Professor Hwang Jang Yop, the twenty-fourth most powerful man in North Korea, whose subsequent defection in February 1997 became a world media event.

Indeed, my final success in a five-year struggle to gain permission for a reciprocal visit for Hwang to the United States might have destabilized his situation. My comprehensive, all-expenses-paid invitation to him, sent on March 29, 1996, advised him that the Department of State had finally agreed to his coming. A month later, at the end of April, the North Korean mission in New York told me the visit had been approved. Excerpts from three letters smuggled out by Hwang in the fall of 1996 show that "the authori-ties began attacking me on May 9, 1996."[407] It was at about this time that the mission representatives began insulting me and saying that Hwang would never come because I was "arrogant."

By this time, I felt I knew, if only slightly, both the U.S. and the Soviet directors of foreign intelligence. Gates had, by that time, been nominated to be director of Central Intelligence. And after the coup attempt, Gorbachev appointed Yevgeny Primakov head of the External Intelligence Directorate of the Interrepublican Council for Security—that is, head of a foreign intelligence service that was "separate" from the domestic KGB (in 1998 he became prime minister).

I had met Primakov when he was the head of the Institute for World Economy and International Relations (IMEMO). When I first met him, he was on his way to China,

In his capacity as the president of the Korean Association of Social Scientists, Hwang Jang Yop (who defected to China and then South Korea), here meeting with the author in North Korea in 1991

and I briefed him on my experiences there in 1972. He was intelligent and pleasant; I found him quite agreeable.

I checked with the North Korea desk in the State Department to see whether they were securing information from the Russians on North Korea because this seemed a perfect issue of common concern to test the possibility of cooperation. It was evident they were not because the desk director, Charles Kartman, agreed with me that it would be fine if I tried to get such information from Moscow.[408] I called the Soviet embassy to see if Borovikov was there. The next day they sent his replacement, Vyatcheslav N. Zhukov. I gave him the background on my interest and a letter to Primakov. The letter stated that I was "acting on my own initiative" but that I wanted information on the Democratic People's Republic of Korea's (DPRK) nuclear weapons program and information on the DPRK government and society. The bomb program, I argued, would "soon hold Vladivostok hostage to another Korean war." It was definitely a matter of common concern.

Zhukov said that he was, indeed, the liaison for Primakov and that he was "authorized to begin talking to the U.S. side on three topics: terrorism, drug peddling, and organized crime." But he said that the talks had not really gotten started. In particular, Gates had not been around to meet with Primakov when Primakov had recently been in the United States. Zhukov promised to send my letter along, with a covering letter from him. And I wrote Gates about it the next day, saying, "I am, I fear, at it again—trying now to get some cooperation on preventing a DPRK bomb."[409]

On January 9, 1992, Zhukov showed up, quite pleased, with a prompt and kind oral answer from Primakov that had come, he said, between Christmas and New Year's (thus, a ten-day turn-around!), while I was out of town: "Your contribution to the cause of nonproliferation of nuclear weapons is highly appreciated in Russia. Mr. Primakov himself knows your highest scientific qualifi-cations [an exaggeration put in, perhaps, for those below Primakov who would see the communication]. The contents of your report to the Senate of the United States [my testimony to the Cranston Subcommittee] will be compared with what information we have in Moscow. After this analysis, it will be possible to plan different contacts between Russian and American representatives. *In any case, we are ready for all forms of constructive cooperation with the USA, including its special services.* [emphasis added] And we are together with the U.S. in wanting to end proliferation."[410]

On January 21, less than two weeks later, I actually received a let-ter from Primakov, who said he was willing to cooperate with any-one or anything:

> I take this opportunity to assure you that Russia is sincere in its desire to cooperate, including cooperation on the confidential basis, with all states, individuals, and organizations in averting of proliferation of weapons of mass destruction. . . . I can not help mentioning that now we can already see results of implementing of some of your recom-mendations by the diplomatic service of your country. [Wow!][411]

On January 29, 1992, I decided to take Primakov up on his offer to cooperate "with all states, individuals, and *organizations.*"

(emphasis added) I asked him to send one of their analysts of North Korean affairs to Washington to hold a suitable off-the-record seminar, under any cover they wanted and with agreed-upon ground rules. Bill Colby, a former CIA director, had agreed to participate, and, of course, I mentioned this alluring fact. (And I kept Gates informed, calling this an "experiment.")[412] As a courtesy, and also as a precaution, I wrote to inform the FBI's assistant director for counterintelligence of what was going on.[413]

But nothing resulted. I thought CIA had contacted Primakov directly or that Primakov really had little to say on this subject. But guess what? Eight months later, on October 14, *The Washington Times* opened an article with this paragraph: "CIA Director Robert Gates begins the first-ever talks in Moscow tomorrow between a U.S. intelligence chief and former Cold War adversaries about joint cooperation against terrorism, drug trafficking, and arms proliferation."[414]

And guess what else? According to the article:

> Yuri Kobaladze, a spokesman for the Russian Intelligence Service, known by its Russian initials as the SVR, said in a recent interview that plans for the Gates-Primakov meeting have been under way for months. "It's a very important meeting," said Mr. Kobaladze, a former KGB operative who worked undercover as a Soviet journalist. "It is my understanding that it took some time to agree on all the details."

It sure had![415]

In fact, I later learned from an impeccable source that the CIA had made intelligence on North Korea a "test case" of Soviet intentions to cooperate on issues of common interest. And this may explain why we never heard back from Primakov about setting up a special meeting, chaired by Colby, to examine North Korea. Encouraged by the CIA's making this a test case, Primakov may have moved to working directly with the relevant official agency rather than with us. In sum, an NGO (nongovernmental organization) initiative may have triggered specific action on a test case of the willingness and ability of the CIA and the KGB to work together on matters of common interest.

.   .   .

For the most part, I had let the security agencies run their business without comment. But sometimes I could not restrain myself. For example, in 1977 I complained to the CIA director, George Bush, that newspaper stories showed that the CIA was not checking the brief-cases of its employees for classified documents upon their exit—this was the same failure of the RAND Corporation that made Daniel Ellsberg's theft of the Pentagon Papers possible.[416]

In 1983, I dared to give military advice to the chairman of the Joint Chiefs of Staff about a danger in Beirut; my telegram to General John Vessey read as follows:

> The Beirut Anonymous Telephone Caller's reference to generating "A real earthquake under their feet" suggests that there has been tun-neling under U.S. positions or installations and explosions emplaced. Please ask Marine security to consider this possibility.[417]

He later thanked me for the telegram. So, in 1987, when General Vessey was part of a commission investigating the security of the U.S. embassy in Moscow, I wrote to him explaining why I thought the Moscow embassy was bugged and how I had tried to warn the State Department. (Soviet officials were asking me not to relay their quiet, not-for-publication, comments to our embassy, which I took to mean that they feared the KGB's finding out about their comments through embassy eavesdropping.)[418] And in 1993, I wrote an article in *The Wall Street Journal* complaining that the FBI was being charged by federal agencies with "the responsibility to elicit and thoroughly explore comments bearing on a job applicant's abil-ity to be fair and free of biases against any class of citizens."[419] These interventions with intelligence community issues were about all I had earlier permitted myself.

But the KGB-CIA connection effort grew so naturally out of efforts to secure travel to the Soviet Union that I could not restrain myself from taking action. I considered it hazardous politically. I well knew the story of the little old lady on a bus during the McCarthy era who was heard to say, "Well, if this McCarthy is a Communist, why don't they put him in jail?" By that standard, any contact with the letters *KGB*, no matter how well-intentioned and well-organized, could be hazardous to one's political health. But the issue seemed too important to be dropped.

Yevgeny Primakov (second on the left) and Robert M. Gates (full profile, right) meet in October 1992

This shift, in midcampaign, from "travel" to the Soviet Union per se to "bilaterals" between the CIA and the KGB on subjects of common concern reflects a general experience of political activism, where one opportunity leads to another if the activists are sufficiently alert and entrepreneurial. The big break came when, as noted, my letter to Dubinin was shown to Gorbachev, who approved it. This is why events began to move swiftly, as noted in Gates's letter of January 17.

When things slowed down, my effort to turn my visit to North Korea into a test of the Soviet KGB's willingness to cooperate was another example of an opportunity seized. And it appears to have turned into a test case of more general cooperation between these two enormous sources of information: the CIA and the KGB.

The moral here is yet another reason why foundation funding for specific efforts, rather than for specific persons, often unduly constrains the results. Like venture capitalists, the philanthropists ought to give priority to people rather than to projects in funding political activism, because the activists do not know what is going to work until they try; indeed, they often don't know what they are going to be trying until they enter the arena.

PART IX

Undermining Extreme Maoist Insurrections in the Third World

CHAPTER **23**

Preventing Overt U.S. Involvement in a Second Indochinese War

A visit to Vietnam and Cambodia stimulates intense interest in preventing the return to power of the genocidal Cambodian faction, the Khmer Rouge, which has been fighting in coalition with two other factions in seeking to overturn the Vietnamese-installed government. Efforts are made to change the U.S. policy of supporting this coalition. Supporters of the policy overreach by seeking to authorize the sending of weapons overtly to parts of the coalition. By energizing a subcommittee of the Senate Foreign Relations Committee, overt U.S. involvement in the Cambodian civil war is prevented.

In May 1979 a Vietnamese surgeon, Ton That Tung, came to the United States as the guest of the American Friends Service Committee (AFSC) and addressed a small seminar convened by FAS on the effects of herbicides sprayed in Vietnam during the war. This was of interest not only to the Vietnamese but also to the American veterans of that conflict.[420] We proposed sending a delegation to Vietnam, and a telegram of July 6 from the National Center for Scientific Research arrived "officially inviting" an FAS delegation. But trouble intervened.

The first obstacle turned out to be the Vietnamese effort to force Chinese residents in Vietnam to leave—"assisted departures," it was called. They had become boat people. The same day, I sent Nguyen Van Hieu, the president of the National Center of Scientific Research, a telegram that stated, "Our scientists disturbed about the expulsion of ethnic Chinese from Vietnam by sea. Regret FAS Delegation must await resolution of boat-people crisis."[421]

257

Our second obstacle was the Cambodian famine. In Christmas of 1978, the Vietnamese had invaded Cambodia in an effort to overthrow the genocidal regime of the Khmer Rouge, led by Pol Pot. It took them only three weeks to overturn the regime, so exhausted was the country and so incompetent, militarily, were the Cambodians, compared to the Vietnamese. The Cambodian people, despite their historic enmity toward the Vietnamese, welcomed them as liberators. The Khmer Rouge had killed 25 percent of the Cambodian population and were continuing their massacres. They had killed off all the experts as Western-trained, including especially anyone who spoke a foreign language. The country was in a nose dive.

Six months after the invasion, the food supply was so meager that famine loomed. The press was calling the situation desperate, and the general tendency was to blame the Vietnamese. On October 3 I went to New York, met with Vietnamese ambassador Ha Van Lau at the UN mission, and put off our visit to Hanoi until we could be assured that the Vietnamese were allowing food into Cambodia.

On October 17 we held a press conference showcasing America's most experienced specialist on famine, Dr. Jean Mayer, the president of Tufts University. Experienced in Biafran and Bangladesh relief efforts, he deplored the efforts on behalf of Cambodia as "wholly inadequate—financially, logistically, and diplomatically." His statement pointed out, in particular, that the situation was complicated by the fact that the Vietnamese were themselves short of food "by as much as 2 million tons."[422]

Our press release said we were "reluctantly deferring the date at which a delegation might be sent [to Hanoi] until FAS could determine that the Vietnamese would cooperate fully with international relief agencies, both themselves and through their influence with the Heng Samrin government in Phnom Penh."[423]

In retrospect, I consider our decision to put off our visit to have been a mistake; it would have been better to go and find out what was happening. But Heng Samrin's Vietnam-imposed regime in Phnom

Penh was refusing to permit humanitarian aid to come in. And I actually thought—and wrote—that Vietnam might be considering a "final solution" to the problem of Cambodia by depopulating it.[424] Fortunately, this article was not published, because I do not believe it now—at all. In fact, I believe that the Vietnamese cut their own rations to help the Cambodians, as Ambassador Ha Van Lau told us.

I am embarrassed that it took a full decade for us to propose another visit to Hanoi. I cannot now recall just what got me started again, but I know that the vehicle was John McAuliffe, the executive director of the U.S.-Indochina Reconciliation Project. He was running, among other things, an entirely legal underground railroad that furnished information to outsiders on how, exactly, one could get to Vietnam despite the various restrictions on traveling there. (For example, one could not book flights for internal travel in Vietnam or even get a travel agent to book a flight to Saigon.) While arranging the trip, John asked me if I wanted to go to Cambodia, too. There was, he said, a war on. 🍃 I instantly agreed; in the end, the war in Cambodia became my three-year obsession, eclipsing my concern with scientific exchange with Vietnam (although I continued to work on that also, as shown below).

In January 1989 I was in Moscow for a meeting of the International Foundation for the Survival and Development of Humanity. My visit to Vietnam and Cambodia was already set for February, and I decided to visit the Cambodian embassy to meet the ambassador, Hor Namhong, who was said to be quite skillful.

He turned out to be candid, intelligent, and charming. I realized that he was at the absolute top of his diplomatic career since for Cambodia, Russia was the most important ally. I decided on the spot to invite him to Washington, and he accepted; I even called on the U.S. ambassador, Jack Matlock, to tell him that I had done so. (His attitude was, "So?" Matlock may have known more than I did. Because of the State Department's resistance, it took me three years to make good on this invitation.)

On my arrival in Hanoi on February 10, 1989, my Vietnamese host,

Nguyen Van Hieu, turned out to be a Lenin Prize winner in elementary particle physics and a member of the Vietnamese Central Committee. The most brilliant of the Vietnamese students had been sent to Russia to sit out the Vietnam War, so he ended up being trained at an elite atomic research laboratory in Dubna. He turned out to be a kind of Vietnamese Velikhov, a genial operator, full of plans and ideas. The Vietnamese, a Sinic people, shared the Chinese aptitude in science. And Nguyen Van Hieu's forty-odd lieutenants, each working in a different field, all seemed quite with it. The state could not support their efforts, and so they were using "free enterprise" to round up funds for their research by selling the products of their ingenuity: new strains of rice, new perfumes, and so on.

It felt strange to be in Hanoi, the target of the "Christmas bombing" during the war, an act that FAS had denounced as "playing Russian roulette with the city of Hanoi" and "immoral and inexcusable."[425] The Christmas bombing had, in fact, closed down an attempt I had made, during the war, to go to Hanoi to assess the damage from U.S. bombings. A Vietnamese official, told of this, advised me that "we knew that an American scholar was trying to come." And I suppose that was me.

The country was so poor that a single bottle of Pepsi was, in fact, a week's wage for a scientist. And when we met with the famous Mrs. Nguyen Thi Binh, who had been the foreign minister for the Provisional Revolutionary Government of the Republic of South Vietnam (i.e., the Vietcong), she was bundled up in a very cold building without heat.

In 1989, the year of my visit to Hanoi, the decade-old Vietnamese-installed government in Phnom Penh was under attack by a coalition of three groups: the Khmer Rouge, still under the command of Pol Pot; a royalist faction under the command of Prince Ranariddh; and a democratic faction led by former prime minister Son Sann. Since the war was still on, it was quite unclear whether the Cambodian forces of the Phnom Penh government could hold up their end of the war without the help of the Vietnamese army.

Under U.S. and Chinese influence, the UN General Assembly had voted that the Khmer Rouge should hold the Cambodian UN seat, and hence the Phnom Penh government was ineligible for developmental UN aid. Cambodia was almost completely isolated and ostracized. When I asked Nguyen Thi Binh whether Vietnam could be depended upon to protect the Cambodians from Pol Pot after their withdrawal, she said, "We have done all in our capacity to help the Cambodians recover from the genocide. The international community has a responsibility now. Only Vietnam has helped Cambodia so far. Other countries,

The author with General Giap, the victor over the French at Dien Bien Phu

including the United States, now have to help. We have done what we can. We have to help ourselves now. Independence means we have to have food and clothing."

Later I met with the internationally respected Nguyen Co Thach, Vietnam's foreign minister since 1970 (and deputy prime minister for the same period), and with General Nguyen Giap, who had led the victorious fight against the French at Dien Bien Phu. The Vietnamese appointed him defense minister during the war with the United States to persuade the Americans that the same thing could happen to them; in fact, others really ran the war. Now, as deputy prime minister, he called my visit "the first birds of spring," saying that the arrival of scientists signified impending normalization of relations. He did not think the Khmer Rouge would succeed in returning because "I have never see the criminals make a successful comeback."

The scientist Nguyen Van Hieu and I traveled together by plane and car from Hanoi to Saigon (now named Ho Chi Minh City), where we visited with the southern part of his establishment under the vice president of the Center for Scientific Research, Ho Si Thoang. It was very pleasant to be back in Asia, with its socially

The author, President Nguyen Van Hieu of the Center for Scientific Research of Vietnam, Senator Ted Kennedy, and Vice President Ho Si Thoang

sophisticated peoples and ethic of hard work. The country was not free, of course, but its press was starting to print unpleasant facts about the government—very carefully. And it seemed like things were easing up.

At the Ho Chi Minh airport, waiting for the weekly flight to Phnom Penh on February 22, I was about to enter a country at only a decade's remove from total devastation. For four years in the seventies, during the reign of Pol Pot, all schooling had been stopped, so there was not a single ten-year-old in the country who could read and write when the regime was deposed by the Vietnamese invaders. Some twenty thousand people had been tortured to death during Pol Pot's murderous reign. Up to two million others had perished in his fratricidal terrors. The possibility that this regime might now be restored to power, backed by outside aid and a coalition, seemed both real and terrifying.

A fellow passenger on my flight to Phnom Penh, who had been Prince Sihanouk's representative to the United States, told me how the two noncommunist opponents of the Vietnam-sponsored government of Hun Sen—the Prince's faction and a democratic faction—had been forced, by Western pressure, to fight in an alliance with the Khmer Rouge, whom they hated.

But few had really expected that this coalition would prevail against a Vietnamese-backed government. Now that the Vietnamese were withdrawing their forces, some Western backers of the coalition were having second thoughts.

After a touring Phnom Penh, and accumulation of background information, I was granted a meeting with Prime Minister Hun Sen on February 27. ▉ The prime minister gave long answers, but they were earnest and friendly and not unskillful. He seemed modest and well informed. There was not a lot of Marxist jargon. He said he was encouraging American Khmer to come home.[426]

On March 1, in hearings before his subcommittee, Congressman Stephen Solarz said he was seriously considering pressing for military aid to the Sihanouk forces on the grounds that the Vietnamese were withdrawing. I thought that the last best bulwark against the "fate worse than death" (i.e., the Khmer Rouge) was certainly the Hun Sen government and *not* Prince Sihanouk, who was in an alliance with the Khmer Rouge and would use the U.S. aid against Hun Sen. On my return to Washington, on March 3, I began a round of consultations with interested parties (Dalena Wright in Congressman Atkin's office; Mo Steinbruner at the Committee on National Policy; Bill Herod of the Indochina Project; the Chinese ambassador, Han Xu; the analyst Fred Brown; and the Soviet embassy counselor Yevgeny Afanasyev). By March 11 I had prepared and released a fifteen-page analysis of what was wrong with our policy.[427] On March 15 I published an op-ed piece in *The Los Angeles Times* entitled "U.S. Policy Punishes Cambodian Survivors."

The State Department was refusing to see me except at the desk level, and since I had interviewed the prime minister, I thought I deserved better. In the end, on March 29, through the intercession of a friend who had a high position at State, I got a hearing with William Clark (the acting assistant secretary for East Asian and Pacific affairs). It turned out that one reason for the delay was State's fear that Hun Sen might have given me a "message" for them that they did not want to receive.

I considered the State Department's policy to be nothing short of criminal—genocidal, in fact—and so the meeting was tense. Clark was very polite, but the deputy assistant secretary, David Lambertson, was not. On April 11, the Open Forum of the Department of State furnished an opportunity for me to give a talk criticizing the department's policy—and even provided lunch afterwards. It was, I think, the third of four such opportunities that this splendid organization had given me over twenty-five years. But no one from Lambertson's staff attended; I heard later that he had called a meeting at the same time to prevent them from being subverted. And at the lunch after my talk, held in the State Department lunchroom, only members of the human rights staff and the Chinese desk were present—but they were very friendly.

On April 12, desperate to sound the alarm, I wrote a letter addressed simultaneously to three former secretaries of state: Henry A. Kissinger, Edmund Muskie, and Cyrus Vance. I felt the issue was above my pay grade and that the burden should be put on the shoulders of my elders. The letter said that based on a recent trip, I had concluded that the Khmer Rouge will "emerge the winner" and that FAS was appealing to them "separately and jointly" to do something to prevent a "second holocaust in Cambodia." The letter made a few suggestions, indicated what line we were taking, and asked them to help Cranston, to oppose military aid, and to take any additional measures they deemed appropriate.

I never received a response from any of the three. But some months later, I read in the newspapers that Muskie was in Hanoi en route to Phnom Penh. I later picked up the news that he had called my friend Alton Frye about my letter and had asked Alton what he thought. From this I deduced that the letter might have helped turn Muskie on.

Finally, on April 14, I secured a meeting with Senator Alan Cranston, the chair of the Asian subcommittee of the Senate Foreign Relations Committee. Alan readily agreed to hold hearings on this issue of "lethal aid," and a big fight broke out on the issue.

Solarz, Cranston's counterpart in the House, was refusing to receive me. We finally met, but on the set of a television talk show—CBS's *Nightwatch*, where he and I debated the issue with the host, Charlie Rose. Solarz called me an "apologist for the Hun Sen Government" and other names. Rose, a friend of Solarz's, did everything possible to help Solarz. Finally, just to get in my two bits, I asked, "Who is running this show?"—a comment which, by

nighttime when the show ran, they managed to suppress electroni-
cally. Afterwards, I asked Solarz if he was going to see me, and he
said, "Why? What do you know about it?" and turned on his heel.

Eventually I organized a meeting with Nina Solarz, the congressman's wife, thanks to the intervention of the FAS's team of women
assigned to congressional exchange. She was then director of the Fund
for Peace. It was embarrassing to be reduced to dealing with the congressman's spouse, but I was determined. I said that if her husband did
propose lethal aid, he would be defeated in the subsequent vote.

On May 8, *The Washington Post* editorialized that it was "far-
fetched to dally with the idea that, at this late date, a hesitant
United States can add substantially and usefully to its own direct
influence by supplying military aid to the weakest military links in the
Cambodian equation." The issue was clearly on the minds of
increasing numbers of people. On May 9, the Asia Society heard
Solarz. Asked by someone from the floor what he thought of the position Bill Colby and I had articulated in several recent op-ed pieces,
he said something insulting about me; I just quietly walked out.

On May 15 I was invited to the Soviet embassy to meet with the
Asian specialist, Afanasyev, and his superior, a man named Kutovoy.
They were visibly excited. They said that President Gorbachev had
received a letter I had written, that I would receive a letter confirming this, and that they wanted to pass along some comments.[428]

It happened this way. On April 5, realizing that Gorbachev was
going to meet with Premier Deng Xiaoping of China—the main
backer of the Khmer Rouge—I had dared to write, urging that
Gorbachev not sell out the Cambodians. ("We hope that . . .
improvement in relations will not come at the cost of a return of the
Khmer Rouge to control of Cambodia.") I quoted Deng Xiaoping's
comments about the Vietnamese ("dogs," "ungrateful" and "cocky")
to show why China was supporting the genocidal Khmer Rouge. And
I detailed the more naive of Prince Sihanouk's comments. (The
Khmer Rouge have "given me their oath that they will observe a
multiparty system . . . with free economy with press freedom.")

My letter proposed that Gorbachev appeal to the U.S. president to agree to the following:

> The central goal of U.S. and Soviet policy toward Cambodia should be to preclude any possibility of a second Khmer Rouge takeover, which would prevent, forever, any further opportunities for democracy and freedom, whether socialist or capitalist or some combination, in that area. Accordingly, both the U.S. and the Soviet Union should encourage, and try to unite, all factions which oppose the Khmer Rouge organization while denying assistance to all Cambodian elements who ally themselves with it.

I urged a non–Khmer Rouge coalition in which Gorbachev would begin supporting Sihanouk to the extent that he left the Khmer Rouge and began joining with Hun Sen. Meanwhile, the United States would move toward supporting Hun Sen while denying support to Sihanouk insofar as the prince failed to leave the Khmer Rouge coalition. My speculation is that his deputy foreign minister for Asia, Igor Rogachev—whom I had met in January 1988 and with whom I had established a warm rapport—liked the idea and helped the letter get through to Gorbachev.

On May 16, at the Council on Foreign Relations, I debated with the deputy assistant secretary of state, David Lambertson. By this time I had read a large fraction of the books in English on Cambodia and was armed with quotations from everybody and his brother; I was ready to debate anyone. And I was very passionate about the issue. Despite the fact that Lambertson had a good many friends in the audience—one who even came forward and seized the podium in an effort to help him—I felt that I had won hands down.

I asked the Arms Control and Foreign Policy Caucus of the House of Representatives to organize a luncheon for me to debate the issue of lethal aid. The Defense Department sent a deputy assistant secretary, Carl Ford. We met before eighteen House and Senate members and, again, I felt I did quite well. I was also having fruitful discussions with Strobe Talbott, who devoted three of his

Time magazine columns to this subject. He urged changing the order of battle on the ground from "three against one," with the one being the Hun Sen, to "three against one," with the one being the Khmer Rouge—the same approach I had urged on Gorbachev.[429] Finally, I persuaded another forum, Face-to-Face, to let me debate the assistant secretary of state, Richard Solomon (unfortunately, we were featured on separate days, since he declined to debate). All the while we were, of course, lobbying the Senate.

June 14 was the birthday of Ann Druyan, who was then the secretary of FAS. Her husband, the astronomer Carl Sagan, had arranged an elaborate three-day cruise for Annie and forty guests on a boat with a sign that read, in extremely large letters, "Carl Loves Annie." B.J. and I were among the guests. On Sunday morning, June 19, while aboard the boat, I saw that *The New York Times* had a front-page story showing that I had won on lethal aid. In view of the fact that thirty-three important senators, including Robert Byrd, were dead set against lethal aid to Prince Sihanouk, the State Department had decided it would not send it. My decision to bypass the House of Representatives, where Solarz reigned supreme, and base the fight against lethal aid on a Senate investigation by Senator Cranston had carried the day. This was the end of my first round on Cambodia.

At the end of Sunday, as we returned to the train station in a taxi, we heard on the radio the news that my father had died. Thus began a tremendous outpouring of commendations, including, in *The Washington Post* alone, at least six op-ed tributes, an editorial, and a very kind obituary. The journalists were at pains to give a respected member of their own fraternity a real send-off. And they were right to do so. I. F. Stone was, among other things, a brilliant and committed commentator, physically and morally courageous, hardworking, and learned. He was also quite a good father, especially in letting his children find their own way. In particular, had he been less tolerant, I might not have been willing to join Herman Kahn at the Hudson Institute, and all these adventures would have died aborning.

CHAPTER 24

Cambodia: A Failed Attempt
to End the War

On a flight to Thailand via Moscow, the real facts about the secret war in

Cambodia are purchased from a source who cannot print them himself, and

they are published in **The New York Times** *in a failed effort to end the war.*

In September 1989, while on a trip to an arms control
school being organized in Moscow by the Committee of Soviet
Scientists for Peace and Against the Nuclear Threat, I decided to go
to Bangkok to see what was happening on the Thai border.

Aeroflot flies from Moscow to Bangkok—but only barely. In the
first place, the plane seemed to find it necessary to stop almost
every two hours for refueling: Tashkent, Bombay, Karachi, Hanoi,
Ho Chi Minh City (Saigon), and Bangkok. The monotony of this
interminable flight was mercifully broken when I was taken off the
plane and was received, in a private room at the airport, by Nguyen
Van Hieu, Vietnam's leading scientist. (I had advised the Vietnamese embassy in Moscow that I would be passing through
Hanoi.)

In Thailand I had talks with the Australians, and especially the
ambassador, Richard Butler, who was also accredited to Cambodia,
now in charge of the UN arms control effort in Iraq. He had seen
an article by Colby and me reprinted in *The International Herald
Tribune*, and he was very sympathetic. I began to realize what an
important diplomatic and moral force Australia was in Asia. Thailand seemed to be governed entirely by generals; the prime minister
was almost invariably a military man (at the time, only two of six-

teen had been civilians), and the attitude toward corruption seemed traditionally indulgent.[430]

The Thais tried to persuade me that Pol Pot and Ta Mok (his most ruthless lieutenant) had changed their ideas lately; the West worried too much about past atrocities. One foreign ministry hard-liner was appalled to read, in the various intelligence reports on the FAS visit, that I had "expressed his opinion to everyone, absolutely everyone," and he called me "inflexible."

But my big find in Thailand was journalist Nate Thayer, an expert on the Khmer Rouge, who spent much of his time on the Thai-Cambodian border, making forays into Cambodia. Nate was young, rough, ready, courageous, and experienced in the field. Even a mine that put him in the hospital had not slowed him down. (He is now famous for his scoop in being the first to interview Pol Pot before Pol Pot's death.)

His report was alarming. In the current struggle, the Khmer Rouge had always won, he said, when they had attacked. And in the few cases when they had been attacked and lost, it was only with the help of Vietnamese forces that were assisting Hun Sen's military. Hence the withdrawal of the Vietnamese forces, then under way, was serious.

Nate thought the real question for the Khmer Rouge was when to shift from guerrilla war to large-scale operations. But they would still need a political solution because they could no more win militarily than could the United States in Vietnam. Nate knew a great deal, it was evident, but he could not publish it, he said, without being thrown out of Thailand. I asked him if I could retain him to send us dispatches that we would publish anonymously in our newsletter or use as material in our reports. He agreed.

On my return, I learned that Assistant Secretary of State Richard Solomon had testified that the department would not accuse the Khmer Rouge of genocide because it might give the Vietnamese justification for their invasion; it would force the United States to take action under the genocide convention to bring them to justice;

and it would make it hard for us to support Prince Sihanouk in his desire to deal with the Khmer Rouge as part of a new Cambodian government. In brief, the U.S. government would not allow the truth to interfere with its policy.[431]

The Indochina Project, a group run by William Herod that spread information about Indochina problems to Washington policy analysts, was coming under attack by Nina K. Solarz, the director of its umbrella group, Fund for Peace. I therefore offered Herod space in one of our buildings. An FAS town house already housed Chang Song, a former minister of the Lon Nol government and a Cambodian who was widely respected on Capitol Hill. Chang, who was always broke, sometimes even lived in the FAS room he rented (shades of Ed Lazansky, the Russian émigré who had slept on one of our couches for three months). In the same building we also housed CORKR, the Campaign to Oppose the Return of the Khmer Rouge, which I had helped establish on return from my first trip to Cambodia.[432]

In addition to these people, the only other main actors on our side of this struggle were Colby (whom I had brought into the fray), Muskie (who had responded, it seemed, to my letter), and Michael Horowitz, a Reagan administration official. Muskie was particularly helpful because the Senate majority leader then was Senator George Mitchell (D, Maine), Muskie's successor and protégé. Muskie interested Mitchell in the issue, and this intervention was very important in rounding up the sixty-six senators who later urged the administration to "open direct contacts" with the Hun Sen government.[433] Horowitz, who was useful as our only Republican, was Chang's lawyer. He became passionately committed to preserving the Hun Sen government as a bulwark against the Khmer Rouge only when Chang did. And Chang did so only because I offered him the money to go back and see Cambodia for the first time in about fifteen years. He came back completely turned on to the Hun Sen government.

I felt, with some justice, that I had mustered and organized nearly all the anti–Khmer Rouge forces—and was sheltering most of them to boot. This accomplishment was confirmed, in an unhappy way, when a *New Republic* article attacking our campaign mentioned only Muskie, Colby, Horowitz, CORKR, and me—the last characterized as "the American campaign's most active publicist."[434]

From October 9 to October 16, I was preoccupied with hosting the men who had hosted me in Vietnam: Nguyen Van Hieu and Ho Si Thoang, the president and vice president, respectively, of the Center for Scientific Research of Vietnam. They had a very successful visit during which they saw Senator Edward Kennedy, Congressman Lee Hamilton, Congressman Jim Leach, and the president of the National Academy of Sciences.

I thought that the State Department had tried, behind the scenes, to discourage Frank Press, the NAS president, from receiving Nguyen Van Hieu. But it was clear that we would loudly cry "foul" if the NAS knuckled under to the State Department in matters of scientific exchange. And so we had a good meeting with Frank. This was my major effort to organize scientific exchange with Vietnam. Nothing could be done until relations were much nearer normalization. But I pointed out to Frank that the Vietnamese had much scientific ability, that their population needed science, and that we all had an obligation, under such circumstances, to bring them into the scientific community. I am sure Frank Press knew all this, but the reality of seeing a particle physicist from a developing country seemed to sharpen his awareness.

On October 17 I held a very poorly attended but nonetheless quite successful press conference to complain that the Bush administration was violating the law by providing military supplies and advisers to allies of the Khmer Rouge. The press conference was successful because it was attended by Barry Schweid, the AP diplomatic writer, and his dispatch was soon winging its way around the world, provoking a response from Prince Sihanouk. I also released a six-page paper entitled "A Dozen Anomalies in U.S. Policy Toward Cambodia," in which I pointed out that Cambodian policy was so complicated that anomalies abounded: for example, Congress had already passed legislation prohibiting aid that would have "the effect of promoting . . . directly or indirectly the capacity of the Khmer Rouge to conduct military operations."[435] Was it not "indirect" help to one member of a coalition to help the other two?

The State Department's response was the irrelevant assertion that the armies did not fight in coordination. But even this claim was regularly denied in newspaper reports, with Sihanouk saying, on October 11, that all three factions "assist one another in every circumstance and cooperate with one another on the battlefield."[436]

On October 23 Bill Colby and I published an article in *The Los Angeles Times* entitled "Thailand Can Become the Key to Restraining the Khmer Rouge." We argued that power-sharing was impossible and that there was no choice but to back Hun Sen and help the Thais disengage from the forces of Pol Pot. A response quickly followed from Congressman Solarz in *The Washington Post*; Solarz also convened a hearing designed to refute our line—but we were not invited to participate.

I had been prodding Nate for information, and he came through with a very important document detailing the nature of the Cambodian operation. The two noncommunist groups in the resistance (Sihanouk's forces and those of Son Sann) had a joint military command that made requests for weapons, matériel, and aid through Thai operatives and agents of the CIA on the Thai border. They reported to a Cambodian working group that coordinated their actions and was composed of CIA operatives from the U.S. embassy in Bangkok and officials from the highest levels of the Thai, Malaysian, and Singaporean governments. The working group's activities were extensive (re-

Nate Thayer in Aranyaprathet before becoming, temporarily, an anonymous FAS stringer

viewing battle plans, approving specific weapons, disbursing direct cash payments, and so on), and the United States paid for nearly everything. It was even suggested that the CIA was providing intelligence information from U.S. reconnaissance satellites to the noncommunist resistance. Thayer's work revealed the heavy reliance of the operation on Thai infrastructure (including an elite Thai intelligence entity called 838) and the fact that Khmer Rouge weapons flowed through Thailand. From what I knew about the situation from my own trips to Cambodia and Thailand, from Washington reports, and from newspapers, Thayer's report sounded very plausible, indeed.

In fact, I now felt a bit like Daniel Ellsberg with the Pentagon Papers. I felt that this information might expose U.S. secret involvement and lead to an end to the war. It was too important to be published in our newsletter over the name "anonymous"—it ought to be in *The New York Times.* But an effort to get them to publish a piece over the name "anonymous" seemed too difficult, and the resultant major uproar after such a piece was published might have led the Thais to Nate. There were not that many muzzled experts. Moreover, in the case of publication by an anonymous person, there would be no focal point to answer questions about it or pursue it.

If Nate had been in Washington, we could have discussed it. But he was normally in the farthest reaches of Thailand, and, in any case, we could not discuss this by phone since his phone was likely tapped. I reworked the article very slightly and I submitted the material, which FAS had purchased, as an op-ed over my own name to *The New York Times.*

The op-ed page editor, Leslie Gelb, called and said that he had checked with his sources in the State Department and that he believed the piece was right. On the other hand, it was *too* good; the op-ed page had a rule that precluded its publishing "hard" news (i.e., new stuff) unless there was an accompanying article in the news section. Accordingly, they would have to generate a news story.

I sweated blood waiting for this article to appear; I had high hopes. When the day, November 16, 1989, approached, an op-ed page editor said to me ominously, "What they are doing to you!" But I had no idea what until the following morning, November 16, 1989. Instead of a front-page news story that would showcase the op-ed piece, the foreign news desk had put out a story on page A16 with the thrilling title "Aid to Cambodia Non-Communists Is Detailed." This suggestion of "nothing new but details" undercut my op-ed, which was entitled "Secret U.S. War in Cambodia."

It turned out that the foreign desk of the *Times* had called their regional reporter, Steven Erlanger, to check out the veracity of the facts in my op-ed essay. He turned to—guess who—Nate Thayer. Nate, who was as much inclined to oppose the Hun Sen government as I was to support it, played down the significance of the information, so Erlanger and the *Times* did as well. The *Times* had also given my piece to Robert Pear, a Washington reporter, and he ran a piece, one day in advance of mine, saying that the intelligence committees were trying to limit the CIA's ability to fund the war.

Thus the scoop—really Nate's scoop—had been chopped up and played down. Ironically, the same day my op-ed piece ran, *The Washington Post* ran an article showing that the State Department had a standard practice of deflating Soviet peace initiatives by leaking them to the press before the Soviets could announce them. I felt that I had been similarly victimized.

It may be that my mistake was in not giving this information to a *New York Times* reporter in the first place. The reporter could have persuaded his or her editors that a new accretion of detail of this kind was a front-page scoop, and that might have moved Washington. Or maybe I should have tried to run it signed by "anonymous"—perhaps that would have been more newsworthy.

As things stood, *one* reporter at the State Department press briefing asked the penetrating question, "Got anything on those two stories this morning on Cambodia?" When the briefer said, "No," the reporter just went away. I had been warned. In a conversation with Les Gelb, I revealed my high hopes. But Les said, "Nothing will happen because Washington is brain-dead," and he was right. Still, I was devastated, and I did not feel much better when I learned that the article had produced angry and anguished cables from State to Bangkok asking where I got the material and requesting an investigation.[437]

Desperate, I played the moral card. On November 21 I prepared a "Memorandum on the Culpability of Persons Implementing the U.S. Policy on Cambodia." It observed that the United States was a signatory to the Convention on the Prevention and Punishment of the Crime of Genocide and that "complicity in genocide" was a crime under Article III. If the Khmer Rouge returned, would American officials like to make their defense that they did not "intend" genocide even though they had done nothing to "prevent" it?

I had something even stronger, which arrived by accident. After the October 18 press conference, one evening I turned on the television and realized that it was showing a documentary on the Holocaust. I was about to turn it off when I heard the narrator summarize a document that Secretary of the Treasury Henry Morgenthau had sent to President Roosevelt during World War II. The document had denounced the Department of State for what amounted to an amalgam of racism, bureaucratic inertia, and geopolitics.

I instantly realized its great significance and relevance to the State Department attitude toward Cambodia. I sent away to the Roosevelt library for this document, "Report to the Secretary on the Acquiescence of This Government in the Murder of the Jews."

On reading it, I was struck by the raw power of its talmudic style of combining sins of omission with sins of commission; this consisted of indictments that were always of the form: "The Department of State has not done [this good thing], and has done [this bad thing]." I had no difficulty transposing this format to Cambodian affairs and wrote a searing nine-point indictment. I was determined to shock the conscience of the higher-ups at State and to make clear, as Morgenthau had made clear to Roosevelt, that the department's actions contained the seeds of a newsworthy scandal. But underlying this was my feeling that if the Khmer Rouge did come back, history would at least record that someone had walked the halls of the State Department and put this charge of genocide on everyone's desk. I felt myself the embodiment of all those frustrated Jews who had walked the same halls during World War II to no avail as Jews died in the Nazi camps.

I put about seven personalized cover letters on the essay and, moving about the building, left a letter and an attached copy with the secretaries of each of the seven highest State Department officials.[438] And then I left. I realized that calls were already moving down the building toward the Cambodian desk as I dropped the last letter there.

I received an answer—but only, I think, because I published the essay in *The Los Angeles Times* on December 3, 1989, under the title "Accomplices to a New Genocide."[439] The department's response, on behalf of all who got the letters, came from the lowest level, the director of the Office of Vietnam, Laos, and Cambodia Affairs, and said, "Unfortunately, the Khmer Rouge are a fact of life in Cambodia and they must be dealt with effectively."[440]

I continued to press the issue with letters to the chairman of the House Select Committee on Intelligence.[441] Clearly nothing much was happening. I decided to return to Cambodia for a second trip to get more information.

CHAPTER 25

Hosting Prime Minister Hun Sen
in Washington

*A second visit to Cambodia, poetic advice delivered to Vietnam, boycotting
China, devising a method—which seems to have been adopted—of breaking
the Cambodian deadlock, a third visit to Cambodia, and, finally, a great success in the hosting of Prime Minister Hun Sen in Washington.*

By the beginning of 1990, we had played a fundamental
role in Cambodian affairs in three ways: in catalyzing a successful
campaign to prevent lethal aid to Prince Sihanouk; in exposing the
full extent of U.S. covert assistance to Sihanouk and Son Sann; and
in organizing a small political resistance in Washington to work on
preventing the return of the Khmer Rouge.

But nothing had really changed. Cambodia was like the core of a
mobile that was constantly fluttering in response to the movement
of outside larger powers. In the outer ring were the largest states:
China, Russia, and the United States, with France trying to play a
role as well. In the next ring, there were the regional states: the
members of the Association of South East Asian Nations
(ASEAN) like Indonesia, the Philippines, Malaysia, Singapore,
and Thailand, and, outside ASEAN, Vietnam and Australia. And,
finally, there were four factions inside Cambodia. There probably
was no more complicated political situation in the world. Looked at
up close, it was kaleidoscopic, fascinating, ever-changing, and enormously colorful. It made European affairs seem duller than dishwa-
ter. But it also meant that FAS was a very minor actor even at its
most effective. What to do?

I was working really hard. I could taste defeat and Khmer Rouge victory. I decided to return to Cambodia in January 1990 and saw with indescribable relief that Phnom Penh still seemed serene and peaceful. In fact, nothing had happened yet! But it easily could have. Later, when I met with the Vietnamese foreign minister, Nguyen Co Thach, he confided that the military of both Hanoi and Phnom Penh had expected, after the Vietnamese withdrawal, to lose 30 percent of Cambodia but had lost only 10 percent.

According to a Russian proverb, "On the first visit to a country, one's eyes open, and on the second visit, one sees." This certainly was true for me. I met with Hun Sen; a cousin of Prince Sihanouk's, Princess Lydia Sisowat; the brother of Pol Pot; former prime minister In Tam of the Lon Nol government; the Cambodian defense minister; and a U.S.-trained deputy prime minister trying to run the economy.

The president of Vietnam's Academy of Sciences, Nguyen Van Hieu, suggested that after visiting Cambodia, I should come to Hanoi to meet with Premier Do Muoi and Foreign Minister Nguyen Co Thach. Since Vietnam is an ethnic offshoot of China, I decided to go with the flow and incorporate my advice to Vietnam in a poem. Without telling Nguyen Van Hieu what I was doing, I demanded that Hanoi provide me with an English-speaking poet. And, laboring for five hours, the poet-translator, Nguyen Gia Lap (a third of the population of Vietnam is named Nguyen, pronounced "win"), turned my poem into Vietnamese. It is larded with a certain amount of soft soap.

The Vietnamese
A Great Nation
Trapped
In a Small Country
Size Attracts Invaders
Vietnamese Dare to Resist
They Win Wars

Lose Friends
Wonder Why
In Ancient Times
They Apologize
For Their Courage
Today They Are
Too Proud to Lie
Not Just One but Two
Superpowers Are Resentful
Ungrateful Says One
Too Clever Says the Other
China Will Change
Before Vietnam
America Will Not
Find the Defeated
Ask Their Help
Psychological Jujitsu
Is Not Weakness
Ask Your Ancestors
Why Not Practice
What You Preach
Will Not Prosperity
Come Faster
From Saving Face
What Emperor Sulks
In New Jersey
What President Saw
The Famous Victory
In America
Who Lost Limbs
Only Those Who Lost
Care Who Won
Who Else Can Forgive
With Oriental Care

Design a Ceremony
Heal the Hearts
But the Personality of a Nation
Is Its Fate
Do As You Will
Perhaps You Cannot
Will as You Will
The Price of Pride
Is Patience
There Is Another Road
To Both Prosperity and Peace
Relax Rules of All Kinds
Get Rich, Win Friends
All At Once
Only Vietnam
Can Decide
In Any Case
Your Future Is Great

The Vietnamese officials were startled and pleased to see the poetic effort, and they informed me that on each Tet, Ho Chi Minh had given his advice to the Vietnamese in the form of a poem. The Vietnamese asked for the right to print my poem and circulate it to the Central Committee but decided, in the end, not to print it because they thought it would offend the Chinese. The notion of relaxing rules and getting rich was consistent with the preference of Do Muoi and must have played well in the internal power struggle there at the time.

Direct scientific exchange with Vietnam was still impossible to organize within U.S. government regulations, so I suggested we receive one of Nguyen Van Hieu's people in our FAS office for a year to study issues of scientific exchange; I chose the forty-seven-year-old Nguyen Huynh Mai, a mature, relaxed, and considerate woman. Mai passed a useful and pleasant year with us.

Having boycotted Russia over the issue of Andrei Sakharov, I had now reached the point of boycotting China over its support of the Khmer Rouge and over its restrictions on student travel to America. Back in Washington, I wrote Premier Li Peng on February 9, 1990, and said I would not attend a disarmament meeting in China, and was already boycotting Chinese embassy receptions, over China's support of the Khmer Rouge. Li Peng was the adopted stepson of Premier Zhou Enlai, and I made much of the fact that I had loved Zhou and felt that Li had departed from Zhou's path.[442]

At a February 13 press briefing, I released a set of five documents showing "Sihanouk Forces Fighting in Cooperation with Khmer Rouge."[443] In May I released a list of thirty-six scientists, including eighteen Nobel Prize winners, who called on all persons and governments to stop assisting the Khmer Rouge.[444] One did not have to be an expert on Cambodia to know that helping the Khmer Rouge did not make sense.

Seizing the opportunity of a request for lectures in Australia, I went there for ten days, October 19–29, 1990, to see what that government was thinking. Australia had played a pivotal role in this struggle ever since late 1989, when the minister for foreign affairs and trade, Gareth Evans, introduced a Solarz plan for a UN "trusteeship" in Cambodia to be followed by free elections. By the time I arrived, the Australian government had been working heroically and tirelessly for a year to make the plan work. But under the surface there was a general feeling among Australian experts that the Khmer people were just too fractious. Some wanted to wash their hands of the whole affair and just recognize the Hun Sen government.

May 20, 1991, was the seventieth anniversary of Sakharov's birth, and I attended a gala celebration in Moscow. Elena Bonner presided. Alexander Dubcek gave a message from President Havel of Czechoslovakia. President Gorbachev and his wife, Raisa, attended, along with such advisers as Yevgeny Primakov, who had tried to settle the Iraqi war; Y. A. Ossipyan, his scientific adviser;

Guriy Marchuk, the president of the Soviet Academy of Sciences; and so on. Boris Yeltsin was there also. I seized the occasion to visit the Soviet Foreign Ministry, and there, on May 22, I met with Sergei Sergevich Razov, the director of the Division of Far Eastern and Indochinese Affairs under the deputy foreign minister, Rogochev. He knew of my previous meeting with Rogochev, and we had a very good meeting.

At this time, the plan of the five permanent members of the UN for Cambodia (the "Perm 5 Plan") was having a rough time. The Permanent 5 Plan was to turn over Cambodian sovereignty to a Supreme National Council (SNC) of the four contending factions—which would be given the UN seat then held by the Khmer Rouge—and which could act by consensus with a view to holding elections.

I told Razov something I had learned from Herman Kahn: Chickens will peck at a fence forever if they see food on the other side without stopping to see if there's a way around the fence. Dogs, more restless and more intelligent, will break off and look around. Why not, then, relax the pressure from the Perm 5 and let the factions try to work it out? I outlined my thoughts. And he added, "And let the Perm 5 draft agreement be tabled without being rejected."

"Yes," I said. In the end, he agreed to try this out on the Chinese, and I agreed to write to Gareth Evans in Australia. It was high-level maneuvering, and I was exhilarated.

Immediately on returning home on May 29, I wrote to the Australian Foreign Ministry, urging a strategy of "transposition." I outlined these points:

(a) The present emphasis on talks between the Perm 5 members would now shift to emphasis on talks between the Cambodian factions on which the main responsibility for agreement would be seen to rest.

(b) The present emphasis on pressuring the Cambodian factions to agree to an existing draft would shift to emphasis on relaxing such pressures—with a view to giving each faction the confidence with which to seek agreement with the others.

(c) The Perm 5 draft agreement would be tabled without being rejected. [Razov's point]

I included the chicken-dog story and said, "Perhaps the time has come to try stepping back." I called the Australian embassy and arranged with the first secretary, Stephen Kentwell, to see that this got to Australia pronto. I wrote and told Razov what I had done.[445] A few months later, the Chinese foreign minister, Qian Quchen, was telling the Japanese government that it was "time for Cambodian chefs to make Cambodian cuisine, not foreign cooks" and that "modifications are possible" in the plan of the great powers. And in a detailed and thoughtful letter of August 8, Foreign Minister Gareth Evans responded to my letter of May 29. He wrote, "As you will know, since you wrote there has been a fundamental and positive shift in the peace process. This shift has, in fact, been in the direction you suggest." This confirmed a much earlier comment from the startled Australian first secretary, who had passed on my letter to Evans: "They have taken your proposal."

Because of the Chinese change of mood and of the decision to let the factions talk it out, the SNC became operational and decided to locate its headquarters in Phnom Penh. This opened, in turn, a possibility for governments to open embassies in Phnom Penh in recognition of the SNC, if not the Hun Sen government. We had urged this on several governments.[446] Australia promptly announced it would do so, and several others followed; certainly they thought of this themselves, but by prodding them all, we may have helped start the stampede.

By 1991 the embargo had dropped off to the point where one could fly directly from Bangkok to Phnom Penh rather than through Ho Chi Minh City in Vietnam, and the plane flew so low that one could see the B-52 bomb craters left throughout Cambodia. There was euphoria in the city about the impending return of

Prince Sihanouk, who had been in exile since 1974. Everyone wanted a new beginning. Sihanouk was saying, "Hun Sen is more liberal than I was," and they were working well together. Indeed Hor Namhong and Hun Sen had traveled with the prince to Pyongyang to meet with Kim Il Sung and were, indeed, invited to come to China on July 24–26, which excited them both.

Formation of the Genocide Project

On this next trip I took along an American University professor, Gregory Stanton, an anthropologist with experience in Africa and in Cambodia. He had two adopted Cambodian children. One was the first adopted immediately after the Vietnamese forces arrived to find the Khmer Rouge had devastated the country; Stanton and his wife were refugee workers, and someone had left the child on a doorstep. During the trip, realizing that there were a few, but only a few, Cambodians left who had personal contact with the top dozen Khmer Rouge officials, we conceived the idea of a "Genocide Witness Project" to interview them.

We secured a letter of July 11 from the foreign minister, Hor Namhong, authorizing the investigation. It stated, "The State of Cambodia agrees to permit you to organize, in Cambodia, historical investigation into the high-level responsibility for the Cambodian genocide, including especially the taking of oral histories of conversations with, and speeches by, top level Khmer Rouge leaders. We consider this project to be important to better understanding the genocide in Cambodia and, above all, to preventing any repetition of this historical tragedy." This was the genesis of the Cambodian Genocide Program now being run at Yale University by Ben Kiernan and funded by a State Department grant.

By the fall of 1991, the Permanent 5 plan had gone so far that I decided to write Solarz a letter on November 13, throwing my support behind the funding of it.[447] His astonished response to my "utterly unexpected, but very welcome letter" said it "meant a lot" that I would throw my "not inconsiderable weight" behind this plan. And he said he would welcome any thoughts I might have, from time to time, about how to enhance it.[448]

At a mid-January meeting at the Carter Center in Atlanta, when I was asked by one participant what I was going to do next, I had the most important brainstorm of the Cambodian period: Why not invite Hun Sen to Washington? The timing was perfect because the issue of funding the Cambodian peace plan, discussed in my earlier correspondence with Solarz, would be on the floor of the House.

This hosting notion began, really, with my invitation to Ambassador Hor Namhong in 1988. To get that rolling, I had organized supporting letters to the secretary of state from the chairman of the Senate Foreign Relations Committee (Senator Pell) and from the chairman of the relevant Senate subcommittee (Senator Cranston).[449] And I had organized an invitation for him to speak at the Council on Foreign Relations. It would be a private but important visit, and the ambassador's agreement was received on March 20.

The State Department resisted the idea. The department's first defense was that there had been no visa application.[450] And when he did apply, the State Department announced that his visit "would have serious adverse foreign policy consequences."[451] We asked the ACLU to file suit. According to two appellate decisions, only spies, traitors, and saboteurs could be denied entry. The State Department had no legal authority to take this position.

By September 1991 State had grudgingly granted permission to Hor Namhong to visit Washington for a day or two, as a detour during a visit to the UN in New York. And so we had had the pleasure of hosting him, and he met with Senator Cranston and a group of specialists at the Council on Foreign Relations. It was thus natural to think of hosting Prime Minister Hun Sen next. It seemed difficult but it might work.

By January 30 I had rounded up the usual suspects to provide me with the invitations. Senator Cranston said he would meet with the prime minister if he were in Washington—the formulation senators use so that they can avoid actually inviting the person *to* Washington—and his letter stated, "Especially because the Senate will be voting this Spring on funding of the U.N. peace plan, I anticipate that interest in getting your opinion on this plan would be high." And the Council on Foreign Relations extended the same invitation to Hun Sen that it had extended, earlier, to Hor Namhong.

By this time, the United States, like Australia and others, had seized the opportunity to send an official to Cambodia in the guise of a representative to the Supreme National Council of all four factions—not to the working government of Prime Minister Hun Sen, which actually controlled the country. Thus the United States had a mission and a chief of mission, Charles Twining, in place.

As I understand it, Hun Sen had shown the letters to Twining, and Twining had recommended acceptance—hence a visa would be available. Thus FAS became the host for Hun Sen's first visit to the United States. The State Department even agreed, at my request, to provide diplomatic protection.

I flew to Chicago to meet Hun Sen's plane and to discuss his itinerary on the flight to Washington. He had brought his wife and seven others. We had written an "appreciation" of his career for distribution at various events. My goal was to ensure that America saw him much as the *1990 Current Biography Yearbook* had described him:

> The leader of that government is Hun Sen, a young and gifted, though uneducated, former guerrilla who in the past decade has metamorphosed from being a diffident puppet of the Vietnamese Communists, lacking even a basic understanding of world affairs, into a confident and articulate nationalist who rivals the venerable prince Norodom Sihanouk in popularity among the seven million people of Cambodia.[452]

For openers I had prepared a kind of poem on a plaque for Hun Sen to leave at the Tomb of the Unknowns in Arlington National

Cemetery. America was consumed, at that time, with a completely phony campaign on behalf of American soldiers who were missing in action in Vietnam and supposedly might still be alive *after twenty years*. One hundred of these missing were missing in Cambodia.

But *every* Cambodian family was an MIA family, with missing loved ones unaccounted for. To make this point of shared despair, the plaque read:

To The Hundred MIA Americans of Cambodia
From the Millions of Cambodian Families
Who Also Lost a Relative
In Some Cambodian Place
They Know Not Where

The plaque caper almost failed at the outset. As we left Hun Sen's opening press conference, the armored vehicle in which we were riding screeched off from the curb (standard procedure, I was told) and left behind the rest of the delegation (they were not considered protected by State Department security). But they were carrying the plaque, and the guards were unwilling to go back; they were, I think, hazing me because they considered the whole thing a commie-pinko operation. The plaque and the others arrived only minutes before we needed to lay it at the tomb. But it read well in the next day's newspapers. I was *very* happy.

During this week, Hun Sen was everywhere, in accordance with our carefully planned itinerary. In Washington, besides his press conference, he addressed the Asia Society, the Center for International and Strategic Studies (CISS), the NGO Forum, and the Council on Foreign Relations. He met with officials of the Center for National Policy, chaired by Muskie and with its president, Madeline Albright, now secretary of state, and including some key senators. He met with Cranston and the Democratic majority leader, George Mitchell. He lunched with Stephen Solarz and also with the editorial board of *The Washington Post*. He breakfasted

Hun Sen during the Washington visit with George McGovern, left, and William Colby, right

with the *Washington Times* editorial board and also met for breakfast with William Colby and George McGovern.

The State Department finally decided to have him to dinner, and he also met with the undersecretary of state for political affairs. He visited the White House and met with the deputy national security adviser, Admiral Jonathan T. Howe. And he met with General John W. Vessey Jr., special emissary for MIA and POW affairs. In a special trip to New York, he met the secretary general of the United Nations, addressed the Asia Society for lunch, and met with the editorial board of *The Wall Street Journal*.

Everywhere he was cool and often humorous. I fed him jokes for openers—but he improved on them. For a provincial from far-off rural Cambodia, he certainly was poised. At *The Wall Street Journal*, he told them he knew he was "at the heart of capitalism." For a former Khmer Rouge, the most left-wing of Communists, he sure had come a long way.

On March 25, halfway into the visit, *The New York Times* ran an article headlined "Cambodia Chief, a Communist Survivor, Is Welcomed in U.S." It stated, "In the Administration and Congress, there is an increasing sense that the young Prime Minister has evolved into a statesman." Imagine that; this was the person derided, until his visit, as a Vietnamese puppet, a Khmer Rouge with blood on his hands.

By Friday, *The Washington Post* had a piece headlined "Washington Sees a New Hun Sen."[453] The reporter wrote, "Many people who have watched him develop . . . describe him as a complicated, pragmatic, highly skilled politician who is sincere about lifting his people out of their poverty and is, like every other living Cambodian, a survivor."

A *Washington Post* editorial revealed how important FAS intervention was. Noting that Hun Sen was here to "encourage Americans to fund the U.N.'s plan," it pointed out that the Bush administration had "hesitated to allow him an American forum" but had "finally" softened its position.[454] This was clearly a case in which our invitation made all the difference.

Hun Sen left on March 28. On April 1 I cabled him in Paris, his next stop, saying, "House of Representatives passed Foreign Aid bill with $270 million for six months to cover all U.S. peacekeeping operations. Senate approval seems imminent and certain. Congratulations. Many believe this might not have happened without you."

.   .   .

It had cost us $27,000, as I recall, to pay for his delegation's round-the-world airfare and hotel fees in Washington. Only one foundation had contributed anything (only $5,000) but it had been, perhaps, our most cost-effective operation.[455]

As the reader will recognize, I worked very hard on Cambodia and with great passion. Little would have been achieved without such intensity. By this measure, public interest activists cannot be hired but only discovered. Committed public interest activists who did not find the particular crisis of Cambodia fascinating and overwhelmingly important could not have penetrated so far into the workings of the crisis. This means that public interest activists cannot be "deployed" by funders or others but must deploy themselves into areas that grip their imagination.

In working on Cambodia, I realized also the pleasures of working on an issue that was *not* being worked on by everyone and his brother. By contrast, my work on the U.S.-Soviet arms race involved milling about with a large number of other actors. The one clear thing about Cambodian studies was that few indeed knew much about them. And, also, I learned it was not that hard to become an expert, at least for policy purposes. All in all, Cambodia taught me that there was a world out there, beyond the arms race, of real people and blood and tears and of ongoing war and possible peace.

The Cambodian election was held in 1992. Prince Rannaridh won by a significant though not overwhelming majority. Hun Sen's coalition complained about irregularities rather than give up all power, and a coalition government was formed with Rannaridh as first prime minister and Hun Sen second prime minister. An uneasy truce continued for five years as each side built up its forces. In July 1997, in a situation characterized by reciprocal fear of surprise attack, Rannaridh fled the country, and Hun Sen attacked and disarmed the opposition. Hun Sen was roundly denounced for this coup, and the international community began trying to organize another election. In August of 1997, in an effort to determine what had happened, I returned to Cambodia and prepared a report published in the September *Public Interest Report*.

In the wake of the August 1997 visit, I sent a confidential message through a well-placed intermediary to the three leaders of the Hun Sen government: the acting chief of state, Chea Sim; the first prime minister, Ung Huot; and the second prime minister, Hun Sen. It made seven suggestions for improving governance and image but may have had no effect whatsoever.[456]

By April 1998 the Khmer Rouge had broken up and Pol Pot passed away. The situation was completely changed. Hun Sen was no longer the "main bulwark" against the Khmer Rouge, and would have to justify any support he might secure by showing that he could govern better than Prince Rannaridh. This is a much closer call than the one I made in supporting Hun Sen to a coalition containing the Khmer Rouge.

Hun Sen did win the election of 1998 in the eyes of international observers. Predictably for Cambodian politics, the losers, Rannaridh and Sam Rainsey, leader of the Khmer Nation Party, cried "foul" (as Hun Sen had cried foul in losing the previous election) and they refused to accept the results. They were in a position to veto the functioning of the government since the results required them to form a coalition to permit the parliament to function. It seemed, based on his actions and on private conversations, that

Rainsey was unwilling to join such a coalition with Hun Sen under any circumstances and preferred to rally the international community (on the basis of one issue or another) to cut off aid to Cambodia until Hun Sen was forced out. In support of this strategy, he organized peaceful demonstrations and put pressure on Rannaridh to refuse to join in such a coalition, so that government could not function in Cambodia. Meanwhile, he organized demonstrations that would implicitly challenge Hun Sen to use violence, or make some other newsworthy mistake—much as Mahatma Gandhi had organized unrest against the British in India until they withdrew. The international community—having forced not just one free election but two, and having been, on the whole, satisfied with the second one—was now being encouraged by losing factions to force post-election reconciliation. Finally, in November 1988, with Rainsey out of the country, Prince Rannaridh and Hun Sen reached agreement on a governing coalition.

According to general indices of well-being, considering health, education, poverty, and so on, the only countries below Cambodia, with the exception of Nepal or Bhutan, are countries in black Africa. Cambodia is being held to higher standards of democracy than these, especially by conservatives in America, and may not be able to fulfill them. Considering the enmity between Cambodia's three parties, their different ways of doing business, and the various pressures of the different rings of countries around it, it was, as usual, very unclear in what direction Cambodia would drift.

CHAPTER 26

The Arrest of Guzman
of Peru's *Sendero Luminoso*

Peru is being torn apart by an extremist Maoist group, **Sendero Luminoso**
(Shining Path). The president, Alberto Fujimori, organizes an autocoup,
overthrowing his congress. Visiting Peru in the wake of the Fujimori autocoup,
the author learns that the U.S. intelligence is not helping capture the leader of
Shining Path; he also learns why not and begins strenuously lobbying to
change the policy, which does, indeed, change. Guzman is captured six months
later, and the insurgency, as predicted, collapses. This chapter reveals, for the
first time, that the Peruvian antiterrorist experts did get help from the United
States in tracking down Guzman and describes the apparent underlying deal.

Until 1992 my work in Latin America was sporadic and
unsustained. There were some achievements. In 1974 we sponsored
a visit to Chile by some Amnesty International officials that seemed
instrumental in arranging the release of about ten political prisoners. In 1977, I went to Brazil in response to the government's mistreatment of Brazilian scientists. The FAS report of November 1977
was well received by the experts. The nonprofit Washington Office
of Latin American Affairs (WOLA) wrote that I had "penetrated
the reality of Brazil today" and done a "superb job of describing the
current Brazilian scene."[457] A newspaper called *The Brazilians*,
printed in New York, republished the entire newsletter.[458] The president of Brazil called in Dr. Oscar Sala, president of the Brazilian
SBPC (i.e., its American Association for the Advancement of Sci-

ence) and asked why I had come and what the problem was, which was certainly helpful to the Brazilian scientists in showing they had outside support.

We may even have helped secure the release of the son of Dr. José Goldemberg, the president of the Brazilian Physics Society. His courageous stand against the Brazilian-German nuclear deal in the 1970s led, he believed, to the arrest and torture of his engineer son Clovis by the Air Force.[459] I had, myself, been detained by police for taking pictures of a student demonstration in Brasília, been driven away, and had been demanded to relinquish my film. (I gave them a blank roll, rather than the one in the camera, and then decided to leave town promptly.)[460]

In 1986, an attractive new president, Alan García Pérez, had been elected in Peru, and I wondered if anything could be done for that desperate country. In particular, I wondered if something could be done to reduce defense spending in the four Latin American states with highest defense spending per capita: Argentina, Chile, Peru, and Ecuador.

Based on a timely travel grant from the Ploughshares Foundation, I organized a traveling party, composed of myself and Colonel Edward L. King (U.S. Army, ret.)—at one time the Latin American expert on the Joint Chiefs of Staff—and produced an FAS report entitled "Peru at a Final Crossroads."[461] But it was hard to see what could be done. My parting question, Columbo-style, to the Peruvian finance minister was, "Just one last thing: If, by some miracle, Peru's $14 billion debt were to be paid off tomorrow, how long would it be before Peru was hopelessly in debt again?" His candid answer: "Not long."

In 1990 Peru turned to a successful Japanese-born businessman named Alberto Fujimori. He had a Ross Perot–type popularity as an outsider who was moving decisively against a corrupt and inefficient government. At first he looked good to the international community and to the international banking and aid institutions because he adopted a tough economic program to stop the Peruvian inflation, putting the economy and the poor through an economic wringer. But then he ordered a coup against the legislature and the judiciary that made him, at least temporarily, a dictator. The actions were wildly popular in Peru, but in the neighboring Latin American states, mindful of the tradition of coups in their own countries, it was a dangerous precedent; they used their influence to threaten sanctions against Peru, and Fujimori agreed to a constitutional rewrite.

I convened a lunch for about a dozen experts on Peru on April 15, 1990. My line was, "Peru has gotten the world's attention, which is, according to Madison Avenue, half the game. Now what can we do for Peru?" Peru had numerous problems: enormous poverty, high-level drug trafficking, governmental corruption, and, most of all, the *Sendero Luminoso* guerrilla movement. *Sendero* was a superleftist Marxist movement, similar to the Khmer Rouge in its dogmatism, but very patient and clever. Its leader, Abimael Guzman, was a shadowy figure, comparable to Pol Pot. The movement's strategy was to destroy the state to save it. Terrorism was its tool, and its goal was the leveling of the state of Peru.

To my astonishment, none of the experts had any ideas worth noting. Many were experts in human rights and appalled by the undemocratic autocoup. They were, of course, no less appalled by *Sendero* than I was, but there being nothing they could think of to do about it, they tended to concentrate their fire on the government authorities. Their line was, when pressed, that one could never protect Peru from *Sendero* without a lawful and proper regime. I doubted this supposition, and indeed, it turned out to be completely false. And I think I had a hand in proving it so.

The main benefit of the lunch was to deepen my acquaintance with a truly valuable expert, Michael Smith, an American sociologist and journalist who had lived in Peru for seventeen years. He had recently returned from Peru and was temporarily unemployed. I hired him to take me to Peru for a guided tour and to work for at least three months, on the grounds that while, at the moment, FAS had no money for a Peruvian project, something might turn up.[462]

From May 15 to May 20, we traveled around Lima and its environs, and I learned a great deal.[463] *Sendero* seemed diabolically effective, as cruel as the ancient Incas had been, and as patient as a glacier. They infiltrated villages by planting people there for three years before they would speak up. They assassinated those who opposed them. And the police and judiciary seemed intimidated by them. Our own assistant secretary of state, Bernard Aronson, had said there was a real possibility of a "third holocaust" in our time, after those of Hitler and Pol Pot. People in Peru were petrified. As usual, I rose to the bait with considerable passion. Saving Peru from *Sendero* became my consuming goal for the next six months, until the situation had been brought under control.

On our return, I proposed that Michael put out a small, specialized newsletter devoted to sounding the alarm about *Sendero*. At the end of this period, he would be better known to the interested community and would be able, at least, to find a job more readily. In July 1992 he began writing, editing, and putting out a monthly called "The Sendero File."

On June 2 I met with Assistant Secretary of State Aronson and his director of Andean Region Affairs, Anne W. Patterson, and gave them a detailed letter with my findings. They offered me the kind of ready cooperation that had been completely absent when I was working on the Khmer Rouge. In this case, they acted as if Michael Smith and I were the only ones around that were beating the drum about *Sendero* besides themselves. Aronson needed and welcomed help. How nice it was not to have to be opposing State Department officials! I briefed and met other knowledgeable officials at State.

Without telling Michael much about it, I also began trying to rouse the interest of the intelligence community, because during the trip I had discovered two startling facts.[464] The first thing I learned was that, incredibly, our intelligence community had been cooperating with the Peruvian government only in the "drug war" while desiring to steer clear of the conflict between the government of

Peru and *Sendero Luminoso*. The policy, based on a presidential "finding," was "to fight drugs but to avoid another Vietnam."

In response I prepared a confidential paper of July 5, 1992, entitled "The Ostrich Strategy: Fighting Drugs While Ignoring *Sendero*," explaining how any equipment made available to Peruvian intelligence by the United States was constrained, by U.S. orders, to work only against drug-trafficking targets. The issue was so controversial that Peruvian officials were told not to provide to the United States any information on *Sendero* that they might, perhaps inadvertently, have picked up with the equipment supplied.

As a consequence of this policy, the United States was giving no advice, help, or intelligence in the search for Abimael Guzman, *Sendero*'s leader. No really high-powered U.S. technology such as satellites or electronic-surveillance systems were being applied to that important task.

My paper ridiculed the notion of "another Vietnam," arguing that there was no interest in America in such direct involvement anyway. I ridiculed the notion that it was wrong to give such help because of human rights considerations; after all, we had wiretapping here in America under national-security rules.

The policy of pursuing drugs rather than *Sendero* was a "marvelous illustration of the dominance of domestic politics over rational analysis." I called for giving Peru help in listening in on radio and telephone conversations that bore on *Sendero*, in monitoring conversations in safe houses, in the use of satellites to track cars in which *Sendero* leaders were traveling, in locating clandestine radio stations, and in learning modern techniques for finding wanted criminals in cities. The paper concluded, "The Administration should convene an interagency group to consider whether and how to draft a suitable finding permitting the U.S. intelligence community to cooperate with the Peruvian intelligence community on efforts devoted to locating *Sendero*'s leadership."

The second thing I picked up from the U.S. grapevine was that some people in the intelligence community were afraid to help because of the following scenario: They would provide information to Peru about Guzman. The Peruvian police would use the information to find Guzman, but on finding him, they would kill him. And then, the U.S. operatives feared, they would be charged with having violated the U.S. law about assassination.

During a meeting in Washington, I found myself speaking to a person who had been a key legal consultant to the CIA. I seized the opportunity to ask about this scenario. The opinion provided was that such information would not be complicity in assassination (but some years later the same person provided a different opinion— that it turned on how the information was going to be used).

On June 9, 1992, the Center for National Policy was holding a lunch at which the CIA director, Robert Gates, was speaking. During the reception I introduced myself again—we had not spoken since the AAAS meeting at which I called him a "virgin" expert on Russia—and asked if I could quickly brief him on my trip. ♫ Right then and there, in a corner of the cocktail party, I told him that Guzman could not leave Lima for the mountains because of a blood disease. Accordingly, he was traveling around from one safe house to another in Lima and had been for *fourteen years.* Indeed, it was thought that he was traveling in a green Mercedes with frosted windows! If this were New York, I said, the CIA would be helping, and we would have caught him long ago. Why were they not helping?

One reason, I surmised—in addition to those of my memo—was that after the Fujimori autocoup, the U.S. intelligence community had broken off relations with the Peruvian intelligence community *in general.* Gates's body language seemed sympathetic, and he seemed to confirm what I had learned about the general cutoff of relations of the intelligence communities.

In conversations in Washington with an informed insider, I was given to understand that the intelligence community would be emboldened if a "liberal" group like our own would urge this kind of intelligence-community collaboration with Peru, and, certainly, it would distinguish it from an issue of assassination.

In fact, twenty years before, my December 1972 FAS newsletter—entitled "The Intelligence Community: Time for Review"—had urged a firm rule against government-sponsored murder or torture and had complained about the Phoenix program in Vietnam, said to involve widespread assassination. We learned only later that CIA director Helms had already issued a directive in March 1972 banning foreign assassinations and that the ban had been expanded under CIA director William Colby in August 1973, to say: "CIA will not engage in assassination nor induce, assist or suggest to others that assassination be employed."[465]

Happy to show by example that this was different, I wrote two letters. One, dated June 19, 1992, was addressed to Assistant Secretary of State Bernard Aronson and began, "Ought not the United States, as a matter of the highest priority, be helping the Government of Peru to locate Abimael Guzman, who is living in Lima in safe houses and in universities?" A copy was sent to Gates, to remind him of our conversation.

On June 30, at 4:00 P.M., I met with Robert Morley, an assistant director of Latin American Affairs at the National Security Council, to express my fears. And at that time I gave him a personal one-page "Dear Brent" letter urging the national security adviser (Brent Scowcroft) to instruct the intelligence community to help the Peruvian government.[466]

On July 6 I met with the assistant secretary of defense for international security affairs, James Lilly, whom I had met when he was the ambassador to South Korea, and sought his help.[467] And on July 9 I was back at the Pentagon raising my concerns with the head of Latin American Affairs for the Defense Intelligence Agency (DIA), Dr. William A. Naughton. I was also in regular touch with State.

I urged *The Washington Post* to have its correspondents spend more time in Lima, and on June 19 the paper sent Don Podesta to talk to me before his departure to Latin America as their new correspondent. On July 13, in his first dispatch from Lima, he referred to our effort: "Jeremy Stone of the Federation of American Scientists, who this month launched a newsletter and lobbying effort in Washington to focus attention on Peru's war, compares Shining Path to Cambodia's Khmer Rouge and says the guerillas are in it for the long haul."[468]

On July 28 *The Washington Post* finally printed my op-ed piece entitled "Save Peru from *Sendero*," and it was run in the August 1–2 issue of *The International Herald Tribune*. The article claimed that the *Sendero* strategy of destroying Peru so that it could rebuild it might work and, indeed, might spread to other revolutionary movements. It concluded that "Peru has become an international problem requiring some kind of collective international help from the community of states—much as the permanent five members of the United Nations undertook to save Cambodia."[469]

By coincidence, the *Post* article appeared on the Peruvian independence day. At their embassy at lunch, amidst the throngs of Peruvian well-wishers, I was greeted as a kind of savior. People were convinced that the *Post* had deliberately printed my op-ed piece on their national day, and they considered it the first thing about Peru printed in a long time that was not hostile to their government.

Indeed, I was promptly taken to task by Americas Watch for not having emphasized sufficiently the human rights deprivations of the Fujimori government: "Stone's oblique reference to the 'human rights outrages of Peruvian society'—which he deems petty compared with the threat from Sendero—suggests that no one, or everyone, is responsible."[470]

On July 31, thinking that *Sendero* might in fact succeed in destroying Peru, I began pondering ways in which Peru and other similarly threatened countries might be helped. The idea was a kind of trusteeship for countries that were reverting to the kind of instabililty and incompetence that motivated the creation of the Trusteeship Council for states emerging from colonialism. The UN Secretariat had explained to me that the entire UN Trusteeship Council was now supervising only one state (Palau); I wondered whether it, or something like it, could be used for states in Peru's predicament that would temporarily cede their sovereignty to a trustee in order to get help and stabilization. The analogy in real estate was a "sale and leaseback," an agreement by which an owner of a failing rental property would sell it to a reputable personage while continuing to administer it and with the right to buy it back after ten years. Sovereignty would be the item "sold and leased back"; the UN trusteeship would persuade the international community that the state was workable, and Peru would recover its sovereignty when its emergency was over.

I went to New York and discussed this, on September 10, with a very relevant Peruvian, the former secretary-general of the United Nations, Javier Pérez de Cuellar—and also with a high-ranking Peruvian in the UN Secretariat, Alvero DeSoto.

Guzman Captured

Two days later Guzman was captured. He was not killed when arrested, and much information was captured with him. It was an enormous success. *The New York Times* quoted Enrique Obando, director of research at the Peruvian Center for International Studies, as saying, "We now finally realize that Peru is not about to fall to Shining Path. And we can say there is reason to believe that the group can be totally destroyed over time." Observers had never seen Peruvians "so ecstatic and optimistic" and said, "People had forgotten they could feel this way."[471]

Guzman's one occasion to express himself publicly occurred when he was given a press conference; he shouted over the heads of the journalists that the movement should "keep to the strategy." Since three-quarters of the *Sendero* Central Committee was in prison or dead by June 1993, the remainder could do little else than follow these instructions from their great leader. (The Central Committee had been reorganized by December of 1992 and had reaffirmed its loyalty to Guzman.) But the old strategy into which they were now locked was not working. Even the activists at the universities wanted a moratorium on bombings, which were, they felt, fostering more resentment than fear. They wanted to work up a new strategy. But this was impossible in the wake of Guzman's injunction. *Sendero* strikes failed when emboldened peasants organized against the guerrillas in the highlands and the movement began losing people faster than it could replace them. (*Sendero* began attacking prisons to liberate old cadres and kidnapping people to force them into the movement.) At the same time, the government offensives were becoming more effective.

So the human rights movement had been proved wrong in their contention that nothing important could be done about *Sendero* without addressing the human rights shortcomings of the Fujimori government. On the contrary, nothing much could be done to improve the human rights behavior of a government under siege by the *Sendero*.

Our effort to hasten the capture of Guzman was thoroughly vindicated. By August 1996 his arrest had, indeed, made it possible to improve civil liberties substantially. *The Washington Post* reported, "Despite some recent bomb attacks, Shining Path and Tupac Amaru [another revolutionary group] are now greatly weakened, and many here argue that it is time to revamp the anti-terrorism statutes."[472]

But did the United States help in his capture and, if so, how did the policy change? I heard that inside the government, the State Department was taking credit for having mobilized the U.S. intelligence community to take action—exactly what I had worked to do and, indeed, had prodded State to do (and, at one stage, vice versa). Later I wrote a White House official a polite, short note thanking him and the government for anything the United States might have done to help to capture Guzman. I received his reply in the mail. It read, "We did a lot." So evidently, the United States did help.

And what of the rule precluding U.S. government employees— or persons working on their behalf—from engaging in, or conspiring to engage in, assassination?[473] How were fears about this finessed? While writing this book, I learned that under the rule, as interpreted by the Department of Defense, those providing the information have an obligation to ensure that the information will not be used wrongly. In a case like this, the policy would probably require assurances that the arresting officers would not kill Guzman—as, indeed, they did not. The CIA may not have had equally developed "regulations" interpreting the rule but probably felt the same way. Furthermore, I have been advised that this entire episode was written up, inside the government, as a "classic case in which things were done correctly."

It could be termed a success only if American intelligence helped to secure the capture of Guzman. But it could be termed a classic case in which things were done correctly, I believe, only if the United States had asked for assurances against the assassination of Guzman, received them, then helped the Peruvians and then found Guzman safely captured. Whether this is true or not, the press will undoubtedly determine in the aftermath of the publication of this book. (In the meantime, as this book goes to press, I believe I have learned the [low-tech] method which the CIA funded and by which Guzman was captured but I have not been able to confirm it.)

PART **X**

New Concepts for the Peaceful
Resolution of Two Territorial Disputes

CHAPTER **27**

Yugoslavia: The Renting of Kosovo

In an effort to make a contribution to resolving the conflict in Yugoslavia, two visits are made to Kosovo. A "realtor" type of interim solution is designed, which, having a certain logic to it, seems a possible part of a future solution. It constitutes a new approach, competing with three existing approaches: redrawing borders, partition, and UN trusteeship.

On December 5, 1992, at our FAS annual council meeting, I was authorized to look into the issue of war and peace in Yugoslavia. I found and photocopied a clipping file on the issue and began reading two back years of news analysis from *The New York Times* and *The Washington Post*. Subsequently, I lunched with Robert Adams and Paul Warnke to explore their views, gained their support for a "lift of the siege of Sarajevo" idea, and petitioned William Colby for support.

Bill and I began collaborating on an op-ed piece. Like some others, we believed that "unless the siege of Sarajevo is broken by outside force, the Serbs will complete the seizure of most of Bosnia and then move on to the 'cleansing' of the autonomous province of Kosovo."[474] Bill felt that a failure to "face down Serbs engaged in such obvious war crimes would demoralize the West" and be reminiscent of the failure of the League of Nations to meet the challenges of Germany and Japan. We inveighed against "closet Chamberlains" hiding behind "worst-case analyses." *The Washington Post* printed our article one week before the inauguration of Bill Clinton, and the issue became, we later heard, the number-one issue on the agenda of the National Security Council. The timing could not have been better.

I decided to make a trip to the region. As with all important projects, I did not wait for funding. But so many people were working on Sarajevo and Bosnia that I decided to look into the problems of a war spilling over into Macedonia and Kosovo.

Under their World War II hero Josip Broz Tito, Yugoslavia developed the world's most complicated constitution. It was a federal system with six subordinate "republics"—Serbia, Slovenia, Croatia, Macedonia, Montenegro, and Bosnia. And Serbia itself had two autonomous provinces, one of which was Kosovo, with a population almost 95 percent ethnic Albanian rather than Serb.

In fact, the constitution was so complicated that it worked only because Tito was able to settle any conflicts by personal fiat. After his death the whole tangled fabric began to unravel. Slovenia, Croatia, and Macedonia seceded in quick succession. Full-scale war broke out over the secession of Bosnia. Yugoslavia was reduced to Serbia and the tiny republic of Montenegro.

Ethnic Albanians inhabited not only Albania but also the western parts of Macedonia and Serbia. As the Jews in Israel have expressed fears about the population growth rate of the Palestinians, so did the Serbs fear that the Albanians were "making love, not war." Also mirroring the attitudes of the Jews in the Middle East was the Serbs' view of land in Kosovo as having great historical significance—in this case as the site of their greatest battlefields against the Ottoman Turks. In Kosovo, 200,000 Serbs were repressing 2,000,000 Albanians, who had declared, a few years earlier, that they had formed an independent state. Only Albania came close to recognizing them.

Because of international sanctions, international flights were forbidden from entering Yugoslavia. So I traveled to Kosovo via Skopje, the capital of Macedonia. There I met with Macedonia's president, Koro Gligorov.[475] He was statesmanlike and thoughtful, grappling with his own problems: Greece was blockading the land-locked Macedonia for its temerity in using a name that Greece claimed. And he also had problems like those the Serbs had in

Kosovo with a rapidly growing ethnic Albanian population that had separatist tendencies. Without Gligorov, I thought, Macedonia might now be engaged in a civil war; he seemed almost forty years older than those who would replace him and, as many other Yugoslav-trained diplomats of the Tito era, far more civilized and constructive. But the whole country still seemed to be walking on eggs.

In Skopje, I was advised that it was too dangerous to go to Pristina, the capital of Kosovo—another visitor there had been arrested, detained, and told to get out of town because "something" was about to happen. I decided to persist. The drive from Skopje to Pristina takes about ninety minutes; at the border the Serb guard studied my papers and, to my relief, waved me through. My main fear was coming home empty-handed.

In Pristina I met with the leader of the Albanians, Ibrahim Rugova. Rugova was a French-trained intellectual and poet and a "realistic pacifist." The Albanians considered it characteristic of the 1,500-year struggle between the incoming Slavs and the earlier-arriving Albanians (Illyrians) that the Albanians were led by a poet and the Serbs by men of far more brutal temperament. The Albanians advised me that when the Slavs arrived in the sixth century, they were "killing machines" and without culture.

While talking to Rugova, I thought of an approach, which, I told him, would combine my subject—mathematics—with his—poetry. In olden days in the region of China, for example, an ethnic group like the Albanians would have conceded the ultimate authority of a state too powerful to resist. But to preserve their autonomy, they would have paid tribute. Had there been any consideration given to "renting" Kosovo from the Serbs? The "rent" would have the effect of an interim concession that the area was Serbian and could replace the taxes now

The author with Ibrahim Rugova

being paid—this would, in theory at least, look good to the Serbs. And the resulting full autonomy would give the Albanians a long-term reprieve from present repression. After a fifty- or hundred-year lease expired, the whole situation might look very different.

He seemed interested—or perhaps he was the sort who treats everyone's ideas with great courtesy. I then went on by bus to Belgrade, where, by prearrangement, I met with an interesting former dissident under Tito, Mihailo Markovic. Markovic had struggled for an open-minded Marxism under Tito and an FAS member had tried to defend him from the repression he suffered at the hands of that regime. Markovic explained how Tito had tried to give Kosovo to Albania to prevent just such future troubles, but the most he had been able to do—because of Stalin, I think—was to make it a wholly autonomous part of Serbia. (This autonomy was annulled by Serbia when Kosovo began to demand the status of a republic inside Yugoslavia, presumably as a step toward outright independence.)

The current Serbian president, Slobodan Milosevic, once asked Markovic to be the largely ceremonial president of residual Yugoslavia (i.e., of the remaining federal union of Montenegro and Serbia). Although he rebuffed this offer, Markovic seemed to me to have the standing and basic attitudes that might make it possible for him to be a player in resolving the Kosovo problem.

On my return home, on March 21, I prepared the trip report for FAS members.[476] I wrote President Ibrahim Rugova a letter asking whether he would be prepared to meet with Professor Markovic for a "preliminary exploration of the possibility of [Markovic's] pursuing an investigation of the human rights complaints of ethnic Albanians in Kosovo," which Markovic said he would be willing to do if I convened the meeting.[477]

At the same time, with the help of a young lawyer hired for these purposes, Steven Rosenkrantz, we began working on a loophole in the U.S. law that denied entry to the United States for Nazi war criminals but said nothing about persons guilty of other war crimes and/or crimes against humanity. It would also facilitate deportation

of war criminals. Such laws, if adopted by all the industrialized states, would be a powerful threat to the freedom of travel and movement of war criminals like the leaders of the Bosnian Serbs.[478]

We also began investigating what could be done to help Radio Sarajevo broadcast beyond its city limits to Bosnia, perhaps through a rebroadcast from some offshore ship.[479] More generally, we designed and sought funding for a study of the following question: "Can modern communications and surrogate broadcasting be used to mitigate the pressures for ethnic cleansing?"[480]

On May 18 we hosted one of Rugova's advisers in Washington at a lunch for some Senate aides and, at this lunch, invited also an American scholar of Serb origins, who was an expert on the region. To my horror, the Albanian adviser was deeply offended that he had been maneuvered into a lunch with a "Serb"—even though this had been telegraphed earlier and the Serb was an American. It was a useful reminder of how difficult the situation was.

On June 2 we released a letter addressed jointly to President Slobodan Milosevic and President Ibrahim Rugova; in it we sketched the "rent" idea and offered to host a dialogue or proximity talks or to find an acceptable convener for such talks.[481] One day later, worried by rumors that incidents might be created in Kosovo by Serb forces more radical than Milosevic—and to his disadvantage—we faxed President Milosevic a letter suggesting that a UN peace force in Kosovo, "if invited by the Serbian government," would not prejudice Serbian claims and rights in Kosovo but might keep the lid on. (No doubt this got nowhere.)

As regards Kosovo, there seemed to be four possibilities for a peaceful solution. There was redrawing Yugoslavian borders, perhaps in the context of border changes in Bosnia and/or Croatia. (But this seemed unlikely because of the widespread antipathy of the international community to countenancing border changes. The international community is composed of states, all of which have borders. So all entities that vote on questions like these are biased against what they see as the threatening precedent of border changes.)

There was the possibility of a UN protectorate thrown over Kosovo. This was advocated by a group of Minnesota lawyers and was akin to what I had been thinking of in the context of Peru's decline.[482] It was wholly consistent with what the Kosovo Albanians wanted; indeed, on June 15 their prime minister, Bujar Bukoshi, called for establishment of a "United Nations Trust Territory of Kosovo."[483] (But there was considerable state resistance to the UN getting involved in such a thing, and it was considered by Serbia to be a first step toward independence for Kosovo.)

There was the possibility of partition. Various maps were circulating from different sides with different percentages of land allotted to the two sides and with the battlefields and monasteries mostly assigned to the Serb side. (The smart money assumed that this would be the solution.)

And there was the FAS idea of rent. On June 17 my wife and I were celebrating our wedding anniversary with our best man (of 1957), Sidney G. Winter, and his wife, the distinguished economist Alice Rivlin. I explained what I was up to and asked Alice how economists would organize such a "rent" idea, considering such matters as the value of resources mined and so on. She said, "Jeremy, you don't need an economist, you need a realtor." ♫

She was absolutely right. I went home and took out a realtor's lease and, transposing the ideas of home and hearth to the problem of Kosovo, found it rather easy to design an agreement. It would begin as follows:

> Whereas the Albanian citizens of Kosovo have not been able to resolve a dispute with the government of the Republic of Serbia over the governance of Kosovo and other related issues, the parties below, solely as an interim method of conflict resolution and without prejudice to their various underlying claims, do agree to moderate the dispute through the following agreement.

What would be leased would be "the right of full autonomy" in an area, which could be (a) Kosovo; (b) Kosovo minus key battle-

fields, monuments, and religious sites; or (c) Kosovo plus other Serb areas with majority Albanians but without specific parts of Kosovo that have Serb majorities. The term of the lease would be twenty-five, fifty, or one hundred years. The rent would be cost-of-living adjusted, and a realtor-analogy clause on the right of quiet enjoyment would here mean "full autonomy in organization and management of the demised area as if it were the government of a state within this area." Kosovo would agree not to "develop or maintain" armed forces capable of securing secession by force.

No laws would be passed that would discriminate against non-Albanian groups. The demised area would be "delivered" without deliberate acts of destruction. It could not be "encumbered," which meant that the Serbs would not be responsible for debts incurred by the Albanians. The parks, monuments, monasteries, religious memorials, and battlefields within the area would be kept in good condition, and free entry would be permitted to all wishing to visit them.

The "lessee" could not "commit waste" on the property (i.e., permanently impair the value of the land) but could harvest the resources. Full human rights would be guaranteed. And eminent domain would not be used to encourage minorities to relocate. Security would be maintained by the Albanians, but the Serbs would have the right to have guards on the borders, along with those of the Albanians, but persons and objects could enter subject to the conditions specified by the Albanians. There would be no discriminatory tariffs. Non-Yugoslavs (e.g., Albanians from Albania) could not become permanent residents. Kosovo could not represent itself as a sovereign state but could become an observer in international bodies where this was appropriate.

I also included clauses on "nonprejudice of claims" on arbitration and on "friendly guarantors." The latter two provided the possibility of having specific states nominated by the two sides, whose good offices and representation "should be sought in the event that subsequently necessary subsidiary agreements, necessary to maintain this leasehold, cannot otherwise be achieved."

I decided to return to the area, this time to visit Albania, where I thought help might be available to influence the Albanians in Kosovo. In a faxed letter of June 21, I sent the draft "lease" agreement on ahead to Rugova so that he could translate it and study it. I wrote, "My purpose is to advance this idea to the point where it may serve as a backup possibility for settlement if conditions warrant."

Albania, with its zillions of toadstool-like cement pillboxes, is an unearthly looking place, just recovering from unprecedented isolation from NATO, the Soviet Bloc, and even the Chinese. I had a meeting at the Foreign Ministry on July 2 and conferred with a parliamentarian on July 3. On July 4, I discovered, by chance, that Bujar Bukoshi, the prime minister of President Rugova's Republic of Kosovo, was in a guest house in Tirana. We had a long and fruitful discussion.

After a ten-hour bus ride from Albania to Macedonia, where I participated in several meetings, I spent two days in Pristina. The Albanians had translated everything, and we had a good discussion. The one portion of my lease they were unhappy with was one that I thought they would like: a clause that said part of the rent could be used for a "relocation" fund for persons who wanted to leave. This, they felt, would provoke Serb fears that they were being encouraged and funded to leave.

After some later discussions in Belgrade, I returned home to await a signal that there was sufficient interest on one side or the other to pursue something like this. A year or so later, I advised a representative of Kosovo that it would be easy to get the most senior interlocutors to help broker a settlement if there was any interest in trying. But the idea just waited for some kind of crisis or breakthrough.

In October 1994 Steve Rosenkrantz surprised me with a memo showing that Israel was applying similar concepts. Israel had signed a "sovereignty and lease-back agreement" with Jordan in which Israel returned 150 square miles of land seized in the 1948 war with a provision permitting Israel families to stay through a lease.[484] It had a number of terms similar to our own draft lease.[485]

He concluded that it showed the Kosovo lease concept was "on the cutting edge of conflict-resolution concepts and that such innovative concepts have real utility and relevance where both sides are seeking variable-sum, as opposed to zero-sum, solutions."

.   .   .

If ever agreed to, the rent would be taken by Serbs as a kind of tribute that they would accept as proof of their "ownership." But the Albanians would understand the same thing as a purchase of temporary autonomy. Of course, logic only takes one so far in the Balkans. The antagonisms between Serbs and Albanians are of such a nature that the very idea of a peaceful settlement seemed hilarious to some. And in 1998 the antagonism deepened with the emergence of an armed Albanian guerrilla force that strikes at Serbs and suffers massive retaliation on Albanian villages.

Withal, conditions change and leaders change, and the intractable might someday become tractable. In matters like these, there are only a few possible theoretical solutions. Every new theoretical possibility is of potential importance. And so, when the stakes are high, even the most outlandish ideas—so long as they are logical—ought be given thoughtful attention. There is always the possibility that "logic will out."[486]

In 1998, as the fighting in Kosovo raged between the Kosovo Liberation Army (KLA) and the Serbian forces, I reached Richard Holbrooke, Ambassador-Designate to the United Nations, who had authority to handle Kosovo, by phone. I told him of my "rent" plan, which was, in fact, a plan for autonomy for a limited period after which the problem would be discussed again. When he expressed skepticism about the plan ("Maybe too late for this"), I responded that our government was urging "autonomy plus" but had no idea what this phrase meant—and my idea was one such way. He promptly agreed and said, in fact, that he had a committee considering creative ideas for Kosovo and that I should fax it to him right away, which I did.[487]

On July 28, three weeks later, R. Jeffrey Smith reported in *The*

Washington Post, "Sources said Washington has already secretly conveyed to both sides the rough outlines of a deal to grant Kosovo provisional autonomy and decide years later whether the province will be granted outright independence." So in what may well be just a confluence of logic, the eventual outcome could turn out to follow some of the lines I was urging. (But by January 1999, the fighting had intensified and a peaceful solution of any kind was hard to envisage.)

CHAPTER **28**

A New Method for Reunifying China

Encouraged by a crisis to travel to Taiwan, a novel scheme is invented for reunifying China in a way that would achieve Taiwan's goals in cooperation with the People's Republic of China rather than over its resistance. Elements in the Taiwanese Foreign Ministry encourage the idea, which is deemed original by them and by a leading U.S. expert. China is briefed on it, but Taiwan, after some study, seems to discourage it.

On a Saturday evening, February 10, 1966, at a cabin on the Chesapeake, I received an unexpected call from Taiwan via call-forwarding from my home. It was Hsieh Shu-yuan, an American citizen of Taiwanese extraction who functioned as a defense-policy adviser to the Democratic Progressive Party (DPP) of Taiwan, the insurgent minority party that wanted independence from China. Because of her American citizenship, she was able, at a very early stage in Taiwan's relations with the mainland, to work in China. And in that capacity she befriended some very interesting Chinese scientists and introduced them to FAS. These scientists were, by 1996, the highest-ranking administrators of the Chinese equivalent of Los Alamos!

Shu-yuan appeared nervous about the threats then emanating from Beijing to engage in military maneuvers in the Taiwan Straits in the month before the March 23 election. "Did I think," she asked, "that America would come to the aid of Taiwan, if it were attacked? The people of Taiwan need reassurance!" 🔊

I had been giving very little thought to Taiwan's problem, but I knew enough not to answer this question directly and spontaneously. The DPP might simply be seeking a quotation that permitted them a release entitled "Scientists Assure Taiwanese That U.S. Will Defend Taiwan." And this, in the context of an election campaign, would help them argue that a vote for independence could be made in the secure assumption that China would not be permitted to invade Taiwan.

Saying I would call back, I decided to visit Taiwan as soon as possible to see what FAS might be able to do. It was, I advised our executive committee, the most dangerous hot spot of the moment; we owed it to ourselves to have a familiarization visit. █

I began reading everything I could find and talking to or visiting some experts. It seemed all but impossible to find a compromise between the avowed goals of the two political movements competing in Taiwan's upcoming presidential election: The ruling Kuomintang (KMT) party said it wanted eventual reunification with China, while the opposition DPP said it wanted eventual independence.

On the plane to Taiwan, I reflected that this was how it appeared in one dimension. But what if one viewed the goal of independence simply as a drive for "more space"? This was, after all, how Taipei's representative in Washington, Benjamin Lu (a KMT member), had described it to me a few days before. In this case, the two drives might not be inconsistent. What if one viewed the two goals as orthogonal in a plane rather than as opposed goals along a line? One might then imagine a strategy of trading off the reunification Beijing wanted for the more space Taiwan desired, with the resolvent of the two forces moving along some approximation of a 45-degree line in a kind of "northeast direction." (See Figure 1.)

FIGURE 1: *Northeast Strategy: A Failsafe Negotiating Process for Achieving Reunification of China Combined With An International Personality for Taiwan.* The points on both axes of this graph are purely illustrative. In reality, there would be many more points in both directions, and some of the current points would be subdivided. Each side might well put the points in a somewhat different order and, perhaps, have quite different points. All this would be subject to negotiation. The entire graph would not be agreed at the outset, but would develop over time. The purpose of the diagram is simply to illustrate how Taipei could stop trying to achieve international status over Beijing's opposition but try, instead, to do so in cooperation with Beijing in return for negotiated progress toward reunification.

Northeast Strategy: A Failsafe Negotiating Process for Achieving Reunification of China Combined With An International Personality for Taiwan

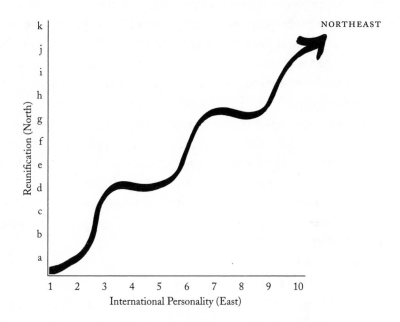

STEPS TOWARD
REUNIFICATION

ROC negotiates:

k. Bilateral Ratification of Reunification
    Constitution

j. Taiwan Plebescite Approves Constitution
    Principles

i. Agreement on Principles of Reunification

h. Agreement on the Non-Use of Force

g. Direct Political Negotiations begin

f. Summit Meeting

e. Bidirectional Exchanges of Officials

d. Bidirectional Exchange of Citizens

c. Relaxation of ROC Limits on Investment

b. Relaxation of ROC Limits on Imports

a. Direct Trade, Shipping, Mail, Air
    and Phone

STEPS TOWARD
INTERNATIONAL PERSONALITY

PRC withdraws opposition to:

1. Taiwan's officials visiting foreign countries
    in private capacity

2. Taiwan joining WTO

3. Taiwan joining IAEA

4. Taiwan having offices in various countries
    where they do not now exist

5. Taiwan joining World Bank

6. Taiwan joining IMF

7. Taiwan joining other subordinate
    U.N. bodies

8. Taiwan officials visiting foreign countries
    in an agreed official capacity

9. Taiwan joining U.N. as Observer

10. Taiwan joining U.N. General Assembly

Thus was born the notion of a "northeast strategy." One immediate corollary of it was that even the Taiwanese drive for membership in the UN—normally considered the quintessence of a two-China policy—could be accommodated by Beijing. Why? Because the UN membership could come at a time after reunification was achieved (i.e., at the top-right corner of the graph). In sum, there could even be *two* Chinese seats in the context of a *one*-China policy—if the timing was right; the USSR, after all, controlled three seats.

Hsieh Shu-yuan met my plane, and we discussed the election and its background. As the Communists were completing their successful overthrow of the Chinese government in 1949, the nationalist government of General Chiang Kai-shek—the Republic of China (ROC)—fled to the island security of Taiwan and awaited an invasion from the new mainland government, the People's Republic of China (PRC).

When the Korean War broke out in 1950 and the U.S. decided to intervene, President Truman used the U.S. fleet to bar an invasion from the mainland, thus saving the ROC remnants on Taiwan from being overwhelmed by the PRC.

General Chiang Kai-shek ruled Taiwan for decades—behind the shield of American might—still claiming to be the head of the government of China when he died in 1975. The mainlanders who came with him repressed the native Taiwanese and controlled the government and society. His son, Chiang Ching-kuo, replaced him and began to bring in some Taiwanese—without whom the government could not function, since the ethnic mainlanders were dying out. In particular, Chiang Ching-kuo had made a Taiwanese agricultural expert, Dr. Lee Teng-hui, vice president. A straight arrow who played the violin, Lee Teng-hui earned a Ph.D. in agricultural economics from Cornell; his dissertation won the annual award of the American Agricultural Economics Association. He was also a Christian who spoke Japanese fluently, having graduated from Kyoto Imperial University in 1946 at the age of twenty-three.

Lee Teng-hui turned out to be the Gorbachev of Taiwan. A

sleeper who had never challenged the ruling party, he could not be prevented from assuming power when Chiang Ching-kuo died. He began to outmaneuver the mainlanders, cleaning house in the manner of Gorbachev. In the words of Tien Hung-mao, the president of the Institute for National Policy Research in Taiwan, "In three rounds of power struggles and leadership reshuffling, Lee consolidated his power over the military, the party, and the government. In the process he has transformed the KMT from an authoritarian party with a revolutionary heritage to a democratic-type party with a strong indigenous character."

Now he was running in Taiwan's first popular election of a president, and as I arrived, the newspapers were reporting that he had been nominated for the Nobel Peace Prize for his political leadership.

At the DPP headquarters, I met Shih Ming-te, then DPP chairman, who had spent twenty-five years in KMT jails and was called the Nelson Mandela of Taiwan. He and his colleagues had sought Taiwanese independence at a time when General Chiang Kai-shek was claiming—as some still claim—that the Taiwanese-based forces were the legitimate government of all China, including Taiwan. Accordingly, they were imprisoned. From their point of view, mainland China had imposed only minimal control over Taiwan in the centuries before 1945. Major Chinese settlement in Taiwan occurred only after 1650, and Taiwan became a province of China only in 1886. In 1895, only nine years later, China ceded Taiwan to Japan. It was only following World War II, when the Allies ceded Taiwan to China, that Taiwan really became part of China. And what interaction they had with the mainland was not, from their point of view, favorable. Repressed by an invading mainland army for decades, they were now facing missile threats from Beijing. They considered themselves Taiwanese, not Chinese. And, as far as the Nobel Prize was concerned, they considered that it was they, not Lee Teng-hui, who had forced the democratization issue in Taiwan.

I began showing my sketch to various KMT public officials. To my amazement, one key analyst in the Foreign Ministry said, "You have opened our eyes to a new approach" and that the "past way of a parallel approach may not be so good and that, perhaps, the same goal could be achieved by cooperation rather than by conflict." This was exactly my view. Taiwan should stop trying to get "more space" over the dead body of the mainland and see how much it could get with the mainland's agreement. If its movement in the eastern direction came with PRC agreement, this movement could, by definition of the PRC, be part of a one-China policy and completely kosher. And the mainland would agree because it would get some kind of quid pro quo of movement in the northern direction.

Would the mainland buy such a policy? In a white paper, it had already declared that in a reunification agreement Taiwan would be permitted not only economic and cultural autonomy but also "certain rights in foreign affairs"—this was the open door to "more space." The mainland claimed it was prepared to discuss "all matters."[488]

Another key government official, of scientific inclinations, said immediately that this Northeast Strategy was "not only a way but the only way" to solve Taiwan's problems in view of the need to maintain a domestic consensus. And a key think-tank observer in Taiwan said it was "an ideal scenario for peaceful evolution."

This was unusual acceptance of a brand new idea. But was it just Chinese politeness? Upon returning home, I consulted with Ralph Clough, whom I considered to be America's greatest expert on Taiwan. I was then preparing a memorandum, at the request of the Taiwanese Foreign Ministry, on my idea. Clough said he could be quoted to them as saying that he "saw no major difficulties and thought the idea very interesting and clever and worth exploring." Of special interest to me was his inability to find more than the most minor and tacit precedents for the ROC and the PRC to trade off points in the two directions. (On reflection I thought this was because serious discussions of reunification were only just emerging as the Taiwanese completed the consolidation of their democratic process.)

I refrained from writing an article about this before the inaugural speech of President Lee Teng-hui on May 20. In case his government wanted to adopt such an approach, it seemed more discreet not to publish it in the Chinese press. However, a Chinese syndicate in Taipei got hold of the FAS newsletter and wrote a review of it that appeared in three related Chinese newspapers. It was surprisingly favorable: "None of these experts in Washington seems to know how to proceed to avoid conflicts and create a more favorable negotiation environment for Taiwan. One American scientist who is not known to the Taiwanese media proposed a bold strategy, the Northeast Strategy. . . . Compared to the impractical 'win-win situation' logo, the Northeast Strategy provides a new way of thinking for both sides who are willing to start peace talks."[489]

Needless to say, a "new way of thinking" was a very gratifying comment, and it seemed to confirm Clough's assessment of its originality. No less surprising was the reaction of the DPP. I had assumed that the DPP would reject this approach out of hand, so I had not sounded out their officials on the idea while I was in Taiwan. They, after all, did not want reunification. But I underestimated two factors. My Northeast Strategy graph had included, on the north axis, a rung labeled "plebiscite." The notion of a plebiscite was a key notion in DPP thinking. Their principled approach set great store in having the island vote on its future course. Also, the DPP was in favor of improving relations with the mainland—as all Taiwanese were. Hence the northern direction, to many of them, just represented "improvement in relations" capped by a plebiscite. As a consequence, the DPP was translating the newsletter and showing it to legislators.

On July 15, 1996, the Taiwanese Foreign Ministry sent me an unexpected letter saying that the theory had been "carefully reviewed by former minister Fredrick Chien and concerned heads of departments in the ministry with much admiration for your foresight." It asked me to work with a former ambassador and senior adviser to the Ministry of Foreign Affairs in developing the idea.

Meanwhile, I prepared to go to China to discuss it with the mainland. In the fall of 1996, I attended an arms control meeting in the area of the atomic weapons laboratory of the Chinese in Chengdu, Sichuan, near the base of the Tibetan mountains. It was here that the Chinese moved their atomic weapons program after a scare in the seventies during which the Soviets were rumored to have asked the United States whether we would mind if they bombed the Chinese nuclear facility, then in Manchuria. On returning to Beijing, I seized the occasion to discuss the Northeast Strategy at five places—all seemed receptive.

At the China Institute of Contemporary International Relations (CICIR), the Northeast Strategy was deemed, by one key participant, as "discussable" and "very constructive." At a dinner with the head of the Beijing Institute of Strategic Studies, the idea of "step-by-step" negotiations was called the "only way," and no objection was heard to the Northeast Strategy. At the Foundation for International and Strategic Studies, the idea was called "very constructive" and an official said it was surprising that a "new idea could be achieved by a mathematical insight." The Institute for Taiwan Studies of the Chinese Academy of Social Sciences was sufficiently interested in the idea that it secured for me an appointment with the very high-placed Taiwan Affairs Office of the State Council.

There I was taken to an elegant lunch in a beautiful guest house where, ordinarily, Taiwanese guests are wined and dined but where, I was told, theretofore, no American had been received. The idea was again deemed constructive, and study was promised.

The former Taiwanese ambassador with whom I was encouraged to stay in contact was Bernard T. K. Joei, now retired from diplomacy but still influential as a columnist for *The China Post* (Taipei). On returning to the United States, I wrote to him to encourage him to devote a column to this idea. Two months later he did so.[490] The good news in the column, entitled "The 'Northeast' Reunification Plan," was in the first paragraph: "Recently there has been a great deal of talk among local scholars and officials about the 'Northeast Strategy,' a method devised by the head of a group of American scholars for Taipei to work out its differences with Beijing."

Apparently, it had been studied! On the other hand, the bad news was that Ambassador Joei felt free to attack it roundly. He concluded that the "core of the issue" was that the people of Taiwan were seeking "primarily security and prosperity, not merely decent status in the international community." I took the whole incident as a sign that the Taiwanese Foreign Ministry had decided—or been instructed by the president—to dump cold water on the scheme.[491]

But ideas like this one do not die, because they embody an underlying logic that cannot be fully ignored. These are ideas that exist in nature, so to speak, "discovered" ideas rather than "invented" ideas and others rediscover them independently later, if not earlier also.[492] When the time is right, the two sides will certainly negotiate "northeast" tradeoffs. The thorough implementation of the Northeast Strategy probably hinges on the attainment of sufficient prosperity and freedom in the PRC to assure the Taiwanese that they would not be joined to a poorer and less democratic country.

How was it possible that a person who was not an "area" expert could come up with an untried plan for reunifying China—one sufficiently new to generate a "great deal of discussion" in Taiwan? In retrospect, it all turned on the timing. Under the first two presidents of Taiwan, Chiang Kai-shek and his son, no one was considering ways of reunifying China through cooperation; on the contrary, the fashion then was to daydream of recapturing the mainland.

In recent years, the emphasis had changed to competing with the mainland in other ways, first economically and then through developing a free society. But the accent has remained on competition and internal political development. My visit came on the eve of the consolidation of democracy in Taiwan, the first election of a president.

This consolidation provided the Taiwanese authorities with the opportunity to consider new approaches to their relations with the mainland. My arrival, through the happenstance of Hsieh Shu-yuan's call, had come at exactly the right time to have this idea seriously, if temporarily, considered.

CHAPTER 29

Unfinished Business:
Atomic Espionage in World War II

A famous living atomic spy of half a century ago is located and the problem arises of what to do about it. This chapter is designed to be part of the solution.

I suppose it all started with the publication, in the spring of 1994, of *Special Tasks*, the memoir of the Soviet KGB spymaster Pavel Sudoplatov; the volume, written with his son, Anatoli, and two American coauthors, Jerrold and Leona Schecter, accused the most famous atomic physicists of the period of the World War II Manhattan Project—Robert Oppenheimer, Enrico Fermi, Leo Szilard, and Niels Bohr—of having "knowingly cooperated" with Soviet espionage to help the Soviet Union (then in a wartime alliance with the United States) to enable them to make progress on an atomic bomb.

Sudoplatov, who died in September 1996, was a highly placed KGB official during the war. From 1939 to early 1942, he seems to have run a special section of the foreign intelligence division that handled "wet affairs": murder, terrorism, sabotage. From 1942 to 1944, he headed the Fourth Directorate of the NKVD, which directed the partisan guerilla operations, including terrorism and sabotage behind German lines. He claimed that Beria made him "director of intelligence" for the Special Committee on the Atom Bomb, though others say that this committee was not formed until August 1945.[493]

In any case, only two sentences in the Sudoplatov book made the allegations against the three Americans. The charge was that

Oppenheimer, Fermi, and Szilard "helped us plant moles in Tennessee, Los Alamos, and Chicago as assistants in those three labs" and that these moles "copied vital documents to which they were allowed access by Oppenheimer, Fermi and Szilard, who were knowingly part of the scheme."[494]

None of these charges could be substantiated, and they were implausible on many grounds, including these simple facts: Oppenheimer was carefully watched, Fermi was a staunch anticommunist, and Szilard was not, as alleged, at Los Alamos. (The Bohr allegations involved a meeting that was wholly watched by Allied intelligence at Bohr's request!) In the end, even *Time* magazine, which initially excerpted the chapter without critical comment, admitted that the critics made a "troubling case" and said the chapter had been "assailed by critics right and left, scientists and historians, American and Russian." The new post–Cold War Soviet intelligence agency, which had full access to the files of the NKVD and the KGB, denounced the book as a "mosaic of truthful events, semi-truths and open inventions." It said that Sudoplatov had "access to atomic problems during a relatively brief period of time, a mere 12 months from September 1945 to October 1946" and that his department "had no direct contact with the agents' network."

I began following this controversy very closely—after all, it involved the original atomic scientists, and FAS was the child of their sense of responsibility. And I daresay my May/June 1994 FAS *Public Interest Report*, entitled "Atomic Spies: The Implosion of the Sudoplatov Charges," became the best summary of the controversy.

But, if those distinguished scientists were not the culprits, then who? In the week of June 20, I recalled and dug up an article from the October 4, 1992, *Washington Post* about a living American spy code-named Perseus. In the next week we unearthed, in the Library of Congress, the Soviet (English-language) journal *New Times* from which the *Post* reporter, Michael Dobbs, had gotten his information about Perseus.

On reading this article, I thought I realized who Perseus was because the article quoted a paragraph that Perseus had uttered, fifty years before, to his recruiting KGB officer. And, despite the fact that this paragraph had been translated into Russian and back into English and then modified at least slightly, there was a statement and a turn of phrase that seemed to me to identify the speaker like a thumbprint.

In the *New Times* article, Perseus claimed to have been offered "material support" and said:

> Oh no, for God's sake. I'm willing to cooperate with them for a cause, not for money. I want to dedicate my life to averting the danger of a nuclear holocaust looming over mankind, because I have just realized how real the threat of such a holocaust is, and this prompted me to counter it in the ranks of the Soviet intelligence service.[495]

Any original atomic scientist who would say that he would "dedicate my life to averting the danger of a nuclear holocaust" would be among FAS's original members, since FAS was set up by the original atomic scientists to do just that and was, indeed, the first organization created for this purpose. If, indeed, such a scientist were still living, then the phrase "dedicate my life" would suggest that he would be helping us still.

In addition, I knew quite well the atomic scientists of conscience who were part of our organization. I had been, after all, their steward for almost a quarter century. I often knew their intellectual physiognomy, better than my brother's. And the third sentence had a formulation, combined with a point of view, that was again as far as I was concerned unmistakable.

Perseus's words were "counter it in the ranks of the Soviet intelligence service." This was the idiom of a scientist who looked at human society in a mechanistic way, as if it were a giant gadget that cried out for appropriate manipulation. I knew only one original atomic scientist whom I could hear, in my mind's ear, expressing himself in that way.

But this was not, of course, evidence. What to do?

I decided to go right to the top of the community of atomic scientists to discuss the general problem of atomic spies. Hans Bethe was a Nobel Prize winner and, as head of the Theoretical Division at Los Alamos, the right-hand man to Robert Oppenheimer. And in the scientific community he was a champion of everything FAS has stood for since 1945. Most important, he was renowned and loved for his decency and integrity. Surely he was the first with whom to discuss this problem.

I had other reasons to visit Ithaca and, in any case, had been regularly consulting with Hans, a sponsor of FAS, about the Sudoplatov case. So there was no problem in justifying a visit without describing my precise concern.

We talked for about six hours about the general situation, including the issue of Alfred Sarant, a Cornell graduate student of physics who had defected to Russia. I read Hans the Perseus "recruiting" exchange without comment. He did not volunteer that it sounded like anyone he knew. And I did not disclose my suspicions.

During a break, when Hans left the room, I had a brainstorm. Since Perseus (and all the other spies of that period) were acting on ideological grounds—and indeed, in their minds, idealistic grounds—not financial ones, why not just invite them to come clean, perhaps after getting suitable assurances from the Justice Department that they would no longer be prosecuted. And since these atomic spies—assuming they were acting out of fear of nuclear war—presumably read our newsletter and/or the *Bulletin of the Atomic Scientists*, an advertisement of this kind might be seen.

Hans agreed that this might be put in the newsletter but "not in too large type." Although he did not say so, I felt he was not keen on having this whole issue of atomic spying raised anew—which was understandable, since this topic is an embarrassment to the scientific community (no doubt some scientists will criticize me for putting this chapter in this book).

Scientist X

Later, in another city, I called on the scientist whom I will call Scientist X—the man I thought was Perseus or, if Perseus was a KGB composite, then part of that composite. I did not confront X with my suspicion but simply began—in the context of my Sudoplatov investigation in the current newsletter—by sharing some of the facts I had learned about Word War II espionage, including the information in the *New Times* article.

As I read and shared this information, he became visibly frightened. (My wife was with me, and her assessment, later, was that his knees were knocking. His wife told B.J. in an aside, "Nothing good will come of this [investigation]." I felt this was intended to warn me off.)

We parted as friends. And I continued talking to a number of the other original atomic scientists (when I could find them) and to a number of people who had reason to be well informed. In particular, I located a Soviet émigré, Dr. Mark Kuchment, formerly of Harvard's Russian Research Center. It was Kuchment who uncovered the fact that a defecting electrical engineer from Cornell, Alfred Sarant, a friend of the atomic spy Julius Rosenberg, had been living in the Soviet Union as Professor Filip Staros until his death in 1979.[496] Asked about the *New Times* article by Chikov, Kuchment said it was either an "indiscretion" or a piece of "disinformation."

The word "indiscretion" hit me like a shock. It was, indeed, indiscreet because it reopened the question of atomic spying. What's more, the KGB had made a mistake. Despite KGB efforts to protect its source, the KGB had left in enough to identify X at least to someone, namely me. (And the notion that the article was "disinformation" seemed clearly wrong because there seemed little disinforming about it and the KGB motive of boosting its reputation seemed clear.)

The article in question—"How the Soviet Intelligence Service

'Split' the American Atom"—was, in fact, a puff piece about a couple, Morris Cohen and Lona Cohen. Its author, Colonel Vladimir Matveyevich Chikov, was a senior officer of the KGB Public Relations Centre. Its obvious purpose was to show that the KGB—not the Soviet atomic scientists—had been the ones who should get the credit for the Soviet atomic bomb.

In the process of lauding the Cohens—who later served Soviet intelligence in Britain as Peter and Helen Kroger—the article recounted the story of how Morris Cohen had recruited Perseus. The KGB had decided to reveal, for the first time, the highly secret recruiting conversation in a file whose notations showed, Chikov said, that it had been seen only by six persons in fifty-five years.

The KGB had obviously doctored the recruiting conversation to protect Perseus because it had an anachronistic reference—Perseus refers to the Pentagon in 1942, before it had been built!

Perseus had been asked by Cohen why he had decided to hand over secret information on the atomic bomb to another country. His response was:

> I am convinced that America's military quarters have cheated nuclear physicists into developing the atomic bomb by telling them that the bomb was intended to save mankind from the danger of Nazism which had engulfed Europe. As a matter of fact, the Pentagon [sic] is of the opinion that it will be quite some time before the Soviet Union harnesses atomic energy. This will take your country decades, it thinks, and in the meantime America will destroy socialism by means of the uranium bomb.

The KGB substituted "the Pentagon" for the *exact* reference made by Perseus lest it tip his identity by revealing his source of information. But Colonel Chikov, or whoever made this substitution for him, did not know, or had forgotten, that the Pentagon was built after the war. I felt sure that the original conversation referred not to the as yet unbuilt "Pentagon" but to "General Groves," head of the Manhattan Project that built the atomic bomb.

Perseus does refer once, in the quoted conversation, to General
Groves. When asked about the "technique of seeing each other," he
says, "I am not supposed to leave Los Alamos without Groves' permission, and Groves has to report my departures to the FBI. . . .
We can be seeing each other not oftener than once a year, while I
am on leave."[497]

Did Perseus have some special relationship to General Groves that
required him to report to Groves—with Groves reporting to the
FBI? It began to make even more sense to me as I learned more about
X and his World War II experience. At one time, he had an office next
door to General Groves. And why the special arrangement with
Groves regarding departures from Los Alamos? This could be
explained by X's left-wing background, which would, inevitably,
produce suspicions requiring a special dispensation, which would, in
turn, suggest a special security arrangement. Or it could simply be
because he worked, or had worked, for General Groves.

Moreover, Groves was just the kind of person whose offhand
comments could easily alarm a young, very left-wing scientist into
believing that America might "nuke" the Soviets. Groves had very
conservative views and was very senior and hence authoritative.

Joseph Rotblat, a British atomic scientist and recent Nobel Peace
Prize winner, had written that General Groves had told him the real
purpose in making the bomb was to subdue the Soviets.[498] Such
talks might have alarmed a young scientist, who might then have concluded—now I put General Groves in place of "the Pentagon"—that
"as a matter of fact, [General Groves] is of the opinion that it will be
quite some time before the Soviet Union harnesses atomic energy.
This will take your country decades, [he] thinks, and in the meantime
America will destroy socialism by means of the uranium bomb."

Indeed, Morris Cohen's response to this observation of Perseus's
was to refer to Groves as if they were talking about Groves rather
than the Pentagon in the original transcript: "I agree with you that
the possession of the atomic bomb will be a strong temptation for
generals like Groves."[499]

Cohen and Perseus then decided that meeting only on scheduled vacations would not do. Perseus proposed that "we can meet in the small neighboring town of Albuquerque. It is a famous health resort, and you can go there under the pretense of needing medical treatment."[500]

Following the thought I had in Bethe's office, I decided to run an advertisement in the FAS *PIR* for people to come forward. But what would it say? Atomic spies were unlikely to come forward if the result were sure to be drastic and certain punishment.

For advice, I called the Justice Department and asked to talk to whoever was in charge of espionage. The head of internal security called, and we discussed the matter on July 5. Espionage, he said, "had no statute of limitations." In fact, there was a special law that turned the crime committed by the Rosenbergs—spying for an ally, which Russia was during World War II—into a capital offense. He said, "Would you want us, the Justice Department, not to pursue murders just because the crime was over fifty years old?" We agreed that Vietnam-era draft dodgers had received an amnesty. But we recognized that amnesty for atomic spies seemed less likely.

Manhattan Project Security

On July 6 I drove sixty minutes out of town to see the man who had headed security for the Manhattan Project, Colonel John J. Lansdale. I used my newsletter on Sudoplatov, which he had read and for which he had expressed admiration, as a calling card. Lansdale, a very honorable man, had testified in support of Oppenheimer at the Oppenheimer hearings and had thereby destroyed his own career.

He confirmed that General Groves thought it would take the Russians a long time to build the atomic bomb because "we didn't think the Soviets had the industrial capacity"—this supported my supposition that General Groves was "the Pentagon" in Perseus's conversation. He remembered X as having been in the Communist Party and said, "Didn't we ease him off the project?" But he wasn't sure.

In fact, it was Lansdale, trained as a lawyer and put in charge of security by General Groves, who "cleared" Oppenheimer. He interrogated Oppenheimer and his wife twice. She, especially, was one of the security community's concerns. But she said, "This is Oppie's big chance, and we're not going to screw it up." He had been persuaded that the Oppenheimers were sincere and had acquiesced in Oppenheimer's being chosen as director.[501]

In those days, as the atomic scientist Robert Serber explained to me later in New York, people were hired first and cleared later—there was, after all, a war on. People who had Communist backgrounds were not necessarily let go. They were, instead, given special scrutiny. (This seemed to me to support the speculation that Perseus's recruiting conversation referred to a special security arrangement.) For example, David Hawkins, a close assistant to Oppenheimer, had been in the Communist Party, and he had been permitted to continue.

I realized also, from later reading, that X also had been a member of the Communist Party and had made no secret of it in earlier times. This could explain why, if X were Perseus, he expressed the concern for socialism by saying that "America will destroy socialism by means of the uranium bomb." Or perhaps X, like Perseus, was just trying to prevent nuclear war.

On July 7, in the early morning hours, I began examining the Sudoplatov book to see if anything in it might bear on this matter. According to Sudoplatov, the material that reached the spy-ring leader, Anatoli Yatskov, came from "Fuchs and one of the Los Alamos moles" and was carried by couriers, "one of whom was Lona Cohen."[502]

Since Harry Gold was the courier for the atomic spy Klaus Fuchs, Lona Cohen was not helping Fuchs but presumably was the courier for Perseus—as would be natural if Perseus had been recruited by her husband. These circumstances also indicate that Lona explained her trips by saying that she was going to a TB sanitarium, a tack that is consistent with the suggestion by Perseus that Albuquerque be justified as a site for health cures.[503]

Advice from a Unique Source: William E. Colby

On that same morning, from 8:30 A.M. to 11:00 A.M., I met with William Colby in his downstairs parlor. I felt things had reached the point where I needed real legal advice and in particular the advice of a lawyer on matters concerning espionage. Who could do this better than my good friend, the lawyer and ex-CIA chief? I told him that I had something so serious to discuss that I wondered if I could retain him as a lawyer and get the benefits of attorney-client privilege.

Since we were friends, I knew better than to offer more than a token and offered him a hundred-dollar bill. He agreed and took the bill. (Some weeks later, he commented wryly on how hard it was to register a "bill" as opposed to a check with his firm.)

As I began to describe the situation, he said, "Don't tell me the name of the person." Otherwise, he listened to a pretty full account. His conclusion was that under American law I had no obligation to come forward. What I had was not "evidence" in strict legal terms, and even knowledge of a crime does not require persons to come forward. But if asked by suitable law enforcement to tell what I knew, I would, of course, have to comply fully and truthfully.[504]

Bill wondered whether I should forget about it. Wouldn't the disclosure and resultant flap wreck my career? He was beginning to give me the kind of avuncular advice that good lawyers give clients. But I interrupted. I said that it was not something that I could, in good conscience, leave alone. The truth should come out, and some way should be found to achieve it. (His reaction to this was that, if I wanted, I could just discuss this in private with a reporter. [Later, reading his autobiography, I learned that he had lived through a quite similar situation as director of the CIA on learning of inappropriate behavior there. His reactions had been quite similar to mine; in order to get the truth out, he had taken measures that required his former superior, Richard Helms, to face charges.])

By this time I knew well why the statute of limitations for most crimes existed (memories fade, evidence is lost, witnesses die). And it was pretty clear that the Justice Department, even if reminded of this problem and informed of everything I knew, was not likely to be able to persuade a jury beyond a reasonable doubt that someone had been a spy half a century ago—especially if the punishment was likely to be severe. Accordingly, it was not likely to indict X or any-one else. So the urgency and purpose of telling the authorities was undermined by this reflection; moreover, I was interested in truth, not punishment. (Later, on July 15, Colonel Lansdale volunteered that the administration would never pursue a case like this at this late date, confirming my view.)

Continuing with the *PIR*

The next day the July/August *Bulletin of the Atomic Scientists* had an interesting article by an *Izvestia* correspondent, Sergei Leskov, who reported on the reaction of younger KGB officials to Sudopla-tov's disclosure. They denied the truth of Sudoplatov's accusations against the big "four" atomic scientists but said that aside from Fuchs, they had gotten help from six other such agents in America and four in Britain.

As this record shows, I was already keeping daily notes of what was transpiring, with a few key things deleted in case the whole thing was lost or read by someone else without permission. And the log shows that, on Monday morning, I had an idea.

The Justice Department was not strong enough, politically, to recommend amnesty for truth. Even the president was not. But a committee of Congress could, and might, give immunity in return for the full and complete truth. And if the Justice Department were asked by the congressional committee whether it objected, the Justice Department would not object because it would have so little chance of a successful prosecution.[505] Moreover, the executive branch had some interest in the truth; after all, the intelligence community always wants to know what really happened in past events of this kind. (A few weeks later it even occurred to me that the committee would have, or could have, as its purpose, clearing the Sudoplatov four—Oppenheimer, Fermi, Szilard, and Bohr—by hearing the truth from a real spy!)

Colby thought this idea was interesting and less academic than my first thought of just asking people to come forward. Most important, he felt it would not do the world an injustice if such a scientist got immunity to tell his story. I immediately began delicate discussions with a high-ranking officer of the Senate who understood the immunity statute, in an effort to learn how the system really worked. Another lawyer I respected with very relevant congressional experience thought the idea was "brilliant," so I began considering it further and pondering various subcommittees.

On July 13 I returned to visit X for about three hours and discussed many relevant things about his past experience in World War II. I mentioned the immunity possibility in the context of my expressed interest in getting the truth out about Perseus. He actually tried to argue against my suggestion of advertising for Perseus to come forward. It was, I think, clear what I wanted. And his wife was very clearly refusing to let us converse alone.

At one point, I told an anecdote of two friends in China awaiting the final capture of Beijing by the armies of Mao Zedong. One friend, a Communist, knows full well what will happen to the other, a non-communist, when Beijing becomes "red." The Communist knows his friend is a person of integrity and that he cannot be persuaded to pretend to be a Communist by outright appeals to self-interest. But he wants him to come in out of the cold. Accordingly, he engages in a dialogue, over a number of visits, urging his friend to consider the benefits of ideological conversion and trying to help him change his spots.

X thought this amusing. I considered it pretty relevant—a kind of political mirror image of our situation and an example of two friends discussing something without admitting to each other what that something was.

I also explained how someone (e.g., a lawyer or a reporter) could defend Perseus—if he existed—who seemed, after all, trying to prevent nuclear war by jump-starting a balance of terror. Even Bertrand Russell, an arch pacifist, once toyed with the idea of preventive war to prevent the Russians from getting so strong with nuclear weapons that the inevitable war would destroy mankind. X thought this view too intellectual.

Finally, I asked if I could talk to him alone. At this point his wife began carrying on, crying and pointing at him in a clear indication that he was "the one" we were discussing—but without an admission. He said nothing. She suggested I reach a "tacit agreement" with him, saying, "He is good at tacit agreements." It was all too obvious.

And I remembered that, when the first Dobbs article in *The Washington Post* appeared, I had called X to discuss it. She had gotten on the phone, an unusual occurrence, and started answering for him how, she thought, the whole thing could be explained. She was then, as now, afraid that a direct question would be put and that he, a scientist, would not know how to handle it.

I left with nothing being said and, no doubt, they both hoped that a tacit agreement had been reached. But I was still thinking about what to do.

On July 14 an informed source told me that X had been petrified by Groves and used to shake in his shoes while Groves chewed people out. On July 16 Herbert F. York told me that Groves was "apocalyptic and anti-Soviet"; the historian Stanley Goldberg said that Groves was, indeed, very apocalyptic. Had he ever said that we should "nuke them," the earlier the better? Goldberg said, "Yes." This was reason enough to persuade a young idealistic left-wing scientist assisting Groves to believe that the way to "counter"

nuclear war would be "in the ranks of the Soviet intelligence service," as Perseus, in the recruiting conversation, had explained of his motives.

A Gentle Appeal to Reason

On July 18, two days later, I sent a two-page memo, "Atomic Spying: Getting at the Truth," to X providing my "mechanism and a theory" at which Perseus "if he exists, could come forward voluntarily, with dignity, and with immunity, to help defend the reputation of Oppenheimer."[506]

My letters to X—drafted on the assumption that they would be read by others at some possibly random time continued to avoid any charge. But the letter noted that the Perseus account in *New Times* "reflects a person trying to respond to the many concerns about strategic imbalance and preventive war from persons like Szilard and John von Neumann." And I observed that General Groves wrote in his memoir, *Now It Can Be Told*, "Not until each of the great powers had produced a full atomic arsenal would the threat of one-sided atomic war pass." So even General Groves, it could be argued, believed that a balance of terror was necessary to prevent "one-sided" nuclear war! The letter offered to help find a lawyer "if through you, or others, the Federation could locate a Perseus" who would come forward.

I was increasingly aware, by this time, that all the left-wingers who had helped the Soviets with atomic espionage during the war seemed to have had similar motivations. The book on the Rosenberg case by Louis Nizer shows the Rosenbergs trying to persuade Ruth Greenglass to acquiesce in spying. Julius Rosenberg said, "You see, Ruth, if all nations had the information, then one nation couldn't use the bomb as a threat against another." Ethel Rosenberg said, "David [Greenglass] has a chance to prevent a third world war. He can help create a balance of power to preserve peace; I think he will want to do this. Why don't you tell him about it and let him decide?"[507]

And later Greenglass decided that, indeed, "if the two great powers had the atomic bomb, they would offset each other. Perhaps this was the best road to peace." He agreed to provide information. In sum, in those days, when I was under ten years of age, the pro-Soviet left, more sympathetic to the USSR than others, and more suspicious of what U.S. "ruling circles" would do with an atomic bomb advantage, must often have felt that the road to peace was a balance of terror.

Others took the view that Fuchs described in his confession, when he said that "the Western Allies deliberately allowed Russia and Germany to fight each other to the death." The far left had its own view of things. And, indeed, there was support for this. Even then-senator Harry Truman had said, two days after Germany attacked Russia, "If we see that Germany is winning, we ought to help Russia, and if Russia is winning, we ought to help Germany, and that way let them kill as many as possible."

On July 19, I began thinking of a second newsletter, a sequel to the issue on Sudoplatov's memoir. And this turned into the July/August 1994 *PIR*, entitled "Conscience, Arrogation and the Atomic Scientist."

By this time, I thought I understood the meaning of the word "cheated" in Perseus's recruiting conversation, where he says, "America's military quarters have cheated nuclear physicists into developing the atomic bomb by telling them that the bomb was intended to save mankind from the danger of Nazism."

It meant that Perseus had figured out, in advance of the other scientists, that the Germans were not about to get the bomb. He knew something that was, in general, kept from Los Alamos lest the scientists stop work—that U.S. intelligence increasingly knew the Germans were not getting the bomb. And he knew it, if Perseus was X, because it was X's job for General Groves, to figure this out. X was engaged in "positive" intelligence (i.e., efforts to determine whether the Germans were getting the bomb). There was, after all, a gap of almost two years between those who were persuaded early, and those convinced late, about the German failure to build the bomb.[508]

The mobilization of scientists to work on the atomic bomb depended importantly on the threat that Hitler might get the bomb first. Without this threat, scientists would have been much less willing to work on a weapon of mass destruction. Since Los Alamos only started in March 1943, the British might have squelched the whole project, had they an interest in doing so, by insisting, in the summer of 1943, that there would be no German bomb. But they had no interest in insisting.

Nor did Groves want to hear any good news of this kind. In 1943, when Michael Perrin, the chief scientific adviser on nuclear matters for British intelligence, took General Groves aside and told him what the British thought, Groves said, "Well, you may be right, but I don't believe you."[509] Instead, General Groves, eager to keep his bomb program on track, took the line that until we "took into custody a number of the senior German scientists, we faced the definite possibility that Germany would produce a number of weapons before we could."[510] This condition meant waiting until the end of the war! And it gave credence to Perseus's reference to American physicists being "cheated" by exaggerated fears of a German bomb.[511]

On August 10, with the newsletter in page proofs, I consulted with a lawyer, now dead, recommended by Colby: it was Mitch Rogovin.[512] He agreed that atomic-scientist spies had a zero chance of being convicted at this stage.

With the newsletter in hand, on August 15 I went to Ithaca and, to my satisfaction, Hans Bethe liked it as did our then FAS secretary Ann Druyan and her husband, the late Carl Sagan. But I told them both that I would not answer direct questions about Perseus. And when Carl persisted, nevertheless, over lunch, in asking whether there was any evidence that Perseus existed that did not originate in Russia, I, forced to say something, misled him by saying, "You can take that line if you want." I did not want to discuss, at that time, the personal evidence that arose in tacitly confronting Scientist X.

(By July 11, 1996, with the release of the VENONA code-breaking material, we see that there was a Soviet spy nicknamed "Pers" who is still unidentified and appears to be Perseus. The National Security Agency refers to "the . . . still unidentified PERS.")[513]

On September 1, X called in response to a letter of August 24 in which I invited him to meet with "FAS's lawyer for Sudoplatov-related affairs" as a way of "orienting him" on such things as "the work you performed for General Groves and your experience during the war." He said he appreciated my letters and agreed to meet, only to call back a bit later to say that his wife objected and that he would respond later.

Nevertheless, the meeting was arranged on September 21 and X arrived. X briefed Rogovin and clearly liked him—and this bonding was the purpose of the meeting as far as I was concerned. Afterward, in the fifteen minutes between Rogovin's departure and X's, X addressed the question of hearings by scientists defending Oppenheimer. Couldn't scientists testify in defense of him and then, if senators accused one of them of being a spy, one could ask then for immunity with which to continue? (This seemed to me, then, to be impractical, since immunity requires a vote of the committee and, later, at least thirty days of waiting. But privately I took it as possibly meaning that he had no strong objection to coming forward if it were forced upon him.)

I decided to assemble the circumstantial evidence against X in an open letter that might get him to come forward. This letter of September 22 was not immediately answered. On October 19, 1994, I received a letter dated October 17 in which X completely denied any legal exposure and said he would expect FAS to defend him if, indeed, he were attacked. I felt my efforts had come to an end and was not sure what to do. But I had not given up.

Accordingly, when, in 1996, I decided to write this memoir, I decided to include a chapter on atomic spying and to reveal what I knew with a view, on publication, to continuing working, in this new atmosphere of interest generated by the book, on the effort to get out the truth.[514]

Of course, the failure of Perseus to come forward has made more complicated the effort to dismiss entirely the charges of Sudoplatov. And it has cast something of a pall over other atomic scientists. For example, Joseph Rotblat, who had the courage to quit the Los Alamos project when the war in Europe was over, was quizzed by *The New York Times* as to whether he was the missing spy. I believe things would become somewhat clearer if X were persuaded to testify, but, no doubt, this would require immunity.

In any case, my speculation to X that the public would understand his position, were it described, was, I felt, borne out in the subsequent release in 1977 of the book *Bombshell* about a similar spy named Ted Hall.[515]

I believe that truth heals all. As Mahatma Gandhi once put it in a postcard to a friend of his, "For me, the whole of philosophy is summed up in truth at any cost." And in this case, what cost is there to the truth? Since X's admissions will be valuable to history and cannot be secured without immunity, and since X cannot now be convicted, why not give him immunity and ascertain, among other things, his motives and whatever else he knows? Accordingly, this is the goal toward which he should work and toward which I intend to work on publication of this book.[516]

PART **XI**

Conclusion

CHAPTER 30

Making a Difference
in the Face of Temporal Inertia

One purpose of this memoir was to determine what did and did not work and why.

In the first place, almost everything herein achieved, except for some early work on the ABM, occurred only because of the base that FAS provided. Had I been at a university, with heavy teaching duties, or at one of the more prestigious, stodgy, think tanks, many of these adventures would have died aborning. Even some of the larger public interest groups would not have permitted or encouraged so much freewheeling activity. For entrepreneurial activists, making a difference requires one of the rarest qualities in modern life—autonomy.

But more is required. A vice president of the J. P. Morgan Bank in charge of venture capital once advised me, "People think that one can get rich with a good idea, but in fact, one needs financing and marketing." The same is true, to a degree, with the merchandising of the kinds of ideas an activist generates. With regard to financing, although I kept my salary constant in inflation-adjusted dollars throughout my tenure, and started at $20,000 per year in 1970, nevertheless, a summing of 33 percent for employee benefits and 50 percent (of salary plus benefits) for travel, telephone, computers, and so on, suggests that I cost the public interest funders and FAS members, over almost thirty years, about $5 million in today's dollars.

A great deal of my work, as with anyone's, achieved nothing special. Over the course of nearly three decades, I wrote more than 150 monthly newsletters on a wide variety of issues, each devoting about eight thousand words, on average, to a specific issue. During the first half of my three-decade FAS tenure, I functioned a bit like Robinson Crusoe, firing rifles from behind a stockade in such a way as to persuade the natives that there were more people inside than in fact there were.

Notwithstanding all the work that went into drafting the news-letters and circulating the editorials to the council and the experts, many of these newsletters had little or no discernible impact. Others were circulated by specially interested public interest groups happy to have a supportive discussion of their issue under the imprimatur of FAS. Most of these essays, like other forms of activism, con-tributed more to a general ferment than to a clearly definable result. Of course, from an organizational point of view, it was necessary to produce a product that could keep the federation members renew-ing their membership.

In reinvigorating FAS in 1970 and administering it since that time, I managed to provide a base that helped some others to carry out their own entrepreneurial activism. The staff expanded from one half-time person (me) with a half-time secretary to about a dozen full-time staff combined with a few senior activists working through us from their home institutions. Our key workers have included Steven Aftergood, David Albright, Deborah Bleviss, Michael Casper, Frank von Hippel, Thomas Longstreth, Lora Lumpe, Michael Mann, Christopher Paine, John E. Pike, and Bar-bara Rosenberg. Most, if not all, of these people made a real differ-ence in their fields—a number now run their own organizations. In 1986 *The Washington Post* called me a "Scientific Foreman in an 'Idea' Factory."[517] I'd like to think that some of these people actually learned something from this foreman, directly or by example. So administration of these entrepreneurs is a way of making a differ-ence, albeit at a remove. The dozen FAS chairmen or FAS Fund chairmen who helped supervise the operation were also helped to advance their works and their public personae through the letters and FAS proposals advanced over their signatures and with their help. The distinguished roster of chairmen includes, in order of service, Herbert F. York, Marvin L. Goldberger, Philip Morrison, Martin Stone (no relation), Jerome Frank, George Rathjens, Matthew Meselson, John Holdren, Frank von Hippel, Richard Garwin, Andrew Sessler, Robert Solow, and Carl Kaysen.

But neither newsletter publishers nor administrators normally get the pleasure of making an overt difference. One influential newsletter author and publisher, when asked what tangible effect he could show for his efforts, mentioned only catching the Atomic Energy Commission when it reported that it could detect seismic events only if they were no more than a few hundred miles away when, in fact, it could do far better.[518] This seems not much for a long and celebrated career. Or to take a different example, when Senator Eugene McCarthy was running for president, he was asked by a thoughtful voter how many Senate bills had his name on them. He observed that most people were unaware how few such bills are named. Even distinguished senators could pass an entire career without having their names affixed to a bill.

In sum, many people make a difference, if they do, without making a perceptible or attributable difference. Success normally has too many fathers for that, and most successes require hiding one's role to permit others to secure sufficient credit to motivate their involvement. Oftentimes one's role, if known, would generate additional opposition. Attributable successes are thus a rarity in most lines of work, even in entrepreneurial activism, and much that occurs has hidden and complicated causes.

Nevertheless, in fulfilling the goal of this memoir, an attempt must be made to assess whether any of the work chronicled herein proved successful and, at least, whether it was a "good try." How should this be done? What is a "good try"?

An entrepreneurial activist starts with a conception of what might be achieved, moves on to activities designed to promote that conception, and hopes, in the end, for favorable consequences. The activist can, therefore, be judged according to three quite different standards.

Was the conception of how to deal with the seemingly intractable problem cleverly adapted to the circumstances at issue, so as to constitute a vision worthy of the dilemma?

With regard to activities, was the activist tenacious and determined; courageous morally, politically, or physically; and ingenious in tactics?

And finally, with regard to results, was the effort favored with good consequences, and how much might the activist's efforts have had to do with such success as may have occured? It would be too much, of course, to demand of the activist that he or she be the sole or even the primary architect of success since, in today's world, many people working together openly, tacitly, or accidentally are required to achieve anything. But it is possible, in some cases, to be a possible or provable primary catalyst.

It is often difficult to apply these standards in real life with its chaos, compounded by the variety of methods being applied to get results. To illustrate, here are some instructive episodes in which I participated that are not recorded in the memoir.

The Vagaries of the Media and the Causal Opacity of Parliamentary Votes: Consider the case of the vote on the B-1 bomber on May 20, 1976, when, for the first time in the then thirty-year history of the Cold War, the U.S. Senate failed, in a floor vote, to approve a major weapon system that emerged from the Armed Services Committee. The month before, my assistant Michael Mann and I had conceived the idea of a really short petition—one sentence—that might capture the names of famous persons in a show of force against the bomber: "The tens of billions of dollars required to build and operate the B-1 bomber are not warranted by any contribution to our security which it might make." As an idea, this could be described, perhaps, as no more than "not bad."

Using a certain amount of enterprise, but not much, we managed to find seventeen famous persons, led by a former secretary of defense, Clark Clifford, to endorse this sentence. But to our dismay, our press release was completely ignored. Fortune then turned completely around. An acquaintance, Marilyn Berger of NBC News, called up and was delighted to hear that it had not yet been referred to in the media because, she said, under her rules, she could then put it on NBC News. Marilyn put Clark Clifford and me on the air, and to our astonishment we heard her intone that this "prestigious opposition" (us!) seemed to be having an effect and there was a "big question" whether the B-1 will ever fly. Advised by us subsequently that no such Pentagon proposal had ever been defeated in the Senate, she said, "Well, you had better get moving, because I have had this job for only three weeks and do not want to lose it." Compared with our modest enterprise, we were now doing better than we deserved in a town where media predictions of victory can be self-fulfilling.

Incredibly, the vote was successful. And the margin of success was narrow—only four votes (44–37). At the time, we credited the success to the special influence that Clark Clifford had with various senators, including his good friend Senator Stuart Symington. A journalistic review of the situation called our petition a "notable factor" in the vote, so this tactic doubtless "worked" in at least a limited sense.[519] But exactly what the vote lineup was before we released the petition—or, perhaps more importantly, when we were able to spread word that Clifford was with us—is not clear to us now. In sum, the consequences were entirely favorable, but we were lucky in how the media played our effort and have no firm reason to conclude—with so many other groups working on the issue—that this event played a last-straw role in creating the narrow margin.

Worst of all, several years later, the B-1 bomber was resurrected and built. So this affair could be audited, insofar as overall consequences were concerned, as somewhere between an unprecedented event in the Cold War (first floor defeat in the Senate) and, on the other hand, something that, at best, achieved nothing lasting. Perhaps, then, the entire B-1 campaign, including all participants, achieved little.

The Meandering of Enterprise: Or take the example of how an Eskimo woman's interest in a nuclear-free zone in the Arctic gave rise, through a chain of circumstance, to the creation of a new animal-welfare organization in the lower forty-eight states. I was invited to help an historic meeting of the world's Eskimos work out nuclear-related issues in the Arctic. But on traveling there, seeing how unrealistic the Eskimos' ideas were, and witnessing the problem of whales and caribou, I decided to write about animal problems instead.

Uncertain how to proceed, I accepted the suggestion of an animal-rights activist and foundation director, Scott McVay, that my newsletter ought to be about animal rights generally. Learning in my month-long investigation that Britain had a scientists' group working on such matters and that America did not, I emphasized the importance of creating a similar U.S. center. At this point another animal-welfare activist, Christine Stevens, mailed thirty thousand copies of my newsletter to biologists in a successful effort to create the Scientists' Center for Animal Welfare.

Clearly, this episode shows little conception—editorializing about the desirability of mimicking a British organization is not rocket science—and little enterprise, since so much was done by others—but the consequences were good (a new organization was created) and the editorial was provably the primary cause. This successful meandering of purpose suggests that there is always something useful for activists to do, just as columnists can always work up a column. And it shows the value of collaborative effort—in this case both in conception and in the final enterprise of mailing out the newsletter to so many scientists.

Part of a Ferment Through Random Events: And what are we to say about the happenstance of a journey to Libya in 1978 when, to my amazement, a high official freely admitted that Libya was seeking nuclear weapons even when I made clear, in advance, that our organization could only engage in scientific exchange with Libya if they were not? Arriving home to discover that Libya had recently signed the Non-Proliferation Treaty—which is to say had proclaimed that they were *not* seeking nuclear weapons—in order to persuade the Russians to sell them a large nuclear reactor, I held a press conference denouncing the Libyans as false adherents to the treaty and wrote to the Russians and the State Department. The Russians reneged on the agreement to sell the reactor, but only eight years later—thus not exactly because of our intervention! (The only thing that did clearly result was a pointed allusion from a visiting Libyan embassy employee to our building blowing up—which led us to have an instructive meeting with the FBI bomb squad on issues of self-defense.)

Here I provided no conception and little sustained enterprise, and no clearly connected success resulted. But our press conference and letters to governments were part of a general agitation that made it harder for the Libyans to build a nuclear weapon. So perhaps it all counted for something. Here we were not making any particularly noteworthy or catalytic difference individually but were just joining in a collective effort.

Particular Issues Surface Generic Problems That Require Sustained Efforts: In August 1973 we noticed in the *Congressional Record* that a highly controversial bill on the law of the sea had been reported out of committee unanimously. It was hard for us and for a disturbed State Department to believe. The bill was brought to the floor of the Senate the day before adjournment. Since the bill had been described as having been approved unanimously by the committee, it could easily have breezed through the Senate. After a Democratic Policy Committee staffer, Charles Ferris (whom we had briefed earlier about the nefarious characteristics of the bill), spotted it, alerted the leadership, and had it stopped, we began to look into the general issue of how the Senate reports bills out of committee; at length we produced a November 1974 *PIR* entitled "Voting in Senate Committees: Unkept Records Reflect Violated Rules."[520]

The committees were required to have a nonproxy vote to report out a bill, but staff could organize a voice vote and fail to record who was present at the time—thus conjuring a quorum when none existed. Our efforts to force tighter rules foundered on an inability to find any senator who wanted to champion an issue so likely to alienate his colleagues. But a larger organization, such as Common Cause, would probably have had the time and energy to make a major issue out of this end run by the backers of the American Mining Congress Bill. During this period I could spend only one week between two monthly newsletters trying to merchandise my publication's conclusion. So here we showed enterprise but not enough energy and had no tangible success.

Perverse Effects and Blackmail: In 1971, FAS played a major role in opposing an underground nuclear explosion so large that it could not be conducted in Nevada and so had to be tested in Amchitka, Alaska. With my well-covered testimony at the Atomic Energy Commission (AEC) hearings in Anchorage, Alaska, and by using our senior scientists, many of whom had been advisers to the White House, we were able to draw attention to the bureaucratic momentum building toward the detonation of a nuclear warhead that the government had already decided it would never use. There was no great new conception to our efforts, some enterprise, but no success in preventing the test.

Worst of all, President Nixon became angry with the scientific community, based partly on its opposition on this issue and partly on its defection over the supersonic transport. He threw the scientists out of the White House by abolishing the President's Science Advisory Committee. It took us two years of sustained lobbying, and the work of other scientific groups, to get them reinstalled in a less prestigious way. So here we had no success and, indeed, a giant generic setback for a group that wants scientific advice to be presented to the government.

In some cases this kind of perverse effect can take the form of blackmail. In 1998 the White House called to say that the Senate majority leader had threatened not to bring the Comprehensive Test Ban Treaty to the floor of the Senate for a ratification vote if I and two others continued our work opposing the ratification of the NATO Treaty. But were we to act in accordance with such threats, our effectiveness as a small voice of conscience would immediately vanish. For better or for worse, FAS staffers are trained not to be easily diverted by tactical considerations.

These orienting examples of real-world applications of activism show that just about anything can happen. Let us turn now to attempts to assess, using the same kind of analysis, the major topics of this memoir.

Arms Control

The efforts recounted in chapters 1–3 on the Anti-Ballistic Missile Treaty seem to deserve high marks in all three categories: conception, enterprise, and results. Someone conceived, independently, a grand notion of two nations agreeing *not* to build anti-ballistic missiles either tacitly or overtly and wrote what may have been the first serious paper on this subject (notwithstanding the general view in his institution and elsewhere that technology cannot be stopped). He worked intently and enterprisingly for ten years to persuade both nations to help ensure the result: publishing many articles and two books, and making self-financed visits to lobby the Soviet Union for five years running. And the outcome was successful.

It was successful because the ABM was so expensive and so ineffective—had it been cheaper or more effective, it would not have been stopped. Luck was also involved as when the Army tried to build the ABM near cities, sparking off the Bombs in the Backyard debate and bringing Senator Kennedy into the fray with his unusual influence. Since the battle over the ABM treaty was very close and could have gone either way, everyone who played a significant role in it—and, of course, there were many, many such people—deserves credit for its success. At least I was one of them and thus made a difference.

With regard to the initiation of real reductions of deployed strategic nuclear weapons between the United States and the USSR (getting the START talks started), there was again an original conception (the Bear-Hug Strategy). It was effectively lobbied in both the United States (where discussions were held with the State Department's Paul Nitze) and the USSR (where discussions with Evgeny Velikhov and a major filmed presentation in Moscow was achieved). And it shows, again, a successful conclusion: insofar as START talks did begin. In this arms control affair, I was, in fact, a more major player than on the ABM issue. And although Andrei Sakharov became the major Soviet activist in persuading Soviet society to accept his version of the bear hug—the Sakharov finesse—the original bear-hug approach won out. Here I feel I provided conception, enterprise, and a fairly tangible linkage to the eventual success.

The other work on arms control was less successful. In the case of "Shrink SALT II," on the positive side, a splendidly simple conception (i.e., percentage reduction) was adapted in original fashion to the limits and sublimits of SALT II. The method was deliberately designed to be simple enough to permit chief executives to agree on it without much ado, if they wished. And this simplicity did make it possible for President Carter to clear this approach with his chairman of the Joint Chiefs of Staff on the plane on the way to the Vienna summit and to offer it to Brezhnev on a legal pad in an elevator.

Also, the work shows enterprise in getting a president to adopt an idea and a Senate Foreign Relations Committee to approve it. But Brezhnev's health and the Soviet invasion of Afghanistan combined to wipe out the SALT talks. So this effort is best characterized as a good try overwhelmed by events beyond the control of even presidents of the United States.

The efforts to create a legislative check on the first use of nuclear weapons failed. My ideas here were not as well conceived as I thought they were at the time. My conception of a crisis committee of Congress with veto over first use was quite original, but I misjudged the desire of Congress to be involved. I took too seriously the periodic hypocritical complaints of leading members of Congress that the executive branch refused to consult them in emergencies. In fact, members of Congress do not want to be consulted if it means they will have to take responsibility for the decision to bomb Libya or invade Grenada or Panama. My efforts to advance this approach—which succeeded fleetingly when a temporary committee was set up to implement the War Powers Act—might get good marks for resourcefulness and creativity, but they were doomed by the lack of constituencies with an urgent interest in pressing the issue. So the lesson is that when the conception is flawed, no amount of enterprise can save the effort from failure.

The second effort to prevent first use of nuclear weapons advanced a more plausible conception involving a dramatic declaratory proposition that would seem to say that the use of any weapons of mass destruction is prohibited. This still seems to me ideal for a World Court. I lobbied the court with quite unusual (procedural) success, but the overall approach failed because of internal court preferences for an entirely unexpected result based on an unpredictable coalition.

In fact, I was too optimistic in concluding that the court had only one place to go between business as usual and flat-out prohibitions on use. Activists need to talk themselves into believing that they have a chance—just as good salesmen talk themselves into believing in their product—but they should, in the back of their minds, retain a sense of the real unpredictability of life. Although my work failed, over many years, to make a dent in the no-first-use-of-nuclear-weapons problem, really no one else made any headway on this issue either—with the exception of President Carter's negative security assurance (which the current administration is trying to walk away from).

Good Government

My efforts to foster good government did not really require much work. Aside from writing a newsletter, no conception and enterprise were necessary in the successful campaign to stop illegal mail opening. But I am provably solely responsible for catalyzing this favorable result. Similarly, the "footnote in history" in Watergate simply arose out of other activities that happened to involve John Dean, but I was the sole catalyst.

I am proud to have come close to preventing the first federal preliminary injunction restricting the freedom of the press to publish, and I hope the method I invented will find future use if other such problems arise. In retrospect, I am glad that I did not show more enterprise in following up hints of the Reagans' interest in astrology, since this interest, had it been fully exposed and repressed, might have prevented their astrologer, in a perverse effect, from selling the Reagans on Gorbachev's virtues. But my work on the mysterious sonic booms shows enterprise, and even some vaguely scientific work, and shows the right result, for which I am solely responsible, in not alarming the East Coast unnecessarily.

Improving Relations Between the Superpowers

The establishment of scientific relations between the United States and China would doubtless have occurred eventually quite apart from my prodding. But it felt good helping, and the conception and enterprise seem worthy and the consequences perfect, except for the failure to get a medical delegation to China to help Zhou Enlai, for which I showed insufficient tenacity, which I thoroughly regret.

With regard to improving relations with the Soviet Union, I should have found Ann Hoopes and her troop of elite women, earlier; this is one case where a larger FAS staff might have produced a more sustained effort—although I am sure that hired staff would not have had the panache and penetrating power of her team. Time was wasted while I floundered around for years, trying one thing or another to get members of Congress and senators to travel to the Soviet Union. The conception was good, but the enterprise was flawed. Still, in the end, there was good success. Here Ann made the difference.

Human Rights

The decision to shift FAS policy, in periods of détente, from a single-minded concentration on arms control into some emphasis on human rights for our Soviet colleagues was an important conception that paid off in the early institutionalization of human rights groups in American scientific societies and in our important defense of Andrei Sakharov. This defense shows independence of mind, and the value of autonomy, in pressuring NAS to do more and ingenuity in helping to resolve various hunger strikes.

I am not sure whether we were right, in 1980, to have downgraded our work on disarmament by boycotting the Soviet Union for three years to protest Sakharov's detention in Gorky. But our idea of having Sakharov freed as a present to Kennedy was a worthy one and might have worked. Here the hard work was done by Senator Kennedy. It came close to working and may have left behind momentum that did help in the eventual release of Sakharov.

Defeating Maoist Insurrections

The work on Cambodia shows an accurate conception—that Hun Sen was the best bulwark against a return of the Khmer Rouge—and it shows an enormous amount of work and enterprise.

In the end, our catalytic appeal to the energetic Senator Cranston to use his subcommittee to mobilize the Senate, against Congressman Solarz's control of the House (combined with related follow-up work by myself and the coalition I had organized), was certainly a key part in keeping the country *overtly* out of a second Indochina war.

But I failed in efforts to divert the United States from its role in the *secret* war. The idea of buying the critical information from a journalist who could not or would not use it and getting it into *The New York Times* op-ed page shows conception and enterprise. But no one in Washington cared. The conception and enterprise in bringing Hun Sen to Washington to help fund the Cambodian peace plan was, certainly, a success in changing his image and helping get money for the peace plan. But change of this kind is not permanent (and, of course, ought not be), and Hun Sen's reputation in Washington now has soured because of his preemptive strike against Prince Rannaridh's forces and his violent suppression of political opponents before and after the last election, which he won.

The work on Peru shows, I think, a significant role in defeating a Maoist insurgency. The idea that the U.S. should be helping Peruvian intelligence, and the discovery that it was not, were both right and important. Chapter 26 shows enterprise in lobbying almost all the relevant bases in the intelligence community and some in the White House and State and Defense Departments who were initially reluctant to take action. And it shows a successful conclusion—which, necessarily, had other fathers inside the bureaucracy even if my lobbying on return from Peru was the catalytic event, which, of course, it might not have been since the State Department was, also, trying to get the United States government to move.

Terrorism, Proliferation, and Crime

How well it is going, no outsider can say, but the effort to forge a CIA-KGB connection cannot help but be important, over time, in helping resolve common problems of the United States and Russia in today's global society. No doubt it would have occurred in time without my two major efforts—reaching Gorbachev on the issue of inviting Gates to Russia, which precipitated so much instant action, and threatening to organize my own intelligence exchange on North Korea if the CIA and the KGB did not. But successes are mostly a matter of hastening likely outcomes. And it has been well said that the inevitable often occurs only through the determined efforts of indefatigable men. So I feel good about this.

Resolving Territorial Disputes Within Countries

With regard to the territorial disputes in Serbia over Kosovo and in China over Taiwan, seemingly original conceptions have been marked by limited enterprise because the time has not seemed ripe enough to sustain more. And no success has resulted. At least Taiwan appears to have considered, albeit rejected for now, the Northeast Strategy. And at least the strategy was briefed throughout the relevant Chinese institutions and received as "important and constructive" at quite a high level.

In Kosovo, the situation has, obviously, deteriorated, with no end in sight. But the "rent" approach of an agreement limited in time provides a framework for autonomy-plus that still might play some role. Still, in general, until the parties are ready to consider *any* reconciliation, there is little that even the U.S. Department of State can do, much less an individual based in an NGO. But where there is logic, there is always the possibility, at least, of future progress.

And so these disputes are unfinished business.

· · ·

Whether, all things considered, this is deemed a lot or a little, for a third of a century of work, depends upon one's expectations. For butterflies, which is to say for outside agitators and entrepreneurial activists, it may seem considerable to some—certainly it covers a kaleidoscopic number of issues and romantic adventures. For certain sufficiently high government officials, vested with the powers of their high office—at least for the limited terms that our democracy permits—it may seem less significant. But at least my fate was better than that of Ibn-Khaldun, who felt that *all* of his constructive efforts had failed. I feel particularly good about the work on arms control, on human rights, and on Maoist movements and the efforts to bring China and Russia into better relations with America.

Human society has become, of course, enormously better organized than it was when Ibn-Khaldun was born, 603 years before me, and it provides more individual scope to many more people. Certainly it would have been much harder, six centuries ago, for a John F. Kennedy to assert, "One man can make a difference, and every man should try."

The Inner Life and Qualities
of Entrepreneurial Activists

Whatever has been effectively attempted, what does it require to undertake the effort? An entrepreneurial activist is often fueled by pride of authorship. My feeling that, in 1963, I had independently conjectured, if not indeed invented, the theory behind the ABM Treaty, and my sense that this might turn out to be *the* most important treaty of the Cold War, motivated me for more than a decade! By the end, many others were involved; but to me, it always seemed *my* campaign, and this was the only reason I could persist for so long. Having a sense of ownership of an idea or issue is a powerful motivator. (As a corollary, it can be, for quite a few reasons, quite disruptive to managing one's campaign to have someone else advance your idea publicly without suitable attribution.)

A certain passion, and perhaps even a touch of mania, is essential because so much work is inevitably involved in the face of low prospects of success. This hypomania, found in many of the world's great artists, inventors, and activists, can give the entrepreneurial activist the (normally false) conviction that he or she might actually create something unique and wonderful despite all odds and despite the full knowledge that others have tried and failed. In particular, the amount of enterprise required to play an outsider's role in Cambodia for three years, or to support Andrei Sakharov, on and off, for fourteen years, requires an intensity of effort that cannot be purchased and is based on this mania.

To be successful, passionate idealism and ego involvement must be combined with a certain pragmatism and moderated by the businesslike approach of a capitalist entrepreneur selling an invention. In particular, one cannot achieve change by oneself, by throwing lightning bolts from one's brow. One has to deal with, and through, others. They will not cooperate unless treated with civility. Without such an approach, I could not have pleaded with the intelligence community for its help in arresting Peru's Guzman—and I would not have known enough people in the administration to get my foot in the door.

Thus, it is much better to be well-liked than disliked. On the other hand, too much good-fellowship, and too much emphasis on maintaining civil relations with all and sundry, can interfere with one's effectiveness; one can become captured by too many people or institutions relevant to the goal. Andrei Sakharov benefitted from the fact that I was not a member of the National Academy of Sciences and, accordingly, was willing to joust with its leadership and chide its members in a fashion that could not be denied. And my freedom of action was backed by an organization sufficiently autonomous that its board could not be suborned by the academy's president.

In my experience, the degree of combativeness of entrepreneurial activists varies greatly in normal ordinary life. But when aroused and armored in the right, they are the difficult people without whom the world cannot be saved. Most seem to be—as I see myself—people who are not eager for combat. But their sense of self is such that, once involved, they would rather run personal moral, political, or physical risks than suffer the consequent harm to their integrity of witnessing their own inaction. At the outset of any adventures that involved a degree of moral, political, or physical hazard, an internal dialogue between my backbone and a tightened part of my stomach informed my brain that the undertaking could not be avoided. At these moments, I well knew how many acquaintances, all eminently moral men, would, instead, just have taken a cold shower. Effective entrepreneurial activists are created and maintained, perhaps, by intense visceral reactions that hold them prisoner.

Entrepreneurial activists must combine, in a single persona, both creativity (a key part of the entrepreneurship) and motivation (a key part of the activism). These must be present simultaneously because great idea-men without the motivation to carry out their ideas have difficulty in finding someone to implement "somebody else's idea." And, on the other hand, motivated persons without ideas, even if they are given an idea to work on, often lack the deep conviction and the understanding necessary to keep the idea going when mid-course corrections are necessary, as they always are.

On the other hand, even when motivation and pride of authorship are linked, even when activists are energetic and well connected and well funded, and follow their best instincts, even when a notion is skillfully advanced, even when worldwide coalitions are built, even when many conditions are right, all too often, nothing lasting happens—and for many reasons. The totality of reasons why lasting change does not occur can perhaps best be summarized as temporal inertia.

Not every rifle shot in snowy mountains brings down an avalanche. Similarly, not every activist foray in public life hits a fracture line that produces important, lasting change. Indeed, if life were this easy to manipulate, change would come too fast for all of us to survive. In its broader dimensions, on the whole, human life seems, in any case, affected more by *trends* (i.e., by combinations of many small similar events) rather than by (single newsworthy) *events.* An exception consists of those scientific discoveries or inventions that have changed the life of Mankind, usually for good but, sometimes, as with Edward Teller's insistence on pursuing the hydrogen bomb during World War II, for perilous bad. (His willful behavior may well have put Mankind into more avoidable jeopardy than that of any other man ever born.)

Certainly the more far-reaching the change, the less probable that it will be achieved by a single act of well-motivated will or, put another way, the less likely it is that a single individual will find himself or herself at a point in space-time of such profound significance that his or her act of will could have such results. And, regrettably, it seems much easier for individuals to precipitate *destructive* change—by misconceived acts of some kind of disruption—than it is for individuals to catalyze *constructive* change.

On the other hand, entrepreneurial activity for good, engaged in by many individuals and groups at the same time, can undoubtedly be a powerful force. Happily we see today the continued institutionalization of altruism in the proliferation of nongovernmental organizations devoted to good purposes and staffed by ever more professional activists. This rising tide of potential for good is offsetting the decreasing capacity of governments to control their own affairs in a world that is coming together. Nothing is more important than to find ways of strengthening this trend by stabilizing the nongovernmental public interest sector on a worldwide basis.

Because so much altruistic human activity cannot be firmly linked to good results, the notion that "one man can make a difference" is best understood, I think, as an article of faith. And its corollary, that "every man should try," should be seen as a companion inspirational injunction. *In sum, seeking to make a difference could be at the core of a new secular religion.* If orchestrated properly, such a quasi-religious movement could enormously increase the number of entrepreneurial activists, could further bring the altruistic instincts of Mankind to the fore, and could reshape the future. Activism could become less a series of isolated events and more of a genuine trend—strengthening its impact.

How to do this remains to be worked out. But if science fiction writer L. Ron Hubbard could deliberately set out to create an alleged religion, the Scientologists, it ought not be beyond the wit of some entrepreneurial activist somewhere to create an intense movement championing John F. Kennedy's assertion and bringing together its adherents.

Obviously, there are limits to the enduring change that even the most inspired, and hardworking, public interest activist can reasonably hope to accomplish by himself or herself or even with others. But happily no one can know what, in particular cases, it is. Social science will never be able to determine, in our chaos-driven world, with what probability any particular activist, or group of activists, might be able to achieve any specific goal. And this weakness of social science should not be deplored because it has a positive side for those who dream implausible dreams. If you ask entrepreneurial activists how much temporal inertia there is in modern life, they may tell you:

God Only Knows,
And for this,
We are grateful.

Afterword:

New Initiatives at Press Time

As this memoir goes to press, two important initiatives of November-December, 1998 are underway.

Efforts to Revive Zero-Ballistic Missiles (ZBM)

In November 1998, in an effort to revive a program started at FAS in 1992 designed to shape a missile-free world—and which is not focused on in this memoir—I visited Beijing, armed with a September/October FAS Public Interest Report entitled *Missile Encirclement: China's Interest In Missile Controls*. The purpose of the report (prepared with staffer Charles Ferguson) was to persuade the Chinese Government that it should bestir itself to work for regional missile control zones in Northeast Asia, in South Asia and in Central Asia by offering to keep parts of China missile-free. We also encouraged China to make such pronouncements as "No first use of ballistic missiles." Examples of actions that the Chinese Government could take were coupled with worst-case analyses of how quickly missiles and anti-missiles could spread around China if prompt action were not taken to encourage missile restraint. We made presentations to the Chinese Foreign Ministry, to an association of Chinese generals (The China Institute for International Strategic Studies), to a representative of the People's Liberation Army's Office of Foreign Affairs, to the Institute for Applied Physics and Computational Mathematics (IAPCM), and to an international conference in Shanghai on arms control sponsored by Fudan University. A number of institutions promised to study the issue. Following the visit to China, I visited Australia in mid-November to seek to persuade the Australian Government to introduce a resolution in the United Nations that would, on a generic basis, critique missiles and their special dangers and provide a basis for work toward a missile-free world. The Australian Government showed keen interest, at two different well-placed staff levels and through a key parliamentarian, and promised to study the issue.

The conventional wisdom in disarmament does not assume the disappearance of nuclear-armed ballistic missiles as a way-station to the achievement of "zero-nuclear weapons". This seems an obvious mistake since nuclear weapons are much easier to maintain than the ballistic missiles that might carry them. Thus, a regime controlling the missiles is likely to be feasible before a regime eliminating the warheads. Certainly the introduction of nuclear-armed ballistic missiles was an important way-station in the U.S.-Soviet arms race. It seems plausible that it will be an equally important way station in the world's eventual disarmament. We hope the readers will support our efforts.

On January 12, 1999, Ambassador Sha Zukang, Director-General of the Chinese Department of Arms Control and Disarmament, to whom I had presented our ideas in China in November, gave a speech at the Carnegie International Non-Proliferation Conference saying: "Devoid of any legal basis in international law, missile non-proliferation is the most under-developed part of the entire international non-proliferation regime. . . . It is time for the international community to take a collective look at the missile proliferation issue, including the Missile Technology Control Regime

(MTCR), and explore better ways to combat this danger." This was a very important development.

Initiating a Scientific Dialogue with Iran

Following up on efforts described in the book to catalyze scientific exchange with China in 1972 (Chapter 12), with Vietnam in 1990 (described in Chapter 24), and with North Korea in 1991 (described in Chapter 22), I organized an FAS scientific delegation that visited the Islamic Republic of Iran—evidently the first American scientific delegation since Iran's 1979 revolution two decades before. It required nine months of complicated negotiations. The plans for a December 1998 visit were further complicated by events of the weekend of November 21–22, 1998 that saw attacks on a bus carrying American businessmen and the killing of an Iranian married couple who led a small opposition party. In street demonstrations, the anti-American group that had attacked the bus put out a press release noting that the next delegation of Americans would be dealt with "more severely". In addition, some group was killing moderate Iranian writers—about one a week.

Persisting, nonetheless, FAS Vice Chairman Robert McCormack Adams (an archeologist with experience in Iran and a former long-time chief executive of the Smithsonian Institution), Iranian-American Professor Massoud Simnad (a member of the U.S. National Academy of Engineering), and I spent the week of December 11–18 in Tehran, returning only after the American bombing of Iraq began. This successful visit turned out to be a promising first step in beginning a scientific dialogue with Iran. The expansion of this dialogue is an important agenda item for FAS in 1999 because it clearly represents the will of the vast majority of the Iranian people and of the new Khatami Government—besieged though it may be by certain forces opposing the "dialogue of civilizations" for which President Khatami called.

Science, and scientific exchange, can be a universal solvent in dissolving animosities and securing normal relations. No country can do without science. The scientists of the world are fully prepared to talk to one another even when their statesmen will not. How successful and effective these Iranian contacts can be, in the short and medium run, remains to be seen. But the effort reminds us all that science can be a force for peace.

Notes

Chapter 1

1. Herman Kahn, *On Thermonuclear War* (Princeton, NJ: Princeton University Press, 1960).

2. The RAND Corporation, *A Mathematical Study of Arbitrage*, P-1478; The RAND Corporation, *The Cross Section Method, an Algorithm for Linear Programming*, P-1490.

3. I declined to discuss the political views of relatives when faced with questions like, "What are your father's views with regard to Communism as practiced in the USSR?" I said, "Relatives are a very close thing, and politics are a very vague thing." Asked if any of my immediate relatives had "ever associated with any individuals whom you have known or suspected were a member of a long list of organizations," I said I was "unwilling to discuss the political associates of any person except myself."

   I said, "Whether I agree with the United States in all its actions or whether I agree with my father in all of his political views, I remain loyal to both." It is hard to believe, today, that security officials would ask sons to provide information on fathers, but this was customary then.

   In 1977, thanks to an FOIA request, I learned with amusement that the background investigation had debated the political character of the New School for Social Research, where, during my high school days, I had taken three night courses in higher mathematics and had been asked, at age seventeen, to teach an adult education course on three-dimensional chess.

4. At Hudson, between Kennedy's quarantine of Cuba (October 22) and Khrushchev's capitulation (October 28), I prepared a paper urging the UN to register strategic weapon transfers around the world. ("An Arms Control Proposal Related to Cuba—Registration of Certain Strategic Weapons Outside of the United States and the Soviet Union," Hudson Institute, October 26, 1962.).

By spring 1963, still worrying about future Cuban missile crises, I thought of a way to strengthen the UN in such crises. Needing some kind of endorsement from the UN Secretariat, and hearing that Secretary-General U Thant actually opened his own mail, I sent him a "proposal to study the intellectual resources which would be available to the United Nations Secretary-General should he attempt to mediate a military confrontation of the two blocs."

He responded with a helpful diplomatic letter of April 26 expressing the "hope that the study which you propose to undertake from an independent standpoint would be of such a nature as to stimulate interest not only of the theorists in international politics and organization but also of the practitioners of diplomacy and mediation." But this fledgling effort to work out and stockpile crisis preparations for terminating a nuclear war had not been funded by the time I left the Hudson Institute.

5. We did secure such a contract, and on August 20, 1963, I balanced my ticket on strategic evacuation with Annex I: "The Question of Crisis Evacuation" in a Hudson Institute study on "Arms Control and Civil Defense" (HI–216-RR). It warned that ACDA would find that crisis evacuation programs "will interfere with traditional methods of achieving arms control and disarmament."

6. Donald Brennan, ed., *Arms Control, Disarmament and National Security* (New York: Braziller, 1961).

7. A review of his book found antimissiles mentioned only twice and in passing and nothing whatsoever about controlling them either tacitly or formally.

8. The table of contents, reprinted below, shows the thrust:
    U.S. Progress
    Likelihood of U.S. Procurement
    Likelihood of Soviet Procurement and the Soviet National Interest
    Would Soviet Restraint in Procurement Be Risky?
    Would U.S. Restraint Be in the U.S. Interest?
    Implications for the Arms Race and Arms Control of
        ABM Systems or ABM Restraint
    Research and Development in ABM
    A No-First Procurement Policy
    The Decision to Deploy
    Verification of No-First-Procurement Policies
    Urgency
    Advances over Terminal-Intercept Systems
    Postdeployment Arms Race
    Progress Toward General Disarmament
    Accidents
    Nth Country Deterrence
    Hard Point Defense of ICBMs
    Destruction if War Occurs
    Separation of Forces and Urban Targets
    Destabilization

Inspection
Limitations of Weapons
Nuclear Diffusion and Denuclearization of Europe
Qualitative Acceleration of the Arms Race
Weapons in Orbit
Catalytic War (or Unauthorized Behavior)
Nuclear Materials Cutoff
Test Ban Treaty
What Is to Be Done?
Observations

9. This later appeared in *World Politics* (October 1964) as "Bomber Disarmament" and, also, as a chapter in *Containing the Arms Race: Some Specific Proposals* (Cambridge: MIT Press, 1966).

Chapter 2

10. The papers covered the verification of a strategic freeze, the mothballing of strategic missile forces, the problem of general disarmament, ABM systems and China, and strategic reductions.
11. Jeremy J. Stone, "Arms Race or Disarmament," *Bulletin of the Atomic Scientists* (September 1964): 23.
12. By 1984, however, after President Reagan announced his Star Wars program, Henry Kissinger wrote an article entitled "We Need Star Wars," in which he encouraged defenses and said, "If only an all-out attack can penetrate defenses and if a strategic defense makes it uncertain what weapons will get through, rational incentives for nuclear war will diminish."

    After the ABM Treaty was signed, Kissinger wrote, "It has become clear that to rely on a strategy of mutual annihilation based on unopposed offensive weapons raises profound moral and political issues." He urged that a commission be created to study Reagan's idea. Henry Kissinger, "We Need Star Wars," *The Washington Post*, September 8, 1986.

    Was he giving lip service to arguments he did not believe just to create and direct a commission as some cynics thought? Or was he was shifting backward under the pressure of Reagan's dream? In a contemporaneous op-ed piece, reciting this history of Kissingerian reversals, I concluded, "Perhaps giving lip service to arguments in which you could not possibly believe is a price of power. How would I know?" See Jeremy J. Stone, "Anti-Missile Defense for Utopia: Kissinger now Plumps for What He Once Negotiated Away," *The Los Angeles Times*, October 25, 1984.
13. Jerome Wiesner wrote a preface for my book calling the chapters on anti-ballistic missile defenses "particularly timely" and expressing the hope that "maybe the Russians will translate and publish it."

14. Jeremy J. Stone, *Strategic Persuasion: Arms Control Through Dialogue* (New York: Columbia University Press, 1967).

15. *The Washington Post* praised the book as "meticulous" and noted that I had made a "detailed case in favor of a 'freeze' and a 'pause' in the procurement of missile and anti-missile systems . . . with a fairness to opposing viewpoints, which is quite rare in the messianic world of the megatons." And *The Los Angeles Times* said the book showed a "degree of thoughtful concentration" that entitled the book to a hearing. My *Bulletin of the Atomic Scientists* piece and other articles had made me a minor figure in the debate.

16. Much later, in the seventies, Don did the one thing that lives on from his work. He deliberately invented the acronym MAD for Mutual Assured Destruction to provide a pejorative characterization of the majority view. In fact, contrary to the views of most casual observers, the policy in question was not described by its supporters as "mutual assured destruction." Instead, two policies were involved: mutual deterrence was one, and assured destruction was the other. In a feat of Madison Avenue enterprise, he had just combined MD and AD into MAD.

    Brennan died of a self-inflicted shotgun wound on April 18, 1980, a day before his appointment by Ronald Reagan to a campaign advisory committee was to have been announced. He left a recorded suicide message at the Hudson Institute that outlined a number of financial and work-related problems, but he cited no political motives or reservations about his positions on national policies or the prospects of working in Reagan's campaign. In the preceding weeks he had rewritten his will, put his affairs in order, and updated his obituaries at several newspapers. See *The New York Times*, April 19, 1980.

17. According to a letter provided to me much later under the Freedom of Information Act, U.S. intelligence had her confused with a ballerina and had no idea what her ideology was.

18. See *Containing the Arms Race*, p. 74.

19. Jeremy J. Stone, "The Scientist and Disarmament," *Moscow News*, October 8, 1966.

20. A CIA official, Thomas W. Braden, persuaded CIA director Allen Dulles to overrule regional subordinates and to permit Braden to run an operation funneling moneys to international student groups and European unions and the like, with a view to helping them hold up their end in the struggle against Communist penetration and control. See Thomas W. Braden, "Speaking Out," *Saturday Evening Post,* May 20, 1967. This became a major issue in April of 1996 with a five-part *New York Times* series entitled "C.I.A.: Maker of Policy or Tool." By March 29, 1967, President Lyndon Johnson accepted the conclusion of a blue-ribbon panel that "no Federal agency shall provide any covert financial assistance or support, direct or indirect, to any of the nation's educational or private voluntary organizations." See *The New York Times*, March 30, 1967. As Chapter 3 shows, the fallout from this debate complicated and shaped my life.

Chapter 3

21. I had been promised by Bernard Feld, on leaving Boston for Moscow, that if Wiesner did not attend the upcoming Polish Pugwash conference, I would be invited. On hearing in Moscow that Wiesner was not, in fact, coming, and seeing that a "Stone" was on the list, I traveled to the meeting place only to discover that the "Stone" was Shepard Stone. Joseph Rotblat, the executive director of Pugwash, invited me to leave. The Americans, arriving thereafter, reached me in Warsaw and urged me to return as an "observer." But I was too proud to agree, and the entire incident was never explained to me beyond its characterization by Feld as a "comedy of errors."

22. Stone, *Strategic Persuasion.*

23. Arbatov was Jewish, or half Jewish, depending upon whether one believed Robert Kaiser's or Hedrick Smith's book on the Russians. He had had this disabling fact deleted from his internal passport, as Soviet law permitted with persons who wanted to abandon their ethnic identity.

24. Georgi Arbatov, *The System* (New York: Times Books, 1993), pp. 262–263.

25. Adelphi Paper #47, Institute for Strategic Studies, April 1968.

26. John W. Wheeler, "Wheeler Doubts Khesanh Will Need Atom Weapons," *The New York Times*, February 15, 1968. Senator J. W. Fulbright, chairman of the Senate Foreign Relations Committee, had been tipped off by an anonymous source that "Professor Richard L. Garwin of Columbia University and other physicists who in the past had had some connection with the development of tactical nuclear weapons had been sent urgently to Vietnam." Rusk had written Fulbright that Garwin had gone "to discuss technical matters of a nonnuclear nature." See "Fulbright Query Attacked by Rusk," *The New York Times*, February 16, 1968. And the next day, President Johnson himself asserted that neither the Joint Chiefs nor the secretary of state had ever considered such a thing. John W. Finney, "Johnson Denies Atom Use in Vietnam Is Considered," *The New York Times*, February 17, 1968.

27. A former science adviser to President Eisenhower, George Kistiakowsky revealed, years later, that he, also, had become concerned when he heard an American general say that nukes could extricate marines if they got in trouble at Khesanh. He rounded up two other senior science advisers, I. I. Rabi and J. R. Killian Jr., and the three of them sent General Eisenhower a telegram on February 16. According to Kisty:

"Luck was with us as President Johnson, unbeknownst to us, was to visit Eisenhower the next day. A day or two later the Secretary of Defense, Robert McNamara [immediately before Clark Clifford replaced him], personally telephoned each of us and 'on instructions of the President' unequivocally stated that there were no contingency plans to use nukes around Khesanh." See G. B. Kistiakowsky, "A New Form of Diffuse Responsibility?" *Bulletin of the Atomic Scientists* (March 1976): 58.

28. Konrad Lorentz, *On Aggression* (New York: Bantam, 1970), pp. 42–43. In describing the banana experiment, Lorentz says, "Robert M. Yerkes made the extraordinarily interesting observation that chimpanzees, animals well known to be capable of learning by imitation, copy only higher-ranking members of their species." I believe this has now been established for certain species of birds.

29. Jeremy J. Stone, "An Experiment in Bargaining Games," *Econometrica*, p. 26.

30. ABM proponents were forced into their third rationale for the system. Having failed to sell an anti-Soviet ("thick") system in the years 1959–1966 and the ("thin") anti-Chinese system announced in 1967, they urged an ABM system to defend land-based missiles.

31. The chapter became "Can the Soviets Deceive Us?" in *An Evaluation of the Decision to Deploy an Anti-Ballistic Missile System* (New York: Harper & Row, 1969).

32. Earlier in May 1969, I had joined with the young liberal Republican Ripon Society to prepare a special "Ripon Forum Supplement on Safeguard." This gave me ten thousand words and a handsome monograph to distribute. It concluded, "It appears that an emotional and divisive Senate confrontation on the Safeguard proposal is shaping up. The certain closeness of the eventual vote may have serious effects on the ability of the new Administration to negotiate around the world." *Ripon Forum Special Safeguard Supplement* (May 1969).

33. I concluded that "the vindication of the opposition is simply a matter of time." Jeremy J. Stone, "End of the Beginning," *Commonweal*, September 5, 1969.

34. Sergei Khrushchev, *Khrushchev on Khrushchev: An Inside Account of the Man and His Era, by His Son* (Boston: Little, Brown, 1990), p. 270.

35. Ibid., p. 279.

36. Letter of May 25, 1990, from Sergei N. Khruschev to the author.

37. To the best of my knowledge, the only charge of espionage made against FAS or me in reverse (i.e., of working for the KGB rather than for the CIA) arose when a low-level Soviet defector claimed, in a little-noticed speech, "Leaders of your 'peace' groups, such as SANE and the Federation of American Scientists, came to Moscow for instructions." *Alexandria Port Packet*, June 2 1982; my answer appears on August 4. When he refused to take my call demanding an explanation, I sent a Soviet émigré, whom I had befriended, to inquire.

    The defector said the KGB had given *him* instructions, in 1967, to tell me, ask me, encourage me, or something like that, to support the invasion of Czechoslovakia—but that this was so absurd that he had never passed these "instructions" along. Thus the charge that an FAS official had come to Moscow for instructions was based on a twisting of words. A third émigré—whose father had been the defector's professor in Moscow and considered the defector completely unreliable—advised me that the defector was telling such exaggerated stories that the CIA had warned those who wanted him to appear before the Senate Foreign Relations Committee that, if he did, the CIA would be forced to disavow him as "extremely unreliable."

    I wrote a letter to CIA director William J. Casey (July 22, 1982) denying this charge and asking that its files reflect the fact that this defector was "extremely unreliable"; had been, in Moscow, "too frightened even to volunteer his own opinions much less to give anyone instructions"; and was, indeed, "precisely the kind of lazy and morally corrupt Soviet official which populates so much of that bureaucracy." (I also wrote the FBI.)

38. Technically, it was legal to take it out since it had been published in an obscure provincial newspaper. It finally appeared in *The New York Times Magazine*, February 15, 1970.

Chapter 4

39. The rule, in 1970–1971, read that unless otherwise expressly stated, "All proceedings at the Council's afternoon and dinner meetings as well as study and discussion groups are confidential; and any disclosure or publication of statements made at such meetings or attribution to the Council of information, even though otherwise available, is contrary to the best interests of the Council and may be regarded by the Board of Directors in its sole discretion as ground for termination or suspension of membership."

40. Indeed, as the council president, Bayless Manning, was interpreting the rule, it was completely unworkable because he felt it meant that council members were precluded from attributing statements made at a meeting even to other (absent) members. With his interpretation, many were in violation of the rule.

41. The new rule reads, "Participants are assured that they may speak openly, as it is the tradition of the Council that others will not attribute or characterize their statements in public media or forums or knowingly transmit them to persons who will."

42. The embarrassed council staff wanted to take the voting in the direction of Communist countries, in which no one would ever lose. Various rationales were provided: securing diversity, including youth; putting others besides famous wealthy persons on the board; securing the nominations of cautious persons who feared to lose; and so on.

43. I explained to the staff why, mathematically, Henry had lost. Consider that fame is, also, notoriety. So if council members are asked, in effect, to blackball just one of nine candidates, the famous are likely to lose—*they* have enemies. And under a system of nine persons running for eight slots, it does not take many blackballs to undermine a candidacy. I recommended that they move to twelve candidates for eight positions and assured them that if they did, all would be well.

44. A fig leaf that was often mentioned by die-hard supporters of this system was that any ten members could put up a "floor nomination." By 1991, in eighteen years of operating the system, only four persons had been so nominated and only two elected. (This was partly because the names of persons nominated this way were marked with, metaphorically speaking, a scarlet asterisk.)

45. I first threatened President Peter Tarnoff with a campaign against the rule if he did not have it changed. His response was to persuade the council board to preempt my campaign by voting unanimously that it did not want to change the rule—something I learned only on receipt of a round-robin letter to all members. I felt unfairly treated when I saw the letter and decided, characteristically, that I would not be squelched in this way.

46. It was the largest insurgency in the history of the council, I have no doubt, since CFR is an organization that runs not just on democratic principles but on consensual ones.

    Warren Christopher, then a former deputy secretary of state, and later secretary of state, was put in charge of the committee. The bylaws were rewritten to permit a board that was half elected (in real elections) and half appointed. My opinion was then solicited, and I warmly approved on behalf of my flock. The board promptly voted unanimously again, but now *for* elections. (By early 1998, the council leadership was again considering abandoning democratic elections, but refrained from doing so after consulting the members.)

47. Jeremy J. Stone, "When and How to Use SALT," *Foreign Affairs* (January 1970): 273.

48. Irving Kristol, "Memoirs of a Cold Warrior," *The New York Times Magazine*, February 11, 1968.

49. Manshel never made a secret of his having worked for the CIA from 1952 to 1954 and was self-described in his vitae as a "former analyst" there. See also "Head of Foreign Policy Magazine Named Ambassador to Denmark," *The New York Times*, May 27, 1978.

50. Thus, at an off-the-record January 8, 1968, panel discussion on Intelligence and Foreign Policy, with a stellar cast of intelligence community attendees, chaired by former secretary of the treasury Douglas Dillon, Richard M. Bissell Jr., a former CIA deputy director, circulated a paper saying, "If the agency is to be effective, it will have to make use of private institutions on an expanding scale, though those relations which have 'blown' cannot be resurrected.

    "We need to operate under deeper cover, with increased attention to the use of 'cut-outs'. CIA's interface with the rest of the world needs to be better protected." See Richard Dudman, "More Secrecy in Spying by CIA Urged in Report," *St. Louis Post-Dispatch*, September 26, 1971. See also James Doyle, "CIA Has Cover Problems," *The Washington Star*, September 27, 1971.

51. Samuel Huntington, Warren's Harvard classmate, told me in late 1992 that he considers it "plausible" that the CIA sent Manshel to the Congress of Cultural Freedom to be its "executive director" after his two years with the CIA in Washington, in light of Manshel's "European background and language skills." So I was right to be concerned that Manshel might have been working for the CIA undercover. Ironically, in 1996, while completing this memoir, I was told by Irving Kristol that the person to whom he was referring was the "executive *secretary*," Michael Josselson, not the "executive *director*," Warren Manshel. But in light of Manshel's earlier

employment with the CIA, Josselson's working for the CIA would have raised the same alarm bells for me with regard to both of them.

With regard to *Foreign Policy* magazine being subsidized by the CIA, Irving Kristol says that, in fact, it was Kristol's idea that Warren start a foreign policy magazine because he, Kristol, advised Manshel that this was the best way to advance Manshel's desire to become an ambassador. So perhaps the idea did not spring from any agency.

What about the money? If the money came from Manshel, he must have been much richer during his period as a stockbroker than he was after his stint as ambassador. He was, according to Sam Huntington, Manshel's coeditor at *Foreign Policy*, providing $65,000 to $70,000, or about a quarter million in today's dollars. If he gave 30 percent of his income to this charity—about the most one can expect to deduct—he would have to be earning about $800,000 a year in today's dollars as a 1970s stockbroker. But Kristol, who was the executor of Manshel's estate, says that Manshel did not die a wealthy man. (Incredibly, Kristol [Manshel's close friend] says he did not know that Manshel had *ever* worked for the CIA, although this fact appears in Manshel's biography with regard to his two-year stint with the CIA in Washington and, indeed, in news clips about Manshel's confirmation as ambassador to Denmark.)

Chapter 5

52. It turned out, however, that the insurance company would not reveal the formula according to which the dividends were determined, which it termed proprietary. There was no "truth in dividends" rule, and one simply took what one was given. I complained to Senator Philip Hart, then chairman of a subcommittee governing insurance companies. He said the subcommittee had finally hired an actuary in its struggle to oversee the obscure calculations of the industry.

53. October's newsletter was modestly entitled "New Improved Federation Management" (i.e., York and Stone); November's newsletter was on "Unemployment of Scientists and Engineers" and on the Supersonic Transport debate.

54. Its other members were the FAS Vice Chairman Marvin L. Goldberger, who had been chairman of a Strategic Weapons Committee of the President's Science Advisory Committee, and Morton H. Halperin, former deputy assistant secretary of defense for arms control and policy planning. This was a team of experts who had enormous authority and distinction.

55. Press conference of October 26; see the FAS newsletter of December 1970.

56. I also wrote to Mr. Frank M. Steadman, general counsel of the C&P Telephone Company, asking more than half a dozen questions about its cooperation with law enforcement. Letters of January 14, 1971, and February 26, 1971. No answer was ever received.

57. As Cotter later advised *Science* magazine, "The list of prominent scientists on the FAS letterhead" who might well be ready to compromise this program" was a

major reason he attached importance to the letter. Scoville's name was certainly one that concerned him. Robert Gillette, "The CIA's Mail Cover: FAS Nearly Uncovered It," *Science* 1 (June 27, 1975): 282.

58. This CIA memo is printed in full in FAS *PIR*, December 1975, pp. 11–12.
59. Everett R. Holles, "Man Who Says He Once Served CIA Asserts Post Office Helped Agency Open Mail," *The New York Times*, January 8, 1975.
60. Page 8 of its June 1975 report.
61. These charges were made in a press release of September 5, 1975. An interview on the subject with Orr Kelly of *The Washington Star* was published on July 23, 1975. See also *U.S. News and World Report*, August 11, 1975.
62. Title 18, Section 1001. Statements or entries generally. "Whoever . . . knowingly and willfully falsifies, conceals or covers up by any trick scheme, or device a material fact, or makes any false, fictitious or fraudulent statements or representations . . . shall be fined under this title or imprisoned not more than five years or both."
63. "Kennedy Proposal Would Make Lying to the Public a Crime," *The Washington Post*, June 19, 1975.

Chapter 6

64. Robert J. Bazell, "Arms Race: Scientists Question Threat from Soviet Military R&D," *Science* (August 20, 1971).
65. "Is There an R&D Gap?" *Congressional Record*, May 10, 1971, p. S6517.
66. John Walsh, "Arms Control and Disarmament: SALT, CCD, CTB, MBFR, Etc.," January 21, 1971.
67. Marvin L. Goldberger was the chairman of the ad hoc committee, and the others were George W. Rathjens, Richard R. Nelson, and F. M. Scherer.
68. George C. Wilson, "Scientists Say Soviet Threat Is Exaggerated," *The Washington Post*, May 6, 1971.
69. *CBS Evening News*, UPI, May 7, 1971.
70. Bazell, "Arms Race: Scientists Question Threat from Soviet Military R&D."
71. *The New York Times* entitled its report "The Age of Hebert: Dissent Now Fostered on Key House Panel." *New York Times*, April 13, 1971. The report observed that a representative who had been on the committee for a decade could recall outside witnesses only once (and I believe it had happened twice). But these individuals were not representing outside organizations. Congressman Michael J. Harrington put my statement on ABM, MIRV, and the B-1 bomber, all fifty pages of it, in the *Congressional Record*, noting that the "potential value" of this new congressional tradition "was made evident immediately" from the quality of the FAS testimony. *Congressional Record*, March 29, 1971, pp. E2430–E2437. And *The Washington Post* entitled its report "Hebert Unit Ruffled by Witnesses" and said the committee's decision to let in some peace advocates had been "an unsettling experience." *The Washington Post*, March 24, 1971.

I believe that my March 11, 1971, testimony before the Special Subcommittee on Bomber Defenses of the Preparedness Investigating Subcommittee of the Armed Services Committee was, similarly, the first testimony by a representative of a public interest group before the *Senate* Armed Services Committee. Chairman Senator John Stennis, startled at my youthful appearance, called me to the dais and said, "Your testimony is very interesting—surely not the work of one mind?" He was assured that I was not a stalking horse for anyone else.

72. Federation of American Scientists statement in testimony before the Ad Hoc Subcommittee on Research and Development, Senate Armed Services Committee, May 19, 1971.

73. Orr Kelly, "Scientists Hit U.S. Claim on Soviet Budget," *The Evening Star*, May 19, 1971.

74. "NATO: A Taste of Soviet Wine," *Time* (June 7, 1971).

75. I. F. Stone, *I. F. Stone's Weekly*, May 28, 1956.

76. A second smear occurred, twenty years later, in 1992, after his death, through the deliberate misinterpretation, by the far right press, of a speech by a former Soviet press attaché named Kalugin, a KGB functionary, who referred to his lunches with a "splendid American journalist." According to the press attaché's later book, what Stone had done, after the 1968 Soviet invasion of Czechlosovakia, was to refuse to let Kalugin pay for Stone's lunch by saying, "No, I will never take money from your bloody government." The smear had arisen when one person deliberately took this to mean "never take money *again*," the implication being that it referred to more than lunch. Oleg Kalugin, *The First Directorate* (New York: St. Martin's Press, 1994), p. 74.

77. Letter of August 16, 1971, from George P. Felleman.

78. In Alsop's personal records, deposited in the Library of Congress, is his daily personal schedule card for June 10 on which, in his hard-to-read handwriting, he recorded personal information about me that someone was giving him—in such detail that it must have been read to him from a dossier rather than from memory.

It may have come from his luncheon partner, the late Andrew John Biemiller, an ex-congressman from Ohio who was, at that time, director of the Department of legislation of the AFL-CIO. The only other people on his printed schedule for that day were a caller for an oral history of Robert Kennedy and a representative from the Netherlands embassy. See the Joseph and Steward Alsop Collection at the Library of Congress.

79. Joseph Alsop, "The Balance of Power," *The Washington Post*, October 27, 1971. *The Los Angeles Times* deleted two references to me before publishing this column, much as it had suppressed the entire first smear. But the syndicate sent the article out as drafted. Alsop repeated the idea that we were trying to "get" Foster in his national column of Wednesday, January 5, 1972, entitled "The Research Gap," which appeared in *The Washington Post*.

Much later, in August, he did quote me accurately: "The Department of Defense has become an inventor and merchandiser of exaggerated fears," which was certainly true for its time. Joseph Alsop, "The Anti-Defense Lobby," *The Washington Post*, August 20, 1972.

Chapter 7

80. FAS newsletter of March 1972.
81. Raoul Berger, *Executive Privilege: A Constitutional Myth* (Cambridge: Harvard University Press, 1974).
82. His study appears in *UCLA Law Review* 12, 1044, and was reprinted in a full 150 pages in the Ervin hearings.
83. The executive secretary position was set up by the National Security Act of 1947 and 1949 and was supposed to be held by a civilian.
84. FAS newsletter of March 1972.
85. Three weeks after our newsletter came out, *The Washington Post*'s Murrey Marder wrote, "That issue was not pressed very sharply in the recent hearings, but it is being pursued more openly by the Federation of American Scientists, who note that some presidential advisers who wear several functional hats do testify before Congress in capacities apart from their confidential relationships with the President. "The Budget for Foreign Policy," March 23, 1972, editorial page.
86. According to Marder's article, Kissinger "occasionally has met with Foreign Relations Committee members at Fulbright's home and elsewhere—and plans to again." So the meetings at Blair House were an upgrading and formalizing.
87. Letter of April 20, 1972, to the author.
88. See the newspapers of the next day; the use of the word "formal" was probably to protect Henry Kissinger's informal meetings.
89. H. R. Haldeman, *The Haldeman Diaries* (New York: G. P. Putnam's Sons, 1994), p. 589. Shows press secretary Ron Ziegler talking nervously to Haldeman about Ervin's threat.
90. And, on March 25, a *Washington Post* article observed that Dean's April 20, 1972, letter to me had been dated two days after the White House agreed to let the presidential aide Peter Flanigan testify on limited aspects of the ITT controversy then standing in the way of Richard Kleindienst's confirmation as attorney general. George Lardner Jr., "Once Doubtful Executive Privilege Expanded in Scope," March 25, 1975.
91. According to Lardner's article, Nixon was demanding, on April 22, 1948, an FBI report on Dr. Edward U. Condon, former head of the Bureau of Standards. Condon had been emphatically cleared by the executive branch but denounced by the House Un-American Activities Committee. President Truman decided to forbid the FBI from providing reports on government employee loyalty to the Congress. Nixon had said this was untenable and would mean that presidents could "arbitrarily" do the same thing in case of corruption.

I had a personal reason for being content that Nixon's harassment of Condon had come back to haunt him. Condon, a universally loved scientist, had, in his important capacity as director of the Bureau of Standards, given me a reference for admission to MIT. And it was later reported to me that his secretary had commented on typing the reference, "If he is so good, why doesn't he go to Harvard?"

92. John Dean, *Blind Ambition* (New York: Simon and Schuster, 1976), p. 210.

93. Dean, op. cit., p. 201.

94. David E. Rosenbaum, "Gray Testifies He Gave Data on Watergate Inquiry to Dean Without Telling Kleindienst of FBI Aides," *The New York Times*, March 22, 1973.

Chapter 8

95. November 1972 was an exception devoted mainly to a report of the Ad Hoc Committee on Science, Technology, and Education, composed of Professors Herman Feshback and Jeffrey Steinfeld of MIT and Harvard junior fellow Joel Primack.

The only other newsletter exception in the seventies was October 1979, after a staff assistant (Deborah Bleviss) was hired to work on conservation. The newsletter was a "Conservation Manifesto" organized by her and signed or prepared by Samuel M. Berman, Anthony C. Fisher, Jack M. Hollander, Arthur Rosenfeld, Marc H. Ross, Robert Socolow, Robert H. Williams, Robert Stobaugh, and Daniel Yergin.

96. "Blot Night," With Apologies to A. E. Housman, *Voodoo Magazine* (April 1954).

97. Edward Cowan, "Scientists Urge Shift on Reactor," *The New York Times*, February 7, 1973.

98. Thomas O'Toole, "U.S. Urged to Revamp Its Energy Agencies," *The Washington Post*, February 7, 1973.

99. Here the experts who had "reviewed and endorsed" were James A. Fay of MIT, Richard Garwin of IBM, Irvin Glassman of Princeton, and Harold Johnston of Berkeley.

100. This editorial was "prepared or reviewed by" Allen V. Kneese, James MacKenzie, Laurence I. Moss, and Philip Morrison.

101. I once asked a scientist why the brilliant Harold Brown, who had graduated from Bronx Science in only two years as a valedictorian and *wunderkind*, had not continued as a research scientist. "Oh," the scientist said, "he made a mistake in his thesis."

102. Letter of January 29, 1974, from Dean Harvey Brooks to S. David Freeman.

103. This quote is from my letter to Joseph L. Sax of February 11, 1974, and represents a reaction at the time.

104. Membership was, in fact, 1,500 in June 1970, 2,300 in June 1971, 3,600 in June 1972, and 6,000 in June 1973.

105. Jeremy J. Stone, "Bread from the Waters," *The New York Times*, April 29, 1978.

106. His key endorsement was, "Closer association with the FAS confirmed my prior

feeling that it meets the essential criteria of an effective organization; scientific objectivity in fact finding, analysis, and impartial but forceful presentation of evidence, together with demonstrated effectiveness in directing its efforts toward realistic and significant goals." Letter of September 14, 1972, from Edward L. Tatum to the author.

107. Jude Wanniski, "Teddy Kennedy's 'Shadow Government,'" *The Wall Street Journal*, March 27, 1973.

108. 1946: 1621 K St., NW; 1948: 1749 L St., NW; 1955: 1805 H St., NW; 1960: 1700 K St., NW; 1963: 223 Mills Bldg.; 17th & Penn. Ave., NW; 1964: 2025 Eye St., NW, Suite 313.

109. The $10,000 donation was from Max Palevsky, $5,000 was from Bernard Lee Schwartz, and another $5,000 was donated by Julian Price II, a young man who one year had sent us an unsolicited donation in the mail that was half of our annual $60,000 budget. In constant 1998 dollars, these donations are all worth more than four times as much.

110. As former presidential science adviser George Kistiakowsky put it, in accepting the Priestly Medal in 1972, "The Federation of American Scientists, for its small membership, plays a major role in challenging self-serving plans of the military-industrial complex. An increase in its membership and resources would enable the Federation to extend its sound political interventions into other socio-technological areas."

111. Philip M. Boffey, "On Scientists as Lobbyists," *The New York Times*, September 4, 1985.

Chapter 9

112. David Binder, "Options Seen on U.S.-Soviet Arms," *The New York Times*, March 17, 1977.

113. On June 19, 1973, in a most unusual situation, Metcalf refused to call me to the witness stand to present my scheduled testimony on the grounds that it represented a "rather vitriolic attack on the sponsor of this legislation" (himself) even though, as my testimony showed, he himself had called the legislation at issue "preposterous" when he introduced it as a sponsor! But I was supported in *The Washington Post* ("Battle Stirs over Seabed Mines Bill," George C. Wilson) and in *Science* ("Ocean Technology: Race to Seabed Wealth Disturbs More Than Fish," May 25, 1973, 851).

114. Jeremy J. Stone and William Colby, "Block the Khmer Rouge," *The Washington Post*, April 28, 1989; and, "Playing Into Pol Pot's Hands," *The Washington Post*, December 10, 1989.

115. February 28, 1990, Subcommittee on East Asian and Pacific Affairs, Committee on Foreign Relations, Senate, Re: Cambodia Policy: Time for a Change.

116. Jeremy J. Stone and William Colby, "Break the Siege of Sarajevo," *The Washington Post*, January 15, 1993.

117. William Colby, *Honorable Men: My Life in the CIA* (New York: Simon and Schuster, 1978).
118. Ibid., pp. 334–335.
119. Under the cover of wanting to help "organize" my files, she had, without instruction, gone through them all and then "borrowed" my Rolodex for an evening to help me "clean it up." My desk drawer had gotten a similar treatment, and she advised me, in a way that Freud would have appreciated, that she had worked as a spy on a notable California personality (this is leakage and a desire to get caught). Although she was a very efficient secretary, I finally decided it was unfair to those who dealt with me to have her facilitating the government's opening files on all of them. (Colby's role in dismantling this illegal CIA operation is described in *Honorable Men*, pp. 314–317.)
120. It was in the community of Scientists' Cliffs, a two-hundred-family community, founded, as a summer colony, by biologists in November 1935.
121. This was the conclusion of the autopsy.

Chapter 10

122. The notion of a U.S.-Soviet ban on the first use of nuclear weapons was discussed in "A Proposal for a Ban on the First Use of Nuclear Weapons" by Morton H. Halperin (*Journal of Arms Control* 1, no. 2 [April 1963]: 112–123). And the notion of having the executive branch unilaterally forswear any plans for first use of nuclear weapons had also been long discussed.
123. This was the explanation provided to Congress in 1975 by Secretary of Defense James R. Schlesinger in "The Theater Nuclear Force Posture in Europe," prepared in compliance with Public Law 93–365.
124. The experts included Herbert F. York, Herbert Scoville Jr., Marvin Goldberger, Adrian Fisher, Morton H. Halperin, Leslie Gelb, Eugene Skolnikoff, and Richard H. Ullman along with the FAS "executive committee," by which mechanism I included myself without specific reference.
125. It would, we said, give the United States a new option, better than the oft-discussed "demonstration nuclear attack"—a vote warning that we were giving the president authorization to use nuclear weapons.
126. The amendment read as follows: "Sec. 3. In the absence of a declaration of war by the Congress, the Armed Forces of the United States may be employed by the President only—
    (1) to respond to any act or situation that endangers the United States, its territories or possessions, or its citizens or nationals when the necessity to respond to such act or situation in his judgment constitutes a national emergency of such a nature as does not permit advance congressional authorization to employ such forces; but the President may not under any circumstances use nuclear weapons first without the prior, explicit authorization of the Congress.

127. First use meant, of course, the introduction of nuclear weapons into conventional hostilities, whereas first strike meant a preemptive nuclear Pearl Harbor. Congressmen in the know promptly introduced a joint resolution to "renounce the strategy of a first strike with nuclear weapons." (H.J. Res. 626, September 3, 1975; Bingham, Spellman, Solarz, and Dodd were cosponsors, among others.)

128. "The First-Use Hubbub," *The Washington Post,* July 8, 1975.

129. Based on our having raised this question during the War Powers debate in 1971–1972, an eminent authority on the commander-in-chief clause, Columbia University law professor Louis Henkin, wrote, "In my view, [the President] would be bound to follow congressional directives not only as to whether to continue the war, but whether to extend it to other countries and other belligerents, whether to fight a limited or unlimited war today, *perhaps even whether to fight a 'conventional' or a nuclear war* [italics added]." ("Foreign Affairs and the Constitution," 108, and footnote 49, pp. 351–352 [Norton Library, W. W. Norton and Company, 1975].)

130. Letter of October 1, 1975, from Thomas A. Halsted, executive director, reporting on the September 30 meeting of the board of directors of ACA.

131. Letter of December 5, 1975, from Charles Price, chairman of the Council for a Livable World, to Senator Alan Cranston, and resolution adopted by the board of the Council for a Livable World at its meeting of December 14, 1975.

132. Jeremy J. Stone, "Presidential First Use Is Unlawful," *Foreign Policy* (Fall 1984): 56.

133. Letter of James P. Wade Jr., director DOD SALT Task Force, to David C. Prince, December 16, 1975.

134. For example, on July 21, 1954, Chet Holifield said, "That particular provision was written in especially so that no trigger-happy general could take one of these atomic bombs and start dropping it anywhere in the world and start an atomic war. We wrote that provision in because we . . . must put a solemn obligation on the President that the President and the President alone can designate when and where an atomic weapon is to be used." 110 Cong., *Congressional Record,* 10687.

135. Stone, "Presidential First Use Is Unlawful," pp. 101–102.

136. Press release, embargoed for September 9, on the September 5 press conference on "Presidential First Use Is Unlawful."

137. They referred to the St. Petersburg Declaration, the Hague Conventions, the Geneva Gas Protocol, the Genocide Convention, and the Geneva Conventions.

138. They warned soldiers that refusal to obey could involve severe penalties, urged them to take legal advice, and invited them to write the group at "Nuremberg, BM Box 8072, London WC1N 3XX."

139. Louis Henkin wrote me later, during the 1984 debate, that one who urged disobedience could raise a free speech claim. "But the court might not give him/her standing to challenge the constitutionality of Presidential use of nuclear weapons; that would depend on whether that question is deemed relevant to the free speech claim. Also, the court might not reach that question if it decided that the national interest in military discipline outweighs the free speech interest, whether or not the order is constitutional." Letter of July 9, 1984.

140. Richard Dudman, "Missile Critic Is Retired," *St. Louis Post-Dispatch*, September 25, 1975.

141. Letter of September 30, 1975, to James R. Schlesinger from the author.

142. Jeremy J. Stone, "An Exchange of Views; Four Observers Evaluate Opposition to the War," *Commonweal*, July 14, 1967, p. 444.

143. Peter Raven-Hansen, ed., *First Use of Nuclear Weapons: Under the Constitution, Who Decides?* (Greenwood Press, 1987).

144. Stone, "Presidential First-Use Is Unlawful," p. 108.

145. See Senator Byrd's submission to the *Congressional Record*, April 15, 1986, S4316.

146. This letter, of which I have a copy, is undated, but I received my copy before April 22, so it was sent in the week after the Libyan raid.

147. Scott Cohen and Jeremy J. Stone, "If Congress Is Afraid to Declare War," *The New York Times*, August 19, 1990.

148. Opening page of Senate *Congressional Record*, October 2, 1990.

149. Letter of June 18, 1984.

Chapter 11

150. There is a school of thought that strongly opposes any suggestion that first use of the already banned chemical and biological weapons be linked to the use of nuclear weapons—even to the point of questioning whether chemical and biological nuclear weapons are really weapons of mass destruction in the same sense as nuclear weapons. (See Wolfgang K. H. Panofsky, "Dismantling the Concept of 'Weapons of Mass Destruction,'" *Arms Control Today* [April 1998].) While it might well be preferable, from the point of view of nuclear arms control per se, to have all countries assert "no first use" of nuclear weapons themselves if this could be obtained—it thus far has not. Under the circumstances, a World Court opinion that first use of nuclear weapons was banned—with the possible exception of a response to chemical or biological weapons—would have been, it seems obvious to me, a step forward. And this is most emphatically so if that opinion was drafted in the way I had in mind, as a flat ban—a way that minimized the significance of the exception and left it as a matter of debate whether the exception existed at all, indeed, whether any use was permitted at all! But others disagree.

151. The idea of a "request for an advisory opinion from the International Court of Justice on the legality of the threat or use of nuclear weapons" was a part of a draft resolution introduced by Indonesia on behalf of the Movement of Nonaligned Countries in November 1993 at the forty-eighth session of the United Nations in its First Committee. And it was raised at the General Assembly itself in 1994. But according to *World Citizen News* (December/January 1996), the nonaligned members of the General Assembly were "successfully lobbied" to do so by several nongovernmental organizations that established the World Court Project in order to establish, according to customary international law, the "illegality of nuclear weapons."

152. Experts endorsing the proposition included such key former officials (with their former titles) as the secretary of the Smithsonian, Robert Adams; the editor of the *Bulletin of the Atomic Scientists,* Ruth Adams; the Nobel laureate and head of the theoretical division at Los Alamos, Hans Bethe; the author Ann Druyan; the Nobel laureate and head of the Atomic Energy Commission, Glenn Seaborg; the president of the California Institute of Technology, Marvin Goldberger; the deputy national security adviser to President Kennedy, Carl Kaysen; the award-winning astrophysicist Richard Muller; the World Federalist president, Charles Price; the assistant director for national security in the White House Office of Science and Technology, Frank von Hippel; and the ambassador to the Comprehensive Test Ban talks, Herbert F. York.

153. Since the court had, earlier, decided not to invite amicus briefs for this occasion, it decided not to accept an unsolicited one. In fact, fearing a deluge of amicus briefs arising from my reference to ours in the *Tribune,* the president of the court, Mohammed Bedjaoui, instructed the court secretary to write *The International Herald Tribune* assuring the readers that "all such documents are given consistent treatment" and that readers should not think that it had been made part of the record. (*The International Herald Tribune,* November 15, 1995.)

154. It read, "The United States will not use nuclear weapons against any non-nuclear-weapons state party to the NPT [Non-Proliferation Treaty] or any comparable internationally binding commitment not to acquire nuclear explosive devices, except in the case of an attack on the United States, its territories or armed forces, or its allies, by such a state allied to a nuclear-weapons state or associated with a nuclear-weapons state in carrying out or sustaining the attack." (*Department of State Bulletin,* August 1978.)

155. It said the court was trying to answer *four* distinct questions, which no one pleading before it had bothered to distinguish. The legality of "threat or use" was, already, two questions, and considering that the circumstances might be retaliation for nuclear use or just "first use," this was really four questions. The paper argued that "threat or use" in first-use circumstances had already been abandoned by the nuclear powers. But threat of second use to deter nuclear use by others kills no one and even helps prevent nuclear attacks; ruling this out, in this time period, seemed politically and morally inappropriate. Carrying out retaliatory threats was quite a different matter—it needed to be questioned.

156. These several papers can be found in FAS *PIR,* January/February 1996.

157. Paragraph 95 of the decision of Judge Bedjaoui.

158. The court did say, unanimously, that threats or use of nuclear weapons must be consistent with not only treaties but also "other undertakings which expressly deal with nuclear weapons"; in that capacity, it presumably included the negative security assurances noted earlier.

159. Section 48 of the Advisory Opinion.

160. This assumes that the United States considered such a response consistent with its "undertaking" in its negative security assurance because the court ruled that such

undertakings had to be maintained. This question also turns on the issue of "belligerent reprisal," in which a state reserves the right to do prohibited things to deter or respond to prohibited acts of another state. Of this the court explicitly said little except that such reprisals would have to be governed by the principle of "proportionality."

161. Section 47 of the Advisory Opinion comments that "no State" had suggested otherwise.

Chapter 12

162. Letter of August 31, 1971, to Dr. Henry Kissinger from the author.

163. Letter of September 13 from Henry Kissinger to the author.

164. I knew that from 1935–1939, NAS was listed in organization charts as part of the *legislative* branch. From 1939–1940, it was listed in the U.S. Information Service records as part of the *executive* branch. From March 1941 to the present, it appeared in the Federal Register as "quasi-official." (Asked to explain this drift, the director of the Federal Register threw up his hands, said he could find no records for the "several changes of treatment" of NAS, and said the "best answer" he could give for NAS being listed among "quasi-official" agencies was "for want of a better place to put it." (Letter of June 26, 1974, from Fred J. Emery to the author.)

165. Jerome Alan Cohen, "Zhou Tiptoes Toward Exchange Visits," *The Washington Post*, June, 1972.

166. Nancy Tang, their best translator, had great stamina; she had translated for four hours in the morning at our meeting with the vice foreign minister and for four hours that evening with the prime minister. She had grown up in New York as the daughter of a Chinese UN undersecretary. At the first meeting, I learned to my great surprise that she knew my uncle, the late Leonard Boudin, a famous constitutional lawyer in New York. (In the 1920s, I. F. Stone and Leonard Boudin had married two sisters, Esther and Jean Roisman.)

167. Harrison E. Salisbury, "Zhou Cites Eisenhower and Korea as Way to End War," *The New York Times*, June 17, 1972.

168. Percy Jucheng Fang and Lucy Guinong J. Fang, *Zhou Enlai—A Profile* (Beijing: Foreign Languages Press). They say that Zhou was discovered to have cancer "in 1972."

169. Li Zhisui, *The Private Life of Chairman Mao* (New York: Random House, 1994), p. 572.

170. Ibid., pp. 572–573.

171. Ibid., pp. 582.

172. Ibid., pp. 583.

173. Ibid., p. 609.

174. See October 20 announcement of the NAS. According to *Science & Government*

Report, NAS had lobbied the Chinese in a variety of ways and, in particular, had advised the Chinese that their medical delegation to the Institute of Medicine (IOM) had, in effect, already been hosted by NAS since, unbeknownst to the Chinese, IOM was part of NAS. *The Science & Government Report* gave the Chinese eagerness for science and technology as the reason why Beijing found "the quasi-official Academy preferable to the semi-dissident Federation." December 15, 1972.

175. I wrote Henry Kissinger on September 7 saying we had a "firm and repeated oral agreement with the PRC" to receive ten Chinese scientists. The government was in the process then of giving us the bad news. (Letter of September 11, 1972, from John H. Holdridge of the NSC staff.)

176. *Nature* (November 3, 1972): 6.

177. See, for example, "A Chinese View of U.S. Technology," *San Francisco Chronicle*, December 15, 1972, or "Chinese Students Learn to Serve," *Washington Evening Star*, November 22, 1972, and, especially, the official *Peking Review*, no. 5, February 2, 1973; at the November 21 banquet given at the National Academy of Sciences for the delegation, the CSCPRC chairman, Emil Smith, gave a toast acknowledging its debt to FAS for helping to make the visit possible.

178. This, I believe, was suggested by the CSCPRC's staffer Ann Keatley to salve the FAS's wounded feelings.

179. Letter of September 13, 1973, from the author to Goldberger asking, "Is there some political reason why we have not gotten any report on your trip?"

180. We had sent a delegation of economists—John Kenneth Galbraith, Wassily Leontief, and James Tobin—who were in China from September 8, 1972. (See FAS *PIR*, January 1973, p. 1.) Tobin wrote a report for *Challenge Magazine* (March/April 1973); and John Kenneth Galbraith wrote a book about it: *A China Passage* (Boston: Houghton Mifflin, 1973).

Chapter 13

181. André Gide, *Back from the U.S.S.R.* (Martin Secker & Warburg, 1937), p. 45.

182. John Steinbeck, *A Russian Journal* (New York: Viking Press, 1948), p. 26.

183. Delia Kuhn and Ferdinand Kuhn, *Russia on Our Minds* (New York: Doubleday, 1970), p. 288.

184. Robert Kaiser, *Russia: The People and the Power* (New York: Atheneum, 1976), pp. 452–453.

185. Press release of October 2, 1958.

186. Undated report on 1974 trip.

187. Press release of December 3, 1978.

188. S.3127 Introduction of a Bill to Provide for the Exchange of Governmental Officials Between the United States and the Union of Soviet Socialist Republics. *Congressional Record*, November 7, 1969, S13944–13947.

189. From 1972 to 1982, the average annual number of U.S. passports shown at the

Soviet border was 78,000. If each of these represented a *different* person, and if this went on for seventy-five years—the average life expectancy of an American—the number of people in this period visiting the Soviet Union would be 6 million, and the percentage of the U.S. population that would have experienced the Soviet Union would stabilize at no more than 2.5 percent. Statistics supplied by Sidney Reiner of Cosmos Travel Service in New York.

190. In badly overestimating the prospects for such a vast program, Gravel was showing a characteristic impulsiveness combined with an instinct for the main chance. This showed itself the next year when he became famous for abusing his prerogatives as chairman of a Public Works Subcommittee to release the secret Pentagon Papers in a late-night, hastily called meeting. (Earlier he had sought to involve me in this by saying, in the privacy of his office, "I want your soul"; I immediately indicated that my soul was not available and departed, happily, without being burdened with the knowledge of what the hell he was talking about—characteristically, I wanted nothing to do with anything that was improper or illegal.) Gravel was protected from Senate expulsion by Democratic Majority Leader Mike Mansfield, but his aid Charlie Ferris, who knew I was appalled by this, said to me later, "Jeremy, I have assured those who have asked me that you had nothing to do with this, but you must face the fact that the horse you have been riding [Senator Gravel] has gone underground."

191. These are average estimates based on the annual *Congressional Quarterly* tabulations beginning in about 1965.

192. *Congressional Record*, Senate, S6020.

193. *Congressional Record*, Senate, November 20, 1985, letter of November 14.

194. In 1971 Gravel was persuaded to strip the bill down (abandoning the mayors, governors, and so on). But it was never reintroduced. Why I do not know.

195. Letter of November 15, 1971. This letter said that it required no answer, and I do not think it received one.

196. "Second, we hope out of this visit [to Beijing] could grow at least a beginning of some exchanges in other than political fields that would permit the two peoples to get to know each other better." November 30 press conference on upcoming trip to China in the *Congressional Record*, Senate, December 1, 1971, S20078.

197. For our analysis, we used their votes on such issues as the B-1 bomber, the confirmation of Paul C. Warnke as SALT negotiator, and the Jackson resolution on missile parity.

198. Jeremy J. Stone, "Let's Send Our Senators to Moscow," *The Washington Post*, December 4, 1977.

199. His letter of January 10, 1983, said in part, "I believe members of the United States Congress should visit the Soviet Union, providing they have an objective of specific information relating to their legislative responsibilities, are fully briefed in advance, and are organized to carry out the purpose of the trip."

200. Former secretary of state Dean Rusk was an exception, saying facetiously that he was not sure that the Soviets would "recover from such a traumatic event" as 535 con-

gressmen turned "loose" in the Soviet Union. He doubted that a "few days' visit could provide any more than a very superficial impression." Letter of January 6, 1983.

In a subsequent letter of February 10, 1983, he raised the issue of congressmen getting "quite miffed" if they were not received by top officials. But, he said, "These leaders in other countries are busy people and simply cannot take the time to visit with a continuing parade of American senators and congressmen, nor would our President meet with considerable numbers of parliamentarians visiting from other countries." (Evidently, Rusk visited the Soviet Union only once, in 1963, for the signing of the Limited Test Ban Treaty. I considered these letters as indications that he was of a very pedestrian turn of mind.)

201. Quoted from *Arizona Daily Star*, March 27, 1983.
202. Of twelve full members of the Politburo and thirteen candidate and secretariat members, only the full members—Gromyko, Kunayev, Shcherbitskiy, and Tikhonov—and four candidate members had been to America.
203. They came from newspapers in Los Angeles, Denver, Hartford, Washington, Detroit, Pittsburgh, Wilmington, Phoenix, Tucson, Memphis, Houston, Milwaukee, Spokane, Newport News, and so on.
204. Jeremy J. Stone, "Let Our Senators Go! (to Russia)," *The Washington Post*, March 27, 1983.
205. His press release was entitled "Another Kind of Travel Abuse" (i.e., *not* traveling). Our files were full of articles condemning congressional "junketing." *U.S. News and World Report* articles were an example: "Our Junket-Happy Congress," June 27, 1977; "The Great American Bureaucratic Junketing Machine," December 18, 1978; "The Great American Bureaucratic 'Perks' Machine," December 17, 1979; "Does Economy Begin at Home? Not in Congress," May 4, 1981; and "Congressional Junketeers On the Wing Again," October 26, 1981.
206. Press release of Dole office of July 25, 1983. The bill, referred to the Rules and Administration Committee, never had hearings and died.
207. The team consisted of Ann Hoopes, Cely Arndt, Nori Huddle, Kathy Kenety, Mary Leegh, Betsy Marshall, Stratton McKillop, Beverly Meeker, Martha Newell, Susan Rappaport, Ann Shirk, and Fran Wells.
208. H. Res. 116 had sixty-one cosponsors and was introduced on March 27, 1985.
209. "Raising the Rate of Exchange," FAS *Report*, p. 27.
210. The percentages were up to 56 percent of the Senate and 36 percent of the House; a major problem in getting these percentages up was the continuing electoral process that produced new members—few had ever been to the Soviet Union *before* their election. Updated internal memo, "US-Soviet Parliamentary Exchanges."
211. This formulation, which I wish I had thought of earlier, came to me during a panel debate with Paul C. Warnke and R. James Woolsey when a woman in the audience asked what *she* could do. The idea came to me on the spot that she could, with just a little courage, stand up at a meeting when her congressman next spoke and ask this embarrassing question.
212. FAS *PIR*, May 1985, p. 5.

213. FAS *PIR*, March 1987.

214. FAS *PIR*, June 1987, p. 12.

215. Jeremy J. Stone, testimony on "Reciprocal Visits by U.S. and Soviet Parliamentarians" to the Commission on Security and Cooperation in Europe, November 17, 1987.

216. R. Jeffrey Smith, "The Dissenter," *The Washington Post*, December 7, 1997.

217. I had hoped they would take me along, but they took Alton Frye! This is the trip referred to in Chapter 28; Cohen and Frye used the trip to promote build-down.

218. When I asked for a copy of this poem, an aide in his office reported that Senator Cohen did not remember writing it. But I saw it.

Chapter 14

219. This paper appears in the FAS newsletter of October 1973.

220. Cable of September 8, 1973, from Philip Handler to Academician M. V. Keldysh, the president of the Soviet Academy of Sciences.

221. Deborah Shapley, "Sakharov: Teetering at the Brink: Part II: How NAS Stepped into Furor over Soviet Dissident 23," *Science* (September 1973): 1231–1232. The key figures preparing the letter were the NAS foreign secretary, Harrison Brown, and, from Harvard, Dean Harvey Brooks and Paul Doty. And, of course, it needed and received the support of President Philip Handler.

222. The reporter continued, saying that American scientists "interpreted this as a sign that open discussion of the Sakharov case would not imperil him further." More likely, they concluded that their intervention would not produce an explosive Soviet reaction since my intervention had not.

223. This is similar to the remarks made by Sakharov two years later, when he received his Nobel Prize: "I am likewise convinced that freedom of conscience, together with the other civic rights, provides . . . a guarantee that scientific advances will not be used to despoil mankind." Nobel Prize Lecture, 1975.

224. "Dr. Jeremy Stone, director of the FAS, acknowledged the apparent contradiction of the scientific community's traditional support of an easing of relations with communist nations. However," he said, "military détente is only a temporary and fragile solution to the arms race, too easily reversible in the absence of internal criticism." *The Washington Post*, September 18, 1973.

225. The petition read, "Mr. Ambassador: I wish to join with FAS in endorsing this statement: Co-existence and détente between East and West make it all the more important that we, as scientists, insist on the right of our Soviet and Eastern European colleagues: to communicate and travel freely for scholarly purposes; to function as scientists inside their countries (or, if not so permitted, to leave them to function as scientists elsewhere); and, in general, to debate their views inside their countries and abroad." See FAS *PIR* 7, September 1974.

226. Hearing before the Committee on Foreign Affairs, House of Representatives, June

5, 1974, on "Détente—Scientific and Technological Relations." By this time there was a group specializing in the problems of Soviet Jewish scientists called "Committee of Concerned Scientists"—not to be confused with Union of Concerned Scientists (UCS)—and they joined me and another witness.

227. This was Chairman Philip Morrison, the most left of all the dozen chairmen I have had and the one who felt most strongly that this would simply ally us with anticommunists and, in other ways, would detract from our main goal of disarmament and peace.

Other senior officials were initially uneasy but saw the light. Thus former chairman Herbert F. York wrote reminding me that he had "expressed some concerns" about this work but that he was "especially moved" by what I and FAS were doing for Russian dissidents and refuseniks and thought that the new policy "makes sense" if we restrict our concern on human rights to "fellow scientists." Letter of December 8, 1975.

228. Andrei Sakharov's first hunger strike—and the only hunger strike that was not in defense of his family—began on June 28, 1974, "in protest against illegal and cruel repression of political prisoners." It was staged to coincide with the visit of President Nixon to Moscow, and it focused on Vladimir Bukovsky and eighty-two others. This is the only Sakharov hunger strike in which FAS was not involved.

229. "Scientists Urged to Boycott Meeting," *The Washington Post,* May 10, 1975.

230. See FAS *PIR* 8, September 1975.

231. In the Soviet system a Ph.D. would be a "candidate." After passing further examinations, one became a (full) doctor. The next level would be election to the Academy of Sciences as a "corresponding member." The highest rank would be "academician," and only a few hundred reached that level.

232. We had written to the Soviet Committee on Human Rights, care of Sakharov, its chairman, on January 9, 1973, to "describe our sympathetic interest in creative and constructive contacts between our two organizations" in an effort to provide Sakharov and his two or three colleagues with foreign support. It was, perhaps, the first Soviet organization that was independent of the Soviet government.

233. While staying at our home in Washington, much later, the eighty-year-old elder Mrs. Bonner described her sufferings in a Stalin-era prison camp, one located in a desert, where thirst was constant and water was rationed. She was released after Stalin's death but was not permitted to return to a major city and was forced to go with her granddaughter Tanya to small towns, where life was very hard. (These restrictions were designed to prevent the bulk of the citizenry from hearing about conditions in the camps. Accounts like these from Elena and her family had had a profound effect on Sakharov.)

234. Recognizing that he would be "snubbed" by his "national delegation"—Pugwash participation is normally decided by each national delegation—we suggested a quota of invitations for persons on an extraordinary basis "at the discretion of the secretariat." Letter from the author to Pugwash Continuing Committee members, December 8, 1975.

235. The text of this five-hundred-word "Sakharov Statement to FAS" appears in FAS *PIR* 7, December 1975.

236. After he finally emigrated to Israel, Azbel published *Refusenik: Trapped in the Soviet Union* (Houghton Mifflin, 1981), in which he wrote, "[Stone] ventured little comment on our Seminar, and we had no way of knowing what he thought of us until, after his return to America, we found he had energetically taken up our cause and become one of our most effective supporters" (p. 429).

237. This statement was made on April 21, 1933, less than three months after Hitler came to power.

238. In accordance with our "adoption" strategy, I personally adopted Turchin and sent him one of my books to translate to prevent him from being charged with "parasitism" (i.e., unemployment). He eventually migrated to the West, but only after being required to say he was Jewish—which he was not.

    Our March 1980 newsletter contains his testimony to the House of Representatives on January 31, in which he argues for "antisymmetry," that is, that the Soviet hawks were emboldened by the existence of Western doves (in arguing for Kremlin adventures) and that the Kremlin doves found useful the existence of Western hawks (in discouraging Kremlin adventures).

239. The last two pages of the newsletter were occupied with publishing the supersecret CIA memo in which its highest officials had tried to keep secret their mail-opening project. (See Chapter 5.) It seemed highly appropriate that our newsletter show us agitating for civil liberties and freedom in *both* countries.

240. We also listed two hundred names of refuseniks and asked members to propose which of these they would be willing to become pen pals with so as to organize some lifelines of correspondence.

241. Direct-mail letter "Dear Member of the Academy of Sciences" of December 17, 1975. I signed this letter.

242. I think it was Gordon MacDonald who confided this to me. I know that when Handler learned that MacDonald was chairman of an environmental committee for FAS, as well as for NAS, he demanded that MacDonald resign from the FAS position and, indeed, asked him to secure a letter from me confirming that Mac-Donald had resigned.

243. Philip Handler, speech of October 11, 1976, to the International Council of Scientific Unions.

244. Philip Handler, interview with *The Wall Street Journal*, April 13, 1975.

245. This was also our expectation, based on which we had urged that this study be done. (See my letter of March 11, 1982, to Robert Ehrlich of George Mason University, saying we may have been the "catalyzing agent" in having the study done.)

246. Much later, a group around Carl Sagan had concluded that "nuclear winter" would be induced by a nuclear war and that temperatures would drop enormously because of the smoke produced from nuclear war detonations and fires. This was a possible "killer" mechanism that NAS either had overlooked or did not agree with.

247. FAS press release embargoed for Saturday, October 4, 1975.

248. This was Marvin Goldberger, later the president of the Institute for Advanced Study and still later of the California Institute of Technology. He is now a dean at the University of California at San Diego.

249. "Atom-War Peril to Ozone Is Seen," *The New York Times*, October 5, 1975.

250. "Nuclear War: Federation Disputes Academy on How Bad Effects Would Be," *Science*, 190.

251. *Science* had it exactly right when it reported, "What happened was that Stone had called Howard J. Lewis, the NAS director of information, to say he had picked up complaints about Handler and the academy in Moscow. But Lewis, who had not been with Handler in Moscow, did not want to hear or to respond to them, and suggested that Stone call Handler directly. Stone countered with the suggestion that Handler, whom Lewis soon told of this conversation, could call him if he wished. This is where the matter was left—neither principal called the other. Most reporters would probably agree that Stone fell short of a good-faith effort to elicit Handler's reaction to the complaints made about him and that the academy made no real effort to provide Stone with Handler's reaction." Luther J. Carter, "Academy v. Federation of Scientists: Handler Accuses Stone of 'Ugly Act,'" *Science* (January 16, 1976).

252. In a letter of January 5, 1976, Chairman Morrison said the comments on nuclear war had been "approved by us in advance with virtual unanimity." A placating offer was made to publish, in our newsletter, more about what NAS had done on Soviet scientists. But Handler was told that "we cannot accept certain complaints made about our Director, to whom we are indebted for the rejuvenation of our organization and in whose integrity we have full and tested confidence."

     I had already written Howard Lewis on December 24 to confirm that we were offering him space in our next newsletter to repair any injustice, but NAS never responded to that letter. In April an NAS spokesman told *Science & Government Report* that NAS was "reluctant" to have details published in the FAS newsletter since most of the negotiations with the Soviets "took place in confidence." (Daniel Greenberg, April 1, 1976, issue.)

253. *Nature* (January 22, 1976).

254. Ibid.

255. I was nervous about how this would come out. But a journalist whose opinion I respected read the article and said, "You won."

256. More than eight hundred members joined us and this paid for the mailing. The 125,000 scientists were the subscribers to *Science* (i.e., essentially the members of the American Association for the Advancement of Science, and the members of the American Physical Society).

257. It concluded, "In short, public representations would strengthen the NAS private representations; would do no serious damage to NAS goals; would not lead to serious Administration chastisement; have no substitute in the activities of other organizations; would not be undermined by repetition; and would not importantly poison the international atmosphere." Undated analysis of eight relevant questions on FAS stationery by the author.

258. On January 21, 1976, Victor Franzusoff sent us a Russian-language broadcast on the recent article of *Science* magazine; it contrasted Handler's approach to mine.

259. FAS press conference of February 20, 1976. To our horror, the American Institute of Biological Sciences (AIBS) and the Federation of American Societies for Experimental Biology (FASEB) both refused to let us rent their lists, at commercial rates, to defend *their* biologist colleague. It took a while for the societies to get the message.

260. Through the help of Lipman Bers, then president of the American Mathematics Society and a leading FAS member, we had access to its mailing list at a reduced rate. Bers later became the first chairman of the NAS Committee on Human Rights.

261. FAS *PIR,* 1976.

262. See William Claiborne, "Senate Blasts Soviet Policy on Dissidents," *The Washington Post,* September 18, 1973, for a report on the NAS press release of a week before.

263. For example, the Nobel Prize winner Howard Temin announced he would not receive Soviet visitors in his laboratory until such time as Kovalev was given a needed operation in the Leningrad prison hospital. This was described to suitable authorities and came, as I recall, at a time consistent with the possibility that it might have been effective. (See the author's *FAS Activities in Defense of Soviet Colleagues: 1973–1977* [a report to the Symposium on Freedom of Science: La Biennale di Venezia, December 1977].)

264. Hearings on H.R. 9466 to establish a congressional commission on the Helsinki Accord before the Subcommittee on International Political and Military Affairs of the Committee on International Relations of the House of Representatives, May 4, 1976.

265. But it did take a while. For example, Sakharov had appealed to Handler about the Kovalev case in February 1975, almost a year before we sent NAS members our trip report. By March 18, 1976, a few months after our uprising, he was still writing FAS sponsors that Kovalev "knew what he was doing and what penalty to expect" and had not gotten in trouble for his scientific activities. Was it, he asked, "appropriate that the Academy support, in another country, some forms of what is there deemed to be political dissidence?" In April 1976 NAS put out new guidelines, which were Delphic in significance. (See Barbara Culliton, "Academy Adopts 'Affirmation of Freedom,'" *Science* [May 21, 1976]. This article errs in describing the Handler-Stone flap; see FAS *PIR* 4, June 1976.)

266. We learned of the creation of the Committee on Human Rights only after inspiring thirty NAS members to write to Handler in defense of the Moscow scientific seminar; to these members he wrote that a committee had been set up for such matters and that the NAS president would abide by its decisions.

267. On May 12 we wrote leading scientific societies asking them to create some kind of committee inside their society that would maintain data on the human rights problems of foreign colleagues—a committee to which interested members could repair for information. We sent copies of the newly adopted NAS guidelines for its

foreign secretary and asked whether these could be adopted as well. (See FAS *PIR* 8, September 1976.)

268. The letter, on the stationary of the Horton Hospital, Epsom, Surrey, England, said she had asked that he write "in a similar vein" to Victor Weisskopf but that Low-Beer did not have the address.

269. Andrei Sakharov, *Memoirs* (New York: Alfred Knopf, 1990), p. 472.

270. Ibid., p. 473.

Chapter 15

271. Andrei D. Sakharov, "This Frightful Situation," *The New York Times*, March 29, 1977.

272. Letter of August 18, 1977, to the FAS chairman, Philip Morrison, and the author.

273. Letter of July 11, 1976, received on August 4, 1976, appealing for help for Sergei Adamovich Kovalev, then in prison and needing an operation.

274. Tape of October 25, 1976; translation received by FAS, November 8, 1976.

275. "Soviets Send Sakharov to Isolated City," *The Washington Star*, January 23, 1980.

276. The *Bulletin of the Atomic Scientists*, famous for its "doomsday clock," was the educational arm of the movement of atomic scientists, while our Federation of American Scientists was the political action arm. The bulletin was created in Chicago, on November 24, 1945, three weeks after our Federation of Atomic Scientists (FAS) was founded in Washington, D.C., on October 31, 1945. (Our name was later changed to the Federation of American Scientists [FAS].) So we were the two original arms of the same atomic scientists' movement.

277. Letter to Anatoly Dobrynin from FAS of January 29, 1980, signed by Stone and Feld.

278. On January 31, we released the names of six Nobel Prize winners who agreed to our (refusenik) pledge not to work with Soviet scientists until Sakharov was released from internal exile. (See *Washington Post*, February 1, 1980.) And we began mailing the "Refusenik" pledge to NAS members as part of a poll. On that same day, January 31, Philip Handler testified that NAS would follow the lead of the State Department in a strategy of deferring "all bilateral seminars and the like, while permitting the activities of individual scientists to proceed on our usual basis, leaving decision to the individual consciences of American scientists." A few days later, on February 5, he sent a private communication to Soviet Academy president Aleksandrov warning that "any further deterioration" of Sakharov's position is "sure to result in termination of all forms of exchange between the U.S. and USSR scientific communities." To meet this problem, on February 26, we released the results of our poll of 1,280 NAS members and sent it to the Soviet Academy; it showed that 75 percent of the 20 percent who responded had chosen the FAS pledge. (See FAS *PIR*, March 1980, and letter of February 12, 1980, from Handler to Frank von Hippel.)

279. Moscow *Tass* in English 1838 GMT, January 28, 1980.

280. Letter from the author to Ambassador Dobrynin of June 5, 1980.

281. We were advised that the jamming in the apartment was so severe that Sakharov had to travel to a local park with a portable radio to hear Voice of America.

282. Letter of January 21, 1981.

283. Letter of February 26, 1981, from the author to Dobrynin.

284. Letter of June 2, 1981, from the author to Dobrynin.

285. Letter of October 5, 1981, from the author to Dobrynin.

286. By this time, stepson Alexei Semyonov had been permitted to emigrate and had been married by proxy, in one of the few states that permitted such marriages (Montana); this is why Andrei could use the word "daughter-in-law." The proxy marriage was performed to strengthen Semyonov's case, under the Helsinki Accord, for reunification of families. In Sakharov's letter he noted that the Soviet authorities did not acknowledge the validity of the proxy marriage—though he argued they could if they wished under Article 32 of the Soviet Matrimonial Code. In the end, the Soviets let her leave on a Soviet passport, with the right to travel abroad, rather than on an emigrant's exit permit, precisely because they feared the gimmick of a proxy marriage might spread. (See p. 3 of FAS *PIR*, January 1982; we learned this from a diplomat who, at our request, had taken the matter up with Dobrynin personally.)

287. In a two-inch article, *The Washington Post* announced, as early as November 10, that Sakharov had released an open letter to scientists in the West that he would begin a hunger strike on November 22. ("Sakharov Sets Hunger Strike," *The Washington Post,* November 10, 1981.)

288. *Nature* (November 26, 1981).

289. This telegram was sent to Lisa with instructions to relay it to Alexei, but it was also copied by Sakharov, in tiny script, with a magnifying glass in an effort to smuggle it out of the Soviet Union through intermediaries. (See Sakharov, *Memoirs*, p. 565.) It was sent not only to me but also to Joel Leibowitz of Rutgers University, who had also sent a telegram to Sakharov urging him to discontinue the hunger strike.

290. This background is drawn from FAS *PIR*, January 1982, p. 3. The December 2 stories were as follows: Dusko Doder, "Sakharov, Wife 'Okay' on 10th Day of Fast," *The Washington Post;* and John F. Burns, "Sakharovs Bearing Up in Their Hunger Strike," *The New York Times.*

291. FAS press release of December 1, 1981.

292. I authored a three-part series of op-ed essays, "The Lonely Battle of Andrei Sakharov," for *The Los Angeles Times* on May 27, 28, and 29, 1984. I did not feel free, however, in those reports to indicate the names of the persons we had rounded up to support Sakharov, but only the titles. Now that fifteen years have passed, it seems appropriate to recognize their good will. Few hesitated at all. Pamela Harriman refused for her husband, with a fairly common reservation—that Sakharov was engaging in a hunger strike to get an exit visa for a relative in a country that

gave nobody exit visas. (This is mentioned in a letter to Paul Warnke of November 30.) But later, on Marshal Shulman's intercession with Averil, he agreed. The three retired presidents were approached through intermediaries. President Nixon took the matter under advisement. (Sakharov had staged a hunger strike in 1974, during Nixon's trip to Moscow, to call attention to the mistreatment of political prisoners.) I believe it was President Carter who sent back word that he would make the call, much as he had supported Sakharov by writing him as president.

293. John M. Goshko, "Reagan Appeals to Soviets to End Sakharov Conflict," *The Washington Post*, December 5, 1981.

294. Sakharov, *Memoirs*, p. 572.

Chapter 16

295. Text of letter is reprinted in FAS *PIR*, May 1983.

296. Actually, in 1975, as noted in Chapter 13, after asking Sakharov's permission in personal conversation at his dacha, I had indeed written the Central Committee of International Pugwash with just this suggestion for Soviet-based Pugwash meetings. Later, the head of the Soviet Academy's Pugwash group advised me, in fatherly fashion, that the academy group had discussed my request and decided that if Sakharov attended, none of them would.

297. The chairman of the NAS delegation, our own former chairman, Marvin Goldberger, denied that they had applied to see her in the first place. And he said they broke off the lunch after hearing that she was planning to hold a press conference at it. In addition, it was the first day of their talks, and they felt it was inappropriate to start off their meeting in such a provocative manner.

298. Looking at Andrei's memoirs, I see that I arrived on the scene in late November, only a month after they began such thinking. Elena had had a heart attack in April. (*Memoirs*, p. 582.) On October 17 her condition had not stabilized. And around noon she said, "I think it's time we had a talk." After the talk, Andrei said, "I'll never betray you, myself, or the children." (*Memoirs*, p. 598.) This was the genesis of the hunger strike idea. But, interestingly, in Elena's talk with me—the last published interview with a foreigner before the hunger strike began May 2—the three conditions that she wanted Sakharov supporters to consider had nothing to do with *her* health. They were (1) improving *his* medical treatment through access to Moscow medical attention; (2) returning Sakharov to his Moscow dacha, where he could have regular contact with Soviet scientists; and (3) defending his right to emigrate.

299. Elena Bonner, *Alone Together* (New York: Alfred Knopf, 1986), p. 54.

300. After thanking me for the present sent via Elena, he said, "Now in the evenings I am getting acquainted with the computer, writing programs for more complicated problems, finding in this not an unconsiderable pleasure." (I *knew* he would!)

    The letter in support of Elena Bonner's trip abroad twice repeated a curious combination of medical need and human desire that cropped up in all subsequent appeals for Bonner thereafter. He said, "You are aware already of the struggle that we started for Elena's trip abroad *for the sake of treatment and to see our dear ones.*"

301. "Sakharov's Stepdaughter Sees Pope for Help with Kremlin," *The Washington Times,* May 24, 1984.

302. NAS press release of May 24.

303. Cables to Sakharov were sent directly to Gagarin 214, Apartment 3, Shcherbinka, 2, Gorky. But, of course, he was in a hospital. We thought the KGB might let this one through.

304. Cable of May 28, 1984, 12:06 P.M. EDT to Vice President E. P. Velikhov from the author.

305. "Soviet, Reacting to Rumors, Denies Sakharov Died," *The New York Times,* June 5, 1984.

306. "US Is Trying 'Quiet' Tactics in Bonner Case," *The Washington Post,* June 8, 1984.

307. *Time* (June 11, 1984).

308. About that time, there were stirrings of the possibility that Sakharov might be allowed to leave. The Soviet justice minister, then in Sweden, said that if Sakharov asked to leave he could go. When this was repeated in Moscow, Bonner told the press that she and her husband indeed wanted to leave. There were subsequent rumors that Sakharov was about to be given to Austria. But, as a key West European figure later told one of our scientists (Weisskopf, I think), the Soviet army vetoed Andropov's effort to send Sakharov abroad because Sakharov knew too much about the internal politics of the Soviet Union.

309. Kennedy said some very nice things about me to the throng and then, taken aside by his staff, was advised that he had better say something nice about the president of the National Academy of Sciences or there might be trouble. He did so.

310. In 1978 an advance team for a Kennedy visit persuaded the Soviets to put eighteen families on a list for "favorable consideration" for emigration.

311. And they were, in May 1985.

312. E.g., "I too have the right to say to Lusia: 'You are my self' (and 'my queen' as well)."(*Memoirs,* p. 576.) "My usual lack of assertiveness and my rather slow reaction time in debates may also have caused me to miss out on several opportunities. Lusia was sorely missed; in these respects, as well as many others, she has a definite advantage over me."

313. I also asked him about a December 7, 1984, *Wall Street Journal* article in which "Soviet émigrés" charged that Velikhov, Yuri Ovchinnikov, and Nikolai Basov had "conspired to misinform the political leadership about the consequences of letting Mr. Sakharov emigrate" because they "apparently have personal reasons to fear that Mr. Sakharov's release could damage their reputations." Velikhov said he had written memos about Sakharov's release but not of that nature. Time has proven that he was right, since Sakharov was eventually released and nothing of this kind happened.

314. Sakharov, *Memoirs,* p. 598.

315. Ibid., p. 600.

316. When Sakharov disappeared from his home on June 7, Larry said, "Imminent." On June 14 Larry received a cable and said he would visit Moscow in July—with the possibility of the senator making his trip in September. On June 25 he said, "Some of our guys demoted, looks bad." On June 28 it was, "cable reports things taking on even more serious aspects than before. Very important that Larry come."

317. Sakharov, *Memoirs*, p. 553.

318. Bonner, *Alone Together*, p. 609.

319. Sakharov, *Memoirs*, p. 612.

320. Ibid., p. 615.

321. Efrem, always relentlessly logical and very hardworking, justified asking me to make this request on the grounds that he was the best possible translator for Sakharov, and he felt there was no harm in asking. But, of course, my purpose for going to the forum was not just to talk to Sakharov. I was always very fond of Efrem. Once he explained to me how I could avoid the police around Andrei's Moscow apartment and see Elena Bonner by climbing in the window in the off-hours, when they were not around. I decided not to try.

322. FAS *PIR*, May 1987.

323. Anatoly Dobrynin, *In Confidence* (New York: Times Books, 1995), pp. 497–498.

Chapter 17

324. Indeed, our very precise correlations showed, for example, when Air France arrivals at JFK airport would boom Nova Scotia directly before JFK arrival. And after their departure from JFK, the secondary booms would be felt in Nova Scotia at predicted times. We found the same thing for British Airways Concordes. (See appendix to FAS press release of March 15, 1978, "FAS Relates Concorde to Mysterious High Altitude Explosions.")

325. Deborah Shapley, "East Coast Mystery Booms: A Scientific Suspense Tale," *Science* 1 (March 31, 1978): 416.

326. Ibid. He later concluded that too much of the boom's energy would be dissipated before it even reached the thermosphere, based on further studies of his own and the Defense Department.

327. Richard A. Kerr, "East Coast Mystery Booms: Mystery Gone but Booms Linger On," *Science* (January 19, 1979).

328. In an interview in July, 1998, Hattie Perry provided this further information: She had been credited, in the early 1970s, with preventing a 12,000 megawatt nuclear station from being built on Stoddart's Island, Shelburne Counrty, near her home and so was well known in political circles. Using this political standing, she had written to (among others) her member of Parliament, Lloyd Crouse, raising the issue of sonic booms based on a contact she had in England. This contact warned her that the Concorde was entering Canada's airspace illegally. Indeed, Crouse

raised the issue of sonic booms in the House of Commons on March 6 (the same day I was calling the Canadian embassy in Washington to advise it of my calculations and conclusions) but, on March 7, officials from Transport Canada called on her and tried to convince her that the booms were caused by military planes and that she should not tell anyone. She was therefore under considerable pressure and writes that my subsequent visit to Barrington on April 12 gave her "additional information and the support I so desperately needed."

Chapter 18

329. The Pentagon Papers received temporary restraining orders—something short of a preliminary injunction. Before World War II there were cases of state courts issuing preliminary injunctions, later found unconstitutional, in support of laws against sedition.

330. This is drawn from the amicus brief submitted to the U.S. District Court, Western District of Wisconsin, reprinted in FAS *PIR*, May 1979, pp. 1–3.

331. Howard Morland, "Judge Bars Hydrogen Bomb Article After Magazine Rejects Mediation," *The New York Times*, March 27, 1979; quotes from the court's opinion are drawn from U.S. of America, Plaintiff, v. The Progressive, Inc., No. 79-C–98, U.S. District Court, W.D. Wisconsin, March 26, 1979.

332. Alexander DeVolpi, G. E. Marsh, T. A. Postel, G. S. Stanford, *Born Secret* (New York: Pergamon Press, 1981), p. 211.

Chapter 19

333. Letter of August 12, 1980, signed by the author, to Governor Ronald Reagan with an enclosure, conveying these sentiments, signed by Nobel Laureates Julius Axelrod, Owen Chamberlain, Robert Holley, Salvador E. Luria, and Burton Richter—and by George B. Kistiakowsky, science adviser to President Eisenhower, and Herman Feshbach, president of the American Physics Society.

334. Joan Quigley, *What Does Joan Say?* (Birch Lane Press, 1990), p. 43.

335. This affair is referred to in the June 1989 *Washingtonian*, "Bush Can Thank His Lucky Stars That Reagan Picked Him for Veep."

336. Letter of August 27, 1980, from Ronald Reagan to the author.

337. Quigley, *What Does Joan Say?*, p. 58.

338. See the review of Nancy Reagan's *My Turn* by Donald Regan in the December 1989 *Washingtonian*.

339. Deaver may not have been much troubled by this, since he had sympathies for astrology; according to Quigley, he called for help, at Nancy's suggestion, when he was being investigated by Congress for lobbying activities (Quigley, p. 121). And Howard Baker, Reagan's later chief of staff, is portrayed as used to this because his

father-in-law, Senator Everett Dirksen, "never made a move without first consulting his astrologer" (Quigley, p. 163).

340. Quigley, *What Does Joan Say?*, pp. 138–139.
341. Ibid., p. 137.

Chapter 20

342. Testimony before the General Advisory Committee of the Arms Control and Disarmament Agency, Thursday, November 9, 1978, 9:00 A.M., on the subject "After SALT, What?" by the author.
343. I was well prepared for this because the November 1978 FAS newsletter, then being printed, had listed "Seven Approaches" to "After SALT II, What?": Cutting Back to What We Really Need; Buying Only What We Need; SALT III with Reductions; SALT III Without Reductions; "Mission" Control; Swaps of Restraint; Strategic Persuasion.
344. When I explained this idea to Alton Frye, he had suggested this excellent slogan.
345. "Despite all that might be said for the usefulness, and indeed necessity, of reductions, it must be admitted that this mode of arms control is certain to encounter strong resistance. The destruction of expensive weapons has about it a touch of the futile and the tragic. This view is strengthened by the very short life of the SALT I option." Paul Doty, "Strategic Arms Limitations After SALT I," *Daedalus* 19 (1972): 72.
346. Letter of November 21, 1978, from Thomas J. Watson Jr. to the author.
347. Letter of December 8 from Thomas J. Watson Jr. to the author.
348. This letter appears in FAS *PIR*, January 1979, p. 1.
349. Jeremy J. Stone, "An Arms Race in Reverse: Letting the Generals Take Over Disarmament Could Give Meaning to SALT," *The Washington Post*, December 31, 1978.
350. This was described in FAS *PIR*, February 1979, p. 6.
351. In an interview in 1996, General Welch said that he had had access to General Jones, chairman of the Joint Chiefs of Staff, and that Jones also "saw the merit in the idea."
352. James Carter, *Keeping Faith: Memoirs of a President* (Little Rock: University of Arkansas Press, 1995), p. 248.
353. Ibid., p. 251.
354. Dobrynin, *In Confidence*, p. 424; Much later, in 1985, when, as will be seen later, I tried to revive the idea, I wrote President Carter a letter about it. He wrote a note on the bottom and sent it back: "Jeremy—I still think this is a good idea. Best Wishes, Jimmy."
355. "Scientists Assail Proposals," *The New York Times*, November 1, 1970.
356. Jeremy J. Stone, "SALT, In Perspective," *The New York Times*, March 11, 1979.
357. Stone, "SALT, In Perspective."

358. According to President Carter's memoir, "We decided that rather than have the treaty defeated or for me to withdraw it from consideration, it would be better to leave it in the Senate Foreign Relations Committee, postpone Senate action on it, and work with the Soviets for maximum observance of its terms by our two countries. By doing this we would be able to keep its provisions intact. With the exception of achieving the requirement for unilateral Soviet dismantling of 250 of their missile launchers, both the United States and the Soviet Union continued to honor the agreement." Carter, *Keeping Faith*, p. 270.

359. *The New York Times*, letter to the editor, April 3, 1979.

360. Private communication from a reporter.

361. Reprinted in FAS *PIR*, May 1979, p. 6, it appeared in *The New York Times* on April 30, 1979; other signers were Nina Byers, John T. Edsall, Denis Hayes, George Silver, Arthur Rosenfeld, Howard M. Temin, and Arch L. Wood.

362. Printed in FAS *PIR*, May 1979, as "Response from Jeremy J. Stone."

363. This release had, as contact person, John Holum, now the director of the Arms Control and Disarmament Agency, and a key adviser to Senator McGovern for many years.

364. For an analysis supporting the last two paragraphs, see FAS *PIR*, September 1979.

365. According to an informed committee source, speaking in 1996, Senator Church was intensely annoyed with Senator McGovern's persistent criticism of SALT II and felt that the last thing he needed or wanted was a hearing to criticize SALT II from the left (or any other side). This confirms my impression at the time that there *was* high-level reluctance to hold the hearings. Whether the committee cared, in particular, what *I* said is not certain.

366. Hearings before the Committee on Foreign Relations, U.S. Senate, 96th Congress, first session, on EX. Y, 96–1 "The SALT II Treaty," Part 4, p. 379.

367. The formulation agreed upon was "to pursue continuous year-by-year reductions in the ceilings and subceilings under the Treaty so as to take advantage of the Treaty already negotiated and to begin a sustainable and effective process of reductions in strategic arms which promotes strategic equivalence and strategic stability." FAS *PIR*, December 1979, p. 3.

368. McGovern and Chafee put in the record numerous examples of what they had in mind—with Library of Congress studies applying the notion of shrinking SALT II all done with a single percentage, of course. *Congressional Record*, October 31, 1979, Senate, pp. S15563–15573.

369. As of 1996, it seems they did not know. Roger Molander, then a White House coordinator for SALT II, says he remembers my visiting him at the White House to advance "Shrink SALT II" and considered it an "interesting proposal among other interesting ones" that had promise for its "simplicity, indefinite continuation, and ease of negotiation." But he says he did not know Carter had made this proposal and is "surprised but not shocked" at not knowing. Asked, in 1996, if he had shared with Senator McGovern the knowledge that President Carter had already proposed this notion at the Vienna summit, General Jones said that, although he

remembered President Carter raising this with him on the plane, he was not later told that it had, indeed, been proposed to the Russians. This was, he said, not so unusual considering the confusion at the summit. But it tends to confirm that the White House staff, negotiating with McGovern, did not know either.

370. Letter from the author to Warnke, September 21, 1979.

371. Carter, *Keeping Faith*, pp. 267–268.

372. But Dobrynin, who considered the whole invasion a "gross miscalculation," says that the invasion was "not the result of a conscious choice between expansionism and detente." At the December 12, 1979, secret Politburo meeting at which the decision was made, Foreign Minister Gromyko said nothing about the possibility of a strong reaction in the West. Nor was Dobrynin consulted, even though he was in Moscow having a medical checkup, as would have been the case if they were interested in what Washington might do. It was, instead, the KGB chief, Andropov, the defense minister, Ustinov, and a Politburo member, Chernenko, who really pushed the invasion—to prevent Western expansion along their southern border with troubled Afghanistan—along with the support of chief ideologist Mikhail Suslov and other ideologues who wanted an expansion of territory under "socialism." (See Dobrynin, p. 442.)

373. *Detente and Confrontation: American-Soviet Relations from Nixon to Regan,* rev. ed. (Brookings Institute, 1994), p. 1010.

Chapter 21

374. "But what if the Soviet Union decided to try to preempt and preclude Star Wars deployment through an agreement on reductions of offensive weapons. For example, the Soviets might propose a program of continuing, progressively deeper cuts in offensive weapons that would continue only as long as the United States refrains from field testing or deploying Star Wars systems prohibited by the 1972 treaty banning anti-ballistic missile systems." I was talked into the formulation of "field testing" and/or "deployment" rather than "compliance with the ABM Treaty" by experts who insisted that the ABM Treaty now had several different interpretations. But in other discussions, I just used compliance with the ABM Treaty and assumed that the differences in interpretation would be one of the issues resolved in the Soviet decision to abrogate.

375. Strobe Talbott, *The Master of the Game: Paul Nitze and the Nuclear Peace* (New York: Alfred Knopf, 1988), pp. 260–263; he has also written *Endgame: The Inside Story of SALT II* (New York: Alfred A. Knopf, 1979) and *Deadly Gambits: The Reagan Administration and the Stalemate in Nuclear Arms Control* (New York: Alfred A. Knopf, 1984).

376. I recall later telling Nitze that Vasiliev, who is now dead, was a very honest and brave man; he said he would like to meet him, and this was arranged when Vasiliev was next in town.

377. Our George Rathjens had written defending him with George's memory of the meeting with the National Council of Churches in 1958 at which Nitze made the relevant remarks. See "Nominations of Paul H. Nitze and William P. Bundy Before the Committee on Armed Services," November 14, 1963, p. 27.

378. According to Strobe's account, "As soon as he returned to Washington, Nitze went to work. The plan he eventually assembled provided for a 'schedule' of percentage reductions in strategic offenses every year for ten years, so that by the end of 1995, each side would have come down by approximately 50 percent from a 1986 'baseline' derived from the various SALT II ceilings and subceilings." (I had given Nitze supplemental testimony which I had provided on May 13, 1982, before the Foreign Relations Committee, showing, three years earlier, that a 50 percent reduction of SALT II limits and sublimits would produce most of the Reagan administration goals. Talbott, *Master of the Game*, pp. 261-262.

379. Talbott, *Master of the Game*, p. 265.

380. Ibid., p. 286.

381. Ibid., p. 287.

382. Ibid., p. 316.

383. Jeremy J. Stone, "Conversations with Andrei Sakharov," FAS *PIR* 5, March 1987.

384. My specific proposal, the first of my six points for the forum was the following:

    (1) As a way of holding the door open in Geneva and to avoid letting itself be provoked by those officials seeking to sabotage agreement by undermining the ABM Treaty and, above all, to get the world on the disarmament road and off the Star Wars road, the Soviet Union should consider announcing its willingness to begin disarmament of offensive weapons without further agreement on Star Wars but with the all-important condition that the Soviet Union would stop its disarmament if and when it saw the United States actually violate the Anti-Ballistic Missile Treaty in ways that could not be resolved through the Standing Consultative Commission.

    Point 2 proposed the appointment of negotiators who would attempt to resolve the ABM issues ad referendum (i.e., without instructions). Number 3 proposed Shrink SALT II by a fixed percentage either on agreed levels or force levels in being. Number 4 encouraged initiatives in openness. Number 5 urged more official travel and a new institution to manage it. Number 6 concerned confidence-building measures in the field of verification.

385. FAS *PIR* 1, October 1987.

386. This seminal paper, "Arms Races: Prerequisites and Results," was reprinted in full in FAS *PIR*, February 1987.

387. He noted that the "formulation by a state of its armaments goal in absolute terms is more likely to reflect the desire to obscure from its rivals the true relative superiority which it wishes to achieve or to obscure from itself the need to participate actively in the balancing process [for which, read, arms control]." In other words, in 1958 he described, very precisely Ronald Reagan's approach to Star Wars in 1983! (See reprint of this absolutely splendid paper in FAS *PIR*, February 1987.)

388. R. Jeffrey Smith, "Debates Erupt over Soviet Arms-Control Proposal: U.S. Officials See New Problems in 'De-Linking' SDI from Strategic Weapons Pact," *The Washington Post*, October 1, 1989.

389. Talbott, *Master of the Game*, p. 296.

390. For example, Talbott recounts how the RAND team called on Nitze on May 14, 1986: "Bud McFarlane asked us to do some work last year on possible tradeoffs between offense and defense. . . ."

    "Oh?" said Nitze, "tell me about it."

    I had been talking to Nitze about this *one year and one week before*, on May 3, 1985. As a former RAND consultant myself, this simple fact gave me considerable food for thought. The larger think tanks can be ponderous.

391. Talbott, *Master of the Game*, p. 295.

392. For example, Talbott talks of a Gorbachev *Time* magazine interview in August 1985 in which, based on talking points from his advisers, Gorbachev moved toward making violations of the ABM Treaty the key desiderata rather than just *any* ABM research (which would be unverifiable). This was the final position.

    According to Strobe, however, their negotiating team got the message only much later. (*Master of the Game*, pp. 277–278, and see also the discussion on p. 295, where he says, "Gorbachev seemed to be relying increasingly on a flying squad of academicians and *institutchiki*.") The situation in the two countries was humorously parallel. Just as Nitze could not trust interagency discussions to work—fearing sabotage by Pentagon civilians, so the Soviets were unable to trust the usual channels to deal with us because the whole fractured U.S. administration was listening in. And this is exactly what they told Max Kampelman. (Talbot, *Master of the Game*, p. 293.) And it is exactly what Dobrynin told FAS when asked about talks ad referendum; he said (confusing them with back-channel discussions): "There are plenty of back channels. The trouble is that we don't know with whom we are dealing in Washington. Everyone is at everyone else's throat." (Letter to Paul Nitze of March 25, 1987, reporting on a conversation that Frank von Hippel had with Ambassador Dobrynin.)

393. Stone, *Strategic Persuasion*.

394. Stephen S. Rosenfeld decided to "say a good word for . . . the Cold War"; Dimitri Simes said we should give Gorbachev "grudging admiration" but not "the support one would give a new-found friend"; Charles Krauthammer said he was the "greatest politician of our time" and called the speech a "masterful mixture of beef and guff"; and George F. Will warned that Gorbachev's rhetoric might produce a "pell-mell, bipartisan U.S. retreat from defense spending," thus achieving a "relative enhancement of Soviet military power."

395. Jeremy J. Stone, op-ed appearing in *The New York Times*, February 6, 1989.

396. Leslie H. Gelb wrote that the piece was "terrific, well-read, and well-received." Letter of March 27, 1989.

Chapter 22

397. *Who's Who in America, 1982–1983.* After a career at ACDA (1964–1976), he had returned to the CIA as director of the Office of Strategic Research (1977–1979).

398. Michael R. Gordon, "C.I.A. Aide Sees Soviet Economy Failing to Gain," *The New York Times*, October 15, 1988.

399. Letter of October 14, 1988.

400. It was resent on November 14, 1988.

401. I reported all this to Gates in a letter of December 19, 1988.

402. Five days later, he gave a speech on terrorism with a line I loved: "Perhaps most important, we must work with our Allies *and with the Soviets* [emphasis added] to develop a unified front to deal with this growing problem." ("The Sounds of Silence," statement of Senator William S. Cohen, January 3, 1989.)

403. Letter of January 3, 1989. My first and only visit to the agency was on the occasion of the swearing-in of R. James Woolsey as director of the CIA in 1993.

404. Michael Dobbs, "U.S. Envoy Calls on Soviet Spymaster; KGB Chief Impresses American Diplomat in 90-Minute Chat," *The Washington Post*, January 5, 1989.

405. See typed and added footnote on the computer-prepared letter by the author to Ambassador Dubinin, February 6, 1989.

406. Ibid.

407. Letter of November 13, 1996, reprinted in the *Chosen Ilbo*, February 14, 1997.

408. Memo of the author, December 18, 1991, after talking to Kartman.

409. Ibid., and letter to Gates of December 19, 1991.

410. Quoted from my letter to Gates of January 9, the same day.

411. Letter to Robert M. Gates of January 21 enclosing undated "Dear Jeremy" letter, unsigned, with typed signature: E. Primakov.

412. Letter of February 5, 1992, to Robert M. Gates with enclosed letter of January 29 to Primakov. I also wrote the FBI (Wayne Gilbert, the assistant director for counterintelligence) a letter of January 30, 1992, saying that I was in correspondence with the head of the foreign intelligence operation of the Russian government and would keep in touch via an agent, Robert M. Kelley, who, for one reason or another (which I have forgotten), knew of FAS.

413. Letter of January 30, 1992, to Mr. Wayne Gilbert.

414. Bill Gertz, "CIA, Russians to Discuss Cooperation," *The Washington Times*, October 14, 1992.

415. According to an October 19, 1992, report, the U.S. embassy released a statement saying, "Possibilities of contact and joint activity" between the two services were discussed. "The talks were cordial, and both sides were satisfied with the results." This subject is still sufficiently sensitive that the meeting is not discussed at all in Gates's 1996 memoir.

    Dr. Gates also met President Yeltsin, and guess what he talked about. It was the raising of the Soviet submarine with the *Glomar Explorer*. Readers will remember, from the last section of Chapter 12, on the Mining Bill, that the CIA's cover story for this dramatic success inadvertently helped the American Mining Congress in its effort, in effect, to seize the ocean bottom and disrupt a Law of the Sea Treaty. (Janet Guttsman, "CIA Director Seeks Russia's Assistance on Terrorism, Drugs," *The Washington Times*, October 19, 1992.)

416. Letter of January 4, 1977, acknowledged in a letter of January 24 at Mr. Bush's request.

417. Telegram of December 23, 1983.

418. Letter of June 2, 1987, from the author to General Vessey at his home in Garrison, Minnesota.

419. Jeremy J. Stone, "Political Correctness Invades the FBI," *The Wall Street Journal*, November 2, 1993.

Chapter 23

420. Nicholas Wade, "Viets and Vets Fear Herbicide Health Effects (a report on the FAS seminar)," *Science* (May 25, 1979).

421. Mailgram sent July 6, 1979, signed by the author.

422. Statement on Starvation in Cambodia by Jean Mayer, president, Tufts University, and vice chairman, Presidential Commission on World Hunger, October 18, 1979.

423. Press release of October 17, 1979.

424. Jeremy J. Stone, "How Cruel Can Vietnam Be?," unpublished article.

425. See Robert Adams, "Scientists Call Bombing Immoral, Inexcusable," *St. Louis Post-Dispatch*, December 29, 1972.

426. This trip report is drawn from the twenty-page FAS *PIR*, April 1989, which includes the text of the interview with Hun Sen on pages 16–19.

427. Jeremy J. Stone, "Preventing the Return of Pol Pot: Conventional Wisdom Versus New Appraisal," March 11, 1989.

428. Ambassador Yuri V. Dubinin sent a letter of the same date, May 16, 1989, saying he was "pleased to confirm" that the letter had been "received by General Secretary M. S. Gorbachev."

429. Among other letters, I wrote him on October 3, 1989; on January 3, 1990; and on July 25, 1990.

Chapter 24

430. Even King Mongut, I noticed, who was the hero of "Anna and the King of Siam" and who was very scientifically inclined, seemed to consider corruption of one's office as natural. When, in 1864, Anna Leonowens approached him for a raise, he said, "Why you should be poor? You come into my presence every day with some petition, some case of hardship or injustice, and you demand 'your Majesty shall most

kindly investigate and cause redress to be made'; and I have granted to you because you are important to me for translations, and so forth. And now you declare you must have increase of salary! Must you have everything in this world? Why you do not make *them* pay you? If I grant you all your petition for the poor, you ought to be rich, or you have no wisdom." *The English Governess at the Siamese Court* (Oxford University Press, 1870). King Mongut did not, in fact, die of a heart attack, as the movie suggests, but of malaria while in the jungle in Southern Siam trying to observe an eclipse, so as to persuade his people that such events were natural phenomena.

431. See the September hearing before the House Subcommittee on Asian and Pacific Affairs, as reported in FAS *PIR*, October 1989. The policy was, as Richard Solomon later wrote me, to "(1) stop the fighting and (2) get a neutral international presence in Cambodia to stabilize the situation—i.e., to get the Chinese and Vietnamese out, and with it aid to the Khmer Rouge and Hun Sen's faction."

432. Michael Haas observes in his book, *Cambodia, Pol Pot, and the United States: The Faustian Pact* (Praeger, 1991), that CORKR was formed "after a meeting [of NGOs] organized by John McAuliffe" and that "the group was formed by Jeremy Stone . . . after a trip to Phnom Penh in 1989" (pp. 104–105).

433. Muskie was kept in play on this issue by the Center for National Policy, of which he was the chairman, and whose vice president, Maureen (Mo) Steinbruner, was a skillful and interested party. Mitchell's success was announced in a newspaper article: Al Kamen, "Senators Seek About-Face in Policy on Cambodia," *The Washington Post*, July 14, 1990.

434. Stephen J. Morris, "Skeletons in the Closet," *The New Republic* (June 4, 1990).

435. H.R. 2655. (b) "Prohibition on Certain Assistance to the Khmer Rouge— Notwithstanding any other provision of law, none of the funds made available to carry out this section may be obligated or expended for the purpose or with the effect of promoting, sustaining, or augmenting, directly or indirectly, the capacity of the Khmer Rouge or any of its members to conduct military or paramilitary operations in Cambodia or elsewhere in Indochina." And the House of Representatives' committee report urged the president to secure "firm and reliable assurances" from the noncommunist forces in Cambodia that they "will not use U.S. assistance in cooperation or coordination with the Khmer Rouge or to benefit the Khmer Rouge in any way."

436. See FAS *PIR* 8, November 1989.

437. I was told this by an involved newspaperman.

438. These included, besides Secretary of State Baker, Deputy Secretary Lawrence S. Eagleburger, Under Secretary Robert M. Kimmitt, and Assistant Secretary Richard Solomon.

439. The first five points in the nine-point bill of indictment read as follows:

   (1) Not only has the Department of State made no substantial effort to prevent the return of the Khmer Rouge but it has worked actively and energetically to force the Vietnamese Army out of Cambodia, thus removing the main bulwark of the Cambodian people against the return of the Khmer Rouge.

(2) Not only has the Department of State failed to oppose Pol Pot's Khmer Rouge but it has strengthened it politically by working to combine the noncommunist resistance in Cambodia with the Khmer Rouge in a so-called Coalition Government of Democratic Kampuchea.

(3) Not only has the Department of State failed to support peaceful initiatives of the Thai government to end the conflict but it has actively tried to sabotage those initiatives by intervening in Thai politics against the prime minister.

(4) Not only has the Department of State failed to support Hun Sen's government against the Khmer Rouge but it is the main element in an economic embargo that denies Cambodia help from the West.

(5) Not only has the Department of State failed to prevent Pol Pot's government of Democratic Kampuchea from holding Cambodia's UN seat, it has—for ten years and still today—supported the Khmer Rouge's retaining UN representation.

The last point, number 9, complained that the department avoided exchanges of views with its critics to maintain a more defensible "low profile."

440. Letter of December 7, 1989, from Charles H. Twining. Richard Solomon observes, "By this time, we had laid in place the game plan to get the UN into Cambodia as the basis for getting all the other foreign presence out and as a vehicle for restoring Constitutional Government and blocking Pol Pot." Private communication to the author, September 6, 1996.

441. Letter to Congressman Anthony C. Beilenson of December 26, 1989, and of July 2, 1990; letter to Congressman Stephen J. Solarz of March 6, 1990; letter to Ms. Jan Heininger of the office of Senator Robert C. Byrd of March 28, 1990.

Chapter 25

442. I later learned that Li Peng had sent a representative of his office to the disarmament conference organizers to find out what was up. One consequence of this decision was to put off, for a few years, a planned visit to North Korea that was scheduled to occur at the same time. And, no doubt, it impaired my relations with the Chinese leadership.

443. It included, in particular, a statement from the Cambodian Defense Ministry, news reports, op-ed essays, excerpts of legislation, and letters from the State Department asserting its position.

444. Jeremy J. Stone, "Scientists Call for All-Out Opposition to Khmer Rouge," FAS press release, May 9, 1990.

445. Letter of June 4, 1991, enclosing a "quiet copy" of the letter I had sent Minister Evans "incorporating ideas which I suggested to you in our recent meeting in Moscow."

446. Letter of September 11, 1990, to Peter Wilensky, ambassador of Australia to the United Nations; letter of September 11, 1990, to Mr. Jean-Marie Guehenno, Chef du centre d'analyse et de prévision, Ministère des affaires étrangères, Paris, France;

Letter of September 11 to Pansak Vinyarat, chairman, Council of Advisers to the Prime Minister, Bangkok, Thailand; Letter of September 11, 1990, to prime minister Hun Sen. These letters said the embassies could be established "with the understanding that the states were recognizing Cambodia, as a State" and would be useful in case the diplomatic process broke down.

447. "Especially because I have been an early and persistent critic of the UN plan for Cambodia that you have championed, I want to be sure you understand that I do, and I will, strongly support the funding of that plan. I congratulate you on having brought your plan this far, and I certainly share your hope that it will now succeed."

448. Letter of November 25, 1991.

449. Pell's letter was dated March 6, 1989, and Cranston's January 25, 1989.

450. Letter from Charles Twining of January 30, 1989.

451. They said it "clearly constitutes an activity which would be prejudicial to the public interest." But how? It would "compromise important United States policy objectives and weaken ASEAN's and our position regarding the legitimacy of the People's Republic of Kampuchea." Letter of March 24, 1989, to the author from Michael W. Marine, acting director, Office of Vietnam, Laos and Cambodia Affairs.

452. *1990 Current Biography Yearbook*, p. 317.

453. Valerie Strauss, "Washington Sees a New Hun Sen," *The Washington Post*, March 27, 1992.

454. "An Obligation to Cambodia," *The Washington Post*, editorial, April 1, 1992.

455. And some people knew it. On April 6 former senator Dick Clark, who had been watching this closely from his perch at the Aspen Institute, wrote these words to me: "Your promotion and management of Hun Sen in Washington is one of the most successful, professional, and inspiring performances in my memory. You are truly to be congratulated. If U.S. policy moves in the direction it now seems to be headed, it will be due in no small part to your efforts."

On April 16 I even got a letter from the Australian foreign minister, Gareth Evans, saying he had been "following with great interest the reports of Hun Sen's successful visit to Washington which, I understand, was organized by the Federation of American Scientists." This letter was in response to a letter of mine of March 30 urging that the Australian government invite Prince Sihanouk to agree to send an ambassador to South Korea—something that was not done until after the prince's friend, President Kim Il Sung of North Korea, died.

456. This was a memo of August 25. It suggested announcing that since the threat of civil war was over, "a new era in human rights" would be at hand. It recommended disciplining certain murderous elements, lowering the government's voice, offering a reward for information leading to the apprehension of the Khmer Rouge leaders, hiring more foreign advisers, avoiding the drug traffic, and announcing that it did not intend to purge the CPP or overthrow the monarchy.

Chapter 26

457. Letter of October 27, 1977, from Joe Eldridge, Bill Brown, and Jo Marie Gries-
graber and signed "Jo Marie."
458. January 1978.
459. Clovis, a brilliant engineering student, had led the student opposition to Air Force
efforts to turn an Air Force–supported technological institute into a true military
school.
460. There were a few other activities in South America outside Peru. In 1987 we had
organized a meeting in Chile between Chilean and Argentinian defense experts to
help paper over the antagonisms of those countries (FAS *PIR,* June 1987). In 1989,
in the interests of nonproliferation, I threatened three world-famous U.S. banks
with a stockholder resolution requiring them to advise Brazilian and Argentinian
officials that a nuclear arms race in Latin America would complicate each bank's
ability to sustain its financial links to that region. (Two had agreed on the condition that we drop the stockholder resolution and keep it private, and one, Citicorp,
put it on the ballot and voted it down at its April 1989 stockholder meeting.)
461. FAS *PIR,* April 1986.
462. Letter of April 21, 1992.
463. The resulting FAS *PIR* was entitled "Peru: Desperately Ill and Confronting a
Maoist Mafia" (July/August 1992).
464. My caution in sharing what I was doing with Michael was my fear that, Latin
America being what it was, it would leak, through him, that I was somehow
"working for the CIA," or something like that. And, in addition, since we would
be returning to Latin America, I feared being targeted by *Sendero* if they believed
that I was, somehow, linked to the intelligence community.
465. George Lardner Jr., "Helms Set Killing Ban in '72 Rule," *The Washington Post,* June
19, 1975.
466. This letter, dated June 29, 1992, said there was "good reason" to believe we could
save "millions of lives, and endless trouble" in the hemisphere by providing the
Peruvian government with intelligence. I advised him that I was also making the
same "quiet appeal" to Gates and Assistant Secretary of State Bernard Aronson.
467. See letter to him dated June 23, 1992, asking for an appointment on a "matter of
some sensitivity."
468. Don Podesta, "Letter from Peru: Lima's Graceful Past Is Overtaken by Ominous
Present in Dusty Slums," *The Washington Post,* July 13, 1992.
469. The chairman of the Senate Foreign Relations Committee, Senator Pell, reinforced my conclusion by putting this in the Congressional Record and saying that
"it is incumbent upon international organizations, the Department of State, and
other relevant organizations to begin thinking now about just such potential disas-
ters, and calls for international help, from Peru and others." August 6, 1992, p.
S11760.

470. Letter to the dditor from Anne Manuel, associate director of Americas Watch, August 1, 1992. She concluded, "Abandoning scrutiny of the human rights record of government forces in Peru is not only morally unacceptable but entirely counterproductive in the struggle against Sendero."
471. Nathaniel C. Nash, "Peru Rebel Group Is Seen as Potent," *The New York Times*, September 15, 1992.
472. Gabriel Escobar, "Rights Group Assails Peru's Anti-Terror Laws," *The Washington Post*, August 7, 1966.
473. Paragraph 2.11 of Executive Order 12333 states, "No person employed by or acting on behalf of the United States Government shall engage in, or conspire to engage in, assassination."

Chapter 27

474. William Colby and Jeremy J. Stone, "Break the Siege of Sarajevo," *The Washington Post*, January 15, 1993.
475. I had earlier befriended Macedonia's representative in Washington, Ljubica Acevska, and helped set up a meeting for a Macedonian official with Foreign Relations Committee staffer John Ritch. Discussion focused on various names for Macedonia and the Macedonian reluctance to accept "New Macedonia," which denied its ancient origins. I suggested having the "new" transposed to modify the word "republic" as in "New Republic of Macedonia." Impressed with this legerdemain, she helped me set this appointment up with her president.
476. FAS *PIR*, May/June 1993.
477. Letter of March 25, c/o Alush A. Gashi.
478. See FAS *PIR*, September/October 1993; see also letter of August 11, 1993, to Philip B. Heymann, deputy attorney general.
479. Letter to Eugene Pell, president of Radio Free Europe/Radio Liberty, Inc., from the author, February 5, 1993.
480. Letter of February 25, 1993, to Stephen J. Del Rosso Jr., Pew Charitable Trust. This approach was never funded.
481. Letter of June 2 to the two presidents from the author.
482. I prepared a relevant paper of August 10, 1992, which was reviewed by a UN expert, Bertrand Ramcharan, but which I ceased to advance when Peru's Guzman was captured.
483. Press release of the Republic of Kosovo, "Kosovo Prime Minister Calls for U.N. Trust Territory of Kosovo."
484. Barton Gellman, "After Tough Week, Israelis Savor Pact with Jordan," *The Washington Post*, October 18, 1994.
485. The "Treaty of Peace Between the State of Israel and the Hashemite Kingdom of Jordan" of October 26, 1994, permitted certain Israeli settlers special rights for a twenty-five-year, renewable period during which Israelis had special rights of

access to the Jordanian territory; protection from discriminatory taxes, harassment, and the dumping of wastes; and certain extraterritorial rights to be free from the application of Jordanian criminal laws. Israel hoped that the "lease innovation" would be taken up by Syria.

486. In July 1996 *The New York Times* reported on a recent paper by a member of the Serbian Academy of Science and Arts, which argued that the Albanians and Serbs should "share power in Kosovo or divide the province into two ethnic enclaves." The dispatch argued that this was significant since "in the past, Mr. Milosevic has often used the academy as a harbinger of policy shifts." Even if the outcome turned out to be "two ethnic enclaves," the lease approach might find utility, as it did with Israel and Jordan, in smoothing anomalies of population location.

487. Letter of July 9, 1998, from the author to Holbrooke.

Chapter 28

488. President Jiang Zemin had said that "on the premise that there is only one China, we are prepared to talk with the Taiwan authority about any issues including all matters of concern to the Taiwan authority." (*China Daily*, February 2, 1995; quoted from a paper of the PRC's Qimao Chen, senior fellow, Institute of Peace.)

489. Chi-June Liu, *World Journal*, April 24, 1996. This article also appeared in the *Economic Daily News* of April 22 and in the United Daily in Taiwan. (These three journals are owned by the same syndicate.)

490. Letter of February 4, 1997, in response to my letter of December 4, 1996, enclosing a copy of the column.

491. A letter to the deputy foreign minister (Tzen Wen-hua) of February 20, 1997, went unanswered, as did a letter of February 19, 1997, to Ambassador Chang Ping-Nan, then in retirement.

492. Thus, in 1998, the former undersecretary of state Joseph S. Nye Jr. prepared a piece "A Taiwan Deal" (according to *The Washington Post*) that incorporated a Northeast Strategy. (*The Washington Post*, March 8, 1998.) Asked on December 7 whether there was any connection, he said, "Yes, I read and learned from your piece, but there are no footnotes in op-eds." He said his article was "read with interest at high levels in Beijing, Taipei, and Tokyo."

Chapter 29

493. See Amy Knight, *Beria: Stalin's First Lieutenant* (Princeton, NJ: Princeton University Press, 1993) or FAS *PIR* 7, May/June 1994.

494. Pavel Sudoplatov, et al., *Special Tasks* (New York: Little, Brown, 1994), pp. 190, 192.

495. Vladimir Matveyevich Chikov, "How the Soviet Intelligence Service 'Split' the American Atom," *New Times* 16 (1991): 38.

496. Associated Press, *The New York Times,* September 19, 1983. See also letter to the editor of October 20, 1983 ("A Rosenberg Friend Prematurely Condemned" by Mark Kuchment). The best discussion of this story appears in the appendix to the Vintage edition of *The Rosenberg File* by Ronald Radosh and Joyce Milton (New York: Holt Rinehart Winston, 1983).

497. Chikov, "How the Soviet Intelligence Service 'Split' the American Atom," p. 38.

498. Joseph Rotblat, "Leaving the Bomb Project," *Bulletin of the Atomic Scientists,* (August 1985): 18.

499. Chikov, "How the Soviet Intelligence Service 'Split' the American Atom," p. 38.

500. Ibid.

501. Lansdale gave me a manuscript that showed the kind of person he was and the approach he took: "One problem, the most difficult of all and never satisfactorily solved, was to keep the military establishment from drawing unreasonable conclusions from insufficient facts." He went on to say that members of the Communist Party or persons "clearly in sympathy with it" were security risks. But "it was difficult to make people understand, however, that membership in communist front organizations or extremely liberal political views were not of themselves evidence of membership in the communist party or sympathy with the communist party." (John Lansdale, Jr., "Military Service," p. 7.)

502. Sudoplatov, *Special Tasks,* p. 190.

503. Ibid., p. 191.

504. He mentioned that clients in such cases are often advised to limit the documents they keep since these can be requested or seized.

505. And Justice could, if it wished, put its evidence in a so-called can—which is to say that it could date-stamp the information to be able to establish, if it did indict, that its evidence had not arisen from information in the hearings for which the immunity had been given.

506. Letter of July 18 to Scientist X from the author.

507. Louis Nizer, *The Implosion Conspiracy* (New York: Doubleday, 1973), pp. 77–78.

508. A basic source on World War II summarizes the fears of the German bomb as follows: "By the summer of 1942 the critical resource allocation decisions had been made; there would be no German atomic bomb. In the summer of 1943 the British were convinced of this, and by the summer of 1944 the Americans had come to the same conclusion, a view reinforced by the special 'Alsos' mission, whose task it was to check on German atomic bomb progress." Gerhard L. Weinberg, *A World at Arms; A Global History of World War II* (Cambridge: Cambridge University Press, 1994), p. 570.

509. Private communication from Arnold Kramish, author of *The Griffin,* who was told this by Perrin before Perrin died.

510. Leslie Groves, *Now It Can Be Told* (New York: Harper & Brothers, 1962), p. 185.

511. Even in late 1944, when, at Strasbourg, the papers of a key German physicist, Carl Friedrich von Weizecker, were closely examined and found to show that the Germans had gotten nowhere, General Groves said, "Unless and until we had positive

knowledge to the contrary, we had to assume that the most competent German scientists and engineers were working on an atomic program with the full support of their government and with the full capacity of German industry at their disposal."

512. I had asked to see him, on Colby's suggestion, in a letter of August 4, 1994. Rogovin was a perfect selection. He had worked for the CIA as general counsel and would have real credibility in a case of this kind.

513. Robert Louis Benson, *Introductory History of VENONA and Guide to the Translations* (NSA, undated but released on July 11, 1996).

514. Completing the manuscript, seeking a publisher, and, in the end, deciding to work with PublicAffairs, which was just being conceived, explains the three-year delay.

515. Joseph Albright, *Bombshell* (New York: Random House, 1997).

516. In the meantime, I fully expect my analysis to be critiqued and denounced from a number of friendly quarters and my motives impugned. But this memoir constitutes the last clear chance for me to "commit truth" in this matter, as in other corners of my life, and so I am doubly determined not to bury this episode.

Chapter 30

517. "Player, Jeremy J. Stone, Scientific Foreman in an 'Idea' Factory," *The Washington Post*, March 24, 1986.

518. This was I. F. Stone.

519. Nicholas Wade, "Battle of the B-1 Bomber," *The Washington Post*, July 31, 1977.

520. As we were investigating this in August and September, creating waves in the Senate, but before the newsletter was released, we learned that the House of Representatives, on October 8, 1974, approved the complete abolition of proxy voting in committee.

Index

actions in Cambodia, 272–273
ban on assassinations, 298
Encounter magazine and, 40–41
Glomar Explorer and, 82
KGB and, 243–253, 358–359
mail-opening program of, 46–50, 85, 356
Peru and, 297, 302
travel to the Soviet Union and, 241–243
William Colby and, 85
See also Intelligence
community, U.S.
Chadha case, 99–100
Chafee, John, 224
Chalidze, Valery, 174
Chang Song, 270
Chea Sim, 290
Chebrikov, Viktor, 184
Chemical warfare, 104–105
Chernenko, Pavel, 177–178, 218
Chiang Ching-kuo, 318, 319
Chiang Kai-shek, 318, 319
Chicago Sun Times, 207
Chien, Fredrick, 321
Chikov, Vladimir, 329
Chile, 292
Chinese boat people, 257
Chirac, Jacques, 185
Church, Frank, 48, 222, 225
CIA. *See* Central Intelligence Agency
Civil disobedience, 98
Clark, William, 263
Clean Air Act, 70
Clifford, Clark, 23, 348, 349
Clinton, Bill, 353
Clough, Ralph, 320
Clyne, Norman, 232
Cohen, Jerome, 121, 123, 124, 128
Cohen, Joan, 121, 123, 124
Cohen, Leona, 329, 332–333
Cohen, Morris, 329, 330–331
Cohen, Scott, 101, 102
Cohen, William, 141, 244, 247, 248
Colby, William, 50
on atomic spy Perseus, 333, 335
Cambodia and, 265, 268, 270, 272, 288
CIA ban on assassinations and, 298
CIA-KGB cooperation and, 251
collaborations with Stone, 81–87
Richard Helms and, 334
on travel to the Soviet Union, 137
Yugoslavia and, 305
Cold War, NATO strategies in, 92

Committee of Soviet Scientists, 229
Committee on Scholarly Communications
with the People's Republic of China, 129
Commonweal (magazine), 98
Comprehensive Test Ban Treaty, 353
Concorde jets, 193–198, 356
Condon, Edward, 63
Congress, U.S.
atomic spy Perseus and, 334-335
Chadha decision and, 99
no first use doctrine and, 101-102, 355
U.S.-Soviet parliamentary exchange and, 30, 131–141
Congress for Cultural Freedom, 41
Congressional Quarterly, 133
Congressional Record, 351
Containing the Arms Race (Stone), 14
Cooper, John Sherman, 27
Cotter, W.J., 47, 50, 51
Council for a Livable World, 94
Council on Foreign Relations, 32, 35–38, 285, 286, 287
Crain, Melvin, 50
Cranston, Alan, 94, 95, 264, 267, 285–286, 287, 358
Cronkite, Walter, 54
Crowe, William, 242
Cuba, 225
Cuban missile crisis, 7
Czechoslovakia, 24

Daedalus (journal), 215
Dash, Sam, 62
Dean, John, 61–63, 356
Deaver, Mike, 208
Defense Department, U.S.
evacuation plans and, 4–5
on first use of nuclear weapons, 95–96
R&D gap and, 53–55
SALT II and, 219
Defense spending, 293
Democratic People's Republic of Korea. *See* North Korea
Democratic Progressive Party, 315, 316, 319, 321
Deng Xiaoping, 265
DeSoto, Alvero, 300
Détente, 145–149
Dingell, John, 139
Direct-mail marketing, 71–72
Disarmament, 11, 14
"Divide the Question Rather Than the Court" (Stone), 111, 114
Dixon, Jeane, 206–207